INDEX CANONUM,

THE GREEK TEXT,

AN ENGLISH TRANSLATION,

AND

A COMPLETE DIGEST

OF THE ENTIRE CODE OF

CANON LAW

OF THE UNDIVIDED PRIMITIVE CHURCH.

SECOND EDITION, REVISED AND ENLARGED;

WITH A DISSERTATION ON THE SEVENTH CANON OF EPHESUS
AND THE CHALCEDONIAN DECREE OF DOCTRINAL LIBERTY.

BY JOHN FULTON, DD., LL.D.,
RECTOR OF ST. GEORGE'S CHURCH, ST. LOUIS, MO.

AND A

PREFATORY NOTICE

BY

PHILIP SCHAFF, D.D., LL.D.

WIPF & STOCK • Eugene, Oregon

Wipf and Stock Publishers
199 W 8th Ave, Suite 3
Eugene, OR 97401

Index Canonum
The Greek Text, An English Translation, and a
Complete Digest of the Entire Code of Canon Law
of the Undivided Primitive Church
By Fulton, John and Schaff, Philip
ISBN 13: 978-1-62564-881-5
Publication date 4/16/2014
Previously published by E. & J. B. Young, 1883

TO

THE REVEREND FATHER IN GOD,

CHARLES FRANKLIN ROBERTSON, S.T.D.,

BISHOP OF MISSOURI,

THIS MANUAL OF CATHOLIC LAW

IS NOW,

BY PERMISSION,

Reverently Inscribed;

IN TOKEN OF

DUTIFUL REVERENCE FOR HIS OFFICE

AND

SINCERE AFFECTION FOR HIS PERSON,

BY

HIS LOVING PRESBYTER,

JOHN FULTON.

CONTENTS.

PROVINCIAL COUNCILS.

PREFATORY NOTICE.

THE ancient Councils were convened for the double purpose of deciding doctrinal controversies, and passing disciplinary canons, on the basis of the Holy Scriptures and the traditional faith and practice of the church. The dogmatic decisions are laid down chiefly in the Nicene and Constantinopolitan Creed (A. D. 325 and 381), and the Christological formulas of Ephesus (431) and Chalcedon (451). They are still held by all orthodox churches, Greek, Latin, and Evangelical, and form the most important heritage of the ancient undivided church.

The first collection of ecclesiastical Canons goes under the name of "Apostolical Canons." They are appended to the eighth book of the "Apostolical Constitutions," and exist in Greek, Syriac, Ethiopic, and Arabic versions. In some manuscripts they number 85, in others 50. The Greek church, at the Trullan Council in 692, adopted the whole collection of 85 as authentic and binding; the Latin church retained 50, which Dionysius Exiguus about A. D. 500 translated from a Greek Manuscript. They consist of brief rules borrowed from the Pastoral Epistles, from early tradition, and the Councils of the first centuries.

Among the Canons of Councils the first place is due to those of the first four œcumenical Councils; and the second to those of several provincial Councils, which were held soon after the Diocletian persecution, namely the Councils of Elvira in Spain (306), Ancyra in Galatia (313), Arles in France (314), Neo Cæsarea in Cappadocia (between 314

and 325). The latter dealt chiefly with questions arising out of the persecutions of the church by heathen Rome, and gave directions for dealing with those who had denied the Lord in the hour of danger and had afterwards repented. The Councils of Laodicea and Gangra, although only provincial, likewise passed important Canons; but while the Canons of Ancyra, Neo-Cæsarea, Gangra, Laodicea, and also of Antioch were approved by the Council of Chalcedon, and thus gained currency in the West as well as in the East, the Canons of Elvira and of Arles were never received as of authority beyond the provinces for the government of which they were adopted.

These ancient canons give us a tolerably complete idea of the practical life, the clerical duties and morals, the state of discipline, and worship of the church during the first five centuries. They form the basis of the canon law, which grew during the middle ages to as large dimensions as the Roman civil law.

A careful collection of these early canons in the original Greek, with a faithful English Version, historical introductions, critical notes and a digest, must be of very great use to every student of ecclesiastical history.

Such a collection is furnished by a competent and conscientious scholar in the present work, based upon the great *Synodicon* of Bishop Beveridge. It is the only book of the kind issued in America, and I know no better one of the same size. It needs no further introduction. It will best recommend itself by practical use.

PHILIP SCHAFF.

NEW YORK, *June, 1883.*

PREFACE TO THE SECOND EDITION.

CONTAINING A DISSERTATION ON THE SEVENTH CANON OF EPHESUS AND THE CHALCEDONIAN DECREE OF DOCTRINAL LIBERTY.*

AS an introduction to this Second Edition I might be content to say that the corrections of the First Edition which have been found to be necessary after ten years of continuous use amount to no more than the change of a dozen words, and the alteration of a few lines in a single paragraph. Such a statement would be strictly true, but it would be very far from telling the whole truth; for, though the number of necessary corrections has proved to be much less than could have been expected in the First Edition of such a work, their importance is exceedingly great. Most of them occur in the translation of the Seventh Canon of Ephesus and the Definition of Chalcedon, and are directly connected with no less important a subject than the extent and limitations of authoritative doctrinal teaching in the Church of Christ. The pretentions of Rome on the one hand, and the investigations of science and of criticism on the other, are compelling men to inquire with eager earnestness whether the Catholic Church itself has never set a limit to its own right of definition, and whether Christianity has ever made itself responsible for the philosophical theories with which scientific discovery and critical research are in open conflict. Now the truth is that the limitations of authoritative doctrinal teaching in the Church of Christ were long ago determined in the

* The substance of this essay was printed, though not published, in June, 1882. At that time Canon Bright's "Notes on the Canons of the first Four General Councils," and the third volume of Bishop Hefele's "History of the Councils of the Church from the original Documents," had not appeared. I trust it is not inconsistent with becoming modesty to say that, after a careful examination of these two learned works, I have found no sufficient reason to change even the details of the argument herein presented.

most emphatic and unequivocal way; and it is a fact which mere inspection will verify, that, with the Catholic Faith, as it was then authoritatively defined by the Catholic Church, not one fact which science or criticism has yet proved, or ever will prove, can by any possibility conflict. I shall be pardoned, I trust, for saying that the succession of causes and events which led to that important act has not heretofore been presented with the exactness which its far-reaching significance demands. Indeed, the connection of these successive incidents with the cardinal fact on which the whole question of the scope and limitations of authorized Catholic doctrine hinges, seems to me to have been strangely overlooked. I therefore avail myself of the opportunity afforded by the present occasion to narrate the interesting series of incidents which I have been compelled to consider while engaged in a critical review of the language and history of the two important documents to which I have referred.

I. When our Lord Jesus Christ declared that the gates of hell should not prevail against His Church, that promise cannot be understood to mean less than this, that however individual men or particular Churches might err, the whole Catholic Body should not err in any matter of faith. Hence we must conclude that Definitions of Faith carefully elaborated by Councils and afterwards approved by the consent of the whole Catholic Commonwealth are infallibly true. If they were not true, the gates of hell must have prevailed against the Church of Christ, contrary to His promise.

Again, when our Lord promised that the Holy Ghost whom He was to send from the Father should guide His Church into all truth, it is very clear that He did not mean all sorts of truth; such, for example, as scientific truth or historical truth. Neither did He mean every sort of truth connected with religion, as, for example, the exact date and the authorship of every book of the Holy Scriptures. Nor did He mean every sort of truth concerning God, as, for example, how God creates. And most assuredly He did not mean all sorts of truth concerning the operations of divine grace through the workings of the Holy Ghost; for these things the Lord Himself declared to be like the wind blowing whither it will—recognizable, but not definable. What our Lord meant could, in reason, have been simply this: that the Holy Ghost should

guide the Church into all necessary and essential truth; and manifestly the very highest function of the Church as a teaching body, guided by her Divine Inspirer, would be to declare what is the necessary and essential truth of Christ, as distinguished from all other truth, whether scientific, historical, critical, philosophical, or even theological. Now if it were a fact that the Catholic Church of Christ had not only declared what the essential verities of the faith are, but had positively forbidden any minister of any rank to set forth anything different as true, or anything else as necessary and essential; if it were, furthermore, a fact that, for her own protection, the Catholic Church had been compelled to set forth the *ipsissima verba* in which alone the essentials of the faith might be authoritatively expressed; and if it were a fact that, from the time when this was done and its value tested, God's wise providence made it impossible that one single additional definition of faith should ever be made by the united voice of the Catholic Church, it seems to me that, unless Christ's promise has failed, and unless the gates of hell have prevailed against His Church, we need be at little pains to ascertain what are the essential verities of the Catholic Faith. And these three things are true, as I proceed to show.

II. (1). Nothing could be more strikingly in contrast with the dogmatical recklessness of assertion exhibited by Churches and by individuals in later centuries than the cautious reluctant with which the primitive Church suffered itself to be compelled to express the verities of the Faith in scientific terms of theological definition. No definition of any article was ever volunteered in advance of some imperious necessity. At first the formula of Holy Baptism was the only Formula of Faith, and its meaning was set forth, not in terms of scientific theology, but in the looser terms of popular teaching. As there seems to be little doubt that the briefest possible abstract of the story of the gospel was reduced to writing at a very early day, and was afterwards the basis of the three larger Synoptical Gospels, so there is little doubt that the formula of Baptism was gradually expanded for catechetical purposes into short Creeds, of which the form known as the Apostle's Creed is probably the best and fullest specimen now extant. It is important, however, to observe that these Baptismal Creeds were set forth as freely in particular Churches

as catechisms of one sort or another are set forth now. They had this in common, that they all set forth the elementary facts of the Faith, in the simplest language, and without theory or comment. In other respects they differed in different Churches.

(2). It is a very common error, but still an error, to suppose that the First General Council of Nicæa set forth a Creed, if by the word *Creed* we mean an exact form of words which was prescribed or recommended as a substitute for the catechetical or Baptismal Creeds which had been previously used in particular Churches. Even if it were true, it would mark the significant fact that it was not until the year 325 that the Catholic Church ever attempted to set forth an exact and authoritative Formula of Faith. But the truth is that the Council of Nicæa did no such thing. The heresy of Arius had denied the eternity, and therefore the essential deity, of the Only-Begotten of the Father, and to correct this heresy the Council of Nicæa set forth the testimony of all the Churches of Christ concerning the true doctrine of the Son of God. It did nothing more than that. The Nicene definition was indeed made in exact and scientific terms, which were meant to be a bulwark of the Faith against the heresy of Arius; and it was the first definition ever made by the consentient voice of the Catholic Church, teaching in the name and by the authority of Christ. But it was not, nor was it meant to be, a perfect or sufficient statement of the Christian Faith. It determined one central truth, and that undoubtedly the greatest and most vital; but it did no more. The reluctance of the Church to make exact definitions of doctrine is strikingly exhibited in the fact that this holy, great and venerable Synod would not, and did not, utter one word beyond what it was required to utter by the manifest necessities of the Church, and by the manifest providence of God. And this, too, is remarkable, that it did not, even then, impose its own form of words upon the Churches. The facts it had declared were eternally true; and whoever should deny them must be cast out of the Catholic Church as one who had denied the Faith of Christ; but there was no intimation whatsoever that the same eternal truths might not, in the future as in the past, be freely, if only faithfully, set forth on any occasion in different language.

(3). More than half a century passed away before the Catholic Church in the first Council of Constantinople was compelled by absolute necessity to add what was lacking to the definition of Nicæa. The Semi-Arians and Pneumatomachi had depraved the doctrine of the Holy Spirit, and the Council of Constantinople added a few brief and pregnant statements to correct the errors of these and other heretics. But still, though the Fathers of that Council spoke in no stammering or hesitating words, they imitated the fathers of Nicæa in this, that they did not forbid the use of any other true words in the exposition of the same truths. This Council, eminent for wisdom and sanctity, was not in form an Œcumenical or General Council of the whole Church, since it was composed exclusively of Oriental bishops; and its definitions had not the stamp of authority which belonged to those of Nicæa until they had been sanctioned, as they were immediately afterwards, by their universal reception and approval throughout the whole Catholic Church. The fact that they had been so sanctioned was emphatically ascertained at the Council of Chalcedon.

(4). Fifty years more passed away before the Catholic Church was called again to declare a matter of doctrine at the Council of Ephesus, but on this occasion the Council merely tested the heresy of Nestorius by the clear signification of the previous definition of Nicæa. The *ecthesis*, i. e., the *statement* or *exposition* of Nicæa, was read, and after it the *symbolon*, or *formula* in which Theodore of Mopsuestia had covered up the essential heresy of Nestorius in terms of pretended orthodoxy. The inconsistency of the new heresy with the old truth was at once apparent; and then the Fathers adopted that famous Seventh Canon* which has been so widely misinterpreted. It is very commonly believed that the Seventh Canon of Ephesus sets forth the Nicene definition as a final Creed, to the neglect of the Constantinopolitan definitions, so that the subsequent decree of the Council of Chalcedon

* It has been objected that the Seventh Canon of Ephesus was not, properly speaking, a canon, but a ὅρος, or determination of the particular matter to which it referred. The objection, however, is of little real force; since the Council, instead of limiting its determination to the particular errors contained in the formula of Theodore, and instead of pronouncing sentence upon the particular persons who maintained those errors, chose rather to render judgment in the form of a general rule, that is to say a *Canon*, which would apply to all persons who should set forth a doctrine different from the Nicene.

seems to be, in effect, an overruling of the previous action of the Council of Ephesus. I confess that the translation given in the first edition of this work entirely fails to bring out the very important truth of the matter, a failure which it has in common with all other translations I have examined. The truth is this, and a glance at the original Greek will verify the assertion: That the Seventh Canon of Ephesus simply reaffirmed the Nicene definition; not even then did it prescribe the Nicene form of words to be used on all occasions; but it declared in effect that any and every form of words which might be used must be consistent with the Nicene definition; and it decreed that if any clergyman should dare to set forth *heteran pistin*, that is to say, a *different faith* from that of the Nicene fathers, he should be summarily cut off.*

* Canon Bright's discussion of the Seventh Canon of Ephesus is very unsatisfactory. He affirms that to explain ἑτέραν πίστιν "as a belief contrary to the Nicene, or a creed expressing doctrine inconsistent with the Nicene" "is to explain it away;" an assertion which simply begs the question. He declares that "πίστις means a *formulary* of doctrine which can be 'written' and 'presented,'—in short, a creed;" a declaration which begs the question in another form of words. He says that "ἑτέρα applied to a creed" (i. e. to πίστις) "*must* bear the sense of verbal difference, not of doctrinal opposition;" a necessity which is not shown, so that the statement is merely a third begging of the question. The learned Canon maintains that the decree of Ephesus "excludes the Apostles' Creed as a baptismal symbol;" a notion which, if it were true, would condemn the baptisms of the Western Church from the Council of Ephesus until now. In order to establish his thesis it would be necessary for the learned professor to show, by at least *one* undoubted instance, that at the time of the Council of Ephesus πίστις had acquired the new meaning of a *verbal formulary* in addition to its old and usual signification of a *faith, doctrine, belief*. No such undoubted instance, I believe, can be produced. If it could, the learned professor must next show that the Council, in laying down a rule for the government of the Catholic Church, deliberately used a common word in a new and unusual sense, which is altogether improbable unless there were no other word in the Greek language to express their meaning. So far from that, however, the word σύμβολον lay ready for that very use; and the fact that they did not use it is sufficient evidence that they did not mean it. It would strengthen Canon Bright's opinion, of course, if he could show that any person ever understood the Council to have used the word πίστις in the new sense of a verbal formulary; but the evidence is altogether to the contrary. If πίστις alone had been understood in that sense, the Fathers of Chalcedon would have found it enough to include the definitions of Constantinople in their confirmation of the decree of Ephesus; but instead of that they first forbade all that had been forbidden by the Council of Ephesus, and then they added *a new prohibition* by extending the decree which already protected the doctrine of the Church to the verbal formula in which it might be offered. If the two decrees are put side by side, it seems to me that the inference is inevitable; and the fact that the Fathers of Chalcedon adopted the very words of the Fathers of Ephesus plainly shows that the additional words were inserted deliberately and on account of some indispensable necessity.

EPHESUS.	CHALCEDON.
"The holy Synod decrees that it is unlawful for any man to propose, or compile, or compose any ἑτέραν πίστιν than	"The holy and œcumenical Synod decrees that it is unlawful for any man to propose, or compile, or compose,

(5). Twenty years later the greatest of all the Councils, numbering six hundred and thirty bishops, assembled at Chalcedon for the correction of recently invented forms of heresy; and as the Council of Ephesus had found that the definition of Nicæa, fairly and grammatically construed in its obvious sense, was a sufficient protection against Nestorianism, so the Fathers of Chalcedon found that in the definitions of Nicæa and Constantinople united, the Church had a sufficient protection against all heresies whatsoever. It was now a hundred and twenty-six years since the Council of Nicæa had assembled, and nearly four hundred and twenty years since the Apostles had received their commission to go and teach all nations. In all that time the Catholic Church had never but twice, and then with great reluctance, exercised her supreme function of exact doctrinal definition. Heretics, on the contrary, had been ever ready with irreverent self-conceit to affirm or deny, as the whim took them; and the absence of a fixed formula or symbol of faith had been severely felt. For want of it, faithful members of the Church had been liable to be led away by heretics who professed the greatest devotion to orthodoxy and the utmost reverence for the

<table>
<tr><td>that established by the holy and blessed fathers assembled with the Holy Ghost at Nicæa.</td><td>or hold, or teach to others any ἑτέραν πίστιν.</td></tr>
<tr><td>But those who shall dare to compose, or to publish, or offer ἑτέραν πίστιν</td><td>But those who shall dare EITHER to compose ἑτέραν πίστιν, OR to publish, or teach, or deliver ἕτερον σύμβολον</td></tr>
</table>

to persons desiring to turn to the acknowledgment of the truth, whether from heathenism, or from judaism, or from any heresy whatsoever, shall be deposed, if they be Bishops or Clergymen; Bishops from the Episcopate, and Clergymen from the Clergy; and, if they be monks or laymen, they shall be anathematized."

The truth is that the language of the General Councils is not loose and inconsistent, but, on the contrary, it is, as might be expected, exceedingly precise and exact, in every utterance which concerns the Faith. It will be found, I think, that in the first four General Councils διδασκαλία signifies doctrine in general; ἔκθεσις, a statement of doctrine; δόγματα, opinions set forth as doctrines of faith; πίστις, faith irrespective of form; σύμβολον, an exact verbal formula of faith, or, in the strictest sense of the word, a *Creed*. The mere fact that the word σύμβολον began to be used at the Council of Chalcedon alone suffices to prove that the idea which it expresses was then first recognized.

Though I have thought it necessary to give my reasons for differing from the learned Professor, I may nevertheless remark that the main argument of the text would be in no way weakened if it could be shown that πίστις in the Seventh Canon of Ephesus was intended to mean an exact verbal formulary of faith. It would then simply follow that the Council of Chalcedon accepted and completed the earlier work of Ephesus; for, whatever might be the force of πίστις alone, it is impossible to deny or doubt that πίστις, clinched by σύμβολον, can mean nothing less than a *Creed* in the strictest sense of an exact verbal formula of faith.

Councils of the Church, but who availed themselves of the unrestrained liberty of exposition to set forth heretical formulas, which were, in fact, *heterai pisteis*, utterly inconsistent with the faith of the Catholic Church. In like manner heathen persons embracing Christianity, and heretics or schismatics desiring to return into the one fold, were liable to be required by pretentious priests to subscribe to formulas which were not only unauthorized, but which were expressly designed to teach heresy in the Church itself. The necessity of having not only sound and sufficient definitions of the Faith, but also a fixed and unalterable form of words in which to express it, had at length become manifest. The definitions of Nicæa, supplemented by the additional definitions of Constantinople, were beyond all question theologically exact in their terms, and they were found to be amply sufficient in their scope to express the Catholic Faith. Therefore the Fathers of Chalcedon, in dealing with the new heresies of their day, imitated the example of the Fathers of Ephesus. They distinctly refused to adopt or to impose new definitions. They tested existing heresies by simply comparing them with the definitions of Nicæa and Constantinople. For the protection of the Church in the future they renewed the prohibition of Ephesus, which forbade the setting forth of any *heteran pistin;* that is to say, any faith which should be inconsistent with the definitions of Nicæa; they extended that prohibition to the definitions of Constantinople; and lastly, they declared that not only the doctrines expressed in those definitions, but the very *ipsissima verba,* the identical words in which they were defined, should be and remain unalterable. The distinction is very clearly brought out in the two words *pistis* and *symbolon; pistis* referring to the doctrine and *symbolon* to the formula of the Creed. Repeating the prohibition of Ephesus, the Fathers of Chalcedon declared "that it is not lawful for any man to propose, or compile, or compose, or hold, or teach to others any different faith (*heteran pistin*);" a prohibition which manifestly applied to the substance of the Faith and to all modes of teaching; and then they proceeded furthermore to enact that "those who dare EITHER to compose a different faith (*pistin*), OR to publish or teach, or deliver a different formula (*symbolon*), to persons desirous of turning to the truth from heathenism, or Judaism, or any heresy

whatsoever, shall be deposed, if they be bishops or clergymen—bishops from the Episcopate and clergymen from the Clergy; and, if they be monks or laymen they shall be anathematized."

(6). In no more striking, positive, or emphatic way would it have been possible for the six hundred and thirty bishops who represented the Catholic Church at Chalcedon to have declared that *the whole Catholic Faith is summarily and sufficiently expressed in the words of the Nicæno-Constantinopolitan symbol; that to tamper with the least jot of its form is to tamper with heresy; and that to add to its definitions, making the acceptance of such additions a condition of communion, is to act without Catholic authority, and to incur the condemnation of the Catholic Church.* And be it well observed that this grand decree of the greatest of all Œcumenical Councils was none other than a law of Christian liberty. It did not require that the baptismal Creeds which had grown venerable by long ages of continuous use in different Churches should be displaced by the exact technical formulas of Nicæa and Chalcedon; it was neither to be expected nor to be desired that children and peasants, that is to say, a large majority of mankind, should be vexed with the subtleties of theological distinctions; it was wholly unnecessary that they should be taught the difference between *homo-ousios* and *homoi-ousios;* therefore the old provincial formulas continued, at least in the Western Church, to be freely used as they had been before; and, in popular use, the Apostles' Creed has never in the West been displaced by the fuller formula. Neither were provincial Churches prohibited from uttering their voices on new questions of doctrine that might come up from time to time. When the Western Churches were constrained by royal meddling and imperial dictation to declare that the Holy Ghost proceedeth from the Father *and the Son,* it was an unfortunate thing to do, and it was done in precisely the most unfortunate way that the spirit of mischief could have devised; but it was not an act of heresy, for the statement was not inconsistent with the Catholic Symbol; it was not at first an act of schism, because the Western Churches did not at first make the reception of the added words a condition of communion; and it was not, nor did it become, an offense against the decree of Chalcedon until it was made a condition of

communion, and so an occasion of schism; for the scope and purport of the Chalcedonian decree was this: that no Church, however great or venerable, and no prelate, however eminent in authority, should impose one syllable of doctrine, however true, as a condition of communion, beyond the *ipsissima verba* of the Nicæno-Constantinopolitan Symbol. Thus the Chalcedonian Decree was emphatically a law of liberty for the whole Christian Commonwealth, and if that law had been obeyed, innumerable scandalous divisions and other evils would have been spared to the Body of Christ.

(7). In the next two General Councils, which completed the number of those that can be called "undisputed" and therefore truly Œcumenical, the sufficiency of the Chalcedonian Decree was effectively tested. New heresies of the subtlest sort, and couched in the subtlest phrases of the subtlest and most flexible of languages, had rapidly appeared in great number; but the second and third Councils of Constantinople found no difficulty in dealing with them. In every instance it was only necessary to compare the new doctrine with the plain meaning of the old formula in order to discover that the new was inconsistent with the old, or, in other words, that it was *hetera pistis*, and therefore false; so that what are incorrectly called the doctrinal definitions of the fifth and sixth General Councils were not, properly speaking, definitions at all; they were in fact judicial declarations that the several heresies which they condemned were inconsistent with the Catholic Faith, as it had been already defined.

(8). No one, I suppose, will doubt that it was of God's wise providence that the Catholic Church was enabled in her General Councils to defend the Faith of Christ against the assaults of heresy. No one, I imagine, can fail to admire the reverent reluctance exhibited by those great assemblies in approaching the duty which God's providence imposed upon them, of choosing human words for the definition of divine truth. No Catholic Christian can deny or doubt that they were divinely guided, as the Lord had promised, in their definitions of the truth; and just as little can we question that they were divinely guided in forbidding definition to be carried further. Surely we must equally believe it to have been of God's wise providence that *from the time when the essential verities of the Faith had thus been clearly and suffi-*

ciently expressed in a form of words which could not have been changed without endangering the Faith itself, no true Œcumenical Council of the whole Catholic Church has ever been convened. Humanly speaking, if General Councils had been held in subsequent ages they would have done what provincial Councils and patriarchal Councils have done everywhere; they would have taken up the passing questions of the time and would have multiplied definitions of unimportant doctrines until the Faith of Christ would have been obscured in a confused mass of inconsistent theological philosophy. Doubtless the Holy Ghost *could* have guided the Church through all such dangers. But the way in which the providence of God actually *has* saved the Church has been by suffering the holding of General Councils to become impossible. Thus the wrath and sinfulness of men has been made to subserve the safety of the Church; and, as we glance back upon the history of the ages, we may well adore the mystery of Providence, when we perceive that every individual and particular Church has sinned and erred in divers ways; that "as the Churches of Jerusalem, Alexandria and Antioch have erred, so also the Church of Rome hath erred," and the Church of England hath erred; and yet the Catholic Church, but the Catholic Church alone, hath not erred, but hath been wonderfully saved from error, and even from danger of error, lo, these many centuries.

III. (1). It is no part of the purpose of this essay to enlarge on the divine truths which are declared in the only authorized Symbol of the Catholic Faith; and it is needless further to insist that the Christian Faith is sufficiently as well as truly defined in that consecrated Symbol. What the Catholic Church has authoritatively defined in that Symbol is true and Catholic; what she has forbidden to be defined may indeed be true, but it is not Catholic, and cannot lawfully be imposed upon any Christian man as a condition of communion in the Church of Christ. Hence the pretended right of the Roman Patriarchate to define new doctrines of Faith, or, in other words, to change the Christian Religion, is a sheer rebellion against the Catholic Church; and every attempt to impose such doctrines as a condition of communion is an act of schismatical usurpation. But the ease of mind and the comfort of faith which a Catholic Christian may enjoy in

these days by remembering what the Chalcedonian law of liberty does not define, and even forbids to be defined as Catholic doctrine, extends to many other matters besides the arrogant pretensions of the Church of Rome. After a brief reference to some of these, the present essay may be fitly closed.

(2). In these days we hear much of the conflict between science and religion. That there unfortunately is, and has been, very much of conflict between scientific men and religious men is unquestionably true; but nothing which the researches of scientific men have proved to be true does even so much as touch the utmost verge of the Catholic Faith. Briefly stated, the whole religious question involved in the vague doctrine of evolution, for example, is this: *How* does God create? On that question the Catholic Faith says nothing. It simply declares that God is, and that He is the "Maker of heaven and earth, and of all things visible and invisible." The Catholic Christian has no conflict with science; rather, he is full of sympathy with those who study the wonderful works of God. He may be slow, perhaps, to adopt the hasty theories of scientific men, but he is always thankful for their facts, and he is utterly fearless of them. What has he to fear from them? Atheism? Atheism is not science! Atheism is a negative proposition which can never be proved, but which every fact of science goes to disprove.

(3). Again, in these days, we hear much about the destructive tendencies of biblical criticism, and it must be confessed that to the mere Protestant, who has only some sentimental sort of belief in the Catholic Church, there has been ample cause for consternation. Not so to the Catholic Christian. On the subject of the Sacred Scriptures his faith cannot be shaken. That deep and pregnant declaration that it was the Holy Ghost "Who spoke by the prophets" will never, indeed, allow him to make light of any part of Holy Scripture, nor to lay irreverent hands upon the pages of The Word. He will not run lightly into new-fangled theories, either of criticism or of interpretation. He will be prone to remember that the Scriptures are very old, and that the science of biblical criticism is a very new and a very capricious and uncertain sort of thing. But from any fact that criticism can establish concerning the books of Holy Scripture, he has no reason to

shrink. On the contrary, he has every reason to desire the increase of kuowledge which will enable him more perfectly to follow the mind of the Spirit "Who spake by the Prophets."

(4). Again, when we consider the endless controversies of philosophical theologians on the subject of soteriology, or the means of man's salvation, and remember the hideous distortions of the divine character which the perverted ingenuity of men has set forth as divine truth, it is profoundly humbling and instructive to recur to the round simplicity of faith which is preserved in the Catholic Symbol. In it there is no exalting of the incarnation so as to make the death and passion of our Lord merely an incident of the incarnation; neither is the incarnation made to be merely the introductory step to the tremendous sacrifice of Calvary. All the truth is given without interpretations that our Lord and His Apostles did did not give, and nothing is depressed from its divine importance. "For us men and for our salvation (δἱ ἡμᾶς κ. τ. λ.) He came down from heaven and was incarnate of the Holy Ghost and the Virgin Mary, and was made man; for our sakes (ὑπὲρ ἡμῶν) He was crucified under Pontius Pilate, and suffered, and was buried, and rose again the third day according to the Scriptures, and ascended into heaven, and sitteth on the right hand of the Father;" (for our sakes) "He cometh again to judge the quick and the dead." It was all from first to last "for us men and for our salvation;" it was all, in whole and in part, "for our sakes." What an amazing contrast have we here to the endless muddle of scientific soteriology set forth by schools and parties in the Church and outside of the Church.

(5). Again, when we consider the embittered controversies which have raged concerning the divine foreknowledge and decrees of God, things which must undoubtedly exist, but which from their very nature are not rightly knowable, and therefore cannot be rightly defined, is not a blessed thing to know that on these subjects not one single word is to be found in the Catholic Symbol? Even into the vestibule of that sanctuary of the secret things of God, which men have profaned with their presumptuous and uncharitable clamor, the Catholic Church of Christ has not presumed to enter.

(6). Not less reverent is she touching the inscrutable oper-

ations of the Holy Spirit in the hearts of men. She adorès Him as the Giver of life; but she does not attempt to parcel out and label His ineffable gifts, nor does she authorize others so to do. She leaves us to learn from the simple language of Scripture: "It is the Spirit that quickeneth;" "by grace are ye saved, through faith, and that not of yourselves; it is the gift of God;" "therefore being justified by faith, we have peace with God." No nicety of definition could add to the instruction or to the comfort of such words; attempts at nicety of definition have in fact done monstrous mischief; but they have never been sanctioned by the Catholic Church.

(7). There are many who might learn a lesson of humility from the reverent silence of the Catholic Church concerning the sacred mystery of sacramental grace. She asserts the reality of sacramental grace in the acknowledgement of "One Baptism for the remission of sins;" but there she stops. The divine mystery and the unspeakable gift of the Holy Eucharist she does not define. The unbroken tradition, and (until recently in the Roman Communion alone) the universal custom of every branch of the Catholic Church has regarded the Holy Eucharist as chief among the *agenda* of the Church, the liturgy and its accessories being left to the discrimination of each particular Church; but no definition of *credenda* concerning it is set forth in the Catholic Symbol. This is a very remarkable fact concerning which more than a few observations might well be made. Enough that it is a fact which should teach us at least three things: 1st, to be cautious in forming positive opinions concerning the doctrine of the Sacraments; 2d, to be yet more cautious not to set forth any opinions we may have formed as if they were catholic truth; and, 3d, always and everywhere to resist and deny the pretense that exact modern definitions, by whomsoever set forth, have the slightest color of catholic authority.

(8). I have now to note a seventh topic on which the Catholic Church did not define, but which has recently engaged the minds of men to a great extent. It is astonishing that on the subject of Eschatology, concerning which whole libraries have been printed, the Catholic Faith gives us in the Greek original only fourteen words in which it declares that our Lord Jesus Christ "cometh again with glory to judge both the quick and the dead," and affirms that "we look for

the resurrection of the dead and the life of the world to come." Once again we are compelled to contrast the simplicity and reserve of the Catholic Church with the volubility of arrogant dogmatism displayed by vastly less respectable authorities. On the subject of future rewards and punishments the abundance of assertion has been in inverse ratio to the littleness of our knowledge. The *doctrina Romanensium*, or the vulgar Romanism of the middle age, went wild in its horrible declarations concerning the state of the lost; and the vulgar Protestantism of later times bated nothing of the Romish horrors; indeed it made them worse, by denying the existence of a purgatory, which in the Romish system left some chance of escape. From the cruel atrocity of Romish and Protestant doctrine concerning the last things, the common sense and instinct of mankind recoiled; and I believe that it has been the horror of those abominable and unauthorized teachings, more than any other one thing, which has caused a multitude of men to renounce Christianity altogether. Of late years the recklessness of denial has been almost as remarkable, if not so atrocious, as the former recklessness of assertion. Now there is declared to be neither hell nor purgatory, nor any judgment at all worth thinking of. The reaction has certainly been extensive and radical; but, standing in our position as Catholic Christians, we are not swayed, and our Church has not been swayed, to the one extreme or to the other. We do not pretend to make void the words of Scripture that "whatsoever a man soweth, *that* shall he also reap." We dare no more reject all meaning from the words, "Depart ye cursed," than we dare to cast away the comfort of those others, "Come ye blessed of My Father." We are not free to misuse our lexicons in such wise as to show that the tremendous word *aionios*, the significance of which transcends imagination, really means nothing of any consequence. But, on the other hand, we hold not, and we have never held, those monstrous calumnies against the moral character of God which vulgar Romanism and vulgar Protestantism have equally set forth. So far as definition goes, the Anglican Churches add not a word to the definition of Constantinople. We care not further to define. It is enough to know that "for our sakes" the Lord Jesus Christ "cometh again with glory to judge the quick and the dead." Enough for us, in the blessed hope of

his merciful award, to "look for the resurrection of the dead, and the life of the world to come."

IV. I conclude with two brief observations:

(1). If any thoughtful man will consider the history of Christ's Church in the ages that are past he will observe this universal fact: that whenever a Church, or a prelate, or an individual theologian, has violated the Decree of Chalcedon, the immediate fruit has been schism, and the aftermath has been an even more abundant harvest of heresy.

(2). If he shall then look forward to the future he will see that the only hope of the restoration of unity to the separated fragments of the Catholic Church is this: that one day or another, and some way or another, as God's good providence shall direct, all of them shall return to the common platform of faith, *which, thank God, is still the common heritage and possession of all.* Constantinople, and Alexandria, and Antioch will never submit to Rome. England and the greater England of English-speaking Churches can never submit to any of their elder sisters. But England, and Alexandria, and Antioch, and Rome can all submit to their common Mother, the Holy Catholic Church of Christ; not by renouncing their provincial traditions, but by obeying the Chalcedonian Law of Liberty which secures the liberties of each by maintaining the rights of all.

JOHN FULTON.

ST. GEORGE'S CHURCH, ST. LOUIS, MO.,
EASTERTIDE, 1883.

PREFACE TO THE FIRST EDITION.

THE preparation of this little Manual of the Canon Laws of the primitive Church was undertaken at the suggestion of several Bishops. It is now laid before the public not only with their sanction, but with that of many others of our chief Pastors who have very cordially approved the plan of the work, and who have generously trusted that the diligence of the compiler would suffice to execute it to the satisfaction of the Church.

Of the utility of such a Manual on such a plan it is not, therefore, necessary for the writer to speak; of the merits or demerits of its execution it is not for him to judge; and the object of this preface is only to give such information to the reader as may tend to make its use more satisfactory.

1. The Greek Text which has been followed in the Apostolical Canons is that of Beveridge's Codex Canonum Ecclesiæ Primitivæ Vindicatus ac Illustratus. In the Canons of the Councils the text is that set forth by authority of the Holy Synod of the Church of Greece under the title ΣΥΝΤΑΓΜΑ ΤΩΝ ΘΕΙΩΝ ΚΑΙ ΙΕΡΩΝ ΚΑΝΟΝΩΝ. The other documents, which, for the sake of greater completeness, it was thought advisable to insert, have been drawn from various sources, and are believed to be correct; though in some few cases the compiler has been obliged to use the privilege of an Editor in deciding between various readings. This, however, has never been done in any case which touches the substance of a doctrine or of a Canon.

2. In the English Version the Translator has aimed at such a conscientious accuracy as might justify its claim upon the reader's confidence. In the choice of English equivalents for Greek words that might be supposed to have a special bearing upon any question doctrinal or ecclesiastical, he has invariably chosen that which is most literal; thus πρεσβύτερος, for example, is always rendered by *presbyter*, never by *priest;* and whenever the word *priest* or *priesthood* occurs, which is exceedingly seldom, it is because the original demands it.

To assure the general exactness of the rendering, former editions and translations, Greek, Latin, French, and English, have been diligently examined and compared; so that wherever this version is found to differ in sense from that of its English predecessors, it is because of some reason which has been deliberately weighed. Happily such instances are few. To the learned reader there is a sufficient safeguard in the presence of the Greek Text side by side with the English; but to many of the honoured laity, and even of the reverend Clergy, to whom the Greek tongue is no longer as familiar as it once was in the consulship of Plancus, it may not have been unnecessary to say thus much of the Version now before them.

3. In the Introduction an attempt has been made to gather together such information as might suffice to a clear understanding of the Canons; and this has been done with the double purpose of avoiding a multiplicity of Notes upon the Text, and of presenting the leading facts in as readable a form as possible. The Index to the Introduction, which has been carefully prepared, will enable the student to refer at his pleasure to any particular point. It is hoped that there is nothing in the Introduction which can justly be objected to on any ground. Nevertheless, the writer thinks it right to say that in this part of his work he has felt himself entitled to a measure of freedom in the expression of opinion which would have been wholly inadmissible in any other part.

4. In the DIGEST the same careful accuracy has been studied as in the Translation; but as the Digest is merely a complete summary and convenient Index of the matters contained in the Canons, it has been felt admissible to use the word *Priest*, which is the word constantly used in the Book of Common Prayer, and customarily used in common conversation as the equivalent of Presbyter.

5. It will be observed that the writer has included in the present work all of the DOCTRINAL DEFINITIONS which were directly set forth by the first four undisputed General Councils; and this he has felt it right to do even in a work which is intended to bear only on the Canons of those Councils; because the Canons themselves frequently presuppose some knowledge of their own doctrinal reasons. Yet it is not to be supposed that the documents here given are all the documents approved by these four Councils; for, to mention no others, the Tome of S. Leo and the doctrinal Canons of S. Cyril, are as fully sanctioned as the disciplinary Canons of Ancyra or the rest of the Provincial Councils whose decrees were sanctioned at Chalcedon. Neither is it meant to be implied that the writer does not recognize the Fifth and Sixth General Councils of the undivided Catholic Church. He has simply given the doctrinal decrees which were directly set forth by the Councils with whose Canons he is here concerned, and he has given nothing from the Fifth and Sixth General Councils, for the single reason that those Councils passed no Canons. If the present work shall be received with favor by the Church, it will encourage him, or some one abler than himself, to bring out a more noble work than this; in which the doctrinal decisions of the undivided Church of CHRIST shall all be given in Greek and English; and their matter be digested and arranged under the sections of the Nicene Symbol.

This volume passes from the writer to the public and the Church with a deep feeling on the writer's part that it might

have been better. With more learning he might doubtless have given more instruction; and with greater leisure he might have avoided inadvertencies that doubtless will be found. Therefore, he asks to be considered by his brethren, not as one who would be thought a *Master*, but as the mere *assistant* of their higher and more fruitful studies. The book before them is not a Thesaurus, but a Manual; it is an Index, not a Cyclopædia; and in their judgment of its faults he prays them to remember that it has been put together in the irregular hours of often-interrupted leisure which are not too frequent in the daily avocations of a working Parish Priest.

CHRIST CHURCH, MOBILE, *June 15th, 1872.*

INTRODUCTION.

CHAPTER I.

THE PROVINCIAL SYSTEM OF THE ROMAN EMPIRE.

NECESSITY OF THIS DISCUSSION. UNIVERSALITY OF ROMAN LAW. THE ORGANIZATION OF ROME AND ITALY THE MODEL OF MUNICIPALITIES AND PROVINCES THROUGHOUT THE WORLD. THE CITY AND ITS ORGANIZATION. THE PARISH. THE PROVINCE. THE DIOCESE. THE PRÆTORIAN PRÆFECTURES. THE SYSTEM OF THE CHURCH NOT A SERVILE COPY OF THE CIVIL DISTRIBUTIONS OF THE EMPIRE.

IN order to have any clear conception of the marvellously simple and perfect system of organization which grew up in the Church of the first centuries, it is necessary, first of all to understand at least the outlines of the system of municipal and provincial government which then prevailed throughout the Roman Empire. The Roman world in which the Church was first established was a world, not of contending Kingdoms and distracted Commonwealths, but of uniform and universal law. Notwithstanding the sagacious policy of Rome, which led her to respect, as far as possible, the local customs and religious preferences of the nations she had conquered, every generation as it saw her power more firmly rooted, likewise saw her system of administration growing to a perfect and undeviating uniformity. The civil law of Rome became the code of every province of the Empire, and the practice of the Roman courts became the code of practice likewise in the provinces. Hence the municipal arrangement of the cities and the governments of provinces were organized throughout the world in strict conformity to those of Rome and Italy, and the administration of justice was conducted by officers invested with like powers to those possessed by officers at Rome; and as at Rome the City Government had jurisdiction both in the City proper and in the suburbicarian districts, so throughout the densely populated regions of the Empire in Europe, Asia and Africa, even where the substantial benefits of Roman Citizenship had not been conferred upon the people, the Cities were made the Centres of Government, and the

magistrates had jurisdiction over the outlying districts of their own immediate vicinity.

The City, therefore, (*urbs*, ἡ πόλις), is the first element of the Roman government that must be observed and borne in mind. "Even in the times of the Apostles," says Bingham, "every city among the Greeks and Romans was under the immediate government of certain magistrates within its own body, commonly known by the name of *βουλή* or *Senatus*, its Common Council or Senate, otherwise called *ordo* and *curia*, the States and Court of the City; among which there was usually one Chief or Principal above the rest whom some call the *Dictator*, and others *Defensor Civitatis*."

The Jurisdiction of the City Courts and Officers, however, extended sometimes far beyond the limits of the City itself. The Suburbs (*προάστεια*) and the surrounding country, often to the extent of many miles, and including villages and lesser towns, were all under the jurisdiction of the City Government. The City, together with its subordinate districts, was in the Greek part of the Empire called *παροικία*, a Parish; and in the villages or towns of a Parish there were not unfrequently subordinate officers or deputy magistrates chosen by the magistrates of the City, and responsible to them for the performance of their trust.

But the Magistrates of the City were themselves responsible for their administration of the Parish to the Prætor or Proconsul or other Officer of like rank who presided over the Province in which the Parish was situated. A Province included all the Cities and Parishes of a certain region of country. The Seat of government was in the Metropolis or chief city of the region, and it was in the Metropolis that appeals were heard against the decisions of the Magistrates of other Cities of the Province.

Under the Commonwealth and in the earlier period of the Empire Provinces were of great extent, and were generally conterminous with the nations which had been subdued by the Roman arms; that is to say, they included the undivided territory of one or more nations, nations which had been wholly conquered, being seldom dismembered or distributed among different Provinces. The number of Provinces at the beginning of the Empire was seventeen; viz., Sicilia; Sardinia et Corsica; Hispania Citerior et Ulterior; Gallia Citerior;

Gallia Narbonensis et Comata; Illyricum; Macedonia; Achaia; Asia ; Cilicia ; Syria ; Bithynia et Pontus ; Cyprus ; Africa ; Cyrenaica et Creta ; Numidia ; Mauritania. Those of a subsequent date were either new Provinces acquired by conquest, or they were erected by dividing older Provinces. Such were Rhætia ; Noricum ; Pannonia ; Mœsia ; Dacia ; Britannia ; Mauritania Cæsariensis et Tingitana ; Ægyptus ; Cappadocia ; Galatia ; Rhodus ; Lycia ; Commagene; Judæa; Arabia; Mesopotamia; Armenia; Assyria.

Gradually, however, the necessities of administrative government in the transaction of local affairs demanded that the area of Provinces should be diminished; and about the time of Constantine their number had been increased by successive divisions to nearly one hundred and twenty. But at the same time unity of administration was secured by the erection of thirteen larger districts called DIOCESES, presided over by officers called Eparchs or Vicars of the Empire. These Dioceses included each from three to seventeen Provinces, over which the Eparch exercised the right of superior jurisdiction, and, indeed, of limited control.

There remains but one officer and one division of this complex and yet simple system to be mentioned. The four Prætorian Præfects, of the East, of Illyricum, of Italy, and of Gaul were the highest officers of the Empire, and exercised the supreme administration of Justice and of the Finances. They controlled all inferior magistrates, "removed the negligent, and inflicted punishments on the guilty. From all the inferior jurisdictions an appeal in every matter of importance, whether civil or criminal, might be brought before the Præfect; but *his* sentence was final and absolute. The Emperors themselves refused to admit complaints against the judgment or the integrity of these magistrates, in whom they reposed unbounded confidence." *

We have thus glanced briefly at the form in which the Empire had come to exist at the time and during the period which requires our attention, because it was to this model that the Church conformed the outward shape of her divinely constituted Order. The Imperial System consisted, as we have seen, of the following elements :

* Gibbon, abridged.

THE EMPIRE,

divided into

FOUR PRÆTORIAN PRÆFECTURES,

which had jurisdiction over

THIRTEEN DIOCESES,

including

ONE HUNDRED AND SEVENTEEN PROVINCES,

in which the local affairs were administered by the Magistrates of

THE CITIES,

and the Cities with their suburbs and outlying districts and villages, over which the City Magistrates presided, were known as

PARISHES.

The attentive student of the early Canons will speedily find that the Church, in following the suggestions of this plan of the Empire, as she unquestionably did, nevertheless did not conform to that plan in a spirit of slavish imitation. The Parochial and Provincial System was everywhere adopted; of the Diocesan System we have some trace in the Canons of the Undivided Church; the later idea of Patriarchates *may* have been taken from the Prætorian Præfectures, though the Patriarchates never corresponded either in location or in jurisdiction with the Præfectures; but of an Imperial Head of the Church on earth it is not too much to say that there is not one trace in any Canon of the Undisputed Councils of the Universal Church.

In the sketch which we are now about to give of the organization of the Church in what might not improperly be called the Age of the Councils, the reader must do us the justice to bear in mind that the sole object of this essay is to illustrate the actual condition of the Church in that Age, as we find it in the Canons of the Councils; that otherwise than incidentally it is not our province to discuss the processes of growth or gradual development by which the various elements were constituted or combined; and that we have even less to do with the corruptions and exaggerations of a later time.

CHAPTER II.

THE CLERGY, OFFICERS, AND RELIGIOUS ORDERS OF THE CHURCH.

MEANING OF THE WORD CLERGY. THE CLERGY LIST. THE PRIESTHOOD. THE BISHOP. HIS ELECTION, ORDINATION, AND PRIVILEGES. THE PRESBYTERS. THE DEACONS. THE MINOR CLERGY. SUBDEACON. ACOLYTHIST. EXORCIST. READER. DOOR-KEEPER. SINGER. COPIATÆ. PARABOLANI. CATECHIST. STEWARD. ADVOCATE OF THE POOR. ADVOCATE OF THE CHURCH. MANSIONARIUS. WARDEN. SCEU-OPHYLAX. HERMENEUTÆ. NOTARII. APOCRISARII. DEACONESSES. THEIR ORIGIN. THEIR ORDINATION. THEIR DUTIES. MONKS. MONASTICISM PERMITTED, NOT EN-JOINED. THE TRUE IDEA AND PURPOSE OF ASCETICISM. THE ANCHORETS. CŒNO-BITES. PILLAR MONKS. STROLLING MONKS. GENERAL UTILITY OF THE MONAS-TERIES. REGULATIONS OF MONASTERIES. RISE OF SACERDOTAL CELIBACY. MAR-RIAGE AFTER ORDINATION FORBIDDEN. THE VIRGINS OF THE CHURCH. THEIR DISTINCT RECOGNITION IN THE SECOND CENTURY. THE NATURE OF THEIR PRO-FESSION. THEIR MARRIAGE AFTER PROFESSION NOT HELD TO BE VOID NOR ADULTEROUS. CEREMONY OF CONSECRATION. CONSECRATED VIRGINS WERE NOT THE SAME AS DEACONESSES. THE SYNEISACTÆ. THE WIDOWS OF THE CHURCH.

THE CLERGY (ὁ κλῆρος), a term which, to us, means only the three great Orders of Bishops, Presbyters, and Deacons, has throughout the Canons a much wider scope. All who were appointed to any subordinate function in the Church, as the Subdeacon, Reader, and Singer, or to the charge of its affairs, as the Œconomus or Steward, were likewise enrolled among the Clergy (ἐν τῷ κλήρῳ).

A LIST OF THE CLERGY (κατάλογος τῶν κληρικῶν), otherwise called THE CANON (ὁ κανών), and still more frequently the SACERDOTAL LIST (κατάλογος ἱερατικός), was kept in every Parish, and included the names of all who served the Church in any official capacity whatever, whether they were ranked among the Priesthood, or belonged to any of the Minor Orders.

THE PRIESTHOOD (ἱερατεῖον), in its various offices of worship and administration, included only the Bishop, Presbyters, and Deacons as the Presiding Orders of the Church (οἱ προεστῶτες τῆς ἐκκλησίας, Ant. I.). They alone could take part in the Sacred Service (λειτουργία) of the Sacrifice (θυσία) ; only the Bishop or a Priest being permitted to offer (προσφέρειν), and

none beneath the rank of a Deacon being permitted to assist at the Oblation (προσφορά). And as none but they might serve at the Altar (θυσιαστήριον), so none but they were permitted to communicate within the Sanctuary (βῆμα), or even to touch the Holy Vessels (ἱερὰ σκεύη). So wide was the line of distinction between the Priesthood and the other Minor Clergy that it was forbidden to the Subdeacon to frequent the Diaconicum or Deacon's Room ; and in short it was distinctly recognized that while the Priesthood was essential to the very being of a Catholic and Apostolic Church, and therefore was ordained by the solemn imposition of hands with prayer and invocation of the Holy Ghost, the other Clergy were appointed merely for convenience and efficiency in the administration of subordinate affairs, and therefore might be multiplied or wholly set aside as individual Churches might see fit.

At the head of the Priesthood in every Church was the Bishop, and a glance at the provisions of the Canons as summed up in the Digest at the end of this volume will suffice to show that every Bishop stood in his own Parish as a Father and a Prince. The earliest Bishops were of course appointed and ordained to their respective Sees by the Apostles or by Apostolic men. How they were appointed or elected in the age immediately succeeding the Apostles, is not clear, and perhaps the custom varied both in different Churches and at different times ; but it may be assumed that the united suffrage of the Clergy and the Laity was in many places long considered necessary to a lawful election.* The disorderly proceedings, however, which accompanied such popular elections, led to a gradual change in the rule, so that the neighboring Bishops, or at a later time the Bishops of the Province, who at first probably gave a bare consent to the election of any orthodox man who might be chosen by the people, were at length invested with the power of electing fit men for this office. Doubtless as a general rule, a Bishop was chosen from among the Clergy of the See, over which he was to preside, and the recommendation of the Clergy and Laity of the See was also doubtless of great weight in determining the choice; but it seems evident that from the Council of Nicæa onward the power of choosing men to fill Sees that fell vacant rested ab-

* For a full discussion of this subject, see Bingham, Bk. IV.

solutely with the Metropolitan and other Bishops of the Province in which such a vacancy occurred.

Until the Council of Nicæa the Bishop-Elect was ordained by two or three Bishops, and from that time by at least three Bishops of the Province in which his See was situated; and from the moment of his ordination he had full jurisdiction over all orders of men, Clergy and Laity, in the City and Parish of which he was Bishop. He alone ordained the Presbyters and Deacons, and appointed Clergymen of Minor Orders; he presided in the public worship of the Church; he had control of all Church funds and properties, though he was bound to take the counsel of his Presbyters and Deacons as to the appropriation of them; the exercise of discipline was in his hands; and with it he had like power of indulgence to the truly penitent. Though, as we shall see, his personal acts were subject to investigation, and his official acts and judgments were subject to revision and reversal in the Synod of his Province, yet within his Parish he had no superior and no equal. The Bishop was no autocrat; he was as much "under authority" as the poorest Reader, or Singer, or Monk within his jurisdiction; but when charged with personal wrong or crime, he had a right to trial by his peers, his Brother Bishops of the Province; and his official acts stood as effectual and canonical until they were reversed by the Provincial Synod.

The Presbyters were next in order to the Bishop. They performed the functions and enjoyed the dignities of the Sacerdotal Office. They had no right to ordain; perhaps not even to confirm; but every other priestly ministry might be performed by them as well as by the Bishop. They were subject to the Bishop's jurisdiction; yet in the administration of his See he was required both to give due consideration to their counsels and to make known to them whatever disposition he might make of moneys or estates belonging to the Church.

In an inferior sense the Deacons were included in the Sacred Order of the Priesthood. Though they might not offer (προσφέρειν), they assisted at the Oblation, and were Ministers of the Altar; they had charge of the Holy Vessels; they communicated at the Altar with the Bishop and the Presbyters; and they administered the Oblation to the inferior

Clergy and the Laity. With the Presbyters they were the Almoners of the Bishop in the distribution of Church charities. The Bishop was required to seek their counsel with that of the Presbyters in the administration of affairs, and to communicate to them his disposition of Church funds.

The MINOR CLERGY ranked far below the Orders of the Priesthood; yet though they were wholly subordinate to the Presbyters and Deacons, they were everywhere recognized as Clergymen. They lived under clerical discipline; they were supported in their office from the revenues of the Church; and though they had no ordination by imposition of hands, they were admitted to their ministry with sacred ceremonies which could be performed by none but the Bishop or Chorepiscopus. First among the Minor Clergy* was

THE SUBDEACON (ὑπηρέτης, ὑποδιάκονος), who was charged with the preparation of the Holy Vessels, and delivered them to the Deacon at the proper time in Divine Service. During the Celebration of the Eucharist they attended at the doors of the Church, though this duty seems to have been sometimes shared with them by Deacons who stood at the men's gate while the Subdeacons stood at the women's gate. Not the least important of the functions of the Subdeacon was that of bearing episcopal messages and letters from one Church to another. The Subdeacons were strictly charged not to encroach on the functions of the Deacons; nor to minister the Holy Gifts to the people; nor to touch the Sacred Vessels during the Oblation; nor to come within the rails of the Altar; nor to have any place in the Diaconicum or Deacon's Room; nor to bid the prayers in Church; nor to wear the Vestment called the *Horarium;* nor even to sit in the presence of a Priest or Deacon without his leave.

THE ACOLYTHIST (ἀκόλουθος), as distinguished from the Subdeacon, was unknown in the Eastern Church until the fifth century, though counted among the Clergy by the Latins at an earlier date. His duty was to light the candles of the Church, and to attend the Ministers with wine for the Eucharist.

THE EXORCIST (ἐφορκιστής) was not regarded as a separate Order before the third century. Origen ascribes the power

* For a full account of the Minor Clergy see Bingham, Bk. III, from which these definitions are mainly abridged.

of casting out devils to the prayers and adjurations of ordinary Christians. Bishops and Presbyters, however, were the ordinary ministers of this power, until the class of Exorcists was established and recognized. Their duty was to lay hands on the energumens, to repeat the forms of prayer prescribed, and to command the evil spirits to depart.

The Reader (ἀναγνώστης) was appointed to read the Gospels and other parts of Scripture from the Ambo or Pulpit which stood in the midst of the Church. This class of Minor Clergy does not appear before the third century.

The Doorkeeper (πυλωρός) seems to have been little more than Sexton and Janitor.

The Singer (ψαλτῆς κανονικός) is first mentioned in the Council of Laodicea. His office was to sing in the Church, in his appointed place, which was the Ambo or Pulpit.

The Copiatæ or Fossarii (κοπιάται, κοπιῶντες) had charge of funerals, and were particularly bound to see that the poor had decent burial.

The Parabolani (παραβολανοί) are counted by some as a distinct Order among the Minor Clergy, while others with better reason believe them to have been a class of men chosen from among the Clergy, but not a distinct Order. Their duty was to take care of the sick, and their name was taken from that of the gladiators (παράβολοι), who fought with wild beasts, on account of the equal danger incurred by the parabolani in encountering infectious disease.

The Catechists (κατηχηταί), were not an order of the Clergy, but were men chosen from among the Clergy superior and inferior on account of their peculiar aptness to teach. Their duty was to receive and instruct the candidates for Baptism. They were also sometimes called ναυτολόγοι. As the Bishop, as ruler in the Ark of Christ's Church, resembles the πρωρεύς or Pilot; the Presbyters, the ναῦται or Mariners; the Deacons, the τοίχαρχοι or Chief Rowers; so the Catechists were called ναυτολόγοι, Ship's Clerks, they being appointed "to receive passengers and contract with them for the fare of their passage;" *i. e.*, to show the Catechumens the contract they were to make, and the conditions on which they were to be received into the ναῦς (*Nave*) which represented the Ship or Ark of the Church.

The Steward of the Church (οἰκονόμος), like the Cate-

chist, was chosen by the Bishop out of the Clergy of the Parish. He was, therefore, always a Clergyman, though the Stewardship was simply an administrative office in the Church, and not an Order of the Clergy. His duty was to manage the revenues of the whole Parish under the inspection of the Bishop, and particularly to take care of the revenues of the Church during the vacancy of the Bishopric.

THE SCEUOPHYLAX (φύλαξ τῶν σκευῶν, or otherwise φύλαξ τῶν κειμηλίων), was commonly a Presbyter, and had charge of the sacred vessels, utensils, and such precious things as were laid up in the sacred repository of the Church. He was also properly the CHARTOPHYLAX, or Keeper of the Rolls and Archives.

THE HERMENEUTÆ OR INTERPRETERS (ἑρμηνευταί), were a class of men of whose existence in Churches where the people differed in language, there is no doubt. In countries like Palestine, for example, where probably some spoke Syriac and others Greek, or in Africa where some spoke Latin and others Punic, their office was to render the one language into the other, as there was occasion, both in reading the Scriptures and in the homilies that were addressed to the Congregation. So careful was the Church of the instruction of the people, that she not only translated the Scriptures into all languages, but provided a standing office of Interpreters that whatever was done in her public worship, might be so done as "to be understanded of the people."

Besides the Clergy whom we have named, there were Offices in the Church which it may be well to mention here, though their incumbents were not counted as forming Orders of the Clergy, and indeed were not always even Clergymen, but might be chosen from the Clergy or the Laity as might seem most expedient.

Such was the ADVOCATE OR DEFENSOR OF THE CHURCH (ἔκδικος τῆς ἐκκλησίας), who is also sometimes called ECCLESIECDICUS (ἐκκλησιέκδικος). It is probable that the duties of this officer varied in different Churches or at different times in the same Church, and it is certain that they were occasionally divided in extensive Parishes between two or more Advocates. In the latter case it was the business of the ADVOCATE OF THE POOR to look to the interests of poor persons, widows, and virgins belonging to the Church, and in case of wrong or

injury being done them by the rich, to act as their attorneys and advisers in seeking redress from the Magistrates.

The Church Advocate, properly so called, was appointed to the same office in behalf of the Church as a corporation, and in behalf of any of the Clergy who were so injured or oppressed as to have occasion for redress in a civil court. It was his duty in case of failure before the ordinary magistrates to appeal directly to the Emperor, and obtain a Rescript in favour of the Church. The Church Advocates were also empowered to admonish idle Monks and Clergy who were in the habit of resorting to Constantinople, and in case of necessity to compel them to return to their own homes. Together with the Stewards they had the superintendence of the Copiatæ and they were required to inform the Bishop of any negligence on the part of Clergy in attending the celebration of Morning and Evening Service in the Church. It is to be observed, however, that the Advocates had no spiritual power, authority, or function whatever.

The Mansionarius (παραμονάριος) was an officer concerning whose functions there has been much dispute; but he seems in the judgment of the weightier authorities to have been the Steward or Bailiff of the lands of the Church.

The Wardens of the Churches (φύλακες τῶν ἐκκλησιῶν) were either the same as the Doorkeepers, or they were a body of men analogous in their position to the Wardens and Vestry of English Churches.

The Notarii or Exceptores (ὀξυγράφοι, ταχυγράφοι) were shorthand writers appointed to attend the trials of Martyrs and Confessors, and minutely to report the circumstances of their examination. It was also their duty to be present at the executions of the Martyrs, and to record whatever passed during the time of their suffering. Such descriptions were called *Gesta Martyrum*, and were the original accounts which every Church preserved of her own Martyrs.

It is not necessary to mention more than one other class of Church Officers, the Apocrisarii or Responsales, who were resident representatives of foreign Bishops and Churches, appointed to act as proctors at the Imperial Court in all causes ecclesiastical wherein their principals might be concerned.

But we cannot leave the subject of the Clergy without taking particular notice of three important classes of persons, viz.: the Deaconesses, the Monks, and the Virgins of the Church.

There is evidence that Deaconesses were of apostolical appointment, since St. Paul, in Rom. xvi, 1, calls Phœbe a Servant (διάκονος, Deaconess) of the Church of Cenchrea. The original word διάκονος, used by St. Paul, is exactly equivalent to the Latin *Ministra*, by which name certain women of the Church are called in Pliny's Epistle in which he speaks of the Christians.*

Tertullian and other early writers call the Deaconesses *Viduæ*, Widows, and their office *Viduatus*, Widowhood, because they were usually appointed from among the Widows of the Church. According to certain regulations they were required 1st, to be Widows; 2d, to have had but one husband; 3d, to have borne children; and 4th, to be of considerable age, as forty, fifty or sixty years. These regulations, however, were not inflexible, since it appears that Virgins as well as Widows were promoted to the office of Deaconess, and that even after Chalcedon, Widows were sometimes at least ordained while under forty years of age; nor is it absolutely certain that a Widow who had lawfully married a second time after being separated by *death*, not by *divorce*, from her first husband, was always excluded from the office of Deaconess.

Concerning the *ordination* of Deaconesses, there has been much dispute among the learned, some affirming and some denying that they were always regularly ordained by the imposition of the hands of the Bishop. Bingham shows convincingly that they did receive imposition of hands, and that not merely in the way of benediction, but as an actual consecration of them to their office in the Church. Among the Paulianists it is probable that the Deaconesses were not so ordained; and among the Catholics it is probable that there were two classes of persons indifferently known as Deaconesses, viz., true Deaconesses who had been regularly ordained; and novices or candidates who had not been actually

* Plin. lib. x. Ep. 97. Quo magis necessarium credidi, ex duabus ancillis, quæ *Ministræ* dicebantur, quid esset veri et per tormenta quærere. *Wherefore I deemed it the more necessary to put to the torture two damsels who were called* Ministers, *and inquire of them what the truth was.*

ordained, but who lived under the rules and appeared in the habit or dress (ἐν τῷ σχήματι) of the Deaconesses. Zonaras states (Com. on Nic. XIX) that Deaconesses were sometimes chosen from the Virgins of the Church, though they were not ordained until they had attained the age of forty; but that Virgins of twenty-five years received from the Bishop a certain habit or dress without imposition of hands; and that these latter were also called Deaconesses (διακονίσσαι) even in the Canons of the Church.

It is to be observed that the ordination or consecration of the Deaconesses conveyed to them no power to execute any part of the Priestly Ministry. This was always forbidden. They were appointed to perform merely some inferior services of the Church, chiefly relating to women, for whose sake they were appointed; and particularly to assist in preparing women for Baptism, and to attend them before and after the immersions with which Baptism was customarily celebrated. They acted as private catechists to female catechumens; they visited women who were sick and in distress; they ministered to the Martyrs and Confessors in prison; in Greek Churches they attended the women's gate in the Church; they preserved order in Church among the women; they presided over the Widows; and it was their duty to introduce to the Bishop any women who had a suit to prefer to him.

Early in the fourth century the MONKS (μοναχοί) began to be a very important class in the Church, but *Monasticism* is not to be confounded with the ASCETICISM which was cultivated and enjoined from the beginning. Asceticism in its true primitive sense meant nothing more than our Saviour meant in his encouragement of "Prayer and Fasting," and in his prediction concerning his disciples when He should be taken away, "Then shall they fast;" or than St. Paul meant when he said, "I keep my body under, and bring it into subjection." It is true that the measures and degrees of mortification practised by private Christians of the early ages were vastly greater than are dreamed of by the Christians of the present day: but the object was the same then that it is now, "to keep under the body and bring it into subjection," and thereby the more easily to mortify their "members upon the earth, fornication, uncleanness, inordinate affections, and evil concupiscence." In the early Church, there were many who

"for the Kingdom of Heaven's sake" renounced the ordinary pursuits of men, such as honour, riches, power and the like, that they might the better give themselves to the studies and pursuits of a holy life. Such self-discipline the primitive Church always approved, and while she never propounded it as a rule, nor prescribed the degrees to which an individual man must practise it, she unequivocally approved the practice and applauded the design. But on the other hand, the primitive Church was the steady foe of that false asceticism which despises or abominates the things that it renounces, as a reference to the article "Asceticism" in the Digest will suffice to show. The uniform language of the Church was: "If any Bishop, Presbyter, or Deacon, or any other of the Clergy shall abstain from marriage, flesh, or wine, *οὐ διὰ ἄσκησιν, ἀλλὰ διὰ βδελυρίαν, not through asceticism* (or self-discipline) *but as abominating the good creatures of God,* let him be deposed and cast out of the Church." Notwithstanding this decided position of the Catholic Church, the various forms of false Asceticism in the early ages were well nigh innumerable, as the early Canons show, so that while it is true that Christianity fostered true Asceticism, it is no less true that the Church was forced to be a resolute adversary of its counterfeit.

In the eye of the Church, therefore, Marriage and Celibacy, considered as states of life, were equally estimable. Marriage was "honourable unto *all* men," Bishops, Priests, and Deacons not excepted; but for him who "could contain" and who for the love of God, that he might better serve the Church or promote his own salvation, kept himself a virgin, it was felt that honour should be given in proportion to the greatness of his sacrifice. Nevertheless it was not till the beginning of the fourth century that Monasticism as a professed state of life began to prevail so widely as to need the regulation of the Church, but from that time it was speedily developed under many forms.

The Anchorets (*ἀναχωρηταί*) were men who retired into the wilderness and dwelt in natural caves, or artificial cells, or even in tents. When many of these were near each other, though separate from each other and independent of each other, their settlement was called a *Laura.*

When the Monks were joined together in one Community they were called Cœnobites (*κοινοβιταί*), and their habitations

were called *Cœnobia* (*κοινόβια*). Such communities were soon established in all parts of Christendom, and became the regular form of Monastic Institutions. They were under regulations of greater or less stringency, according to the rules which they professed, and they were in all things subject to the Bishop, who was required by the Canons to provide for their decent maintenance. It was also his duty to maintain a godly discipline over the Monks, and in case of their contumacious persistence in any forbidden courses, to expel them from their Monasteries.

Of the many extravagant and capricious forms of monastic life none was more extraordinary than that of the STYLITÆ or Pillar Monks who were so called because of their living perpetually on the top of a pillar. Naturally enough the professors of this way of life were extremely few, but the accounts of their prolonged endurances are certainly astonishing. It does not appear that they were in any very great or general esteem.

Far more pernicious to the Church and to the State were the bands of *Strolling Monks*, who lived in companies of two or three together, making their profession a pretext for idleness, and their pretence of ascetic sanctity a plea for setting at defiance all authority except their own. They were the pests of the Cities, fomenting contentions and disturbances, slandering the Clergy, challenging and receiving superstitious veneration from the multitude, affecting an unusual habit, making frequent visits to the Virgins, fasting to absurd excess at fasting times, but on the feast-days drunk and riotous to beastliness, when, as St. Jerome says, *saturabantur ad vomitum.* In the correction of such disgraceful rioters it is evident that spiritual censures were of small avail, and it sometimes became necessary to call in the civil power for the abatement of the nuisance.

Happily this corruption of Monasticism was the exception, not the rule. The early Monasteries were, in general, of real and valuable service to the Church. It was no trifling matter in an age like that, when Christianity had still to struggle with the virus of hereditary heathenism in the hearts of the baptized themselves, that houses should be found in every city filled with men of faith so strong that they renounced the world in order that they might win CHRIST. And it is

beyond a doubt that in the great majority of cases, making due allowance for the frailty of humanity, the Monks were in their lives and conversation wholesome patterns to the members of the Church. The religious simplicity of their daily life was only equalled by the unwearying fervency of their devotions. Their houses were abodes of learning, industry, and piety, and it was often in the Monastery that the truest life of Christianity was lived and its most perfect spirit breathed.

Yet in spite of the reputation they acquired, and of the reverence in which their virtues caused them to be held, the Monks had no rank in the Church but that of simple laymen. As they had embraced an exceptional state of life, which needed more than ordinary safeguards, they were protected and restrained by a more strict and watchful discipline than ordinary laymen ; but they had, beyond this, no rights, rank, nor titles in the Church that any layman might not claim. They were stringently forbidden to meddle with ecclesiastical affairs ; and it was a well-known point of order that, however learned he might be, no Monk nor other layman might usurp that right of public teaching and preaching which is the prerogative of the Priests of God.*

Whenever, therefore, a Monk was for any cause promoted to be a Priest or Bishop, says Bingham, he was obliged to go through all other Orders of the Church, as it was then customary for laymen to do, before the superior Orders were conferred upon them ; and in this respect, adds the same learned author, "the difference between a Monk and any other layman was only this, that a Monk by virtue of his education in a school of learning and good discipline (such as Monasteries then were) was supposed to be a better proficienr than other laymen, and therefore allowed the benefit of a quicker passage through the inferior Orders than other candidates of the Priesthood." It does not appear that the Monks ordinarily aspired to the Sacerdotal Dignity, though there were several instances in which it was customary to promote them to the Priesthood. In the Lauras the Priest was naturally taken from among the Hermits, and a like rule was followed in all Monasteries of any considerable size. Indeed in

* Leo, Ep. 60 al. 62. Illud quoque convenit præcavere, ut præter eos qui sunt Domini Sacerdotes, nullus sibi jus docendi et prædicandi audeat vindicare, sive sit ille monachus, sive laicus, qui alicujus scientiæ nomine glorietur.

the Cities, where the Monastic Houses were often very large and had Churches attached to them, the Archimandrite or Abbot was Priest of the Church, and was even permitted to have four or five of the other Monks likewise ordained to the Priesthood for the service of their Church. On account of the learning and piety which prevailed in the Monasteries it also came to be common for Bishops who had need of Clergy to take Monks out of their Monasteries with the consent of the Abbot, and ordain them for the service of the Church. The men thus chosen commonly continued in the world that ascetic way of life which they had practised in the cloister; and on this account both these and the Priests of Monasteries were by the Greeks called *ἱερομοναχοί* or Priest-Monks, to distinguish them on the one hand from Monks who were not Priests, and on the other from Priests who were not Monks. It happened, too, sometimes, that a Bishop and all his Clergy embraced an ascetic way of life, having all things common, renouncing individual property, living in one house, eating at one table, and being all clothed at the common expense. This happened oftener in early times at the East than at the West, St. Ambrose being the first who brought this way of living into the Western Church. St. Austin himself says that he introduced it into Hippo, where, as he declares, he made his Bishop's-house a Monastery of Clergymen who, like the Apostles, had all things common.* Thus in a third way it came about that Monasticism was professed and practised by the Priesthood. Celibacy, however, was by no means exacted from the Clergy in general. A declared contempt for marriage was considered cause sufficient for the deposition of a Bishop or other Minister or for the excommunication of a layman. Marriage was no impediment to ordination even as a Bishop; and Bishops, Priests, and Deacons, equally with other men, were forbidden to put away their wives under pretext of religion. The case was different when a man was unmarried at the time of his ordination. Then he was held to have given himself wholly to God in the office of the Holy Ministry, and he was forbidden to take back from his offering that measure of his cares and his affections which must necessarily be given to

* Aug. Serm. 49 de Diversis. Volui habere in istâ domo Episcopi meum monasterium clericorum. Ecce quomodo vivimus. Nulli licet in societate habere aliquid proprium.

the maintenance and nurture of his family. In short, the married man might be ordained, but with a few exceptions no man was allowed to marry after ordination.

It could not be that the devout practice of celibacy by Christian men of every order lay and clerical should thus prevail, without a corresponding tendency among the women of the Church. Rather we might look for greater and more marked developments in this direction among women than among men. For in every age and country the chastity of women has been the one virtue without which all other virtues were of no avail; and even among the heathen of the older world the VIRGIN consecrated for her life or for a term of years was the most sacred type of womanhood. In a religion which declares as one of its most fundamental articles that the ETERNAL SON OF GOD, being conceived of the HOLY GHOST, did not abhor the Virgin's womb; but that, being GOD of the Substance of the FATHER, He became Man of the Substance of the Blessed Virgin Mary His Mother; in such a religion, it could not but be that from the first many holy women should give themselves to the Service of GOD in the estate of Perpetual Virginity. Such at least is the established fact; and as ascetic celibacy was frequently embraced among men for centuries before monastic institutions became common in the Church, so among women there were many recognized as Virgins of the Church though dwelling at their own homes and in the midst of their own families before conventual communities of women had been thought of. Early in the second century we know from Tertullian that there were Virgins who made open and public profession of Virginity, and dedicated themselves to CHRIST in that estate; that such Virgins were specially recognized by the Church; that they were enrolled on the Sacred List of the Church (*ἀναγεγραμμέναι ἐν τῷ τῶν ἐκκλησιῶν κανόνι*); and that their customary distinction was that of Virgins of the Church or Ecclesiastical Virgins (*Παρθένοι ἐκκησιαστικαί*). "So that," as Bingham says, "it is now out of dispute that as the ascetics for the first three hundred years were not [cloistered] Monks, so neither were the Sacred Virgins of the Church monastical Virgins or Nuns confined to a cloister as in after ages."

On what terms the profession of Virginity was permitted

to be made is not by any means clear. It is admitted on all hands that there must have been on the woman's part some declaration of her purpose to continue in that state throughout her life; but whether this was in the form of a simple declaration or in that of a solemn and irrevocable vow to God is not so certain. Perhaps in this as in so many other instances the custom was different in different Churches; perhaps the custom was different at different times even in the same Church; perhaps there was a choice left to the woman of the form in which she should profess; and perhaps in some cases there may have been a novitiate introduced by a simple profession of intention to remain a Virgin, followed when the woman was of riper years by a more solemn vow. It is evident, however, that a solemn and irrevocable vow was not universally required in the age of St. Cyprian, who expressly says of the Virgins of the Church: "If they have given themselves to Christ through faith, then let them abide so in modesty and chastity without pretence; and so let them await in strength and stableness the wages of Virginity. But if they either cannot or if they will not abide, then better were it that they marry than that they should burn through their offences." * Yet it is equally evident that the tendency of the Church's legislation was always to greater and not less strictness in this matter, so that the penalty of excommunication was visited on professed Virgins who contracted marriages. It is to be observed, nevertheless, that such marriages were never declared to be null or void. The parties to them fell under the censures of the Church, and might not be absolved without a long continued penance; but their act was not disannulled nor cancelled, neither was their union held to be adulterous. And it is further to be observed that by the imperial laws as well as by the Canons of the Church, the Consecration of a Virgin was not reputed valid till she was forty years of age, but that if done earlier it was in her power to disavow her profession and enter lawfully into the married state.

* Cypr. Ep. 62 al. 4. ad Pompon. Si ex fide se Christo dicaverunt, pudice et caste sine ullâ fabulâ perseverent; ita fortes et stabiles præmium Virginitatis exspectent. Si autem perseverare nolunt, vel non possunt, melius est nubant, quam in ignem suis delictis cadant.

When a Virgin desired to be consecrated she made known her wish to the Bishop, who either himself or by one of his Presbyters met the woman in the Church, and there publicly invested her with the Virgin's Habit, a peculiar dress by which she might at once be recognized as a consecrated person. To this was added the Veil, the usual badge of marriage, but in this case signifying the giving of herself to God. She also received a head-dress called the *Mitre*, and as there was a form, usual in secular marriages, of unbinding the woman's hair in token of her subjection to her husband, so the Virgin's hair was unbound in token of her unreserved submission of herself to Christ. It will be noted that the consecration of a Virgin differs greatly from the ordination of a Deaconess. The Deaconess had an *Office* in the Church to which she was ordained by the Bishop only. The Virgin entered on a *State of Life* which the Church approved; and in her public self-consecration she was recognized and invested with the symbols of her state by the Bishop himself, or by a Priest of his appointment. In a word, the Virgin stood to the Deaconess in the same relation in which the Monk stood to the Clergy, and the ceremonies of her consecration necessarily differed in a marked degree from the ordination of the Deaconess.

The great esteem and veneration in which the Virgins of the Church were held, and the inviolable chastity which all believed them to maintain, led in the third and fourth centuries to an abuse which is repeatedly forbidden in the Canons. Unmarried Clergymen, requiring supervision for their households, employed women who were not kinswomen to live in their houses and take charge of their affairs. The desire of society and the fear of scandal often led them to prefer the Virgins of the Church for this position. The Virgins so entertained were naturally chosen from a preference on the Clergyman's part—a preference which was not at all concealed, but on the contrary was openly professed. A chaste love and a wholly spiritual affection were declared to be the cause of the connection. The Virgins, or others, so living with Clergymen, were therefore called *ἀγαπηταί* or beloved; and it would be uncharitable not to believe that in many instances the connection was, at least at first and in the purpose of the parties, pure and chaste. Yet in the nature of things it could

not but lead to great scandal and no small amount of actual sin even on the part of those whose first designs were innocent; and when the impure availed themselves of such a license the effect might readily have been foreseen. "For it appears," says Bingham, "from the complaints of St. Cyprian, St. Jerome, and others, that the practice of some was very intolerable; for they not only dwelt together in the same house, but lodged in the same room, and sometimes in the same bed; and yet would be thought innocent, and called others uncharitable and suspicious that entertained any hard thoughts of them." With such an excess of charity as these lewd persons required, the Church declined to treat them, and proceeded against them as scandalous libertines who were unworthy of communion with her. And that such things might forever cease, it was absolutely forbidden to any Clergyman of any order to have *any woman* (not of his near kindred) dwelling with him (*συνείσακτον*). Grave as this scandal was, it would be difficult to find a better or more singular proof of the general estimation of the chastity of the Virgins of the Church than that such an outrage upon common decency should ever have been possible under such pretexts.

THE WIDOWS of the Church were in regard to their habit, profession, consecration, and the like, under the same laws as the Virgins. They were required to have been only once married, and before profession to have long lived chastely and irreproachably after the death of their husbands. When they were admitted, they made to the Bishop openly in the Church a profession of their purpose to continue in the state of Widowhood, and were then invested by the Presbyter with the Widow's garment. The ceremonies of their consecration differed in some respects from that of Virgins, but the chief point of distinction was that Widows were forbidden either at their consecration or thereafter to assume the Virgin's veil.

We have thus glanced at the officers and other persons who were recognized in a peculiar manner by the Church, and had their names enrolled in the SACERDOTAL LIST or Sacred Canon of the Church. The whole, as we have seen, comprises

I. The Priesthood, including the Bishop, Presbyters, and Deacons.

II. The Minor Clergy, including the Subdeacons, Acolythists, Exorcists, Readers, Doorkeepers, Singers, and the Copiatæ or Fossarii. Here, too, perhaps, we ought to class the Deaconesses.

III. Clerical Officers, that is persons chosen from the whole list of the Clergy, superior and inferior, to fulfill some special function. Such were the Parabolani, the Catechists, the Steward, the Sceuophylax, and the Hermeneutæ.

IV. Officers who might be either Clergymen or Laymen, viz., The Advocate or Defensor, the Mansionarius, the Wardens, the Notarii, and the Apocrisarii.

V. The Ascetics, including Monks, Virgins, and Widows.

CHAPTER III.

ANCIENT CHURCHES AND THE APPOINTED STATIONS OF THE VARIOUS CLASSES OF THE LAITY.

CHURCHES IN THE AGE OF PERSECUTIONS AND AFTERWARDS. THE CATHEDRAL AND THE SEE. ORATORIES. MARTYRIES. CEMETERIES. THE BISHOP'S THRONE. THE ALTAR. THE BEMA. THE PROTHESIS. THE DIACONICUM. THE CHANCEL. THE HOLY GATES. THE NAVE. PLACE OF THE MINOR CLERGY AND THE FAITHFUL. THE CO-STANDERS. THE AMBO. PLACE OF THE READERS AND SINGERS. PLACE OF THE PROSTRATORS. THE WOMEN'S GALLERY. THE INTERIOR NARTHEX. THE ROYAL GATES. PLACE OF THE HEARERS AND CATECHUMENS. PRIVILEGES OF THE HEARERS. CATECHUMENS, THEIR AGE, THEIR PROBATION, THEIR FOUR CLASSES. THE GREAT GATES. PLACE OF THE HYEMANTES. PENANCE IN THE PRIMITIVE CHURCH WAS A DISCIPLINE, NOT A PUNISHMENT NOR A MERITORIOUS EXPIATION.

AFTER the account of the Clergy and Ascetics of the early Church which has been given in the previous chapter, it will be expected that we should give some account of any classes or distinctions that were recognized among the Laity; and possibly the best way to do this acceptably will be to combine a brief description of the Sacred Edifices of that age with some slight outline of the ancient discipline.

During the centuries of persecution Christian Churches were extremely simple in their form and structure. The necessities of the time often compelled the Christians to perform the Holy Mysteries of their religion in whatever place seemed likeliest to afford security from the intrusion of their enemies; yet it is evident that from the first they had their consecrated places for the worship of Almighty God, and that their use of common dwellings, caves, and catacombs was caused by mere necessity, not from a disregard of the proprieties and decencies of God's House. The moment they were free from danger, Churches (κυριακά) appeared in every City; and where the number of believers needed more than one, they were indefinitely multiplied. The chief Church of the City was the Bishop's Church, not that he had less authority in one Church than another, but because in that he had his special throne (θρόνος), or seat of office, which was therefore called the Bema (βῆμα), or Tribunal, because it was there

that he pronounced his sentences and made known his decisions. The Bishop's throne was called by the Latins *Sedes* and by the Greeks *Cathedra,* whence we derive our English word SEE to designate the City from which he takes his title, and CATHEDRAL as the name of his chief Church.

Besides the Cathedral there were frequently other Churches that demand some special notice.

Such were ORATORIES (προσευκτήρια, οἶκοι εὐκτήριοι), a name which is often indiscriminately applied to all Churches whatever, but which more strictly belongs to private chapels which were always dependent on the Parish Church, and were licensed only for the purpose of Common Prayer, and not for the Celebration of Holy Communion.

MARTYRIES (μαρτύρια) were Churches erected over the graves of Martyrs or called by their names; but if the person in memory of whom the Church was built was a Prophet or Apostle, then it was called PROPHETEUM (προφητεῖον), or APOSTOLEUM (ἀποστολεῖον).

CEMETERIES (κοιμητήρια), were the same as Martyries, except in origin. During times of persecution the Christians were accustomed to assemble in private vaults or burying places, and particularly at the graves of Martyrs and Confessors; and when the persecutions ended they erected Churches on the places which had thus been doubly consecrated and endeared to them both by the ashes of the Saints, and by the consolations of religion. Such Churches received the name of Cemeteries, that is, *sleeping-places,* which had previously been given to the burying-ground or vault above which they were built.

But by whatever name known, and however simple or however ornate in their structure, all Churches were arranged in much the same way as the Eastern Churches of the present day; and this fact is an evidence not only of the prevalence of liturgies which closely corresponded with each other, but also, as the reader will ere long perceive, of a uniform order of discipline.

Let us then proceed to examine the ground plan of an ancient Church as it is exhibited in the engraving opposite to the title-page of this book.

Following the order suggested by the figures on the drawing we find first of all (1) at the East end, in the center of a

great arc, the Bishop's THRONE (θρόνος) which was also sometimes called the Bema (βῆμα); and to the right and left of this are the lower thrones or sedilia of the Presbyters.

Immediately in front of the Bishop's Throne is the ALTAR (2) called in Greek Θυσιαστήριον, that is, an *Altar of Oblation* or *Holy Table*, but never called βωμός, a name which was exclusively applied to heathen altars. This distinction suffices to explain the fact that while in their Canons and other writings the ancient Fathers habitually spoke of the Holy Table as an Altar, θυσιαστήριον, they indignantly denied that they had βωμούς, that is, such altars or for such purposes as the heathen had.

The enclosed space around the Altar (3) took its name from the Bishop's Throne, and hence was commonly called the BEMA; but it was also sometimes, though seldom, called the ALTAR. Into the Bema none but Bishops, Priests, and Deacons were permitted to enter.

Opening into the Bema by a door on its North side is (4) the PROTHESIS (πρόθεσις), or room in which the offerings of the people were received, and particularly the Bread and Wine which were to be consecrated at the Altar.

On the South side of the Bema, is (4′), the DIACONICUM (διακονικόν), or Deacon's Room, in which were kept the Sacred Vestments and Holy Vessels which were used in Divine Service.

The entrance from the Body of the Church to the Bema is (5) through the HOLY GATES (ἅγιαι πύλαι), which stand in the middle of a partition (6) of lattice-work or rails (κιγκλίδες, Lat. *Cancelli*, whence our English *Chancel*).

Passing through the Holy Gates Westward we come (7) into the Body or NAVE (νάος) of the Church; and here, next to the Chancel, was the place for the MINOR CLERGY and FAITHFUL LAITY (πιστοί, τέλειοι), who were in the enjoyment of the full Communion of the Church.

With these a class of PENITENTS was permitted to stand during the service of the Church, on which account they were called CONSISTENTES (συνιστάμενοι), or CO-STANDERS. These persons were permitted to communicate in prayers with the faithful; that is, to be present at all parts of the service, even the Oblation or Celebration of the Holy Eucharist. They were therefore in one sense Communicants, but they were not

permitted to partake of the Holy Gifts, and were not reputed as Communicants, until they were restored to the full Communion (τὸ τέλειον) of the faithful at the Altar.

In the Nave stood the AMBO (ἄμβων), an elevated platform for the Readers and Singers who ascended to it by a flight of steps, and

Behind the Ambo was the place appointed for the second class of Penitents called PROSTRATORS or KNEELERS (ὑποπίπτοντες, γονυκλίνοντες) from the attitude of kneeling or prostration which they were required to preserve during the prayers of the Church. They were excluded not only from receiving, but even from being present at the Celebration of the Eucharist, and were dismissed with the benediction of the Bishop, after special prayers had been offered in their behalf, but before the Oblation was begun.

On the North and South of the Nave there was generally (8) a Portico on the ground-floor, and above this a Gallery occupied exclusively by the women.

West of the Nave, but still within the Body of the Church was (9) the INTERIOR NARTHEX (νάρθηξ, προνάος), opening into the Nave by (10) the Beautiful or Royal Gates (πύλαι ὡραῖαι, πύλαι βασιλικαί), and in this was the appointed place of the third class of Penitents called HEARERS, as well as of the CATECHUMENS, and of Jews, Heathens, Heretics, or Schismatics who desired from any cause to hear the doctrines of the Church.

The HEARERS (ἀκροώμενοι) were not permitted to enter the Nave, nor to join even in Common Prayers with the rest of the Congregation. They were admitted only to the Interior Narthex and allowed to listen to the reading of the Scriptures, the recitation of the Psalms, and the Sermons which were commonly delivered by the Bishop only, but sometimes by a Presbyter of his appointment : and when the Prayers began the Hearers were commanded to withdraw.

The CATECHUMENS (κατηχούμενοι) were persons receiving elementary instruction in the Christian religion, with a view to Holy Baptism. When they had made formal application for Baptism they were acknowledged in an imperfect sense as Christians, and were admitted to the state of Catechumens with some solemnity and ceremony, including prayers, imposition of hands, and the Sign of the Cross.

The *age* at which Catechumens might be received varied according to circumstances. The heathen were received at any age at which they might present themselves; unbaptized children were received even under seven years of age; and the baptized children of the Faithful were considered as Catechumens from the moment that they were capable of receiving instruction.

The *length of time* that the Catechumens were required to wait before they were baptized varied in like manner. Not unfrequently Baptism was administered almost or quite immediately; but more than one Provincial Council found it expedient to require a probation of considerable length, as two or even three years.

There were, probably, four recognized Classes of the Catechumens, though many of the learned make but two. Hammond, following Bingham, gives them as follows: 1. Those who were under private instruction only, and not yet publicly received as Catechumens in the Church. 2. The Hearers, who were permitted to hear the Scriptures read and the Sermon preached, but not to remain for any of the Prayers, not even for those which related to the other classes of Catechumens. 3. The Kneelers, who remained during the Prayers for the Catechumens which immediately followed the Bishop's Sermon, together with those for the Energumens and Penitents. After these prayers they received the imposition of hands, kneeling. 4. The Competentes or Electi, called in Greek βαπτιζόμενοι or φωτιζόμενοι, who were the immediate candidates for Baptism, and had received the Bishop's examination and approval.

Again proceeding Westward from the Interior Narthex we pass (10′) through the Great Gates into the Exterior Narthex, or area included within the wall which inclosed the whole circumference of the outer courts. In front of the Great Gates there was an open area (αἴθριον) of greater or less extent (11) surrounded by a portico (στοαί), and having somewhere, generally near the middle, a fountain (φίαλα) or spring (φρέαρ) of pure water.

In our engraving which is copied from Beveridge, the fountain is perhaps incorrectly represented in the Interior Narthex (12); though it may be that this was its actual place in some Churches. It was in the open area that the lowest

class of penitents were found. They were such as had been guilty of heinous crimes, and were not so much penitents in the ecclesiastical sense of that word, as candidates for re-admission to the Church by means of the established discipline of public penance. They were called MOURNERS or WEEPERS (συγκλαίοντες) and stood or lay without the Great Gates with visible tokens of mortification and distress, begging the prayers of the Clergy and of the Faithful as they entered. This class of penitents is also sometimes called *χειμαζόμενοι*, Hiemantes, or Hibernantes, on account of their being compelled to remain exposed to the weather outside the shelter of the Church.

Of the penitential discipline of the Primitive Church, it cannot be out of place even in a work of this kind to observe that it was emphatically a system of *discipline.* It was in no sense a system of punishment inflicted by the Church on her offending members. On the contrary, it was always asked by the returning sinner, and was granted to him as a grace ; the Church endeavouring, by a long-continued course of spiritual exercises suited to his weakness, to advance him prudently to higher and still higher privileges ; till at length she might again embrace him in the full communion of the Blessed Sacrament without the apprehension of a second fall. So, too, the course of penance through which he was called to pass was in no sense conceived to be a meritorious expiation of his past offences. The state of penance in its very nature involved a renunciation of all pretence of merit, and its object was not to atone for the abuse of past grace, but by means of discipline to frame the heart and life to a worthier use of more grace which was in due time to be again received.

A reference to the numerous Canons on this subject will show that the appointed times of penance were exceedingly protracted, sometimes reaching even to the hour of death. Yet a certain discretion was almost always left with the Bishop to dispense with some part of the penance if he saw in the demeanour of the penitent such signs of true repentance as sufficed to justify such leniency ; and whatever might have been the crime for which the penance was imposed, no dying sinner was permitted to depart without the consolation of the Blessed Sacrament, " the last, most indispensable provision for his journey," as it is called by the Council of Nicæa.

It is needless to observe to the attentive reader of these Canons that they contain no trace, however slight, of any compulsory or obligatory confessions required from members of the Church on any occasions or for any reasons whatever. Yet to the careful reader, and even to the curious, these documents are not without some indications of a voluntary opening of spiritual griefs to an appointed Minister of God.

CHAPTER IV.

PARISHES, PROVINCES, AND DIOCESES OF THE CHURCH.

PARISHES. COUNTRY DISTRICTS. CHOREPISCOPI. THEIR ORDINATION. THEIR PRIVILEGES AND DUTIES. THEIR VALUE. EFFICIENCY OF PRIMITIVE ORGANIZATION. POWER OF THE BISHOP. SOLIDARITY OF THE EPISCOPATE. JURISDICTION OF THE WHOLE OVER THE PART; OF THE PROVINCE OVER THE PARISH. PROVINCIAL SYNODS. METROPOLITANS. THEIR PRIVILEGES AND DUTIES. EARLY DATE OF THE METROPOLITICAL SYSTEM. ITS UNIVERSALITY. THE DIOCESE A PROVINCE OF PROVINCES. DIOCESAN SYNODS AS COURTS OF APPEAL. THE ARCHBISHOP OR EXARCH. PATRIARCH A LATER TERM. DUTIES AND PRIVILEGES OF THE ARCHBISHOP. ALL ARCHBISHOPS EQUAL. PRECEDENCE GIVEN TO ROME AND CONSTANTINOPLE FOR POLITICAL REASONS. NO TRACE OF THE ROMAN PAPACY TO BE FOUND IN THE CANONS.

I. Parishes and Country Districts.

WHEREVER the civil power had erected a municipal organization, it was the policy of the Church to create a See, and to establish a Bishop; and the jurisdiction of the Bishop was made co-extensive with the Parish of which the City was the political centre. So strong, indeed, was the tendency to multiply Bishoprics in places where there was even the appearance of a real need of episcopal oversight, that at a very early period it was necessary to forbid Bishops to be consecrated for the villages or lesser towns. Yet, as the Parishes connected with the Cities were often of considerable size, including widely separated and extensive districts which it was impossible for any City Bishop to attend to, it was customary in the primitive age, and particularly in the East, for the City Bishop to appoint and ordain Bishops of such country districts to act as his representatives. Such country Bishops were called Chorepiscopi. They had no independent power or jurisdiction whatsoever, but were merely the representatives and deputies of the City Bishop, by whom they were appointed, and to whom they were responsible. So limited, in fact, was their authority, that not a few of the learned have supposed them to have been merely Presbyters;

but there seems to be no doubt that they were true Bishops, though their appointment might be made and their ordination might be performed by only one Bishop; while the appointment of the City Bishop required the concurrent choice of the Bishops of the Province, and his ordination required the presence and participation of at least three of their number.

The Chorepiscopus was charged with a general oversight of the Clergy of his district; and he might ordain Clergymen of Minor Orders, such as Sub-Deacons, Readers, and Exorcists, without being required to consult the City Bishop in every particular instance. Presbyters and Deacons they were strictly prohibited from ordaining without the express consent of their Bishop. They had the right to confirm persons who had been baptized in the Churches of their districts, and they were permitted to grant letters dimissory to such Clergy of their districts as desired to remove to another district or Parish. They were permitted, when in the City, to officiate in the presence of the Bishop and Presbyters of the City—a privilege not granted to the country Presbyters; and in Councils of the Church they had a right to sit, to vote, and to subscribe the decrees which might be enacted—a right enjoyed by no Presbyter. Yet it is probable that the functions of the Chorepiscopus were not at all times and in all places the same; but rather that they very greatly varied, sometimes approaching, if not equalling the independence and authority of the City Bishop; and sometimes falling so nearly to the level of the Presbyter as to be performed by one of that order. So, too, the number of the Chorepiscopi varied very greatly in different ages; for while in the fourth and fifth centuries they are constantly noticed in ecclesiastical documents, they seem as early as the ninth to have passed nearly, if not quite, out of existence. Of the usefulness of such assistants to the Bishop of an extensive Parish there can hardly be a doubt; and it may well be considered whether the creation of some such officers as the Chorepiscopi is not the best way now of meeting the imperative demand for increased episcopal efficiency among ourselves, and also whether in a country like our own the Chorepiscopus in his District would not be the best agent to prepare the way for the subsequent establishment of the Bishop in his See. Let it be borne in mind, however, that the

Chorepiscopus was never meant to do away with the direct and personal supervision of the Bishop. On the contrary, the Bishop was expected to visit every district of his Parish frequently, and never less than once a year. It was only when a multiplicity of duties or unusual extent of territory hindered him from doing more than this, that he was expected to appoint a Chorepiscopus for his outlying districts. Nothing, indeed, can be more admirable than the practical sagacity and nice address with which the Bishop's personal power and influence was made to permeate and be felt through every portion of his jurisdiction. In the City, his well-ordered corps of Presbyters, Deacons, Minor Clergymen, and other officers was daily carrying the influences of his power, of his authority, and of his charity to representatives of every class of men ; and in the Country, where it was impossible that he should come into as frequent contact with the members of his charge, the Chorepiscopus, his own, appointed, confidential representative, in like manner conveyed his admonitions or obeyed his orders. Thus, common sense and tact arranged a system of organization nearly perfect in the then existing circumstances ; and intelligent organization soon achieved and long sustained the triumphs of the Church. Indeed, no little of the wonder with which one reads of the marvellous rapidity with which the faith spread among the heathen population, in a measure disappears when we consider the efficiency with which the Church's power was made to reach to every sort and condition of men. Give the Church now her Bishops *in every City*, and let them take the primitive Church for the model of their action, rather than for the convenient topic of homiletic panegyric, and the same results will follow from like causes of success.

II. The Province.

We have now seen in the present as well as in the previous chapters of this Introduction the immense powers, spiritual, moral, and temporal, which were entrusted to the Bishops of the primitive age ; and if it seem at first sight that such powers were too great to be committed to the head of any body of free men, we must remember that the Bishop was himself,

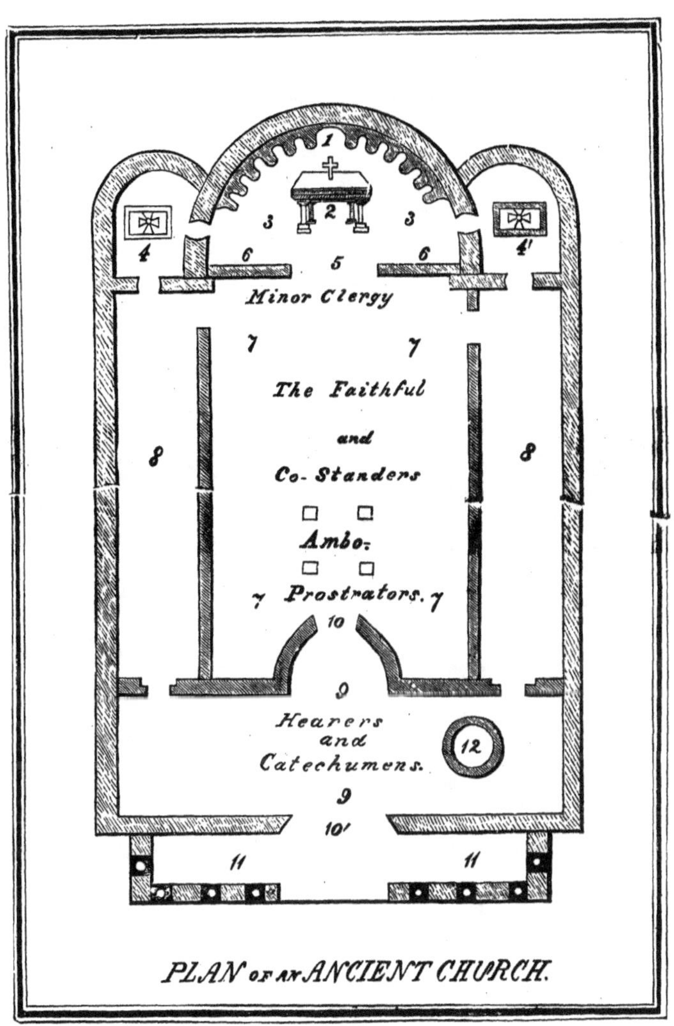

PLAN OF AN ANCIENT CHURCH.

in fact as well as theory, the executive and representative of an authority superior to his own. The Episcopate of the whole world was held to be a unit to which, as to a never-dying College of Apostles, was committed the ingathering and safe-keeping of the Flock of Christ. Of this Sacred College every Bishop in his Parish was the representative. It was his duty to instruct his people in the doctrine that was held by all, to strengthen them with means of grace enjoyed by all, to rule them upon principles approved by all of the Episcopate. His government was therefore never meant to be a merely arbitrary or personal government; it was part of the charge of the undivided Episcopate; and what he did, he did as the executive of its authority rather than his own.

And as the power of the Episcopate was exercised by one Bishop over the people of one Parish, so the Bishops of every Province, acting in their corporate capacity, exercised the power of their united Episcopate over every Bishop and every Parish within their jurisdiction. When a See was vacant, no election by the people was sufficient to the installation even of a man who had already been elsewhere ordained and consecrated as a Bishop. Jurisdiction over the See was inherent, not in the people of the See, but in the Bishops of the Province in which the See was situated; and no Bishop might pretend to jurisdiction over any portion of the Province who had not had jurisdiction given to him by the Bishops of the Province. Even when he had been validly elected, duly consecrated, and canonically constituted Bishop of his See, they still retained the power to try him for malfeasance, to reverse his unwise judgments, and if need were, to withdraw the jurisdiction they had given him. The Provincial Synod, therefore, in which the Bishops of the Province assembled twice a year, was a real power in every Parish. In it lay the true safety of the members of the Church against attempted usurpation or injustice by the Bishop; and in it, too, lay the safety of the Church against corruptions of her doctrine; for it was one special purpose of these frequent Synods that the Bishops might make mutual examinations of each other as to purity of doctrine.

The Synods usually assembled in the Metropolis of the Province, and then courtesy alone would require that the Bishop of that City should preside. It seems, however, to

have been settled from the first that the right to preside in a provincial Synod was vested in the Bishop of the Metropolitan See, and the Canons subsequently decreed that no Provincial Synod should be held to be validly constituted, unless he should be present and preside. It was also the right of the Metropolitan to take charge of all vacant Sees within his Province; to administer their affairs; to secure their revenues; to procure the speedy election of Bishops and to ordain them, or appoint some other to ordain them; it was his duty to interpose and endeavour to settle controversies or disputes that might arise among them; to summon them to attend his Synod at such canonical times and at such places as he might designate: to cite before the Synod any Bishop who might be accused of error in doctrine, viciousness of life, or maladministration in office; to make due publication of such imperial laws or ecclesiastical canons as might from time to time be passed by competent authority; and to give letters commendatory to Bishops about to travel; without which, indeed, no Bishop was at liberty to leave his Parish. Yet in the Synod over which he presided, the Metropolitan had no more power than any other Bishop. He was simply *primus inter pares*, and might speak and vote no otherwise than as his peers. In short, he had that amount of influence and prestige which attaches to the permanent President and Executive Head of any eminent body of legislators; and no more.

The Provincial and Metropolitical System of the Church dates from the earliest time. One of the early Apostolical Canons, dating possibly from the beginning or middle of the Second Century, before the persecuted Church had dared to show herself at all points side by side with the imperial authorities, expressly declares the principle of the System. The language is as follows: "It is necessary that the Bishops of every *nation* should know who is chief among them, and should recognize him as their head by doing nothing of great moment without his consent; and that each of them should do such things only as pertain to his own Parish and the districts under him. And neither ought he (who is chief) to do anything without the consent of all; for thus shall there be unity of heart, and thus shall God be glorified through our Lord Jesus Christ." The use of the word *nation* instead of

Province, and the absence of all mention, *eo nomine*, of a Metropolitan, suffice to show the early date of this Canon; while its whole tenor, followed by the solemn conclusion, sufficiently proves that the gathering of neighboring Bishops round one recognized chief of their own order for mutual counsel and support, was a thing which might indeed have been neglected, but which was yet recognized as of the customary order of the Church.*

From the moment that the Church emerged from her sore persecutions she is found to have been, as universally established, with her Provinces and Metropolitans, as with her Bishops, Priests and Deacons; and the single exception of those African Provinces, in which circumstances had led to the adoption of the rule that the Bishops should preside in the order of their Seniority, without regard to the location of their Sees, is not a happy one. For when the hordes of Islam fell upon the Christians of the East and on the North of Africa, the Churches of the East stood fast in their integrity; while those of Africa, having no head, no centre, and no mutual bond of union and support, were swept off as in a day by hundreds, and left not a trace behind.

III. The Diocese.

The Province, with its Metropolis, its Synod, and its executive officer and President, the Metropolitan, which probably existed from the first foundation of the Church, contained

* The present essay is not the right place in which to enter into the discussion of historical questions even when their bearing upon matters of undoubted practical importance is immediate and direct. But if these questions were proposed: Whether the Provincial and Metropolitical System, as we find it universally established in the Fourth Century, was formed on grounds of human reason by the voluntary aggregation of isolated Sees, round the Metropolis as a convenient Centre: Or whether, on the contrary, the Metropolis, from the beginning and of divine purpose, was intended to be, as in point of historical fact it actually was, the Mother Church of the Country or Province, with which every other See within her area was from the first connected as a spiritual daughter:—the writer is prepared on grounds of Holy Scripture, history, and common sense, to prove the former proposition to be false, and the latter, with one possible exception, to be true. He commends the consideration of this subject to his learned readers: for in this, as he conceives, is matter for reflection nearly touching the great problem of the missionary agency of "this Church" on this Continent and elsewhere. As things stand now, the question is between ourselves with all our justly boasted purity of primitive truth, and Rome with her sagacious following of primitive organization; but at our present rate of progress she will leave us out of sight before the present century is ended.

within itself the idea of the larger coöperation of the Bishops of the Diocese when the division of the Empire into Dioceses came to be made. In our first chapter we have shown that the Provinces of the Empire were at first comparatively few and of immense extent, and that for certain reasons they were gradually subdivided till their number had increased to nearly one hundred and twenty. These successive subdivisions were, apparently, invariably followed by the Church, so that wherever the State erected a new Province with its own Metropolis, there the Church established her Synod and recognized the Metropolitan. In like manner, the subsequent erection of the Dioceses of the Empire, with the Exarchs or Vicars at the head of their administration, was at once accepted by the Church as the convenient geographical arrangement of Superior Synods and Tribunals of the Church. Whenever, therefore, it was found impossible for the Synod of a Province to arrive at moral unanimity in the determination of a matter of importance that had been submitted to it, the whole matter could be brought before a Greater Synod of the Diocese in which the Province was. Or if a Bishop had been condemned to any punishment by his Provincial Synod, he was free to carry up his cause to the Superior Court of the Diocesan Synod; and whatever cause was there determined could be brought before no higher Court.

The erection of Dioceses dates only from about the time of Constantine, and the Chief Bishop of the Diocese was originally called Archbishop—a word which now means merely a Metropolitan Bishop, but which then meant not merely a Metropolitan, but the acknowledged head of all the Metropolitans whose Provinces had been included by imperial decree within one Diocese. In the Canons he is also called the Exarch of the Church, this being the word which also designated the Chief Civil Magistrate of the Diocese. It was not until a later period that the name Patriarch began to be applied to certain of the Archbishops.

The Archbishops generally were ordained by the Synod of the Diocese over which they were appointed to preside; and it was their privilege to ordain all other Metropolitans of the Province; to call the Synods of the Diocese and to preside

therein; to receive appeals from the decisions of Metropolitans and of Metropolitan Synods; and to take cognizance of charges brought against Metropolitans, or even against the Provincial Bishops in case their Metropolitans were lax or remiss in discipline. In addition to these general privileges which were enjoyed by all Archbishops, the local customs of certain Sees permitted other privileges which were neither claimed nor granted elsewhere. But whatever power they might enjoy at home among the Metropolitans and other Bishops of their several Dioceses, the Archbishops had no power whatever over each other; no appeal lay from any one of them to any other; they had no superior but a General Council of the Catholic Church. Yet for political reasons which are plainly stated in the Canons which decreed it, the Bishop of Rome as being Bishop of what was then the Capital of the world and seat of the imperial dignity, was permitted a certain precedence of honour among other Archbishops. For a like reason the Archbishop of Constantinople, whose See was then the Second Capital of the world and seat of the imperial dignity in the East, enjoyed the second place of honour. The third place seems to have been held by the Archbishop of Alexandria. This precedence was entirely a matter of Canon, and how little it depended on even the most sacred traditions may be inferred from the fact that the See of Jerusalem, where the Apostolic office was created by our Lord Himself, and whose first Bishop S. James the Just presided over the First Council of the Sacred College of "Apostles, Elders, and Brethren," was for a long time not allowed even the dignity of a Metropolis, but was subordinate to the See of Cæsarea, under whose Metropolitan the Bishop of Jerusalem enjoyed only such precedence of rank over the other Bishops of the Province, as is now enjoyed by Bishops of London over their fellow-suffragans of the Province of Canterbury. To trace how the greater Patriarchates grew out of the Dioceses, and how the Patriarchate of the West grew up into the present arrogance and insolence of the Roman Papacy, with its absurd pretence of personal infallibility and universal jurisdiction, is not necessary to the student of the early Councils of the Christian Church. In them he will discover not a sign of any universal jurisdiction save that of the universal Catholic Episcopate when gathered in a General Council. Of

the personal infallibility of any individual Bishop, which would have made General Councils and all controversies in behalf of truth unnecessary, he will also find no sign. In other words, he will discover that throughout the age in which the undisputed General Councils of the Church were held, the Roman Papacy had not been born, nor had it even been conceived.

CHAPTER V.

HISTORY OF THE COUNCILS OF THE CHURCH.

NATURAL TENDENCY TO COUNCILS IN THE EARLY CHURCH. ORIGIN OF THE APOSTOLICAL CANONS. THEIR ANTIQUITY. THEIR AUTHENTICITY. SYNODS PROVINCIAL, DIOCESAN, AND GENERAL. AUTHORITY OF GENERAL COUNCILS. TEST OF THEIR ŒCUMENICITY. SANCTION OF THE FIVE PROVINCIAL SYNODS BY THE COUNCIL OF CHALCEDON. COUNCILS OF ANCYRA, NEO-CÆSAREA, NICÆA. PRESIDENTS AT NICÆA. CONDUCT OF CONSTANTINE. ARIUS. EXPANSION OF APOSTOLICAL CANONS. CANONS OF SARDICA. HISTORY OF THE SARDICAN COUNCIL. COUNCILS OF GANGRA, ANTIOCH. TRICK OF THE ARIANS. LAODICEA.

THE very nature of the Episcopate as a body represented by individual men, rather than an aggregation of individuals, must, independently of every other cause, have led the Bishops of the early ages to take frequent counsel with each other; and particularly when some case of general interest to the Church, or to their order, might, from time to time, occur. In ages of persecution, the number of Bishops who could conveniently or even safely meet together for such consultations, would be very limited; and then the spirit of charity as well as a desire of approbation from their brethren would lead to the communication of their acts to other Bishops who had not been able to be present. On the other hand, previous decisions thus communicated, would have great weight with all later gatherings of Bishops; and so, gradually, it might be expected that a kind of common Code would grow into existence and command the general obedience of all orders in the Church. Such, beyond a reasonable doubt, was the precise way in which the most ancient code of Canons in existence came to be compiled. The Canons called Apostolical, though there is not the slightest evidence that they were written in the age of the Apostles, are of very high antiquity; and Beveridge (in his Codex Canonum Eccles. Prim.) clearly shows that they had grown up into general acceptance in successive Synods; that they had been gathered into one collection by some unknown hand before the termination of the second century, or certainly, at latest, in the first part of

the third; and that before the Council of Nicæa they were recognized as universally obligatory everywhere throughout the Church. Some persons, indeed, as Hammond well sums up a lengthy controversy, "are disposed to consider the first fifty of these Canons as of more authority than the remainder, and Beveridge himself does not appear decidedly against this opinion. There does not, however, seem to be any sufficient foundation for it. It appears to have originated in the circumstance of the first fifty only having been translated into Latin by Dionysius Exiguus, and inserted into his collection of the Canons about A. D. 500; which collection was used in the Latin Church. The whole eighty-five exist in the contemporary collection of John of Antioch; they were acknowledged and approved as ancient and authoritative by Justinian who began to reign A. D. 526; and they are received and commented upon by all Greek writers and commentators without distinction. There is no apparent break or dissimilarity of style between the two portions; but what is the most conclusive proof of their unity is, that the references to the Canons by both Fathers and Councils, are made as distinctly and unhesitatingly to the Canons in the latter part of the Collection as in the former. Neither does there appear to be any reason for suspecting that the collection or addition of these Canons, as we have it, was made by Arians or other heretics. On the contrary, the circumstance of the Arians, in the Council of Antioch, having formed their own Canons upon these, and under cover of them made their attack upon Athanasius and Paul, is a strong argument of their previous reputation and authority in the Church." It seems, indeed, impossible to entertain a doubt of the antiquity, the universality, or the general integrity of the Apostolic Canons, after reading Beveridge's masterly vindication and illustration of that ancient Code; and though the Councils in which they were gradually set forth have been long ago forgotten, yet they are, on that account, in no degree less venerable. For, like the Common Law of England, these Canons were accounted in the universal Church as of such antiquity that the memory of man ran not to the contrary; and thus they were accepted from the Council of Nicæa downwards as a fundamental portion of the Canons of the Catholic Church.

When the Provincial System of the Church had been

clearly established, and the cessation of persecutions had made it possible to carry out that system with some slight approach to its integrity, the Synods of the Church, as we have seen, were Synods of the Province, of the Diocese, or of the Universal Church in all its Provinces. The authority of a Provincial Synod extended over the Province in which it had jurisdiction. The authority of a Diocesan Synod, in like manner, extended over the Diocese in which it was held. It is not, however, to be therefore inferred that a General Council had of necessity an equal jurisdiction over the universal Church. For, not to enter into any doctrinal or theological reasons, General Councils were sometimes extremely meagre in the disproportion of their numbers, to the Episcopate of the whole Church. Thus, at Nicæa there were present only 318 Bishops; at Constantinople only 150; and at Chalcedon the far larger number of 630; though even this was but a fragment of the total number of Bishops in the Universal Church. In such assemblies, where whole Provinces, Dioceses, nations, were entirely unrepresented, it is evident that there was no true presence of the Catholic Episcopate, even by representation; and particularly as the Bishops who were actually present came of their own personal pleasure, not by the election of their comprovincial Bishops. Since, then, the presence of the universal Episcopate would have been necessary to give universal jurisdiction to a Council, and universal authority to its decrees, it follows that no General Council had in virtue of that name, or of its numbers, or of the circumstances of its meeting, any universal jurisdiction or authority throughout the Church of CHRIST. The assembly of Bishops at Ephesus, A. D. 449, had as many of the visible tokens of a General Council of the Catholic Church as the Council of Constantinople; while the latter has been universally accepted by the Universal Church, while the former has as universally been branded with the title of a *Band of Robbers*. What, then, is the test of the authority of General Councils? Simply their general recognition as true General Councils and the general reception of their doctrines and decrees throughout the Universal Church. By this test every General Council stands or falls. By this test the doctrines of the Six Great Councils of Nicæa, Constantinople, Ephesus, Chalcedon, and the Second and Third of Constantinople, stand, being to this day undis-

puted by any Catholic Church. Perhaps it were as well for Christendom if the Canons of the First Four had in later times been as religiously regarded as the doctrines of the Six.

With the Second and Third Councils of Constantinople we have no concern in this work, for those Councils passed no Canons, but were occupied exclusively with doctrine. We shall therefore confine the brief historical outline we are now about to give, to the First Four General Councils, and the Five Provincial Councils of Ancyra, Neo-Cæsarea, Gangra, Antioch, and Laodicea, whose decrees received the sanction of the General Council of Chalcedon.*

Council of Ancyra.

The Council of Ancyra was held A. D. 314 or 315; that is to say, about ten or eleven years before the First General Council of Nicæa. Ancyra was the Metropolis of one of the

* The writer has been requested to discuss the question whether no other Canons than those of the Five Provincial Councils above-named were approved at Chalcedon. As it is the purpose of the present work to include only what is universally received by East and West, it would be beyond its purpose to discuss that question. Nevertheless, the writer cannot withhold from his readers the hints suggested by a reverend and very learned correspondent.

"It is a very important point," he observes, "to determine what Canons are authorized by Canon I. of Chalcedon. I think that all Canons of orthodox Synods and Councils, East and West, which were held prior to Chalcedon, are authorized: those of local Councils being approved—not indeed as of œcumenical force; but as of force within the jurisdiction of the local Synod which enacted them. Hence, such Canons as those of Eliberis in Spain are, by Canon I. of Chalcedon, recognized as of force *there*. Provincial Councils and those which were Diocesan, as, for example, that of the six Provinces of North Africa under Carthage, were, as you know, recognized as having the power to enact Canons, long before the Fourth Œcumenical Council. The erudite Beveridge does, indeed, favour the view that the only Canons of local Councils approved by the Canon of Chalcedon are those of Ancyra, Neo-Cæsarea, Gangra, Antioch, and Laodicea; and Hammond, pp. 148 and 149, seems to follow his notion, as I myself once did; but I now think otherwise. For those from the West who approved this enactment would naturally, in the absence of any sufficient proof to the contrary, understand all Canons before Chalcedon, Western as well as Eastern, to be approved."

Without entering into further detail on this point, the writer would simply observe—

1. That Canon I. of Chalcedon denies the force of no Canon previously passed by any competent Synod for the government of the Church within its jurisdiction; but that

2. No Canons except those of Ancyra, Gangra, Neo-Cæsarea, Antioch, and Laodicea, are universally recognized, East and West, as having received a universal force from the endorsement of Chalcedon; and

3. That no Western Province would have a right to think that its provincial rules had been specially approved, unless it had positive evidence that they had been specially examined.

Provinces of Galatia, and was chosen as a convenient place of meeting for the Bishops of Asia Minor, Pontus, Cappadocia, Armenia, Cilicia, and Syria; though the number who actually attended was only eighteen. The principal object of their meeting was to consider the case of those who had lapsed into idolatry during the persecution of Maximin, and who now sought restoration to the communion of the Church. It is to such cases chiefly that the twenty-five Canons of this Council relate. Nevertheless, there are Canons of this Council which are exceedingly interesting and valuable on account of doctrine as well as discipline.*

The Council of Neo-Cæsarea

Was held in the same year as that of Ancyra, and was attended by thirteen Bishops; of whom certainly some, and possibly all, had been in attendance at the former Council. This Council enacted Fifteen Canons.

THE FIRST GENERAL COUNCIL OF NICÆA

Was assembled by the Emperor Constantine, A. D. 325, to settle the prevailing discords which had been excited by the impious and novel doctrines of Arius † and his partisans. Courteous letters were addressed by the Emperor to all the Bishops of the world inviting them to attend the Council at

* This Council is not to be confounded with an assembly of Semi-Arians who met in the same place, A. D. 358, under the auspices of George of Laodicea, and adopted a Creed into which they admitted the word *Substance*, but not the word *Consubstantial.*

† Arius was a Presbyter of the Church of Alexandria, and a man of subtle turn, and remarkable for his eloquence. He maintained various erroneous opinions in religion; but that for which he is most notorious was the assertion of the inferiority of the Son, in nature as well as dignity, to the Father, and the denial of his divinity. These opinions spread rapidly throughout Egypt and the neighbouring Provinces, and found many supporters; in consequence of which Alexander, the Bishop of Alexandria, summoned two Councils at Alexandria, A. D. 315 and 319, in which the tenets of Arius were condemned, and he himself excommunicated.

Arius upon this retired to Palestine, where he found many abettors, and amongst them Eusebius, Bishop of Nicomedia, a man of great influence and authority in the Church.

The troubles and commotions consequent upon these events increased so much, and caused such great confusion in the Church, that Constantine at length assembled the Council of Nice to put an end to the controversy.

Arius being condemned by this Council, was banished to Illyricum; but some years afterwards one of his followers found means to persuade Constantine that his

Nicæa in Bithynia, and offering the means of transportation to and from their Sees both to the Bishops and to their attendants. Three hundred and eighteen Fathers came together at this summons; and among them were the Presbyters Vincentius and Vitus as the representatives of the Bishop of Rome. The Presidents of the Council were Alexander of Alexandria (who was attended by his Deacon Athanasius), Eustathius of Antioch and Hosius of Cordova.

The Bishops met in the imperial Palace, when their session was opened by the Emperor Constantine in person, who assured the Bishops, in a courteous address, that he affected no power of determining ecclesiastical questions, but left the decision of such matters to them. He then invited the Presidents to open the discussions, though he seems himself to have been very active in the Sessions of the Council. "The Emperor," says Eusebius (Life of Constantine, Bk. III., Chap. XIII.), "gave patient audience to all alike, and received every proposition with steadfast attention; and by occasionally assisting the argument of each party in turn, he gradually disposed even the most vehement disputants to a reconciliation. At the same time, by the affability of his address to all and by his use of the Greek language, with which he was not altogether unacquainted, he appeared in a truly attractive and amiable light; persuading some, convincing others by his reasonings, praising those who spoke well, and urging all to unity of sentiment; until at last he succeeded in bringing them to one mind and judgment respecting every disputed question."

Arius also made his appearance in the Council, and set forth his doctrines, which he defended at length in speeches which are said to have contained horrible blasphemies. His arguments were met and answered by the Fathers, and par-

condemnation was unjust; in consequence of which the Emperor recalled him from banishment, A. D. 330, repealed the laws which had been enacted against him, and permitted his chief protector Eusebius, Bishop of Nicomedia, and his faction, to vex and oppress the maintainers of the Nicene Council in various ways. Athanasius, who had succeeded Alexander in the See of Alexandria, was one of those who suffered most from these vexations. Having resolutely refused to restore Arius to his former rank and office in the Church of Alexandria, he was deposed by the Council of Tyre, A. D. 335, and banished into Gaul.

The people of Alexandria, however, could not be prevailed upon to receive Arius, upon which the Emperor invited him to Constantinople, A. D. 336, and ordered Alexander, Bishop of that city, to receive him to communion. Before, however, this order could be put into execution, Arius died at Constantinople, and Constantine survived him but a short time."—Mosheim, Cent. IV., P. 2, C. 5.

ticularly by Athanasius the Deacon of Alexandria; and then his heresies were condemned by the Council, and Arius himself was excommunicated.

The Council next proceeded to abate the disorders which had attended the schism of Meletius,* Bishop of Lycopolis in Egypt; and afterwards brought the long-continued controversy concerning Easter † to a satisfactory conclusion.

The important documents of this Council are the Symbol or Creed which was adopted in opposition to the heresy of

* "MELETIUS was Bishop of Lycopolis in Egypt. He was accused and convicted of having offered incense to idols, and was in consequence deposed by Peter, Bishop of Alexandria, whose jurisdiction extended throughout all Egypt. Meletius upon this became the head of a schism in the Church, by assuming to himself the power of ordination, which was vested in the Bishop of Alexandria, and exercised by him in all the Egyptian Churches. Epiphanius, Hær. 68, attributes the dissensions between Meletius and Peter to another cause. He says that the rigorous proceedings of Peter against Meletius were occasioned by the latter's refusing to readmit into the Church those who had fallen from the faith during Diocletian's persecution, before their penitential trial was entirely finished. The former opinion, however, is supported by the superior authority of Socrates and Theodoret. The confusion which Meletius introduced into the Church by his illegal ordinations was rectified by the Council of Nice, as appears by the Sixth Canon, in which it was ordained that the ancient privilege of the Church of Alexandria should be preserved, and the general authority of the Metropolitans over the Bishops of their several provinces was declared and confirmed."—Mosheim, *Ib.*, note by Dr. Maclaine.

† The controversy respecting the proper time of celebrating the Easter festival was of very early origin in the Church. The generality of the Asiatic Churches kept the festival as the Jews did their Passover, on the fourteenth day of the first moon in the new year, whatever day of the week that happened to be. The Western Churches generally deferred it to the first Sunday after the first full moon. The former alleged the authority of St. Philip and St. John for their practice, the latter that of St. Peter and St. Paul, and of a revelation made by an angel to Hermas, brother of Pius I., Bishop of Rome. Polycarp, Bishop of Smyrna, came to Rome about the middle of the second century, to confer with Anicetus, Bishop of Rome, upon the subject; but they could not come to any agreement as to the proper day. They agreed, however, in this, that the peace and communion of the Church were not to be broken on account of the difference. Some years after, Victor, Bishop of Rome, being unable to persuade the Asiatics to adopt the Western custom, excommunicated the Asiatic Churches, and sent circular letters to all the Churches which agreed with him respecting Easter, that they should hold no communion with the Asiatics. This proceeding of Victor's was, however, condemned by all the wise and sober men of his own party, several of whom wrote sharply to him upon the subject, and particularly Irenæus, who wrote to him in the name of the Churches of Gaul. The dispute still prevailed till the time of Constantine, who, wishing to terminate it, sent, in the first instance, Hosius, Bishop of Corduba in Spain, into the East, to endeavor to bring those Churches which still retained the Asiatic custom to an agreement with the rest of the Church. The mission, however, proving fruitless, the subject was submitted to the decision of the Council of Nice, which decreed that from thenceforth all Churches should keep the feast on the same day, *i. e.*, the first Sunday after the full moon, which happens upon, or next after, the vernal equinox, *i. e.*, the 21st day of March. The great reverence which was paid to the decrees of this Council produced a mere general agreement, which was further enforced by the decrees of other Councils, and thenceforth those persons who kept the feast according to the old Asiatic practice were accounted heretics, and subjected to ecclesiastical punishment.—Bingham, B. XX. C. 5.

Arius, the Synodical Epistle in which the Acts of the Council were communicated to the Churches of Egypt, and twenty Canons on various subjects. Of these twenty Canons there are five which distinctly appeal to an earlier code of ecclesiastical law on as many different points; and on investigation we discover these same points clearly expressed in the Apostolical Canons. In these instances and in at least two others the Canons of Nicæa are evidently mere expansions or applications of the rule or principle which is more briefly expressed in the Apostolical Canons on the same subject.

Among the Canons of Nicæa are regulations for the reconciliation of the Cathari * and the Paulianists,† and for the restoration of persons who had lapsed during the persecutions of Licinius.‡

* The CATHARI were Novatians, a sect so called from Novatian, a presbyter of the Church of Rome, who having adopted very severe notions respecting those who had lapsed in persecution, and also respecting other offenders, and having in vain opposed the ordination of Cornelius, who was elected Bishop of Rome, A. D. 250, separated from the Church, and brought to Rome three Bishops from the further part of Italy, whom he compelled by force to ordain him Bishop. He then erected a new society, and ordained Bishops and Presbyters in it. There was no difference in point of doctrine between the Novatians and Catholics: what particularly distinguished this sect was their refusing to readmit to communion those who after baptism had fallen into grievous sins; and to communicate with those who had married twice; and other such-like severities of discipline. They pretended to an extraordinary degree of purity, and therefore called themselves Cathari, or the pure; and obliged such as came over to them from the general body of Christians, to be rebaptized on entering into their society. One of the chief partisans of Novatian was Novatus, a Carthaginian presbyter, who passed over to Rome from Carthage to avoid the excommunication of Cyprian, his Bishop.—Hammond, pp. 43, 44; Bingham, Scholastic Hist. of Lay Baptism, p. II., C. II., s. 2. Mosheim, B. I., p. II., C. V., s. 17.

† The PAULIANISTS derived their name from Paulus Samosatensis, who was elected Bishop of Antioch, A. D. 260. He maintained, amongst other errors, that our LORD was a mere man, and had not come down from heaven. He was condemned and deposed by a Council at Antioch, A. D. 272. The Canon requires the Paulianists to be rebaptized, because in baptizing they did not use the only lawful form, according to our SAVIOUR's command, "In the name of the FATHER, the SON, and the HOLY GHOST." This, indeed, was a general rule in the ancient Church applicable to all heretics, that those who did not use that form should be baptized on their admission into the Church, but that those who did use it should be admitted by imposition of hands without any fresh baptism.—Hammond, pp. 51, 52.

‡ LICINIUS, who, after the defeat and death of Maxentius, A. D. 312, and of Maximin, A. D. 313, shared the empire with Constantine, was at first favorably disposed towards the Christians, and, in conjunction with Constantine, issued a decree, A. D. 312, granting to them full power to live according to their own laws and institutions; which power was specified still more clearly in another edict, drawn up at Milan in the following year. The joy of the Christians at these favorable events was, however, soon interrupted by the war which broke out between Licinius and Constantine. Licinius being defeated, A. D. 314, made a treaty with Constantine, which he observed for some years, but then broke out in another war. In order to engage the friends of the old superstition on his side, he cruelly persecuted the Christians. This persecution commenced about A. D. 320, and lasted till the final overthrow of Licinius, A. D. 324, the year before the assembling of the Council of Nice.—Hammond, p. 46.

As early as the beginning of the Fifth Century an attempt was made by Zosinus, Bishop of Rome, to pass off the Canons of Sardica as genuine Canons of this Council in addition to the twenty which are universally acknowledged to be genuine. At a later period the Roman Canonists have alleged the same Canons of Sardica in evidence of the Pope's pretended right of hearing appeals; and they have affirmed that these Canons are to be considered as at least a sort of appendix to the Canons of Nicæa. Some account, therefore, of the Council of Sardica seems to be necessary in connection with the Council of Nicæa; and we accordingly append what follows as abridged from Johnson and Hammond.

Council of Sardica.

"Athanasius, Bishop of Alexandria, and several others, being deposed by the Arian party, which prevailed in the East through the countenance of the Emperor Constantius, took refuge at Rome. Julius, Bishop of that city, heard their cause in a Synod assembled for that purpose, A. D. 340, and decided in their favor; and wrote to the Eastern Bishop, requiring them to be restored. When this was refused, Constans, Emperor of the West, espoused their cause, and threatened Constantius with a war in case he did not oblige the Bishops to permit Athanasius and his associates to return to their bishoprics. Hereupon, by the joint consent of both Emperors, a Synod was appointed to meet at Sardica in Illyricum to give a final decision to this dispute. The Eastern Bishops, to the number of seventy-six, came to Sardica; but the great majority of them being Arians, refused to assemble with the Western, who were orthodox, and went and formed an assembly of their own, at Philippopolis in Thrace. The Western, with Athanasius and the other refugees, held a Synod at Sardica, A. D. 347, where they absolved Athanasius and the other orthodox Bishops from the sentence of deposition, and for their further security made the Canons in question. This Council was intended to be a general one, being called by the Emperors both of the East and the West, and being designed to consist of the Bishops of both parts; but, by the secession of the Eastern Bishops, it came to pass that it was really a Western Synod only; and therefore its Canons were never received into the code of the Universal Church."—Johnson's Clergyman's Vade Mecum, Vol. II., p. 157.

Amongst other things enacted by these Canons, it was provided, that in the event of any Bishop considering himself aggrieved by the sentence of the Bishops of his Province, he might apply to the Bishop

of Rome, who would write to the Bishops in the neighborhood of the Province of the aggrieved Bishop, to rehear the cause; and should also, if it seemed desirable to do so, send some Presbyters of his own Church, to assist at the rehearing. These privileges indeed were not allowed to the Bishop of Rome by the Sardican Fathers as a matter of right, but of favor; as appears from the words of Hosius, Bishop of Corduba, in proposing the Canon to the Synod. "Hosius, Bishop, said: If any Bishop thinks that his cause has been misjudged, in order that it may be judged again, if it seems right to your love, let us honor the memory of the Apostle Peter, and let those who have judged the cause write to Julius, Bishop of Rome, in order that a new trial may, if proper, be had." And at the end of the Canons relating to the subject it is added: "The Bishops answered, We approve of what has been said." It is probable, indeed, as Richerius in his History of Councils observes, that these Canons were only provisional, and intended for the security of the Eastern orthodox Bishops against the Arians, and that the privilege conferred upon the Bishop of Rome in them, was not meant to be given to the See of Rome, but only to the then Bishop Julius, who is expressly mentioned in them; and consequently that they were only designed for the case then before the Council.

An attempt, however, was made at the beginning of the fifth century, by Zosimus, Bishop of Rome, to establish his authority in the African Churches, by means of these Canons, on the following occasion.

Apiarius, a Presbyter of the Church of Sicca in Africa, having been deposed by his Bishop for gross immoralities, fled to Rome, A. D. 415, and was received to communion by Zosimus. Zosimus further sent legates into Africa, to the Bishops there, desiring that Apiarius's cause should be heard over again, asserting that the Bishops of Rome had the privilege of requiring such rehearings conferred upon them by the Canons of Nice. The African Bishops to the number of two hundred and seventeen, being assembled in Synod at Carthage, received these legates, who declared the cause of their coming, and, in proof of the authority claimed by the Pope, quoted the Sardican Canons, which they alleged as genuine Canons of the Council of Nice. The African Bishops said in their answers that they acknowledged the authority of the Nicene Canons, and were ready to abide implicitly by them; but that as regarded those which the legates alleged, they were not to be found in the copies of the Nicene Canons, which were brought to Africa by Cæcilian, Bishop of Carthage, who was present at the Council of Nice, nor in any other copies that they had ever seen. That, however, they would send to the Bishops of Constantinople, Antioch, and Alexandria, who must have the genuine Canons, and if it should appear

that the alleged Canons were genuine, they would submit to them. They sent accordingly, and received answers from Atticus, Bishop of Constantinople, and Cyril of Alexandria, with copies of the genuine Canons.

By these answers it was indisputably proved that the twenty Canons alone were genuine, and that no others had ever been known or heard of. The matter, however, was not finally settled for several years, in the course of which Zosimus and his successor Boniface died, and it was closed by a letter from the African Bishops to Celestine, then Bishop of Rome, in which they assert the independence of their own, and all other Churches, and deny the pretended right of hearing appeals claimed by the Bishop of Rome; and further exhort him not to do or attempt anything contrary to the Canons of the Church, either by receiving into communion persons who had been excommunicated by their own Bishops, or by interfering in any way with the privileges of other Churches. For a full account of the particulars contained in this note, see the account of the Synod of Sardica, and of those of Carthage, in the collections of Councils. The Canons of Sardica are translated by Johnson, and inserted in the Clergyman's Vade Mecum.—Hammond, pp. 55, 56.

Council of Gangra.

The exact date of this Council is unknown. If Eusebius, whose name stands first among the signatures of the Bishops who attended it, was, as some suppose, Bishop of Cæsarea in Cappadocia and predecessor of Saint Basil, then the Council must have been held during the Episcopate of Eusebius, which extended from A. D. 362 to 371. The more probable opinion is that it was held between the Council of Nicæa and that of Antioch, that is, sometime between A. D. 325 and 341.

The Twenty Canons of this Council are chiefly directed against the practices of a spurious asceticism which had been propagated by a certain Eustathius whose heresies are fully detailed in a Synodical Letter. Lest, however, the Canons which were then enacted to meet an unavoidable necessity and to abate an intolerable scandal should be misconstrued into a condemnation of true asceticism, a valuable protestation is appended to the Canons, in which protestation the Bishops disavow every such purpose, and declare the real distinction between true asceticism and its pretentious counterfeit.

Council of Antioch.

The Council of Antioch was held A. D. 341, on the occasion of the assembling of many Bishops at the dedication of the Church known as the Golden Church of Antioch, which had been founded by Constantine, and completed by Constantius. The Bishops numbered nearly one hundred, most of whom were Arians, or Semi-Arians. They did not, however, attempt to make the Council an occasion of propagating their peculiar tenets by any mode of direct teaching. Indeed, they set forth more than one confession of faith, and one, at least, of these St. Hilary maintains to be susceptible of an orthodox construction. The Synodical Letter, brief as it is, boasts much of the unanimity and peace which had prevailed at the Council, and the phraseology is studiously chosen so as to give no offence to Catholics. Their object was, in short, to gain authority among the Catholics by seeming to be Catholics, in order that they might the better serve the cause of heresy. Accordingly they professed in their First Canon the most perfect obedience to the "holy and great" Council of Nicæa; then they proceeded to establish other Canons which in fact, are very valuable applications and expansions of the ancient code of Canons called Apostolical; and then, still never seeming to touch doctrine, but to be aiming only at true principles of Canon Law, they enacted their famous XI. and XII. Canons, which were intended to apply to Athanasius, the great defender of the Catholic Faith against the heresies of Arius. Athanasius had become Archbishop of Alexandria, where he had first served as a Deacon; but heresy which he had seemed to crush by his transcendant genius now assailed him with its usual weapons of most infamous slander. To set these at rest the Emperor Constantine, A. D. 335, summoned a Council, to convene at Tyre, and when it had convened it was discovered that a large majority of the assembled Bishops were adherents of the Arian party. Hence it is not to be wondered at that though the innocence of Athanasius of every charge alleged against him, was sufficiently established, yet he was condemned to be deposed from his Archbishopric, and banished from his See. Against this infamous sentence Athanasius protested and appealed to Constantine, who interposed, and the Archbishop was restored. The bearing of the XI.

and XII. Canons of Antioch upon this case will readily be perceived; for the former was, and was in fact designed to be, a new decree of deposition against Athanasius, while the latter was intended to prevent all possibility of future restoration by a subsequent rehearing of his cause before a higher and more competent canonical tribunal. A like purpose is apparent in the XIV. and XV. Canons; and the XVI. and XVII. were enacted to cover the case of Paul, Archbishop of Constantinople, a Catholic whose election to that See had been bitterly resisted by the Arians, and, as they now alleged, had been accomplished without the concurrence of Theodore of Heraclea, Metropolitan of Thrace. Passing the XVIII. Canon, all the others of this Council are mere expansions of Apostolical Canons, and were doubtless intended to impose upon the Church by their appearance of devotion to the ancient statutes of the Church. It is also to be noticed that this Council adopts in its XX. Canon the rule of the Apostolic Canons in reference to the time of holding the Spring Councils, rather than that of the Council of Nicæa—a circumstance which seems to indicate that such matters, even when regulated by a General Council, were never intended nor understood to override the ancient, well-established customs of particular Churches.

On the whole, though the purpose of the Council of Antioch was clear enough both to the orthodox and to the heretic; yet as it did not set forth any heresy in any formal manner; as, on the contrary, it professed entire submission to the only General Council that had then been held; and as the Canons it enacted were entirely unobjectionable, and indeed extremely valuable additions to the previous legislation of the Church; they were therefore universally received into the Code of the Church, and having been approved by the General Council of Chalcedon, they have now as much authority as if they had been passed in a true General Council instead of by a Council of Semi-Arians.

Council of Laodicea.

This Council was held at Laodicea in Phrygia, but the year in which it was held is not known. Baronius maintains that it was held A. D. 314; others date it in 319; others yet

think that it was held during the pontificate of Liberius who was elevated to the See of Rome A. D. 352 ; Beveridge argues that it was held A. D. 365 or thereabouts. The opinion of those who would date this Council before that of Nicæa, is sufficiently disproved by the mention of the Photinians in Canon VII., since that sect did not appear till after the Council of Nicæa ; and the mere fact that in Collections of the Councils it has always been placed after that of Antioch is presumptive evidence that it was later than that Council. We may therefore assume that it was held certainly later than A. D. 325. Of the particulars of this Council nothing further is known than what may be gathered from its Canons.

CHAPTER VI.

HISTORY OF THE COUNCILS, CONTINUED.

THE SECOND GENERAL COUNCIL. ITS DATE. ITS PRESIDENTS. MELETIUS NOT IN COMMUNION WITH ROME. ADDITIONS TO THE CREED OF NICÆA. THE FILIOQUE AFTERWARDS INSERTED THROUGH THE INFLUENCE OF SECULAR POWER. COUNCILS OF TOLEDO, ROME, AIX-LA-CHAPELLE. ACTION OF CHARLEMAGNE AND LEO III. ROME ADOPTS THE INTERPOLATION UNDER NICHOLAS I. COUNCIL OF EPHESUS. DOCTRINE OF NESTORIUS. ACTION OF POPE CELESTINE AND S. CYRIL. CONDEMNATION OF NESTORIUS. ARREST OF NESTORIUS AND CYRIL. DECISIONS OF THE COUNCIL. SUBMISSION OF JOHN OF ANTIOCH AND OTHERS. COUNCIL OF CHALCEDON. EUTYCHES AND HIS DOCTRINE. THE "LATROCINIUM EPHESINUM." MARTYRDOM OF FLAVIAN. CONDUCT OF POPE LEO. CONDEMNATION OF EUTYCHES. PRIVILEGES CONFERRED ON CONSTANTINOPLE. APPROVAL OF EARLIER PROVINCIAL COUNCILS.

THE SECOND GENERAL COUNCIL,

WHICH IS

THE FIRST COUNCIL OF CONSTANTINOPLE.

THE Second General Council was called by the Emperor Theodosius, A. D. 381, for the purpose of deciding on the strange and heretical doctrine which had been recently maintained by the Arians, the Macedonians, and others mentioned in the first Canon of the Council, who had erred from the Catholic Faith.* It was com-

* Of these heretics the following were the chief:

The EUNOMIANS, so called from Eunomius, a disciple of Aëtius (from whom this sect were also sometimes called Aëtians), and Bishop of Cyzicus, the Metropolis of the Province of Hellespont. The tenets of Eunomius were those of the more rigid Arians. He taught that the SON was of a different substance from the FATHER (whence the name of Anomæans or dissimilar), that the SON was created by the FATHER, and the HOLY GHOST by the SON, and that the HOLY GHOST is destitute of all divinity, or creative power.—Hammond, p. 68.

The EUDOXIANS derived their name from Eudoxius, who was Bishop first of Germanicia in the Province of Euphrates, afterwards of Antioch, and lastly of Constantinople. Their tenets were in all respects the same as those of the Eunomians.—Hammond, p. 69.

The SEMI-ARIANS or PNEUMATOMACHI were properly those who neither agreed with the Catholics in holding that the SON is of the same substance, ὁμοούσιος, with the FATHER, nor with the rigid Arians in asserting that he is altogether dissimilar, ἀνόμοιος, but maintained that he is, although a creature, yet of a different nature from all other creatures, and in a peculiar manner like to the FATHER, ὁμοιούσιος, but that the HOLY GHOST is in all respects a creature, and different from the FATHER and the SON.

posed of One Hundred and Fifty Bishops, among whom it is remarkable that not one was from the West. Damasus, the Bishop of Rome, was not represented even by legates. This Council was successively presided over by

On this account they are classed with the Pneumatomachi in the Canon. The Pneumatomachi, properly so called, were orthodox in their opinions respecting the FATHER and the SON, and held that they were of one and the same substance, but they would not acknowledge this of the HOLY GHOST, whom they asserted to be a mere creature. Augustin, Hær. 52, says that some persons called them Semi-Arians on this account, as agreeing partly with the orthodox and partly with the Arians. The founder of this sect was Macedonius, Bishop of Constantinople, from whom they were commonly called Macedonians. It was chiefly against these heretics that the Council of Constantinople was assembled by Theodosius, and two of the principal leaders of the sect, Eleusius, Bishop of Cyzicus, and Marcian of Lampsacus, were present at it.—Hammond, p. 69.

The SABELLIANS, from Sabellius, a native of Lybia, held that the SON and the HOLY GHOST are not only the same GOD with the FATHER, but the same person; so that the Godhead is not only one in substance, but one in Person, and FATHER, SON, and HOLY GHOST, only three appellations of the same person, who appeared or manifested himself at different times as FATHER, SON, and HOLY GHOST, and who is therefore sometimes called the FATHER, sometimes the SON, and sometimes the HOLY GHOST. They are therefore called by the Latin Fathers, Patripassians, since it necessarily follows from their doctrines that the FATHER was incarnate, and suffered on the cross.—Hammond, p. 69.

The MARCELLIANS, were so called from Marcellus, Bishop of Ancyra, in Galatia, who lived about or shortly after the time of the Council of Nice. He asserted that at the end of the world CHRIST would give up his kingdom and his subsistence, so that he would neither reign nor subsist for ever, but be dissolved at the last into the FATHER. He founded his opinion upon 1 Cor. xv. 24-28. It was apparently to meet this heresy that the Constantinopolitan Fathers made that addition to the Nicene Creed, "of whose kingdom there shall be no end," as it was to meet the Macedonian heresy that they added the articles relating to the HOLY GHOST.—Hammond, p. 10.

The PHOTINIANS, took their name from Photinus, a disciple of Marcellus, and afterwards Bishop of Sirmium. He maintained the absolute unity of the Godhead, denying any Trinity of Persons, or the Personality of the Word, or the HOLY GHOST. He asserted that CHRIST was a mere man, and that he had the beginning of his existence from the Virgin Mary.—Hammond, p. 70.

APOLLINARIUS, from whom the Apollinarians took their name, was a native of Laodicea, and taught that our LORD took our body without a rational or intellectual soul; and that his divine nature supplied the place of a soul, or at any rate of the intellectual faculty.—Hammond, p. 70.

The SABBATIANS were so called from Sabbatius, a Presbyter, who adopted the sentiments of Novatianus.

ARISTERI, is probably a false reading for Aristi, *i. e.*, the best; as we also find *Cathari* and *Catheroteri*, *i. e.*, the pure and the more pure.

The QUARTODECIMANS, or TETRADITES, were those persons who persisted in observing the Easter festival with the Jews, on the fourteenth day of the first month, whatever day of the week it happened to be.—Hammond, p. 74.

The MONTANISTS, one of the older sects, were so called from Montanus, who embraced Christianity in the second century. He professed to be inspired in a peculiar way by the HOLY GHOST, and to prophesy. He was supported in his errors by two women, Priscilla and Maximilla, who also pretended to prophesy. His heresy infected many persons, amongst others Tertullian, but being condemned by the Church, his followers formed a sect remarkable for extreme austerity. But although they asserted that the HOLY GHOST had inspired Montanus to introduce a system of greater perfec-

Meletius * of Antioch, Gregory Nazianzen, Timothy of Alexandria, and Nectarius of Constantinople.

The Fathers of Constantinople reaffirmed the Nicene Creed in its integrity, and they further appended to it the clauses concerning the HOLY SPIRIT, which seemed necessary in addition to the Creed of Nicæa, in order to meet new forms of heresy that had sprung up. The Creed of Constantinople was never, however, supposed or intended to teach doctrine which had not been fully and explicitly held by the Fathers of Nicæa; but as the earlier controversies had been chiefly concerning the person of CHRIST, so the later controversies had been chiefly concerning the HOLY GHOST; and so it had been found advisable to adopt clauses which by general sanction should define the doctrine of the HOLY SPIRIT as precisely as the Council of Nicæa had defined the doctrine of the SON of GOD. Hence, as these Creeds are not two, but in fact one and the same, the Creed of Constantinople was universally adopted, and is now customarily called the Nicene Creed.

But here we have unhappily to note a variation by the Western Churches from the pure text of the Creed of Constantinople, that has confessedly been the chief cause of the great schism between the East and the West. The Fathers of Con-

tion than the Church had before known, and condemned those who would not join them as carnal, they did not at first innovate in any of the Articles of the Creed. This sect lasted a long time, and spread much in Phrygia and the neighbouring districts, whence they were called Phryges and Cataphryges, and latterly adopted the errors of Sabellius respecting the Trinity.—Hammond, p. 74.

Here also we may mention the case of Maximus the Cynic, which is the subject of the Fourth Canon.

MAXIMUS the Cynic was an Egyptian by birth, and a cynic philosopher. He was converted to the faith by Gregory Narzianzen, and baptized and ordained by him. Afterwards being led by ambition to desire the Bishopric of Constantinople, he suborned certain Egyptian Bishops, and brought them to Constantinople to elect and ordain him Bishop. Before, however, the ordination was completed, they were driven out of the church by the people, and retired into a private house, where they performed the ordination. This whole transaction, however, was so completely at variance with all the laws and customs of the Church, that the Synod would not recognize it in any way, and therefore did not decree that Maximus should be deposed, but that all ecclesiastical acts done towards him, or by him, were utterly void and of none effect.—Hammond, p. 71.

* For a long time there had been a schism at Antioch. That city had two Bishops, Meletius and Paulinus. The Bishop of Rome was in communion with the latter, and consequently regarded Meletius as schismatic. . . . . . The Second Œcumenical Council was therefore under the presidency of a Bishop who was not in communion with Rome. Meletius died during the sitting of the Council. Those who were well known for eloquence among the Fathers pronounced his eulogy. . . . . . He was regarded by all as a Saint; and when his body was transported to Antioch, the journey was an uninterrupted ovation.—The Papacy by Abbé Guettée. Engl. Ed., p. 110.

stantinople, following the exact words of our SAVIOUR, say that the HOLY GHOST "proceedeth from the FATHER." In the version now used universally throughout the West the clause is: EX PATRE FILIOQUE procedentem, "Who proceedeth from the FATHER *and the SON*." It is not within the scope of such a work as this to discuss the theological importance of this corruption or variation: nor to show the inveterate confusion in the Western mind of the idea of *procession* in the order of nature with *mission* in the order of time; nor on the other hand to show the inveterate prejudice of the Easterns, who as it seems, are unwilling to believe that one can say "Who proceedeth from the FATHER and the SON," without meaning that He proceeds *in the same way or in the same sense* from the SON as from the FATHER.

But without at all entering into the theological merits of this question, or even touching upon the kindred question of the duty of Western Churches at the present day, it will not be out of place to mention the historical succession of facts connected with this matter.

It has been attempted by the Latins to prove that the present Western version is in fact the true version of the Creed: but not one Greek copy has ever been produced in which the interpolated words FILIOQUE, "and from the SON," are to be found. The earliest authentic instance of their use is in some copies of the Latin Version of the Creed which is found in the Acts of the Third (*Provincial*) Council of Toledo, A. D. 589. It is therefore evident that the Creed of Constantinople, which was afterwards confirmed with an anathema by the General Council of Chalcedon, did not contain these words. The use of the words in some Latin copies of the Council of Toledo is to be traced to a singular cause: no other, indeed, than the indiscreet zeal of a royal convert from Arianism, Reccaredus, King of the Spanish Goths, who on renouncing Arianism insisted on the introduction of FILIOQUE into the Creed as an act of greater homage to the SON of GOD.

From this time onward the expression is found in the records of several Spanish Councils of the Sixth and Seventh Centuries. In an English Council held A. D. 679 the SPIRIT is said to proceed in an ineffable manner from the FATHER and the SON. The Council of Friuli, A. D. 791, adopts the words in its version of the Creed. In the only other Latin Council

which contains a copy of the Creed, that is, in a Council of Rome held under Martin I., A. D. 642, Filioque is not found.

As it was the influence of a royal layman which had caused this interpolation at first, so it was again the influence of an imperial meddler that prevailed over the Church's own authority to make the interpolation permanent. In A. D. 809 a Council was held by Charlemagne at Aix-la-Chapelle from which deputies were sent to the Pope, Leo III., to obtain his sanction to the singing of the Creed with the interpolated words which had not then been adopted at Rome. The Pope peremptorily refused ; and in testimony of the true Creed as he had received it, he caused two silver tablets to be hung up in the Basilica of S. Peter at Rome, on which there were engraved the Greek text and the Latin version of the Creed of Constantinople, both without the Filioque. Popes, in those days, were not thought to be infallible, and the imperial theologian carried matters with a high hand. The interpolated version of the Creed was sung in spite of Leo's prohibition, and before long, probably in the Pontificate of Nicholas I., the Church of Rome itself adopted the interpolation.

THIRD GENERAL COUNCIL.

EPHESUS.

The Council of Ephesus was assembled, A. D. 431, by the Emperor Theodosius the Younger, for the trial of Nestorius, Bishop of Constantinople, who had permitted a Presbyter called Anastasius and a Bishop called Dorotheus to preach and maintain that the Blessed Virgin may not lawfully be called Theotocos ; Dorotheus in fact going so far as to pronounce an anathema against all who should apply that title to her.* The Clergy and people of Constantinople declared

* The word Theotocos, which properly signifies the Bringer-forth of God, was originally introduced, not as a title of honor to the Blessed Virgin, but in order to assert the true and proper divinity of our Lord Jesus Christ, and that fundamental doctrine of our faith, that "undoubtedly even the nature of God itself in the only Person of the Son is incarnate, and hath taken to itself flesh."—(Hooker.) In the words of Basil of Seleucia, "The Virgin having brought forth God incarnate, is named Theotocos," Θεὸν σαρκωθέντα τεκοῦσα Θεοτόκος ὀνομάζεται. It is not known who

against Nestorius, and the quarrel having been reported abroad, S. Cyril of Alexandria and Celestine of Rome both held provincial Councils in which the doctrine of Nestorius and his party was condemned. Nestorius, however, still continued to maintain his heresy; the tumults at Constantinople were continued; and therefore, at the instance of Nestorius himself, as well as of Celestine and Cyril, Theodosius called a General Council to be held at Ephesus. On the day appointed for the meeting, Cyril with Bishops of Egypt, Syria, and Asia assembled, and Nestorius also came with ten Bishops in his train; but owing to the absence of a number of the Eastern Bishops and the representatives of Rome, the opening of the Council was postponed from day to day for fifteen days. When that time had expired the Council was convened, although the absentees had not arrived; and then

first introduced the term, but it is to be met with in many of the most eminent Fathers of the Church, who lived before the time of the Council of Ephesus, as Athanasius, Basil, Gregory Nazianzen, Gregory Nyssene, Eusebius, Alexander of Alexandria, Dionysius of Alexandria, Chrysostom, and others, whose words are quoted by Beveridge and by Suicer, in v. Θεοτόκος. Indeed, it appears that Nestorius or Anastasius were the first persons who expressly denied that the Virgin might properly be called Theotocos, because they could not reconcile this title with their particular opinions respecting our LORD's incarnation. The Council of Ephesus, however, having solemnly approved of the word, it was from that time constantly used not only by Greek, but also by Latin writers. In later times, indeed, the word Deipara was introduced as a translation of Theotocos, but it was not used by the earlier Latin writers, such compounds not being agreeable to the idiom of their language. They therefore retained the Greek word Theotocos, as they did the other famous Greek compound Homoousios; or if they wished to explain the term, they used the word Genitrix, which properly signifies the Bringer-forth, and not Mater, in doing so. Thus Peter the Deacon: "We believe rightly and according to the truth, that the Blessed Virgin is Theotocos, *i. e.*, the Bringer-forth of GOD (Dei genitricem)." And Leo I., Bishop of Rome, "We anathematize Nestorius, who believed the Blessed Virgin Mary to be the Bringer-forth (genitricem) not of GOD, but only of man." Ephraim of Theopolis translating these words of Leo into Greek, uses the word μήτηρ to express the Latin genitrix, and therefore says in another part of his works, that Leo was the first person who called the Holy Theotocos, Mother of GOD, Μήτηρ Θεοῦ, which none of the Fathers before him had done in express words. From this it appears, as Beveridge observes, that the Greeks first called the Blessed Virgin Theotocos; the Latins afterwards interpreted that phrase by the Latin Genitrix Dei; the Greeks then rendered the expression Genitrix Dei by Μήτηρ Θεοῦ, which being retranslated into Latin became Mater Dei, the Mother of GOD. To this I would add, that the expression, Mother of GOD, having thus originated in a mistranslation of the original word, and having, as we know, been in after-ages perverted from its primary intention of an assertion of our LORD's divinity, and used to exalt the privileges of the Blessed Virgin beyond those bounds within which (blessed and highly to be honored as she is) they ought to be confined; and being on this account likely to give offence, and lead to error, it seems desirable that it should be avoided, and that either the original word Theotocos should be retained, or some such rendering as that of The Bringer-forth of GOD, be adopted in its stead. *Vid.* Suicer in voce Θεοτόκος, and Pearson on the third Article of the Creed.—Hammond, pp. 79–81.

Nestorius was summoned to appear before it for the trial of his cause. On various pretexts he refused to attend. The Council proceeded in the strictest obedience to the letter of the Canon provided for the trial of a Bishop; and Nestorius still remaining contumacious, his publications were examined in his absence, and he was condemned to be deposed. To this sentence he refused submission.

Five days afterwards the Eastern Bishops, numbering twenty-six, arrived with John of Antioch at their head; these joined the party of Nestorius and held a Counter-Council which proceeded on its part to hurl a sentence of excommunication against Cyril and the orthodox who had united in the condemnation of Nestorius.

Soon afterwards, again, the representatives of Rome arrived, when the previous condemnation of Nestorius was confirmed; John of Antioch with the other dissidents was also excommunicated; sundry Canons were adopted; and several ecclesiastical affairs were settled.*

* Of these affairs, by far the most important were the condemnation of Celestius (Canon I), the condemnation of the documents submitted by Charisius (Can. VII), and the complaint of Rheginus (Can. VIII).

Celestius was a disciple of Pelagius, and held the same opinions with his master, and, therefore, the sect of Pelagians were also called Celestians. The common opinion of both was, that the sin of Adam only injured himself, and not the human race; and that infants when they are born are in the same state in which Adam was before he sinned. Some of the Bishops who joined with John of Antioch in his schism, were, as it appears, followers of Celestius, and, therefore, this Council, although originally assembled only against Nestorius, joined the Celestians with the Nestorians in their sentence of condemnation, noticing the Celestians by themselves in the first Canon, and in conjunction with the Nestorians in the fourth.—Hammond, p. 86.

The seventh Canon of this Council as well as the next are not found in the Synodal Epistle which contains the six former, but are decrees of the Council which were made respecting other matters which came before it. As regards the present Canon, it was occasioned by an application made to the Council by Charisius, who was a Presbyter, and Œconomus of the Church of Philadelphia. He informed the Fathers who were assembled in Council, by a writing which he exhibited to them, that a certain James who had come from Constantinople, and had been recommended as orthodox to the Bishops of Lydia by Anastasius and Photius, two Nestorian Presbyters, had, in despite of the Creed of the Nicene Council, composed another profession of faith, and had persuaded some of the more simple of the Clergy to subscribe to it, and had proceeded so far as to require of those persons who were converted from heresy to the Catholic Church, that they should, before they were admitted, subscribe this Creed, which had been introduced by him, and which was filled with heretical, *i. e.*, Nestorian opinions. The Fathers who were assembled in Council, having heard the charge of Charisius, and read the new Creed, immediately made the present decree, which afterwards came to be reckoned amongst the Canons of the Council. From this account appears what is meant by the words at the beginning of the Canon, "These things having been read," that is, the writing of Charisius, and the new Nestorian Creed, upon hearing which the Fathers made this decree. The full account of this transaction is to be found in the 6th Action of the 2d part of the Acts of this Council,

In the meantime, Theodosius, learning the dissensions which prevailed at Ephesus, ordered that both Cyril and Nestorius should be arrested, and that all the other Bishops of both parties should assemble in one Council. Both sides refused; Nestorius was sent back to his Monastery; Cyril was detained under arrest; and then, the Emperor himself having heard deputies from both sides, gave his judgment that Nestorius had been righteously deposed; that Cyril

in any of the collections of Councils. The Nestorian Creed which is referred to in it is very artfully composed, and calculated to deceive persons not thoroughly alive to the niceties of expression which render an exposition of the doctrine of the Incarnation orthodox or heretical. It begins with great apparent deference to the ancient faith, and gives rather an amplified form of the Catholic doctrine respecting the Trinity, thus preparing the way for a more lengthened statement of the doctrines respecting the Incarnation of The Word, in which the Nestorian hypothesis of two Persons is stealthily introduced, so that the heresy might escape discovery at first. Afterwards, however, it is stated more openly, by way of recapitulation, as follows: "We, therefore, say that there is one SON and LORD JESUS CHRIST, by whom all things were made: considering primarily GOD the Word, the SON of GOD and LORD according to substance; and further considering with him that which was assumed, JESUS of Nazareth, whom GOD anointed with the Spirit and Power, as partaking of the Sonship and dominion by the connection with GOD the Word, &c." In the Acts of the 5th and 6th General Councils this Creed is ascribed to Theodosius of Mopsuestia, and was recited amongst other extracts from his works which were read to the former of these Councils, and upon which the sentence of condemnation pronounced against him was founded.—Hammond, p. 87.

The Eighth Canon of Ephesus, as well as the Seventh, was in the first instance passed in the form of a decree, but afterwards numbered amongst the Canons. The occasion of it was this. Rheginus, Bishop of Constantia, the Metropolis of Cyprus, and Zeno, Bishop of Curium, and Euagrius, Bishop of Soli, in the same island, presented a memorial to the Council, in which they complained of the attempts which had been made by the Bishop of Antioch, to usurp authority over the Bishops of Cyprus, "contrary to the Apostolical Canons (Can. Apost. 35), and the decisions of the most holy Synod of Nice." They further stated, that Dionysius, the imperial governor of Antioch, had, at the suggestion of the Bishop of that city, written to the commander of the troops at Cyprus, as well as to the Clergy of Constantia, requiring the former to prevent the ordination of a Bishop of Constantia, in the room of Troilus, who had lately died, till the question as to the right of ordination had been settled by the Council at Ephesus: and cautioning the latter not to receive any person as their Bishop who should in the mean time be ordained by any one. The Bishops produced these letters before the Council, and prayed that the privileges which they had always enjoyed even from the times of the Apostles, might be preserved, and that the Council would pronounce a sentence in their favor which might prevent their being again invaded. The Council had the letters read before them; and having, by the examination of the Bishops, ascertained that there was no instance to be produced, from the times of the Apostles, of the Bishop of Antioch ordaining the Metropolitan of Constantia, or any other Bishop in Cyprus, and that Troilus, the late Metropolitan, and his predecessors, Sabinus and Epiphanius, had been ordained by the Bishops of their Province, they passed this decree in favor of the Province of Cyprus, and extended it to all similar cases which might occur in other Provinces and Dioceses. The authority, therefore, which the Bishops of Rome, in after-ages, claimed and usurped over the British and other Western Churches, is clearly contrary to this Canon, as well as to those of the Council of Nice. The account of this transaction is contained at length in the Acts of the Council, Part II., Act 7.—Hammond, pp. 88, 89.

should retain his See ; that all the other Bishops of both parties should return home to their several Churches ; that there was no heresy on the one side nor the other ; and that therefore all should strive on both sides for the restoration of a godly unity and peace.

The Council instantly broke up, and for a time it seemed as though a permanent schism had been inaugurated; for the orthodox stood firm in their adherence to the doctrine of the Council, while the dissidents continued to adhere to the opinions of Nestorius. Happily the separation was of short continuance. John of Antioch himself subscribed a document in which he recognized that the Blessed Virgin is Theotocos; and not long afterwards the other Eastern Bishops joined in the confession of the Catholic doctrine as declared at Ephesus, and so were reconciled to the great body of the Church. Thus unity was speedily restored ; the doctrine and Canons of the Council were accepted everywhere by all the Churches; and the Council of Ephesus has ever since been recognized as the Third General Council of the Catholic Church.

FOURTH GENERAL COUNCIL.

CHALCEDON.

After the condemnation of Nestorius in the General Council of Ephesus, Flavian, Archbishop of Constantinople, held a Council A. D. 448, at which Eusebius, Bishop of Dorylæum in Phrygia, presented a memorial against Eutyches, the Archimandrite or Abbot of a Monastery at Constantinople who had fallen into an error opposite to that of Nestorius by obstinately denying that there are two natures in the Person of CHRIST. The Council condemned the doctrine; but Eutyches, having gained the ear of Dioscorus, Bishop of Alexandria, Flavian himself was cited before a Council which was intended to be General, and which was summoned by imperial authority to meet at Ephesus, A. D. 449. This Council, over which Dioscorus presided, was so violent and merciless that it has borne the name of *Latrocinium Ephesinum*, or the Ephesian Band of Brigands. It approved the heresy of Eutyches.

Flavian was condemned, scourged, and so cruelly maltreated that he died soon afterwards at Epipas in Lydia, to which place he was banished.

Before his death, however, Flavian had appealed for help to Leo, Bishop of Rome. Leo espoused his cause, and endeavoured to induce Theodosius the Younger to convoke another Council which should meet in Italy, and might rehear the cause. The Emperor refused, and Leo was obliged to content himself with holding a Provincial Synod at Rome, wherein the Latrocinium of Ephesus was condemned. After the death of Theodosius, his successor Marcian granted the request of Leo, and called a General Council to meet at Nicæa, though, for the convenience of the Emperor it was speedily transferred to Chalcedon; and there the Bishops assembled to the number of 630 or 636 in the Church of S. Euphemia on the 8th day of October, A. D. 451.

The heresy of Eutyches was unhesitatingly condemned; Dioscorus was deposed, and thirty Canons were enacted. The Bishop of Rome was represented by the Bishops Paschasinus, Lucentius, and Julian, and by the Presbyter Boniface, who formally opposed the XXVIII. Canon which granted to the Church of Constantinople, under the title of New Rome, the same privileges as had been conceded to the Elder Rome, and conferred upon the same Church jurisdiction over Pontus, Asia, and Thrace, as well as over Missionary Churches which might lie beyond the limits of the Empire. Notwithstanding the objection of the representatives of Rome, the Canon was adopted by the Council and approved by the imperial authority.*

* The account of what took place at the passing of the Canon is given at length among the Acts of the Council, in the 16th Action: and as the matter is of some importance in its bearing upon the question of the Papal supremacy, an abridged account of it may not be uninteresting.

Upon the meeting of the Council (on the day when the discussion took place), Paschasinus and Lucentius, the Roman Legates, addressed themselves to the imperial Judges, and complained, that on the preceding day, after they, as well as the Judges, had left the meeting, certain things had been brought forward and decreed, contrary to the Canons of the Church, and they requested the Judges to institute an inquiry respecting them. Upon this, Aëtius, Archdeacon of the Church of Constantinople, said that it was the common practice in Synods, after settling the more important and necessary matters relating to the Faith, to make also such regulations in other matters as were necessary. That on this occasion the Church of Constantinople had had certain matters to transact, and that they had requested the Roman Bishops to take part in their proceedings, but that those Bishops had refused to do so, alleging that

The Definition of Faith set forth in this Council is a document of great importance, reaffirming, as it does without exception, the decrees and doctrines of the General Councils of Nicæa, Constantinople, and Ephesus, and setting forth, with

they had no authority for this purpose from the Bishop of Rome. That they had then referred the matters to the imperial Judges, who had desired them to proceed with their business, and they had accordingly done so fairly, openly, and canonically. The Judges desired the account of the proceedings to be read; and Beronicianus, Secretary of the Consistory, read this 28th Canon, with the subscriptions of all the Bishops who attended the Council annexed to it. Lucentius then asserted that the Bishops had been forced to subscribe against their inclinations; but all the Bishops cried out immediately that no one was forced. Lucentius then objected further, that this Canon was contrary to that of the Nicene Council, and founded only upon the decisions of the Constantinopolitan Fathers, which had been passed only eighty years before, and which were not reckoned amongst the Synodical Canons. Aëtius, the Archdeacon of Constantinople, then asked the Legates whether they had received any instructions relating to this matter from the Bishop of Rome; and the Presbyter Boniface, who was joined with Lucentius and Paschasinus in their mission, said that amongst other things they were charged by the Pope, not to suffer the decisions of the holy Fathers to be in any way infringed, but to maintain his dignity; and, "if any persons, presuming upon the splendor of their cities, should make any attempt at usurpation, to resist them with proper firmness." The Judges upon this desired both parties to read the Canons of Nice: and the Roman Legates then read the 6th Canon, beginning it with these words, "That the Church of Rome has always had the Primacy." Constantine, Secretary of the Consistory, then read the same Canon from a copy furnished by Aëtius, as it is read in the genuine Canons. He then proceeded to read from the Synodical book of the Council of Constantinople, the three first Canons of that Council. The Judges then asked the Bishops of the Asian and Pontic Dioceses, whether they had been in any way compelled to subscribe the Canon in question; and they all declared that they had signed it voluntarily, and without any compulsion. Upon this the Judges gave their decision to the following effect: "That the Primacy and the chief honor should by all means be preserved, according to the Canons, to the Archbishop of Old Rome, and that the Archbishop of the imperial city of Constantinople, New Rome, should enjoy the same privilege of honor. That he should also have power of his own authority to ordain the Metropolitans in the Asian, Pontic, and Thracian Dioceses, who should be elected by the Clergy, and proprietors and most illustrious persons of each Metropolis, and by all the Bishops of the Province, or the greater part of them; and that he should have the option of bringing the persons so elected to Constantinople, and ordaining them there, or of allowing them to obtain the decree confirming their election to the Bishopric in the Provinces. That, however, as regarded the Bishops of the different Provinces, they should be elected (or *ordained*, χειροτονεῖσθαι), by all the Bishops of the Province, or the greater part of them, the Metropolitan having the right of confirmation according to the Canon of the Fathers, the Archbishop of Constantinople taking no part in such ordinations." This, the Judges said, was their decision upon the subject, but they desired that the holy and Œcumenical Synod would deign to inform them what was their decision. Upon this all the Bishops cried out at once, that they approved and ratified this decision; but Lucentius entered his protest against all that had been done in his absence, which he said he would report to the Bishop of Rome, who was chief Bishop of the whole Church, that he might declare his sentiments respecting the wrong done to his own See, and the subversion of the Canons.

This was the termination of the Council; but Leo afterwards wrote various letters to the Emperors, to the Bishop of Constantinople, and others, in which, whilst he expressed his complete approval of the proceedings of the Council in matters of faith, he strongly condemned this Canon, which he declared was contrary to the Nicene

still more clearness than before, the Catholic doctrine of the Incarnation.

It was from the Council of Chalcedon that the Canons of the earlier Provincial Councils received the stamp of œcumenical approval.

Canons, and a most unjust usurpation on the part of the Bishop of Constantinople of the privileges of other Bishops, and particularly of those of the Bishops of Alexandria and Antioch, who were next in rank to the Bishop of Rome. He went so far, in one of his letters to the Empress Pulcheria, as to say that "by the authority of the Apostle Peter, he annulled all that was contrary to the Nicene Canons;" but it is worthy of remark how in all his letters, though he is disposed to magnify his own authority, the whole burden of his charge against the Bishop of Constantinople is, that the privileges which he claimed were contrary to the Nicene Canons, and an invasion of the independency and rights of other Churches.—Hammond, pp. 123-125.

THE CANONS CALLED APOSTOLICAL;

THE CANONS OF THE GENERAL COUNCILS;

THE CANONS OF PROVINCIAL COUNCILS,

WHICH WERE

APPROVED AT CHALCEDON.

IN GREEK AND ENGLISH.

THE APOSTOLICAL CANONS.

ΚΑΝΟΝΕΣ

ΤΩΝ

ΑΓΙΩΝ ΚΑΙ ΠΑΝΣΕΠΤΩΝ ΑΠΟΣΤΟΛΩΝ.

Codex Canonum Ecclesiae Primitivae,

QUI VULGO

Canones SS. Apostolorum

APPELLANTUR.

ΚΑΝΩΝ Α'.

Ἐπίσκοπος χειροτονείσθω ὑπὸ ἐπισκόπων δύο ἢ τριῶν.

ΚΑΝΩΝ Β'.

Πρεσβύτερος ὑπὸ ἑνὸς ἐπισκόπου χειροτονείσθω, καὶ διάκονος, καὶ οἱ λοιποὶ κληρικοί.

ΚΑΝΩΝ Γ'.

Εἴ τις ἐπίσκοπος, ἢ πρεσβύτερος, παρὰ τὴν τοῦ Κυρίου διάταξιν τὴν ἐπὶ τῇ θυσίᾳ, προσενέγκῃ ἕτερά τινα ἐπὶ τὸ θυσιαστήριον, ἢ μέλι, ἢ γάλα, ἢ ἀντὶ οἴνου σίκερα ἐπιτηδευτὰ, ἢ ὄρνεις, ἢ ζῶά τινα, ἢ ὄσπρια, παρὰ τὴν διάταξιν, καθαιρείσθω· πλὴν νέων χίδρων, ἢ σταφυλῆς τῷ καιρῷ τῷ δέοντι. Μὴ ἐξὸν δὲ ἔστω προσάγεσθαί τι ἕτερον εἰς τὸ θυσιαστήριον ἢ ἔλαιον εἰς τὴν λυχνίαν, καὶ θυμίαμα τῷ καιρῷ τῆς ἁγίας προσφορᾶς.

ΚΑΝΩΝ Δ'.

Ἡ ἄλλη πᾶσα ὀπώρα εἰς οἶκον ἀποστελλέσθω, ἀπαρχὴ τῷ ἐπισκόπῳ καὶ τοῖς πρεσβυτέροις, ἀλλὰ μὴ πρὸς τὸ θυσιαστήριον. Δῆλον δὲ, ὡς ὁ ἐπίσκοπος καὶ οἱ πρεσβύτεροι, ἐπιμερίζουσι τοῖς διακόνοις, καὶ τοῖς λοιποῖς κληρικοῖς.

CANONS

OF THE

PRIMITIVE CHURCH,

COMMONLY CALLED

THE APOSTOLICAL CANONS.

CANON I.

Let a Bishop be ordained by two or three Bishops.

CANON II.

Let a Presbyter, or Deacon, and the other Clergy, be ordained by one Bishop.

CANON III.

If, contrary to the Lord's ordinance of the Sacrifice, any Bishop or Presbyter shall offer any other things at the Altar, whether honey, or milk, or manufactured strong drink instead of wine; or birds, or any living creatures, or vegetables, contrary to the ordinance; let him be deposed: except only new ears of grain, and clusters of grapes in their season. But it shall not be lawful to offer any other thing at the Altar, save oil for the lamp, and incense for the time of the Holy Oblation.

CANON IV.

All other first fruits shall be sent to the house of the Bishop and Presbyters, not to the Altar; and it is understood that the Bishop and Presbyters share with the Deacons and other Clergy.

ΚΑΝΩΝ Ε'.

Ἐπίσκοπος, ἢ πρεσβύτερος, ἢ διάκονος, τὴν ἑαυτοῦ γυναῖκα μὴ ἐκβαλλέτω προφάσει εὐλαβείας· ἐὰν δὲ ἐκβάλλῃ, ἀφοριζέσθω· ἐπιμένων δὲ, καθαιρείσθω.

ΚΑΝΩΝ ϛ'.

Ἐπίσκοπος, ἢ πρεσβύτερος, ἢ διάκονος, κοσμικὰς φροντίδας μὴ ἀναλαμβανέτω· εἰ δὲ μὴ, καθαιρείσθω.

ΚΑΝΩΝ Ζ'.

Εἴ τις ἐπίσκοπος, ἢ πρεσβύτερος, ἢ διάκονος, τὴν ἁγίαν τοῦ Πάσχα ἡμέραν πρὸ τῆς ἐαρινῆς ἰσημερίας μετὰ Ἰουδαίων ἐπιτελέσει, καθαιρείσθω.

ΚΑΝΩΝ Η'.

Εἴ τις ἐπίσκοπος, ἢ πρεσβύτερος, ἢ διάκονος, ἢ ἐκ τοῦ καταλόγου τοῦ ἱερατικοῦ προσφορᾶς γενομένης μὴ μεταλάβοι, τὴν αἰτίαν εἰπάτω, καὶ ἐὰν ᾖ εὔλογος, συγγνώμης τυγχανέτω· εἰ δὲ μὴ λέγοι, ἀφοριζέσθω, ὡς αἴτιος βλάβης γενόμενος τῷ λαῷ, καὶ ὑπόνοιαν ἐμποιήσας κατὰ τοῦ προσενέγκαντος, ὡς μὴ ὑγιῶς, ἀνενέγκαντος.

ΚΑΝΩΝ Θ'.

Πάντας τοὺς εἰσίοντας πιστοὺς καὶ τῶν γραφῶν ἀκούοντας, μὴ παραμένοντας δὲ τῇ προσευχῇ καὶ τῇ ἁγίᾳ μεταλήψει, ὡς ἀταξίαν ἐμποιοῦντας τῇ ἐκκλησίᾳ ἀφορίζεσθαι χρή.

ΚΑΝΩΝ Ι'.

Εἴ τις ἀκοινωνήτῳ κἂν ἐν οἴκῳ συνεύξηται, οὗτος ἀφοριζέσθω.

ΚΑΝΩΝ ΙΑ'.

Εἴ τις καθῃρημένῳ κληρικὸς ὢν κληρικῷ συνεύξηται, καθαιρείσθω καὶ αὐτός.

ΚΑΝΩΝ ΙΒ'.

Εἴ τις κληρικὸς ἢ λαϊκὸς ἀφωρισμένος, ἤτοι ἄδεκτος, ἀπελθὼν ἐν ἑτέρᾳ πόλει δεχθῇ ἄνευ γραμμάτων συστατικῶν, ἀφοριζέσθω καὶ ὁ δεξάμενος, καὶ ὁ δεχθείς.

CANON V.

No Bishop, Presbyter or Deacon shall put away his wife, under pretext of religion; but if he put her away, let him be suspended; and, if he persist, let him be deposed.

CANON VI.

No Bishop, Presbyter, or Deacon, shall engage in worldly business; and, if he do, let him be deposed.

CANON VII.

If any Bishop, Presbyter, or Deacon, shall celebrate the holy day of Easter before the vernal Equinox, as the Jews do, let him be deposed.

CANON VIII.

If any Bishop, Presbyter, or Deacon, or any one on the Sacerdotal List, shall not partake, when the Oblation is made, he shall tell the cause; and, if it be sufficient, he shall be excused: but, if he will not tell the cause, let him be suspended, as one who causes offence to the people, and brings suspicion on the offerer, as though he had not rightly offered.

CANON IX.

All the faithful who enter [the Church], and hear the Scriptures, but do not remain for prayer and the Holy Communion, shall be suspended, because they cause confusion in the Church.

CANON X.

If any one shall join in prayer with an excommunicated person, even in a private house, let him be suspended.

CANON XI.

If any Clergyman shall join in prayer with a deposed Clergyman, let him also be deposed.

CANON XII.

If any Clergyman or layman who has been suspended, or ought not to be received, shall depart and be received in another City, without letters commendatory, let both the receiver and the person received be suspended.

ΚΑΝΩΝ ΙΓ'.

Εἰ δὲ ἀφωρισμένος εἴη, ἐπιτεινέσθω αὐτῷ ὁ ἀφορισμός.

ΚΑΝΩΝ ΙΔ'.

Ἐπίσκοπον μὴ ἐξεῖναι καταλείψαντα τὴν ἑαυτοῦ παροικίαν ἑτέρᾳ ἐπιπηδᾶν, κἂν ὑπὸ πλειόνων ἀναγκάζηται· εἰ μή τις εὔλογος αἰτία ᾖ τοῦτο βιαζομένη αὐτὸν ποιεῖν, ὡς πλέον τι κέρδος δυναμένου αὐτοῦ τοῖς ἐκεῖσε λόγῳ εὐσεβείας συμβάλλεσθαι· καὶ τοῦτο δὲ οὐκ ἀφ' ἑαυτοῦ, ἀλλὰ κρίσει πολλῶν ἐπισκόπων, καὶ παρακλήσει μεγίστῃ.

ΚΑΝΩΝ ΙΕ'.

Εἴ τις πρεσβύτερος, ἢ διάκονος, ἢ ὅλως τοῦ καταλόγου τῶν κληρικῶν ἀπολείψας τὴν ἑαυτοῦ παροικίαν, εἰς ἑτέραν ἀπέλθῃ, καὶ παντελῶς μεταστὰς διατρίβῃ ἐν ἄλλῃ παροικίᾳ παρὰ γνώμην τοῦ ἰδίου ἐπισκόπου· τοῦτον κελεύομεν μηκέτι λειτουργεῖν· εἰ μάλιστα προσκαλουμένου αὐτὸν τοῦ ἐπισκόπου αὐτοῦ ἐπανελθεῖν, οὐχ ὑπήκουσεν, ἐπιμένων τῇ ἀταξίᾳ· ὡς λαϊκὸς μέντοι ἐκεῖσε κοινωνείτω.

ΚΑΝΩΝ Ιϛ'.

Εἰ δὲ ὁ ἐπίσκοπος παρ' ᾧ τυγχάνουσι, παρ' οὐδὲν λογισάμενος τὴν κατ' αὐτῶν ὁρισθεῖσαν ἀργίαν, δέξηται αὐτοὺς ὡς κληρικούς, ἀφοριζέσθω, ὡς διδάσκαλος ἀταξίας.

ΚΑΝΩΝ ΙΖ'.

Ὁ δυσὶ γάμοις συμπλακεὶς μετὰ τὸ βάπτισμα, ἢ παλλακὴν κτησάμενος, οὐ δύναται εἶναι ἐπίσκοπος, ἢ πρεσβύτερος, ἢ διάκονος, ἢ ὅλως τοῦ καταλόγου τοῦ ἱερατικοῦ.

ΚΑΝΩΝ ΙΗ'.

Ὁ χήραν λαβών, ἢ ἐκβεβλημένην, ἢ ἑταῖραν, ἢ οἰκέτιν, ἢ τῶν ἐπὶ σκηνῆς, οὐ δύναται εἶναι ἐπίσκοπος, ἢ πρεσβύτερος, ἢ διάκονος, ἢ ὅλως τοῦ καταλόγου τοῦ ἱερατικοῦ.

CANON XIII.

But if he be already suspended, let his suspension be prolonged.

CANON XIV.

It is unlawful for a Bishop to leave his own Parish, and cross over to another, though he may be importuned by many [so to do]; unless there be some reasonable cause compelling him to do it; as, for example, if he can by the word of piety confer some greater benefit on them that dwell there: and then it should be done not of his own motion, but by the judgment and at the most urgent entreaty of many Bishops.

CANON XV.

If any Presbyter, or Deacon, or any one whatever on the list of the Clergy, shall forsake his own Parish, and depart with another, and, having wholly changed his residence, shall remain in another Parish contrary to the will of his own Bishop, and particularly if he be summoned by his Bishop to return, and shall persist in his irregularity, refusing to obey, we decree that he shall no more be permitted to officiate. Nevertheless, let him communicate there among the laity.

CANON XVI.

And if the Bishop with whom [such Clergy] are, shall disregard the decree of suspension against them, and shall receive them as Clergymen, let him be suspended, as a teacher of disorder.

CANON XVII.

He who, after Baptism, has been twice married, or has had a concubine, cannot be a Bishop, Presbyter, or Deacon, nor be on the Sacerdotal List at all.

CANON XVIII.

He who has married a widow, or a divorced woman, or a harlot, or a slave, or an actress, cannot be a Bishop, Presbyter, or Deacon, nor be on the Sacerdotal List at all.

ΚΑΝΩΝ ΙΘ'.

Ὁ δύο ἀδελφὰς ἀγαγόμενος, ἢ ἀδελφιδὴν, οὐ δύναται εἶναι κληρικὸς.

ΚΑΝΩΝ Κ'.

Κληρικὸς ἐγγύας διδοὺς, καθαιρείσθω.

ΚΑΝΩΝ ΚΑ'.

Εὐνοῦχος εἰ μὲν ἐξ ἐπηρείας ἀνθρώπων ἐγένετό τις, ἢ ἐν διωγμῷ ἀφῃρέθη τὰ τῶν ἀνδρῶν, ἢ οὕτως ἔφυ, καί ἐστιν ἄξιος, ἐπίσκοπος γινέσθω.

ΚΑΝΩΝ ΚΒ'.

Ὁ ἀκρωτηριάσας ἑαυτὸν, μὴ γινέσθω κληρικὸς· αὐτοφονευτὴς γάρ ἐστιν ἑαυτοῦ, καὶ τῆς τοῦ Θεοῦ δημιουργίας ἐχθρός.

ΚΑΝΩΝ ΚΓ'.

Εἴ τις, κληρικὸς ὢν, ἑαυτὸν ἂν ἀκρωτηριάσει, καθαιρείσθω· φονεὺς γάρ ἐστιν ἑαυτοῦ.

ΚΑΝΩΝ ΚΔ'.

Λαϊκὸς ἑαυτὸν ἀκρωτηριάσας ἀφοριζέσθω ἔτη τρία· ἐπίβουλος γάρ ἐστι τῆς ἑαυτοῦ ζωῆς.

ΚΑΝΩΝ ΚΕ'.

Ἐπίσκοπος, ἢ πρεσβύτερος, ἢ διάκονος ἐπὶ πορνείᾳ, ἢ ἐπὶορκίᾳ, ἢ ἐπὶ κλοπῇ ἁλοὺς, καθαιρείσθω, καὶ μὴ ἀφοριζέσθω. Λέγει γὰρ ἡ γραφὴ, Οὐκ ἐκδικήσεις δὶς ἐπὶ τὸ αὐτό. Ὡσαύτως καὶ οἱ λοιποὶ κληρικοί.

ΚΑΝΩΝ Κϛ'.

Τῶν εἰς κλῆρον προσελθόντων ἀγάμων, κελεύομεν βουλομένους γαμεῖν ἀναγνώστας καὶ ψάλτας μόνους.

CANON XIX.

He who has married two sisters, or a niece, cannot be a Clergyman.

CANON XX.

If a Clergyman become security for any one, let him be deposed.

CANON XXI.

If any one has been made a eunuch by the wanton injury of men, or if he has been deprived of his virile organs in time of persecution, or if he has been born a eunuch, and is worthy, he may be made a Bishop.

CANON XXII.

If any one shall mutilate himself [that is by castration], let him not be made a Clergyman, for he is a self-murderer and a hater of God's workmanship.

CANON XXIII.

If any Clergyman shall mutilate himself [that is by castration], let him be deposed, for he is a self-murderer.

CANON XXIV.

If any layman shall mutilate himself [that is by castration], let him be suspended for three years, for he is an enemy of his own life.

CANON XXV.

Let a Bishop, Presbyter, or Deacon, convicted of fornication, perjury, or theft, be deposed, but not excommunicated. For the Scripture saith [Nahum I. 9, LXX Version], Thou shalt not punish twice for one offence. Likewise the other Clergy.

CANON XXVI.

Of those who have been advanced to the Clergy, while unmarried, we ordain that none but Readers and Singers shall be permitted to marry, if they so will.

ΚΑΝΩΝ ΚΖ'.

Ἐπίσκοπον, ἢ πρεσβύτερον, ἢ διάκονον, τύπτοντα πιστοὺς ἁμαρτάνοντας, ἢ ἀπίστους ἀδικήσαντας, καὶ διὰ τοιούτων φοβεῖσθαι θέλοντα, καθαιρεῖσθαι προστάττομεν· οὐδαμοῦ γὰρ ὁ Κύριος τοῦτο ἡμᾶς ἐδίδαξε· τοὐναντίον δὲ, αὐτὸς τυπτόμενος, οὐκ ἀντέτυπτε· λοιδορούμενος οὐκ ἀντελοιδόρει· πάσχων οὐκ ἠπείλει.

ΚΑΝΩΝ ΚΗ'.

Εἴ τις ἐπίσκοπος, ἢ πρεσβύτερος, ἢ διάκονος, καθαιρεθεὶς δικαίως ἐπὶ ἐγκλήμασι φανεροῖς, τολμήσειεν ἅψασθαι τῆς ποτὲ ἐγχειρισθείσης αὐτῷ λειτουργίας, παντάπασιν ἐκκοπτέσθω τῆς ἐκκλησίας.

ΚΑΝΩΝ ΚΘ'.

Εἴ τις ἐπίσκοπος διὰ χρημάτων τῆς ἀξίας ταύτης ἐγκρατὴς γένηται, ἢ πρεσβύτερος, ἢ διάκονος, καθαιρείσθω καὶ αὐτὸς καὶ ὁ χειροτονήσας· καὶ ἐκκοπτέσθω καὶ τῆς κοινωνίας παντάπασιν· ὡς Σίμων ὁ Μάγος ὑπ' ἐμοῦ Πέτρου.

ΚΑΝΩΝ Λ'.

Εἴ τις ἐπίσκοπος κοσμικοῖς ἄρχουσι χρησάμενος, δι' αὐτῶν ἐγκρατὴς ἐκκλησίας γένηται, καθαιρείσθω καὶ ἀφοριζέσθω, καὶ οἱ κοινωνοῦντες αὐτῷ ἅπαντες.

ΚΑΝΩΝ ΛΑ'.

Εἴ τις πρεσβύτερος, καταφρονήσας τοῦ ἰδίου ἐπισκόπου, χωρὶς συναγάγῃ, καὶ θυσιαστήριον ἕτερον πήξῃ, μηδὲν κατεγνωκὼς τοῦ ἐπισκόπου ἐν εὐσεβείᾳ καὶ δικαιοσύνῃ, καθαιρείσθω ὡς φίλαρχος· τύραννος γάρ ἐστιν. Ὡσαύτος δὲ καὶ οἱ λοιποὶ κληρικοὶ, καὶ ὅσοι ἂν αὐτῷ προσθῶνται. Οἱ δὲ λαϊκοὶ ἀφοριζέσθωσαν. Ταῦτα δὲ μετὰ μίαν, καὶ δευτέραν, καὶ τρίτην παράκλησιν τοῦ ἐπισκόπου γινέσθω.

ΚΑΝΩΝ ΛΒ'.

Εἴ τις πρεσβύτερος ἢ διάκονος ὑπὸ ἐπισκόπου γένηται ἀφωρισμένος, τοῦτον μὴ ἐξεῖναι παρ' ἑτέρου δεχθῆναι, ἀλλ' ἢ παρὰ

CANON XXVII.

If a Bishop, Presbyter, or Deacon shall strike any of the faithful who sin, or any unbelievers who have acted wrongfully, desiring by this means to terrify them, we ordain that he be deposed. For the Lord hath not so taught us, but contrarywise; for when He was smitten, He did not smite again; when He was reviled, He reviled not again; and when He suffered, He threatened not.

CANON XXVIII.

If any Bishop, Presbyter, or Deacon, righteously deposed after public accusations, shall presume to touch the ministry formerly committed to him, let him be wholly cut off from the Church.

CANON XXIX.

If any Bishop, Presbyter, or Deacon, shall have obtained his office for money, let both him and his ordainer be deposed, and let him be wholly cut off, as was Simon Magus by me Peter.

CANON XXX.

If any Bishop shall have obtained his Church through secular rulers, let him, and all who communicate with him, be deposed and excommunicated.

CANON XXXI.

If any Presbyter, despising his own Bishop, shall gather a separate congregation, and raise another Altar, his Bishop having been convicted of nothing contrary to religion or morals, let him be deposed as an ambitious person; for he is an usurper. Likewise of the other Clergy and as many as adhere to him; and let the laity be suspended. But let these things be done after a first, second, and third admonition from the Bishop.

CANON XXXII.

If any Presbyter or Deacon shall be suspended by his Bishop, it shall not be lawful for him to be restored by any

τοῦ ἀφορίσαντος αὐτὸν, εἰ μὴ ἂν κατὰ συγκυρίαν τελευτήσῃ ὁ ἀφορίσας αὐτὸν ἐπίσκοπος.

ΚΑΝΩΝ ΛΓ′.

Μηδένα τῶν ξένων ἐπισκόπων, ἢ πρεσβυτέρων, ἢ διακόνων ἄνευ συστατικῶν προσδέχεσθαι· καὶ ἐπιφερομένων αὐτῶν, ἀνακρινέσθωσαν· καὶ ἐὰν μὲν ὦσιν κήρυκες τῆς εὐσεβείας, προσδεχέσθωσαν. Εἰ δὲ μή γε, τὰ πρὸς χρείαν αὐτοῖς ἐπιχορηγήσαντες, εἰς κοινωνίαν αὐτοὺς μὴ προσδέξησθε. Πολλὰ γὰρ κατὰ συναρπαγὴν γίνεται.

ΚΑΝΩΝ ΛΔ′.

Τοὺς ἐπισκόπους ἑκάστου ἔθνους εἰδέναι χρὴ τὸν ἐν αὐτοῖς πρῶτον, καὶ ἡγείσθαι αὐτὸν ὡς κεφαλὴν καὶ μηδέν τι πράττειν περιττὸν ἄνευ τῆς ἐκείνου γνώμης· ἐκεῖνα δὲ μόνα πράττειν ἕκαστον ὅσα τῇ αὐτοῦ παροικίᾳ ἐπιβάλλει, καὶ ταῖς ὑπ' αὐτὴν χώραις. 'Αλλὰ μηδὲ ἐκεῖνος ἄνευ τῆς πάντων γνώμης ποιείτω τι· οὕτω γὰρ ὁμόνοια ἔσται, καὶ δοξασθήσηται ὁ Θεὸς διὰ Κυρίου 'Ιησοῦ Χριστοῦ, καὶ ὁ Πατὴρ διὰ Κυρίου ἐν 'Αγίῳ Πνεύματι. 'Ο Πατὴρ, καὶ ὁ Υἱὸς, καὶ τὸ Πνεῦμα τὸ Ἅγιον.

ΚΑΝΩΝ ΛΕ′.

'Επίσκοπον μὴ τολμᾶν ἔξω τῶν αὐτοῦ ὅρων χειροτονίας ποιεῖσθαι, εἰς τὰς μὴ ὑποκειμένας αὐτῷ πόλεις, ἢ χώρας· εἰ δὲ ἐλεγχθείη τοῦτο πεποιηκὼς παρὰ τὴν τῶν κατεχόντων τὰς πόλεις ἐκείνας ἢ χώρας γνώμην, καθαιρείσθω καὶ αὐτὸς καὶ οὓς ἐχειροτόνησεν.

ΚΑΝΩΝ Λϛ′.

Εἴ τις χειροτονηθεὶς ἐπίσκοπος μὴ καταδέχοιτο τὴν λειτουργίαν καὶ τὴν φροντίδα τοῦ λαοῦ τὴν ἐγχειρισθεῖσαν αὐτῷ, τοῦτον ἀφωρισμένον τυγχάνειν, ἕως ἂν καταδέξηται· ὡσαύτω, καὶ πρεσβύτερος καὶ διάκονος. Εἰ δὲ ἀπελθὼν μὴ δεχθῇ, οὐ παρὰ τὴν ἑαυτοῦ γνώμην, ἀλλὰ παρὰ τὴν τοῦ λαοῦ μοχθηρίαν, αὐτὸς μενέτω ἐπίσκοπος, ὁ δὲ κλῆρος τῆς πόλεως ἀφοριζέσθω, ὅτι τοιούτου λαοῦ ἀνυποτάκτου παιδευταὶ οὐκ ἐγένοντο.

other than the Bishop who suspended him, unless, indeed, the Bishop who suspended him should die.

CANON XXXIII.

Let no Bishop, Presbyter, or Deacon, be received from abroad without commendatory letters; and even when they bring these, let them be examined, and if they be teachers of godliness, let them be received; but, if otherwise, let them be supplied with what is necessary, but not admitted to communion; for many things are done surreptitiously.

CANON XXXIV.

It is necessary that the Bishops of every nation should know who is chief among them, and should recognize him as their head by doing nothing of great moment without his consent; and that each of them should do such things only as pertain to his own Parish and the districts under him. And neither let him [who is chief] do anything without the consent of all, for thus shall there be unity of heart, and thus shall God be glorified through our Lord Jesus Christ; even the Father through the Lord in the Holy Ghost: [that is] the Father and the Son and the Holy Ghost.

CANON XXXV.

Let no Bishop presume to hold ordinations beyond his own boundaries in Cities or districts not within his jurisdiction; and if he should be convicted of having done this without the consent of the Bishop having jurisdiction in such Cities or districts, both he and those whom he has ordained shall be deposed.

CANON XXXVI.

If any one who has been ordained Bishop will not enter upon the ministry and charge over the people committed to him, let him be suspended until he shall enter thereupon. Likewise also a Presbyter or Deacon. But, if he shall have gone [to his cure] and shall not have been received, not through his own will, but through the perversity of the people, let him remain Bishop; but let the Clergy of the City be suspended, because they have not corrected such an insolent people.

ΚΑΝΩΝ ΛΖ'.

Δεύτερον τοῦ ἔτους σύνοδος γινέσθω τῶν ἐπισκόπων, καὶ ἀνακρινέτωσαν ἀλλήλως τὰ δόγματα τῆς εὐσεβείας, καὶ τὰς ἐμπιπτούσας ἐκκλησιαστικὰς ἀντιλογίας διαλυέτωσαν· ἅπαξ μὲν, τῇ τεττάρτῃ ἑβδομάδι τῆς Πεντηκοστῆς, δεύτερον δὲ Ὑπερβερεταίου δωδεκάτῃ.

ΚΑΝΩΝ ΛΗ'.

Πάντων τῶν ἐκκλησιαστικῶν πραγμάτων ὁ ἐπίσκοπος ἐχέτω τὴν φροντίδα, καὶ διοικείτω αὐτὰ ὡς τοῦ Θεοῦ ἐφορῶντος· μὴ ἐξεῖναι δὲ αὐτῷ σφετερίζεσθαί τι ἐξ αὐτῶν, ἢ συγγενέσιν ἰδίοις τὰ τοῦ Θεοῦ χαρίζεσθαι· εἰ δὲ πένητες εἶεν, ἐπιχορηγείτω ὡς πένησιν, ἀλλὰ μὴ προφάσει τούτων τὰ τῆς ἐκκλησίας ἀπεμπωλείτω.

ΚΑΝΩΝ ΛΘ'.

Οἱ πρεσβύτεροι καὶ διάκονοι ἄνευ γνώμης τοῦ ἐπισκόπου μηδὲν ἐπιτελείτωσαν· αὐτὸς γάρ ἐστιν ὁ πεπιστευμένος τὸν λαὸν τοῦ Κυρίου, καὶ τὸν ὑπὲρ τῶν ψυχῶν αὐτῶν λόγον ἀπαιτηθησόμενος.

ΚΑΝΩΝ Μ'.

Ἔστω φανερὰ τὰ ἴδια τοῦ ἐπισκόπου πράγματα (εἰ δὲ ἴδια ἔχει) καὶ φανερὰ τὰ κυριακά· ἵν' ἐξουσίαν ἔχῃ τὰ ἴδια τελευτῶν ὁ ἐπίσκοπος, οἷς βούλεται, καὶ ὡς βούλεται, καταλεῖψαι, καὶ μὴ προφάσει τῶν ἐκκλησιαστικῶν πραγμάτων διαπίπτειν τὰ τοῦ ἐπισκόπου, ἔσθ' ὅτε γυναῖκα καὶ παῖδας κεκτημένου, ἢ συγγενεῖς ἢ οἰκέτας. Δίκαιον γὰρ παρὰ Θεῷ καὶ ἀνθρώποις, τὸ μήτε τὴν ἐκκλησίαν ζημίαν τινὰ ὑπομένειν ἀγνοίᾳ τῶν τοῦ ἐπισκόπου πραγμάτων, μήτε τὸν ἐπίσκοπον ἢ τοὺς αὐτοῦ συγγενεῖς προφάσει τῆς ἐκκλησίας δημεύεσθαι, ἢ καὶ εἰς πράγματα ἐμπίπτειν τοὺς αὐτῷ διαφέροντας, καὶ τὸν αὐτοῦ θάνατον δυσφημίας περιβάλλεσθαι.

ΚΑΝΩΝ ΜΑ'.

Προστάσσομεν τὸν ἐπίσκοπον ἐξουσίαν ἔχειν τῶν τῆς ἐκκλησίας πραγμάτων· εἰ γὰρ τὰς τιμίας τῶν ἀνθρώπων ψυχὰς αὐτῷ πιστευτέον πολλῷ ἂν δέοι περὶ τῶν χρημάτων ἐντέλλεσθαι,

CANON XXXVII.

Twice in the year let a Synod of the Bishops be held; and let them mutually examine each other concerning the doctrines of religion; and let them settle the ecclesiastical disputes that have arisen. And let the first be held in the fourth week of the Pentecost, [*i. e.*, of the *fifty days* next after Easter], and the second on the twelfth day of October.

CANON XXXVIII.

Let the Bishop have charge of all ecclesiastical goods, and manage them as in the sight of God; but it is unlawful for him to alienate anything, or to bestow on his own relatives the things which are God's. If they are poor, let him relieve them, like [the rest of] the poor; but let him not on their account sell what belongs to the Church.

CANON XXXIX.

Let the Presbyters and Deacons do nothing without consent of their Bishop; for it is he who is entrusted with the people of God, and who shall render an account of their souls.

CANON XL.

Let the private goods of the Bishop, if any he has, be kept distinct from those of the Lord, so that the Bishop may be able when he dies to leave his own [estate] to whom he will, and as he will; and so that the Bishop's property may not be lost through an appearance of its being [part] of the Church funds, when the Bishop, perhaps, has a wife, or children, or other relatives, or slaves. For it is right towards God and man, that neither the Church should suffer loss through ignorance of the Bishop's affairs, nor the Bishop or his relatives be injured for the sake of the Church, nor those who belong to him be involved in lawsuits and cast reproaches on his death.

CANON XLI.

We ordain that the Bishop shall have authority over the funds of the Church. For, if men's precious souls may be committed to him, much more ought he to be entrusted with

ὥστε κατὰ τὴν ἑαυτοῦ ἐξουσίαν πάντα διοικεῖσθαι, καὶ τοῖς δεομένοις διὰ πρεσβυτέρων καὶ διακόνων ἐπιχορηγεῖσθαι μετὰ φόβου Θεοῦ καὶ πάσης εὐλαβείας· μεταλαμβάνειν δὲ καὶ αὐτὸν τῶν δεόντων (εἴ γε δέοιτο) εἰς τὰς ἀναγκαίας αὐτοῦ χρείας καὶ τῶν ἐπιξενουμένων ἀδελφῶν, ὡς κατὰ μηδένα τρόπον αὐτὸν ὑστερεῖσθαι. Ὁ γὰρ νόμος τοῦ Θεοῦ διετάξατο, τοὺς τῷ θυσιαστηρίῳ προσεδρεύοντας, ἐκ τοῦ θυσιαστηρίου τρέφεσθαι· ἐπείπερ οὐδὲ στρατιώτης ποτὲ ἰδίοις ὀψωνίοις ὅπλα κατὰ πολεμίων ἐπιφέρεται.

ΚΑΝΩΝ ΜΒ′.

Ἐπίσκοπος, ἢ πρεσβύτερος, ἢ διάκονος, κύβοις σχολάζων, καὶ μέθαις, ἢ παυσάσθω, ἢ καθαιρείσθω.

ΚΑΝΩΝ ΜΓ′.

Ὑποδιάκονος, ἢ ἀναγνώστης, ἢ ψάλτης, τὰ ὅμοια ποιῶν, ἢ παυσάσθω, ἢ ἀφοριζέσθω· ὡσαύτως καὶ λαϊκοί.

ΚΑΝΩΝ ΜΔ′.

Ἐπίσκοπος, ἢ πρεσβύτερος, ἢ διάκονος, τόκους ἀπαιτῶν τοὺς δανιζομένους, ἢ παυσάσθω, ἢ καθαιρείσθω.

ΚΑΝΩΝ ΜΕ′.

Ἐπίσκοπος, ἢ πρεσβύτερος, ἢ διάκονος, αἱρετικοῖς συνευξάμενος μόνον, ἀφοριζέσθω· εἰ δὲ καὶ ἐπέτρεψεν αὐτοῖς ὡς κληρικοῖς ἐνεργῆσαί τι, καθαιρείσθω.

ΚΑΝΩΝ Μϛ′.

Ἐπίσκοπον, ἢ πρεσβύτερον, αἱρετικῶν δεξαμένους βάπτισμα, ἢ θυσίαν, καθαιρεῖσθαι προστάσσομεν. Τίς γὰρ συμφώνησις Χριστῷ πρὸς Βελίαρ; ἢ τίς μερὶς πιστῷ μετὰ ἀπίστου;

ΚΑΝΩΝ ΜΖ′.

Ἐπίσκοπος, ἢ πρεσβύτερος, τὸν κατ' ἀλήθειαν ἔχοντα βάπτισμα, ἐὰν ἄνωθεν βαπτίσῃ, ἢ τὸν μεμολυσμένον παρὰ τῶν ἀσεβῶν ἐὰν μὴ βαπτίσῃ, καθειρείσθω, ὡς γελῶν τὸν σταυρὸν τοῦ Κυρίου, καὶ τὸν θάνατον, καὶ μὴ διακρίνων ἱερέας ψευδιερέων.

money; so that he may manage all things according to his privilege; and, in the fear of God, and with all piety may supply the needy through the Presbyters and Deacons; and take what he requires for his own necessary use and that of brethren sojourning with him, so that he may no way fall short. For the law of God hath ordained that they who serve the Altar shall be nourished of the Altar, and not even a soldier goeth a warfare at his own cost.

CANON XLII.

A Bishop, Presbyter, or Deacon, given to dice or drunkenness, shall either desist or be deposed.

CANON XLIII.

A Subdeacon, or Reader, or Singer, doing the same thing, shall either desist or be suspended. Likewise the laity.

CANON XLIV.

A Bishop, Presbyter, or Deacon, exacting usury from debtors, shall either desist or be deposed.

CANON XLV.

Let a Bishop, Presbyter, or Deacon, who joins merely in prayers with heretics, be suspended; and if he commit anything to be done by them as Clergymen, let him be deposed.

CANON XLVI.

We ordain that any Bishop or Presbyter who shall admit the Baptism or the Sacrifice of heretics shall be deposed; for what communion hath Christ with Belial? or what part hath the faithful man with an unbeliever?

CANON XLVII.

If a Bishop or Presbyter shall rebaptize one who has true Baptism, or will not baptize one who has been polluted by the impious, let him be deposed, as one who mocks the Cross and death of Christ, and who makes no distinction between true Priests and false.

ΚΑΝΩΝ ΜΗ'.

Εἴ τις λαϊκὸς τὴν ἑαυτοῦ γυναῖκα ἐκβαλὼν, ἢ ἑτέραν λάβοι, ἢ παρ' ἄλλου ἀπολελυμένην, ἀφοριζέσθω.

ΚΑΝΩΝ ΜΘ'.

Εἴ τις ἐπίσκοπος ἢ πρεσβύτερος, κατὰ τὴν τοῦ Κυρίου διάταξιν μὴ βαπτίσῃ εἰς Πατέρα, καὶ Υἱὸν, καὶ Ἅγιον Πνεῦμα, ἀλλ' εἰς τρεῖς ἀνάρχους, ἢ τρεῖς Υἱοὺς, ἢ τρεῖς Παρακλήτους, καθαιρείσθω.

ΚΑΝΩΝ Ν'.

Εἴ τις ἐπίσκοπος ἢ πρεσβύτερος μὴ τρία βαπτίσματα μιᾶς μυήσεως ἐπιτελέσῃ, ἀλλὰ ἓν βάπτισμα εἰς τὸν θάνατον τοῦ Κυρίου διδόμενον, καθαιρείσθω· οὐ γὰρ εἶπεν ὁ Κύριος. Εἰς τὸν θάνατόν μου βαπτίσατε· ἀλλὰ, Πορευθέντες μαθητεύσατε πάντα τὰ ἔθνη, βαπτίζοντες αὐτοὺς εἰς τὸ ὄνομα τοῦ Πατρὸς, καὶ τοῦ Υἱοῦ, καὶ τοῦ Ἁγίου Πνεύματος.

ΚΑΝΩΝ ΝΑ'.

Εἴ τις ἐπίσκοπος, ἢ πρεσβύτερος, ἢ διάκονος, ἢ ὅλως τοῦ καταλόγου τοῦ ἱερατικοῦ, γάμου, καὶ κρεῶν καὶ οἴνου, οὐ δι' ἄσκησιν ἀλλὰ διὰ βδελυρίαν ἀπέχεται, ἐπιλαθόμενος, ὅτι πάντα καλὰ λίαν, καὶ ὅτι ἄρσεν καὶ θῆλυ ἐποίησεν ὁ Θεὸς τὸν ἄνθρωπον, ἀλλὰ βλασφημῶν διαβάλλει τὴν δημιουργίαν, ἢ διορθούσθω, ἢ καθαιρείσθω, καὶ τῆς ἐκκλησίας ἀποβαλλέσθω· ὡσαύτως καὶ λαϊκός.

ΚΑΝΩΝ ΝΒ'.

Εἴ τις ἐπίσκοπος, ἢ πρεσβύτερος, τὸν ἀποστρέφοντα ἀπὸ ἁμαρτίας οὐ προσδέχεται, ἀλλ' ἀποβάλλεται, καθαιρείσθω· ὅτι λυπεῖ τὸν Χριστὸν, τὸν εἰπόντα, Χαρὰ γίνεται ἐν οὐρανῷ ἐπὶ ἑνὶ ἁμαρτωλῷ μετανοοῦντι.

ΚΑΝΩΝ ΝΓ'.

Εἴ τις ἐπίσκοπος, ἢ πρεσβύτερος, ἢ διάκονος, ἐν ταῖς ἡμέραις τῶν ἑορτῶν οὐ μεταλαμβάνει κρεῶν καὶ οἴνου, βδελυσσόμενος, καὶ οὐ δι' ἄσκησιν, καθαιρείσθω, ὡς κεκαυτηριασμένος τὴν οἰκείαν συνείδησιν, καὶ αἴτιος σκανδάλου πολλοῖς γινόμενος.

CANON XLVIII.

If any layman put away his wife and take another, or if he marry a woman divorced by another man, let him be suspended.

CANON XLIX.

If any Bishop or Presbyter shall disregard the Lord's ordinance, and not baptize into the Father and the Son and the Holy Ghost, but into three Beings without beginning, or three Sons, or three Paracletes, let him be deposed.

CANON L.

If any Bishop or Presbyter does not make the three complete immersions of the one Initiation, but gives one immersion into the death of the Lord, let him be deposed. For the Lord said not, Baptize ye into My death; but, Go and make disciples of all nations, baptizing them in the Name of the Father, and of the Son, and of the Holy Ghost.

CANON LI.

If any Bishop, Presbyter, or Deacon, or any at all of the Sacerdotal List, shall abstain from marriage, or flesh, or wine, not for discipline, but because he abhors them; forgetting that all things are very good, and that God made man male and female; but blasphemously slandering God's work; let him amend, or be deposed and cast out of the Church. Likewise a layman.

CANON LII.

If any Bishop or Presbyter will not receive one who turns from his sins, but rejects him, let him be deposed; for he grieves Christ, who said, There shall be joy in heaven over one sinner that repenteth.

CANON LIII.

If any Bishop, Presbyter, or Deacon, will not partake of flesh and wine on festival days, because he abhors them, and not on account of discipline, let him be deposed as a man who has seared his own conscience, and who is a cause of offence to many.

ΚΑΝΩΝ ΝΔ'.

Εἴ τις κληρικὸς ἐν καπηλείῳ φωραθείη ἐσθίων, ἀφοριζέσθω· πάρεξ τοῦ ἐν πανδοχείῳ ἐν ὁδῷ δι' ἀνάγκην καταλύσαντος.

ΚΑΝΩΝ ΝΕ'.

Εἴ τις κληρικὸς ὑβρίσει τὸν ἐπίσκοπον, καθαιρείσθω. Ἄρχοντα γὰρ τοῦ λαοῦ σου οὐκ ἐρεῖς κακῶς.

ΚΑΝΩΝ Νϛ'.

Εἴ τις κληρικὸς ὑβρίσει πρεσβύτερον, ἢ διάκονον, ἀφοριζέσθω.

ΚΑΝΩΝ ΝΖ'.

Εἴ τις κληρικὸς χωλὸν, ἢ κωφὸν, ἢ τυφλὸν, ἢ τὰς βάσεις πεπληγμένον χλευάσει, ἀφοριζέσθω· ὡσαύτως καὶ λαϊκός.

ΚΑΝΩΝ ΝΗ'.

Ἐπίσκοπος, ἢ πρεσβύτερος ἀμελῶν τοῦ κλήρου, ἢ τοῦ λαοῦ, καὶ μὴ παιδεύων αὐτοὺς τὴν εὐσέβειαν, ἀφοριζέσθω· ἐπιμένων δὲ τῇ ἀμελείᾳ καὶ ῥαθυμίᾳ, καθαιρείσθω.

ΚΑΝΩΝ ΝΘ'.

Εἴ τις ἐπίσκοπος, ἢ πρεσβύτερος, ἢ διάκονος, τινὸς τῶν κληρικῶν ἐνδεοῦς ὄντος, μὴ ἐπιχορηγεῖ τὰ δέοντα, ἀφοριζέσθω· ἐπιμένων δὲ, καθαιρείσθω, ὡς φονεύσας τὸν ἀδελφὸν αὐτοῦ.

ΚΑΝΩΝ Ξ'.

Εἴ τις τὰ ψευδεπίγραφα τῶν ἀσεβῶν βιβλία, ὡς ἅγια, ἐπὶ τῆς ἐκκλησίας δημοσιεύει, ἐπὶ λύμῃ τοῦ λαοῦ καὶ τοῦ κλήρου, καθαιρείσθω.

ΚΑΝΩΝ ΞΑ'.

Εἴ τις κατηγορία γένηται κατὰ πιστοῦ, πορνείας, ἢ μοιχείας, ἢ ἄλλης τινὸς ἀπηγορευμένης πράξεως, καὶ ἐλεγχθείη, εἰς κλῆρον μὴ προσαγέσθω.

CANON LIV.

If any Clergyman shall be detected eating in a tavern, let him be suspended; unless, when on a journey, he has been compelled to lodge at an inn.

CANON LV.

If any Clergyman shall treat his Bishop with insolence, let him be deposed; for, Thou shalt not speak evil of the ruler of thy people.

CANON LVI.

If any Clergyman shall treat a Presbyter or Deacon with insolence, let him be suspended.

CANON LVII.

If any Clergyman shall mock a person who is lame, or deaf, or blind, or who halts in his steps, let him be suspended. Likewise a layman.

CANON LVIII.

If a Bishop or Presbyter shall neglect the Clergy or the people, and not teach them religion, let him be suspended; and if he continue in negligence and self-indulgence, let him be deposed.

CANON LIX.

If a Bishop, Presbyter, or Deacon, shall not supply what is necessary, when one of the Clergy is in need, let him be suspended; and if he persist, let him be deposed, as one who murders his brother.

CANON LX.

If any one, to the destruction of the Clergy and people, shall publicly in the Church read the falsely superscribed books of impious men, as if they were Holy Scripture, let him be deposed.

CANON LXI.

If any accusation of fornication, or adultery, or any other forbidden act, should be brought against one of the faithful, and he should be convicted, let him not be promoted to the Clergy.

ΚΑΝΩΝ ΞΒ'.

Εἴ τις κληρικὸς διὰ φόβον ἀνθρώπινον Ἰουδαίου, ἢ Ἕλληνος, ἢ Αἱρετικοῦ, ἀρνήσεται, εἰ μὲν τὸ ὄνομα τοῦ Χριστοῦ, ἀποβαλλέσθω· εἰ δὲ τὸ ὄνομα τοῦ κληρικοῦ, καθαιρείσθω. Μετανοήσας δὲ, ὡς λαϊκὸς δεχθήτω.

ΚΑΝΩΝ ΞΓ'.

Εἴ τις ἐπίσκοπος, ἢ πρεσβύτερος, ἢ διάκονος, ἢ ὅλως τοῦ καταλόγου τοῦ ἱερατικοῦ φάγῃ κρέα ἐν αἵματι ψυχῆς αὐτοῦ, ἢ θηριάλωτον, ἢ θνησιμαῖον, καθαιρείσθω. Τοῦτο γὰρ ὁ νόμος ἀπεῖπεν. Εἰ δὲ λαϊκὸς εἴη, ἀφοριζέσθω.

ΚΑΝΩΝ ΞΔ'.

Εἴ τις κληρικὸς, ἢ λαϊκὸς, εἰσέλθῃ εἰς συναγωγὴν Ἰουδαίων, ἢ Αἱρετικῶν προσεύξασθαι, καὶ καθαιρείσθω, καὶ ἀφοριζέσθω.

ΚΑΝΩΝ ΞΕ'.

Εἴ τις κληρικὸς ἐν μάχῃ τινὰ κρούσας ἀπὸ τοῦ ἑνὸς κρούσματος ἀποκτείνῃ, καθαιρείσθω διὰ τὴν προπέτειαν αὐτοῦ· εἰ δὲ λαϊκὸς, ἀφοριζέσθω.

ΚΑΝΩΝ Ξς'.

Εἴ τις κληρικὸς εὑρεθῇ τὴν κυριακὴν ἡμέραν νηστεύων, ἢ τὸ σάββατον (πλὴν τοῦ ἑνὸς μόνου) καθαιρείσθω. Εἰ δὲ λαϊκὸς, ἀφοριζέσθω.

ΚΑΝΩΝ ΞΖ'.

Εἴ τις παρθένον ἀμνήστευτον βιασάμενος ἔχοι ἀφοριζέσθω· μὴ ἐξεῖναι δὲ αὐτῷ ἑτέραν λαμβάνειν, ἀλλ' ἐκείνην κατέχειν ἣν ᾑρετίσατο, κἂν πενιχρὰ τυγχάνῃ.

ΚΑΝΩΝ ΞΗ'.

Εἴ τις ἐπίσκοπος, ἢ πρεσβύτερος, ἢ διάκονος, δευτέραν χειροτονίαν δέξεται παρά τινος, καθαιρείσθω καὶ αὐτὸς καὶ ὁ

CANON LXII.

If any Clergyman, from the fear of man, whether of Jew, or heathen, or heretic, shall deny the name of CHRIST, let him be cast out; and if he deny the name of a Clergyman, let him be deposed; but if he repent, let him be received as a layman.

CANON LXIII.

If any Bishop, Presbyter, or Deacon, or any one whatever of the Sacerdotal List, shall eat flesh with the blood of the life thereof, or which has been slain by beasts, or which has died a natural death, let him be deposed; for this the law has forbidden. And if it be a layman, let him be suspended.

CANON LXIV.

If any Clergyman (or layman) shall enter a synagogue of Jews or heretics, to pray, let him be both deposed and suspended [*i. e.*, let the layman be suspended, but let the Clergyman be both deposed from his ministry, and also suspended from Communion].

CANON LXV.

If a Clergyman in a quarrel shall strike a man, and kill him at one blow, let him be deposed for his violence; and if it be a layman, let him be suspended.

CANON LXVI.

If any Clergyman be found fasting on the LORD'S day, or on any Sabbath except one only [*i. e.*, on Easter Even], let him be deposed. And if it be a layman, let him be suspended.

CANON LXVII.

If any one shall force and keep a virgin not betrothed, let him be suspended. And let him take no other woman to wife, but keep her whom he has chosen, even though she be poor.

CANON LXVIII.

If any Bishop, Presbyter, or Deacon, shall receive from any one a second ordination, let both him and his ordainer be

χειροτονήσας· εἰ μήγε ἄρα συσταίη, ὅτι παρὰ αἱρετικῶν ἔχει τὴν χειροτονίαν. Τοὺς γὰρ παρὰ τῶν τοιούτων βαπτισθέντας, ἢ χειροτονηθέντας, οὔτε πιστοὺς, οὔτε κληρικοὺς εἶναι δυνατόν.

ΚΑΝΩΝ ΞΘ'.

Εἴ τις ἐπίσκοπος, ἢ πρεσβύτερος, ἢ διάκονος, ἢ ἀναγνώστης, ἢ ψάλτης, τὴν ἁγίαν τεσσαρακοστὴν τοῦ Πάσχα οὐ νηστεύει, ἢ τετράδα, ἢ παρασκευὴν, καθαιρείσθω, ἐκτὸς εἰ μὴ δι' ἀσθένειαν σωματικὴν ἐμποδίζοιτο. Εἰ δὲ λαϊκὸς εἴη, ἀφοριζέσθω.

ΚΑΝΩΝ Ο'.

Εἴ τις ἐπίσκοπος, ἢ πρεσβύτερος, ἢ διάκονος, ἢ ὅλως τοῦ καταλόγου τῶν κληρικῶν, νηστεύει μετὰ Ἰουδαίων, ἢ ἑορτάζει μετ' αὐτῶν, ἢ δέχεται παρ' αὐτων τὰ τῆς ἑορτῆς ξένια, (οἷον ἄζυμα, ἤ τι τοιοῦτον) καθαιρείσθω. Εἰ δὲ λαϊκὸς εἴη, ἀφοριζέσθω.

ΚΑΝΩΝ ΟΑ'.

Εἴ τις Χριστιανὸς ἔλαιον ἀπενέγκοι εἰς ἱερὸν ἐθνῶν, ἢ εἰς συναγωγὴν Ἰουδαίων, ἐν ταῖς ἑορταῖς αὐτῶν, ἢ λύχνους ἅπτει, ἀφοριζέσθω.

ΚΑΝΩΝ ΟΒ'.

Εἴ τις κληρικὸς, ἢ λαϊκὸς ἀπὸ τῆς ἁγίας ἐκκλησίας ἀφέληται κηρὸν, ἢ ἔλαιον, ἀφοριζέσθω.

ΚΑΝΩΝ ΟΓ'.

Σκεῦος χρυσοῦν, ἢ ἀργυροῦν, ἁγιασθὲν, ἢ ὀθόνην, μηδεὶς ἔτι εἰς οἰκείαν χρῆσιν σφετεριζέσθω· παράνομον γάρ. Εἰ δέ τις φωραθείη, ἐπιτιμάσθω ἀφορισμῷ.

ΚΑΝΩΝ ΟΔ'.

Ἐπίσκοπον κατηγορηθέντα ἐπί τινι παρὰ ἀξιοπίστων ἀνθρώπων καλεῖσθαι αὐτὸν ἀναγκαῖον ὑπὸ τῶν ἐπισκόπων. Κᾂν μὲν ἀπαντήσῃ, καὶ ὁμολογήσῃ, ἢ ἐλεγχθείη ὁρίζεσθαι τὸ ἐπιτίμιον· ἐὰν δὲ καλούμενος μὴ ὑπακούσῃ, καλείσθω καὶ δεύτερον, ἀποστελλομένων ἐπ' αὐτὸν δύο ἐπισκόπων· ἐὰν δὲ

deposed, unless it should be proved that he had his ordination from heretics; for it is not possible that they who are baptized or ordained by such can be either of the faithful or of the Clergy.

CANON LXIX.

If any Bishop, Presbyter, Deacon, Reader, or Singer shall not fast in the holy forty days of Lent, or on Wednesdays and Fridays, let him be deposed, unless he be hindered [from fasting] by bodily weakness. And if it be a layman, let him be suspended.

CANON LXX.

If any Bishop, Presbyter, or Deacon, or any one whatever on the List of Clergy shall fast with the Jews, or observe festivals with them, or receive from them gifts, such as unleavened cakes, or the like, from their feasts, let him be deposed. And if it be a layman, let him be suspended.

CANON LXXI.

If any Christian shall bring oil into a temple of the heathen or a synagogue of the Jews, at their festivals, or if he shall light their lamps, let him be suspended.

CANON LXXII.

If any Clergyman or layman shall carry off wax or oil from the Holy Church, let him be suspended.

CANON LXXIII.

No one shall appropriate to his own private use any consecrated vessel of gold or of silver, or linen; for this is a crime. And if any one be found so doing, let him pay the penalty of suspension.

CANON LXXIV.

If a Bishop be accused of anything by trustworthy men, it is necessary that he be summoned by the Bishops; and that if he appear and confess, or be convicted, they should determine the penalty. But if he be summoned, and will not obey, let two Bishops be sent to him, and let him be summoned a

καὶ οὕτω μὴ ὑπακούσῃ, καλείσθω καὶ τρίτον, δύο πάλιν ἐπισκόπων ἀποστελλομένων πρὸς αὐτόν. Ἐὰν δὲ καὶ οὕτως καταφρονήσας μὴ ἀπαντήσῃ, ἡ σύνοδος ἀποφαινέσθω κατ' αὐτοῦ τὰ δοκοῦντα, ὅπως μὴ δόξῃ κερδαίνειν φυγοδικῶν.

ΚΑΝΩΝ ΟΕ'.

Εἰς μαρτυρίαν τὴν κατὰ ἐπισκόπου αἱρετικὸν μὴ προσδέχεσθαι, ἀλλὰ μηδὲ πιστὸν ἕνα μόνον. Ἐπὶ στόματος γὰρ δύο ἢ τριῶν μαρτύρων σταθήσεται πᾶν ῥῆμα.

ΚΑΝΩΝ Oϛ'.

Ὅτι οὐ χρὴ ἐπίσκοπον τῷ ἀδελφῷ, ἢ τῷ υἱῷ, ἢ ἑτέρῳ συγγενεῖ χαριζόμενον, εἰς τὸ ἀξίωμα τῆς ἐπισκοπῆς χειροτονεῖν ὃν βούλεται. Κληρονόμους γὰρ τῆς ἐπισκοπῆς ποιεῖσθαι οὐ δίκαιον, τὰ τοῦ Θεοῦ χαριζόμενον πάθει ἀνθρωπίνῳ· οὐ γὰρ τὴν τοῦ Θεοῦ ἐκκλησίαν ὑπὸ κληρονόμους ὀφείλει τιθέναι. Εἰ δέ τις τοῦτο ποιήσει, ἄκυρος μὲν ἔστω ἡ χειροτονία, αὐτὸς δὲ ἐπιτιμάσθω ἀφορισμῷ.

ΚΑΝΩΝ ΟΖ'.

Εἴ τις ἀνάπηρος ᾖ τὸν ὀφθαλμὸν, ἢ τὸ σκέλος πεπληγμένος, ἄξιος δέ ἐστιν ἐπισκοπῆς, γινέσθω· οὐ γὰρ λώβη σώματος αὐτὸν μιαίνει, ἀλλὰ ψυχῆς μολυσμός.

ΚΑΝΩΝ ΟΗ'.

Κωφὸς δὲ ὢν καὶ τυφλὸς, μὴ γινέσθω ἐπίσκοπος· οὐχ ὡς μεμιασμένος, ἀλλ' ἵνα μὴ τὰ ἐκκλησιαστικὰ παρεμποδίζοιτο.

ΚΑΝΩΝ ΟΘ'.

Ἐάν τις δαίμονα ἔχῃ κληρικὸς μὴ γινέσθω· ἀλλὰ μηδὲ τοῖς πιστοῖς συνευχέσθω. Καθαρθεὶς δὲ προσδεχέσθω, καὶ, ἐὰν ᾖ ἄξιος, γινέσθω.

second time. And if he will not then obey, let two Bishops be again sent to him, and let him be summoned the third time. And if he shall even then despise [the summons], and will not appear, let the Synod pronounce against him what they think right, that he may not evidently be a gainer by avoiding a trial.

CANON LXXV.

No heretic, nor even a single communicant, is to be received as the accuser of a Bishop; for, By the mouth of two or three witnesses shall every word be established.

CANON LXXVI.

It is unlawful for a Bishop desiring to gratify a brother or a son, or some other relative, to ordain whom he will to the dignity of the Episcopate. For it is not just to make heirs of his episcopal office, and through natural affection to give away the things which are God's. It is not lawful to bequeath the Church of God to heirs; and if any one shall do this, let the ordination be void, and let himself be punished with suspension.

CANON LXXVII.

If any one who is otherwise worthy of the Episcopate be blind of an eye, or lame of a leg, let him be made [Bishop]; for it is not a blemish of the body, but a pollution of the soul, that defiles a man.

CANON LXXVIII.

But if any one is [wholly] deaf or blind, let him not be made a Bishop, not because he is defiled, but that the affairs of the Church may not be hindered.

CANON LXXIX.

If any man have a devil, let him not be made a Clergyman; neither let him pray with the faithful; but if he be dispossessed, let him be received [to prayers]; and if he be worthy, let him be made [a Clergyman].

ΚΑΝΩΝ Π'.

Τὸν ἐξ ἐθνικοῦ βίου προσελθόντα, καὶ βαπτισθέντα, ἢ ἐκ φαύλης διαγωγῆς, οὐ δίκαιόν ἐστι πάρ' αὐτὰ προχειρίζεσθαι ἐπίσκοπον. Ἄδικον γὰρ, τὸν μηδέπω πεῖραν ἐπιδειξάμενον, ἑτέρων εἶναι διδάσκαλον· εἰ μήπω κατὰ θείαν χάριν τοῦτο γένηται.

ΚΑΝΩΝ ΠΑ'.

Εἴπομεν ὅτι οὐ χρὴ ἐπίσκοπον, ἢ πρεσβύτερον καθιέναι ἑαυτὸν εἰς δημοσίας διοικήσεις, ἀλλὰ προσευκαιρεῖν ταῖς ἐκκλησιαστικαῖς χρείαις. Ἢ πειθέσθω οὖν τοῦτο μὴ ποιεῖν, ἢ καθαιρείσθω. Οὐδεὶς γὰρ δύναται δυσὶ κυρίοις δουλεύειν, κατὰ τὴν Κυριακὴν παρακέλευσιν.

ΚΑΝΩΝ ΠΒ'.

Οἰκέτας εἰς κλῆρον προχειρίζεσθαι ἄνευ τῆς τῶν δεσποτῶν συγγνώμης οὐκ ἐπιτρέπομεν, ἐπὶ λύπῃ τῶν κεκτημένων· οἴκων γὰρ ἀνατροπὴν τὸ τοιοῦτον ἐργάζεται. Εἰ δὲ ποτὲ καὶ ἄξιος φανείη ὁ οἰκέτης πρὸς χειροτονίαν βαθμοῦ, οἷος καὶ ὁ ἡμέτερος Ὀνήσιμος ἐφάνη, καὶ συγχωρήσουσιν οἱ δεσπόται, καὶ ἐλευθερώσουσιν, καὶ τοῦ οἴκου ἐξαποστείλωσι, γινέσθω.

ΚΑΝΩΝ ΠΓ'.

Ἐπίσκοπος, ἢ πρεσβύτερος, ἢ διάκονος στρατείᾳ σχολάζων, καὶ βουλόμενος ἀμφότερα κατέχειν, Ῥωμαϊκὴν ἀρχὴν καὶ ἱερατικὴν διοίκησιν, καθαιρείσθω. Τὰ γὰρ Καίσαρος, Καίσαρι, καὶ τὰ τοῦ Θεοῦ τῷ Θεῷ.

ΚΑΝΩΝ ΠΔ'.

Ὅσ τις ὑβρίσει βασιλέα, ἢ ἄρχοντα παρὰ τὸ δίκαιον τιμωρίαν τιννύτω. Καὶ εἰ μὲν κληρικὸς, καθαιρείσθω· εἰ δὲ λαϊκὸς, ἀφοριζέσθω.

ΚΑΝΩΝ ΠΕ'.

Ἔστω ὑμῖν πᾶσι κληρικοῖς καὶ λαϊκοῖς βιβλία σεβάσμια καὶ ἅγια· τῆς μὲν Παλαιᾶς Διαθήκης, Μωυσέως πέντε, Γένεσις, Ἔξοδος, Λευϊτικὸν, Ἀριθμοὶ, Δευτερονόμιον. Ἰησοῦ υἱοῦ Ναυῆ,

CANON LXXX.

It is not right that one who has come over from heathenism, or from a dishonorable course of life, should immediately be made a Bishop; for it is unjust that he who has not yet given proof of himself, should be the teacher of others, unless this should happen of Divine grace.

CANON LXXXI.

We have said that a Bishop or Presbyter ought not to let himself down to public business, but should occupy himself with the affairs of the Church. Let such, therefore, either be persuaded not to do so, or let them be deposed; for no man can serve two masters, as the Lord hath taught.

CANON LXXXII.

We do not permit slaves to be promoted to the Clergy without the consent of their masters, so as to trouble their owners. For such a course would bring households into confusion. But if at any time a servant should appear worthy of ordination, as did our Onesimus, and if the master should agree and manumit him, and dismiss him from his house, let it be done.

CANON LXXXIII.

Bishop, Presbyter, or Deacon, serving in the army and desiring to retain both the Roman command and the priestly ministry, shall be deposed; for the things which are Cæsar's, belong to Cæsar; and the things which are God's, to God.

CANON LXXXIV.

If any one shall wrongfully treat the Emperor or a Magistrate with insolence, he shall pay the penalty, and if he be a Clergyman, he shall be deposed. If he be a layman, let him be suspended.

CANON LXXXV.

Let these books be accounted holy and venerable by you all, Clergy and laity, namely,

Of the Old Testament: Five of Moses; Genesis, Exodus, Leviticus, Numbers, Deuteronomy; One of Joshua, the son of

ἕν. Κριτῶν, ἕν. Ῥουθ, ἕν. Βασιλειῶν, τέσσαρα. Παραλειπομένων τῆς βίβλου τῶν ἡμερῶν, δύο. Ἐσδρά, δύο. Ἐσθὴρ, ἕν. Μακκαβαίων, τρία. Ἰὼβ, ἕν. Ψαλτηρίου, ἕν. Σολομῶντος τρία, Παροιμίαι, Ἐκκλησιαστὴς, Αἶσμα Αἰσματων. Προφητῶν, δεκαδύο. Ἠσαΐου, ἕν. Ἰηρημίου, ἕν. Ἰεζεκιὴλ, ἕν. Ἓν Δανιήλ. Ἔξωθεν δὲ ὑμῖν προσιστορείσθω μανθάνειν ὑμῶν τοὺς νέους τὴν σοφίαν τοῦ πολυμαθοῦς Σιράχ. Ἡμέτερα δὲ, τοῦτ' ἐστὶ, τῆς Καινῆς Διαθήκης, Εὐαγγέλια τέσσαρα, Ματθαίου, Μάρκου, Λουκᾶ, Ἰωάννου. Παύλου ἐπιστολαὶ δεκατέσσαρες. Πέτρου ἐπιστολαὶ δύο. Ἰωάννου, τρεῖς. Ἰακώβου, μία. Ἰούδα, μία. Κλήμεντος ἐπιστολαὶ δύο. Καὶ αἱ διαταγαὶ ὑμῖν τοῖς ἐπισκόποις δι' ἐμοῦ Κλήμεντος ἐν ὀκτὼ βιβλίοις προσπεφωνημέναι, ἃς οὐ χρὴ δημοσιεύειν ἐπὶ πάντων, διὰ τὰ ἐν αὐταῖς μυστικά. Καὶ αἱ Πράξεις ἡμῶν τῶν Ἀποστόλων.

Nun ; One of Judges ; One of Ruth ; Four of Kings ; Two of [Paralipomena, that is of] the Book of Days Omitted ; Two of Esdras ; One of Esther ; Three of Maccabees ; One of Job; One, The Psalter ; Three of Solomon, Proverbs, Ecclesiastes, The Song of Songs ; Twelve of the Prophets, One of Isaiah, One of Jeremiah, One of Ezekiel, One of Daniel. Besides these, let it be understood that your children ought to learn the Wisdom of the most learned Sirach.

[The Books] of our own, that is, of the New Testament : Four Gospels ; of Matthew, Mark, Luke, John ; Fourteen Epistles of Paul ; Two Epistles of Peter ; Three of John ; One of James ; One of Jude ; Two Epistles of Clement ; and the Constitutions addressed in eight books by me Clement to you Bishops (which books are not to be published to all, on account of the mystical things contained therein). And the Acts of us Apostles.

FIRST GENERAL COUNCIL.

NICÆA.

ΣΥΝΟΔΙΚΗ ΕΠΙΣΤΟΛΗ.

Ἡ ἁγία καὶ μεγάλη σύνοδος τῇ ἁγίᾳ καὶ μεγάλῃ Θεοῦ χάριτι Ἀλεξανδρέων ἐκκλησίᾳ, καὶ τοῖς κατὰ τὴν Αἴγυπτον, καὶ Πεντάπολιν, καὶ Λιβύην, καὶ τοῖς κατὰ τὴν ὑπ' οὐρανὸν, ἀγαπητοῖς ἀδελφοῖς, κλήροις τε καὶ λαοῖς ὀρθοδόξοις, οἱ ἐν Νικαίᾳ σύνοδον συγκροτήσαντες ἐπίσκοποι ἐν κυρίῳ χαίρειν.

Ἐπειδὴ τῆς τοῦ Χριστοῦ χάριτος καὶ τοῦ θεοφιλεστάτου βασιλέως Κωνσταντίνου συναγαγόντος ἡμᾶς ἐκ διαφόρων ἐπαρχιῶν καὶ πόλεων, ἡ μεγάλη καὶ ἁγία σύνοδος ἐν Νικαίᾳ συγκροτηθεῖσα τὰ περὶ τῆς ἐκκλησιαστικῆς πίστεως διείληφεν, ἅ τινα ἀναγκαῖον ἡμῖν ἐφάνη ἀποσταλῆναι παρ' ἡμῶν πρὸς ὑμᾶς διὰ γραμμάτων, ἵνα εἰδέναι ἔχοιτε, τίνα μὲν ἐκινήθη καὶ ἐξητάσθη, τίνα δὲ ἔδοξε καὶ ἐκρατύνθη.

Πρῶτον μὲν οὖν ἁπάντων ἐξητάσθη τὰ κατὰ τὴν ἀσέβειαν καὶ παρανομίαν Ἀρείου καὶ τῶν σὺν αὐτῷ ἐπὶ παρουσίᾳ τοῦ θεοφιλεστάτου ἡμῶν βασιλέως Κωνσταντίνου· καὶ παμψηφοὶ ἔδοξαν ἀναθεματισθῆναι αὐτὸν, καὶ τὴν ἀσεβῆ αὐτοῦ δόξαν, καὶ τὰ ῥήματα, καὶ τὰ νοήματα αὐτοῦ τὰ βλάσφημα, οἷς ἐκέχρητο, βλασφημῶν τὸν τοῦ υἱὸν Θεοῦ, λέγων ἐξ οὐκ ὄντων εἶναι, καὶ πρὶν γεννηθῆναι μὴ εἶναι, καὶ ἦν ποτε ὅτε οὐκ ἦν, καὶ αὐτεξουσιότητι κακίας καὶ ἀρετῆς δεκτικὸν τὸν υἱὸν τοῦ Θεοῦ· λέγοντος, καὶ κτίσμα· ταῦτα πάντα ἀνεθεμάτισεν ἡ ἁγία σύνοδος, οὐδὲ ὅσον ἀκοῦσαι τῆς ἀσεβοῦς δόξης, καὶ τῆς ἀπονοίας, καὶ τῶν βλασφήμων ῥημάτων αὐτοῦ ἀνασχομένη· καὶ τὰ μὲν κατ' ἐκεῖνον οἷου τέλους τετύχηκε, πάντως ἢ ἀκηκόατε, ἢ ἀκούσεσθε, ἵνα μὴ δόξωμεν ἐπεμβαίνειν ἀνδρὶ δι' οἰκείαν ἁμαρτίαν ἄξια τἀπίχειρα κομισαμένῳ. Τοσοῦτον δὲ ἴσχυσεν αὐτοῦ ἀσέβεια,

SYNODICAL LETTER.

To the Church of Alexandria, by the grace of God, Holy and Great; and to our well-beloved brethren, the orthodox Clergy and Laity throughout Egypt, and Pentapolis, and Lybia, and every nation under heaven; the Holy and Great Synod, the Bishops assembled at Nicæa, wish health in the Lord.

Forasmuch as the Great and Holy Synod, which was assembled at Nicæa through the grace of Christ and our most religious Sovereign, Constantine, who brought us together from our several Provinces and Cities, has considered matters which concern the Faith of the Church, it seemed to us to be necessary that certain things should be communicated from us to you in writing, so that you might have the means of knowing what has been mooted and investigated, and also what has been decreed and confirmed.

First of all, then, in presence of our most religious Sovereign, Constantine, investigation was made of matters concerning the impiety and transgression of Arius and his adherents; and it was unanimously decreed that he and his impious opinion should be anathematized, together with the blasphemous words and speculations in which he indulged, blaspheming the Son of God, and saying that He is from things that are not, and that before He was begotten He was not, and that there was a time when He was not, and that the Son of God is by His free will capable of Vice and Virtue; saying also that He is a creature. All these things the Holy Synod has anathematized, not even enduring to hear his impious doctrine and madness and blasphemous words. And of the charges against him and of the results they had, ye have either already heard or will hear the particulars, lest we should seem to be oppressing a man who has in fact received a fitting recompense for his own sin. So far indeed has his

ὡς καὶ παραπολέσαι Θεωνᾶν τὸν ἀπὸ Μαρμαρικῆς, καὶ Σεκοῦνδον τὸν ἀπὸ Πτολεμαΐδος· τῶν γὰρ αὐτῶν κἀκεῖνοι σὺν τοῖς ἄλλοις τετυχήκασιν.

Ἀλλ' ἐπειδὴ ἡ τοῦ Θεοῦ χάρις τῆς μὲν κακοδοξίας ἐκείνης καὶ βλασφημίας, καὶ τῶν προσώπων τῶν τολμησάντων διάστασιν καὶ διαίρεσιν ποιήσασθαι τοῦ εἰρηνευομένου ἄνωθεν λαοῦ, ἠλευθέρωσε τὴν Αἴγυπτον, ἐλείπετο δὲ τὸ κατὰ τὴν προπέτειαν Μελητίου καὶ τῶν ὑπ' αὐτοῦ χειροτονηθέντων· καὶ περὶ τούτου τοῦ μέρους ἃ ἔδοξε τῇ συνόδῳ, ἐμφανίζομεν ὑμῖν ἀγαπητοὶ ἀδελφοί. Ἔδοξεν οὖν Μελήτιον μὲν, φιλανθρωπότερον κινηθείσης τῆς συνόδου, κατὰ γὰρ τὸν ἀκριβῆ λόγον οὐδεμιᾶς συγγνώμης ἄξιος ἦν, μένειν ἐν τῇ αὐτοῦ πόλει, καὶ μηδεμίαν ἐξουσίαν ἔχειν, μήτε χειροτονεῖν, μήτε χειρίζειν, μήτε χειροθετεῖν, μήτε ἐν χώρᾳ, μήτε ἐν πόλει ἑτέρᾳ φαίνεσθαι ταύτης τῆς προφάσεως ἕνεκα· ψιλὸν δὲ τὸ ὄνομα τῆς τιμῆς κεκτῆσθαι· τοὺς δὲ ὑπ' αὐτοῦ κατασταθέντας, μυστικωτέρᾳ χειροτονίᾳ βεβαιωθέντας, κοινωνηθῆναι ἐπὶ τούτοις· ἐφ' ᾧ τε ἔχειν μὲν αὐτοὺς τὴν τιμὴν, καὶ λειτουργεῖν, δευτέρους δὲ εἶναι ἐξάπαντος πάντων τῶν ἐν ἑκάστῃ παροικίᾳ καὶ ἐκκλησίᾳ ἐξεταζομένων, τῶν ὑπὸ τὸν τιμιώτατον καὶ συλλειτουργὸν ἡμῶν Ἀλέξανδρον προκεχειρισμένων. Ὡς τούτοις μὲν μηδεμίαν ἐξουσίαν εἶναι τοὺς ἀρέσκοντας αὐτοῖς προχειρίζεσθαι, ἢ ὑποβάλλειν ὀνόματα, ἢ ὅλως ποιεῖν τι χωρὶς γνώμης τῶν τῆς καθολικῆς καὶ ἀποστολικῆς ἐκκλησίας ἐπισκόπων τῶν ὑπὸ Ἀλέξανδρον τελούντων, τὸν ὁσιώτατον συλλειτουργὸν ἡμῶν. Τοὺς δὲ χάριτι Θεοῦ καὶ εὐχαῖς ὑμετέρας ἐν μηδενὶ σχίσματι εὑρεθέντας, ἀλλὰ ἀκηλιδώτους ἐν τῇ καθολικῇ καὶ ἀποστολικῇ ἐκκλησίᾳ ὄντας, ἐξουσίαν ἔχειν καὶ προχειρίζεσθαι, καὶ ὀνόματα ἐπιλέγεσθαι τῶν ἀξίων τοῦ κλήρου, καὶ ὅλως πάντα ποιεῖν καὶ κατὰ νόμον καὶ θεσμὸν τὸν ἐκκλησιαστικόν. Εἰ δέ τινα συμβαίνῃ ἀναπαύσασθαι τῶν ἐν τῇ ἐκκλησίᾳ, τηνικαῦτα προσαναβαίνειν εἰς τὴν τιμὴν τοῦ τετελευτηκότος τοὺς ἄρτι προληφθέντας, μόνον εἰ ἄξιοι φαίνοιντο, καὶ ὁ λαὸς αἱροῖτο, συνεπιψηφίζοντος αὐτῷ, καὶ ἐπισφραγίζοντος τοῦ τῆς Ἀλεξανδρείας ἐπισκόπου. Τοῦτο δὲ τοῖς μὲν ἄλλοις ἅπασι συνεχωρήθη· ἐπὶ δὲ τοῦ Μελητίου προσώπου οὐκέτι τὰ αὐτὰ ἔδοξε, διὰ τὴν ἀνέκαθεν αὐτοῦ ἀταξίαν, καὶ διὰ

impiety prevailed, that he has even destroyed Theonas of Marmarica and Secundus of Ptolemais; for they also have received the same sentence as the rest.

But when the grace of God had delivered Egypt from that heresy and blasphemy, and from the persons who have dared to make disturbance and division among a people heretofore at peace, there remained the matter of the insolence of Meletius and those who have been ordained by him; and concerning this part of our work we now, beloved brethren, proceed to inform you of the decrees of the Synod. The Holy Synod, then, being disposed to deal gently with Meletius, (for in strict justice he deserved no leniency), decreed that he should remain in his own City, but have no authority either to make appointments, or to administer affairs, or to ordain; and that he should not appear in any other City or District for this purpose, but should enjoy the bare title of his rank; but that those who have been placed by him, after they have been confirmed by a more sacred appointment, shall on these conditions be admitted to communion: that they shall both have their rank and the right to officiate, but that they shall be altogether the inferiors of all those who are enrolled in any Church or Parish, and have been appointed by our most honourable colleague, Alexander. So that these men are to have no authority to make appointments of persons who may be pleasing to them, nor to suggest names, nor to do anything whatever, without the consent of the Bishops of the Catholic and Apostolic Church, who are serving under our most holy colleague, Alexander; while those who, by the grace of God and through your prayers, have been found in no schism, but on the contrary are without spot in the Catholic and Apostolic Church, are to have authority to make appointments and nominations of worthy persons among the Clergy, and in short to do all things according to the law and ordinance of the Church. But, if it happen that any of the Clergy who are now in the Church should die, then those who have been lately received are to succeed to the office of the deceased; always provided that they shall appear to be worthy, and that the people elect them, and that the Bishop of Alexandria shall concur in the election and ratify it. This concession has been made to all the rest; but, on account of his disorderly conduct from the first and the rashness and precipitation of

τὸ πρόχειρον καὶ προπετὲς τῆς γνώμης, ἵνα μηδεμία ἐξουσία ἢ αὐθεντία αὐτῷ δοθείη, ἀνθρώπῳ δυναμένῳ πάλιν τὰς αὐτὰς ἀταξίας ἐμποιῆσαι.

Ταῦτά ἐστι τὰ ἐξαίρετα καὶ διαφέροντα Αἰγύπτῳ καὶ τῇ ἁγιωτάτῃ Ἀλεξανδρέων ἐκκλησίᾳ. Εἰ δέ τι ἄλλο ἢ ἐκανονίσθη ἢ ἐδογματίσθη συμπαρόντος τοῦ κυρίου καὶ τιμιωτάτου συλλειτουργοῦ καὶ ἀδελφοῦ ἡμῶν Ἀλεξάνδρου, αὐτὸς παρῶν ἀκριβέστερον ἀνοίσει ταῦτα πρὸς ὑμᾶς, ἅτε δὴ καὶ κύριος καὶ κοινωνὸς τῶν γεγενημένων τυγχάνων.

Εὐαγγελιζόμεθα δὲ ὑμᾶς καὶ περὶ τῆς συμφωνίας τοῦ ἁγίου πάσχα, ὅτι ὑμετέραις εὐχαῖς κατωρθώθη καὶ τοῦτο τὸ μέρος, ὥστε πάντας τοὺς ἐν τῇ ἑῴᾳ ἀδελφοὺς, τοὺς μετὰ τῶν Ἰουδαίων τὸ πρότερον ποιοῦντας, συμφώνως Ῥωμαίοις καὶ ὑμῖν, καὶ πᾶσιν τοῖς ἐξ ἀρχαίου μεθ' ἡμῶν φιλάσσουσι τὸ πάσχα, ἐκ τοῦ δεῦρο ἄγειν τὴν αὐτὴν ἁγνοτάτην ἑορτὴν τοῦ πάσχα.

Χαίροντες οὖν ἐπὶ τοῖς κατορθώμασι, καὶ ἐπὶ τῇ κοινῇ εἰρήνῃ καὶ συμφωνίᾳ, καὶ ἐπὶ τῷ πᾶσαν αἵρεσιν ἐκκοπῆναι, ἀποδέξασθε μὲν μετὰ μείζονος τιμῆς καὶ πλείονος ἀγάπης τὸν συλλειτουργὸν ἡμῶν, ὑμῶν δὲ ἐπίσκοπον Ἀλέξανδρον, τὸν εὐφράναντα ἡμᾶς τῇ αὐτοῦ παρουσίᾳ, καὶ ἐν ταύτῃ τῃ ἡλικίᾳ τοσοῦτον πόνον ὑποστάντα ὑπὲρ τοῦ εἰρήνην γενέσθαι παρά τε ὑμῖν καὶ πᾶσιν. Εὔχεσθε δὲ καὶ περὶ ἡμῶν ἁπάντων, ἵνα τὰ καλῶς ἔχειν δόξαντα, ταύτα βέβαια μένοι, κατ' εὐδοκίαν γεγενημένα, ὡς πιστεύομεν, παρὰ τοῦ παντοκράτορος Θεοῦ, καὶ τοῦ μονογενοῦς υἱοῦ αὐτοῦ τοῦ κυρίου ἡμῶν Ἰησοῦ Χριστοῦ, καὶ τοῦ Ἁγίου Πνεύματος, ᾧ ἡ δόξα εἰς τοὺς αἰῶνας. Ἀμήν.

his character, the same decree was not made concerning Meletius himself, but that, inasmuch as he is a man capable of committing again the same disorders, no authority nor privilege should be conceded to him.

These are the particulars, which are of special interest to Egypt and to the most holy Church of Constantinople; but if in the presence of our most honoured lord, our colleague and brother Alexander, anything else has been enacted by Canon or other decree, he will himself convey it to you in greater detail, he having been both a guide and fellow-worker in what has been done.

We further proclaim to you the good news of the agreement concerning the holy Easter, that this particular also has through your prayers been rightly settled; so that all our brethren in the East who formerly followed the custom of the Jews are henceforth to celebrate the said most sacred feast of Easter at the same time with the Romans and yourselves and all those who have observed Easter from the beginning.

Wherefore, rejoicing in these wholesome results, and in our common peace and harmony, and in the cutting off of every heresy, receive ye with the greater honour and with increased love, our colleague, your Bishop, Alexander, who has gladdened us by his presence, and who at so great an age has undergone so great fatigue, that peace might be established among you and all of us. Pray ye also for us all, that the things which have been deemed advisable may stand fast; for they have been done, as we believe, to the well-pleasing of Almighty God and of his only Begotten Son, our Lord Jesus Christ, and of the Holy Ghost; to whom be glory for ever. Amen.

SYMBOLUM NICÆNUM,

AD EXEMPLAR QUOD EXTAT IN ACTIS

CHALCEDONENSIS CONCILII.

Πιστεύομεν εἰς ἕνα Θεὸν, Πατέρα, παντοκράτορα, πάντων ὁράτων τε καὶ ἀοράτων ποιητήν·

Καὶ εἰς ἕνα Κύριον Ἰησοῦν Χριστὸν, τὸν Υἱὸν τοῦ Θεοῦ, γεννηθέντα ἐκ τοῦ Πατρὸς, μονογενῆ, τουτέστιν ἐκ τῆς οὐσίας τοῦ Πατρός· Θεὸν ἐκ Θεοῦ, φῶς ἐκ φῶτος, Θεὸν ἀληθινὸν ἐκ Θεοῦ ἀληθινοῦ, γεννηθέντα, οὐ ποιηθέντα, ὁμοούσιον τῷ Πατρί· δι' οὗ τὰ πάντα ἐγένετο, τάτε ἐν τῷ οὐρανῷ καὶ τὰ ἐν τῇ γῇ· τὸν δι' ἡμᾶς τοὺς ἀνθρώπους, καὶ διὰ τὴν ἡμετέραν σωτηρίαν κατελθόντα, καὶ σαρκωθέντα, καὶ ἐνανθρωπήσαντα, παθόντα, καὶ ἀναστάντα τῇ τριτῇ ἡμέρα, ἀνελθόντα εἰς τοὺς οὐρανοὺς, καὶ πάλιν ἐρχόμενον κρίναι ζῶντας καὶ νεκρούς.

Καὶ εἰς τὸ Πνεῦμα τὸ Ἅγιον.

Τοὺς δὲ λέγοντας· ἦν ποτε ὅτε οὐκ ἦν, καὶ πρὶν γεννηθῆναι οὐκ ἦν, καὶ ὅτι ἐξ οὐκ ὄντων ἐγένετο, ἢ ἐξ ἑτέρας ὑποστάσεως ἢ οὐσίας φάσκοντας εἶναι, ἢ τρεπτὸν, ἢ ἀλλοιωτὸν τὸν Υἱὸν τοῦ Θεοῦ, τούτους ἀναθεματίζει ἡ καθολικὴ καὶ ἀποστολικὴ ἐκκλησία.

THE NICENE CREED

AS CONTAINED IN THE ACTS OF THE COUNCIL OF

CHALCEDON.

We believe in one God, the Father, Almighty, Maker of all things visible and invisible:

And in one Lord Jesus Christ, the Son of God, Begotten of the Father, Only Begotten, that is, of the substance of the Father; God of God, Light of Light, Very God of Very God, Begotten, not made, Being of one substance with the Father; By Whom all things were made, both those in heaven and those in earth; Who, for us men and for our salvation, came down, And was incarnate, and was made Man, Suffered, And rose again the third day, Ascended into heaven, And cometh again to judge the quick and the dead:

And in the Holy Ghost.

But them that say that there was a time when He was not; and that He was not before He was begotten; and that He was made of things which are not; or who say that He is of another substance or essence; or that the Son of God is subject to conversion or mutation; these the Catholic and Apostolic Church anathematizes.

CANONES

NICÆNI CONCILII UNIVERSALIS.

A. D. 325.

ΚΑΝΩΝ Α'.

Εἴ τις ἐν νόσῳ ὑπὸ ἰατρῶν ἐχειρουργήθη, ἢ ὑπὸ βαρβάρων ἐξετμήθη, οὗτος μενέτω ἐν τῷ κλήρῳ. Εἰ δέ τις ὑγιαίνων ἑαυτὸν ἐξέτεμε, τοῦτον καὶ ἐν τῷ κλήρῳ ἐξεταζόμενον, πεπαῦσθαι προσήκει· καὶ ἐκ τοῦ δεῦρο, μηδένα τῶν τοιούτων χρῆναι προάγεσθαι. Ὥσπερ δὲ τοῦτο πρόδηλον, ὅτι περὶ τῶν ἐπιτηδευόντων τὸ πρᾶγμα, καὶ τολμώντων ἑαυτοὺς ἐκτέμνειν εἴρηται· οὕτως, εἴ τινες ὑπὸ βαρβάρων, ἢ δεσποτῶν εὐνουχίσθησαν, εὑρίσκοιντο δὲ ἄλλως ἄξιοι, τοὺς τοιούτους εἰς κλῆρον προσίεται ὁ κανών.

ΚΑΝΩΝ Β'.

Ἐπειδὴ πολλὰ, ἤτοι ὑπὸ ἀνάγκης, ἢ ἄλλως ἐπειγομένων τῶν ἀνθρώπων, ἐγένετο παρὰ τὸν κανόνα τὸν ἐκκλησιαστικὸν, ὥστε ἀνθρώπους ἀπὸ ἐθνικοῦ βίου ἀρτὶ προσελθόντας τῇ πίστει, καὶ ἐν ὀλίγῳ χρόνῳ κατηχηθέντας, εὐθὺς ἐπὶ τὸ πνευματικὸν λουτρὸν ἄγειν, καὶ ἅμα τῷ βαπτισθῆναι προσάγειν εἰς ἐπισκοπὴν, ἢ εἰς πρεσβυτέριον, καλῶς ἔδοξεν ἔχειν, τοῦ λοιποῦ μηδὲν τοιοῦτο γίνεσθαι· καὶ γὰρ καὶ χρόνου δεῖ τῷ κατηχουμένῳ, καὶ μετὰ τὸ βάπτισμα, δοκιμασίας πλείονος. Σαφὲς γὰρ τὸ ἀποστολικὸν γράμμα, τὸ λέγον· μὴ νεόφυτον, ἵνα μὴ τυφωθεὶς εἰς κρίμα ἐμπέσῃ, καὶ παγίδα τοῦ διαβόλου. Εἰ δὲ, προϊόντος τοῦ χρόνου, ψυχικόν τι ἁμάρτημα εὑρεθείη περὶ τὸ πρόσωπον, καὶ ἐλέγχοιτο ὑπὸ δύο, ἢ τριῶν μαρτύρων, πεπαύσθω ὁ τοιοῦτος τοῦ κλήρου. Ὁ δὲ παρὰ ταῦτα ποιῶν, ὡς ὑπεναντία τῇ μεγάλῃ συνόδῳ θρασυνόμενος, αὐτὸς κινδυνεύσει περὶ τὸν κλῆρον.

CANONS OF NICÆA.

CANON I.

If any [Clergyman] has been subjected by physicians to a surgical operation, or if he has been castrated by barbarians, let him remain among the Clergy; but, if any one in sound health has castrated himself, it behoves that such an one, if [already] enrolled among the Clergy, should cease [from his ministry], and that from henceforth no such person should be promoted. But, as it is evident that this is said of those who wilfully do the thing and presume to castrate themselves, so if any have been made eunuchs by barbarians, or [being slaves] by their masters, and should otherwise be found worthy, such men the Canon admits to the Clergy.

CANON II.

Forasmuch as, either from necessity, or through the urgency of individuals, many things have been done contrary to the Canon of the Church, so that men just converted from heathenism to the Faith, and who have been instructed but a little while, are straightway brought to the spiritual laver, and as soon as they have been baptized, are advanced to the Episcopate or the Presbyterate, it has seemed right to us that for the time to come no such thing shall be done. For to the Catechumen himself there is need of [more] time and of a fuller trial after Baptism. For the apostolical saying is clear, "Not a novice; lest, being lifted up with pride, he fall into condemnation and the snare of the devil." But if, after the lapse of time, any sensual sin should be found out about the person, and he should be convicted by two or three witnesses, let him be deposed from the Clergy. And whosoever shall transgress these [enactments] will imperil his own clerical position, as a person who presumes to disobey the Great Synod.

ΚΑΝΩΝ Γ'.

Ἀπηγόρευσε καθόλου ἡ μεγάλη σύνοδος, μήτε ἐπισκόπῳ, μήτε πρεσβυτέρῳ, μήτε διακόνῳ, μήτε ὅλως τινὶ τῶν ἐν [τῷ] κλήρῳ, ἐξεῖναι συνείσακτον ἔχειν, πλὴν εἰ μὴ ἄρα μητέρα, ἢ ἀδελφὴν, ἢ θείαν, ἢ ἃ μόνα πρόσωπα πᾶσαν ὑποψίαν διαπέφευγεν.

ΚΑΝΩΝ Δ'.

Ἐπίσκοπον προσήκει μάλιστα μὲν ὑπὸ πάντων τῶν ἐν τῇ ἐπαρχίᾳ καθίστασθαι· εἰ δὲ δυσχερὲς εἴη τὸ τοιοῦτο, ἢ διὰ κατεπείγουσαν ἀνάγκην, ἢ διὰ μῆκος ὁδοῦ, ἐξ ἅπαντος τρεῖς ἐπὶ τὸ αὐτὸ συναγομένους, συμψήφων γινομένων καὶ τῶν ἀπόντων, καί συντιθεμένων διὰ γραμμάτων, τότε τὴν χειροτονίαν ποιεῖσθαι· τὸ δὲ κῦρος τῶν γινομένων δίδοσθαι καθ' ἑκάστην ἐπαρχίαν τῷ μητροπολίτῃ.

ΚΑΝΩΝ Ε'.

Περὶ τῶν ἀκοινωνήτων γενομένων, εἴτε τῶν ἐν τῷ κλήρῳ, εἴτε τῶν ἐν λαϊκῷ τάγματι, ὑπὸ τῶν καθ' ἑκάστην ἐπαρχίαν ἐπισκόπων, κρατείτω ἡ γνώμη, κατὰ τὸν κανόνα τὸν διαγορεύοντα, τοὺς ὑφ' ἑτέρων ἀποβληθέντας, ὑφ' ἑτέρων μὴ προσίεσθαι. Ἐξεταζέσθω δὲ, μὴ μικροψυχίᾳ ἢ φιλονεικίᾳ, ἤ τινι τοιαύτῃ ἀηδίᾳ τοῦ ἐπισκόπου, ἀποσυνάγωγοι γεγένηνται. Ἵνα οὖν τοῦτο τὴν πρέπουσαν ἐξέτασιν λαμβάνοι, καλῶς ἔχειν ἔδοξεν, ἑκάστου ἐνιαυτοῦ, καθ' ἑκάστην ἐπαρχίαν δὶς τοῦ ἔτους συνόδους γίνεσθαι· ἵνα κοινῇ πάντων τῶν ἐπισκόπων τῆς ἐπαρχίας ἐπὶ τὸ αὐτὸ συναγομένων, τὰ τοιαῦτα ζητήματα ἐξετάζηται, καὶ οὕτως οἱ ὁμολογουμένως προσκεκρουκότες τῷ ἐπισκόπῳ, κατὰ λόγον ἀκοινώνητοι παρὰ πᾶσιν εἶναι δόξωσι, μέχρις ἂν τῷ κοινῷ τῶν ἐπισκόπων δόξῃ τὴν φιλανθρωποτέραν ὑπὲρ αὐτῶν ἐκθέσθαι ψῆφον. Αἱ δὲ σύνοδοι γινέσθωσαν, μία μὲν πρὸ τῆς Τεσσαρακοστῆς, ἵνα πάσης μικροψυχίας ἀναιρουμένης, τὸ δῶρον καθαρὸν προσφέρηται τῷ Θεῷ· δευτέρα δὲ, περὶ τὸν τοῦ μετοπώρου καιρόν.

CANON III.

The Great Synod has stringently forbidden any Bishop, Presbyter, Deacon, or any one of the Clergy whatever, to have any woman dwelling with him, except only a mother, or a sister, or an aunt, or such persons only as are beyond all suspicion.

CANON IV.

It is by all means proper that a Bishop should be appointed by all the Bishops in the Province; but should this be difficult, either on account of urgent necessity or because of distance, three at least should meet together, and the suffrages being taken, those of the absent [Bishops] also being communicated in writing, then the ordination should be made. But in every Province the ratification of what is done should be left to the Metropolitan.

CANON V.

Concerning those, whether of the Clergy or of the laity, who have been excommunicated by the Bishops in the several Provinces, let the provision of that Canon prevail which provides that persons who have been cast out by one Bishop are not to be readmitted by another. Nevertheless, inquiry should be made whether they have been excommunicated through captiousness, or contentiousness, or any such like ungracious disposition in the Bishop. And, that this matter may have due investigation, it is decreed that in every Province Synods shall be held twice every year; in order that, all the Bishops of the Province being assembled together, such questions may by them be thoroughly examined; that so those who have confessedly offended against their Bishop, may be seen to be for just cause excommunicated by all, until it shall seem fit to the common assembly of the Bishops to pronounce a milder sentence upon them. And let these Synods be held, the one before Lent, (that the pure Gift may be offered to God after all bitterness has been put away); and let the second be held about Autumn.

ΚΑΝΩΝ ϛʹ.

Τὰ ἀρχαῖα ἔθη κρατείτω, τὰ ἐν Αἰγύπτῳ, καὶ Λιβύῃ καὶ Πενταπόλει, ὥστε τὸν ἐν Ἀλεξανδρείᾳ ἐπίσκοπον πάντων τούτων ἔχειν τὴν ἐξουσίαν· ἐπειδὴ καὶ τῷ ἐν [τῇ] Ῥώμῃ ἐπισκόπῳ τοῦτο σύνηθές ἐστιν. Ὁμοίως δὲ καὶ κατὰ τὴν Ἀντιόχειαν, καὶ ἐν ταῖς ἄλλαις ἐπαρχίαις, τὰ πρεσβεῖα σώζεσθαι ταῖς ἐκκλησίαις. Καθόλου δὲ πρόδηλον ἐκεῖνο· ὅτι εἴ τις χωρὶς γνώμης τοῦ μητροπολίτου γένοιτο ἐπίσκοπος, τὸν τοιοῦτον ἡ μεγάλη σύνοδος ὥρισε μὴ δεῖν εἶναι ἐπίσκοπον. Ἐὰν μέντοι τῇ κοινῇ πάντων ψήφῳ, εὐλόγῳ οὔσῃ, καί κατὰ κανόνα ἐκκλησιαστικὸν, δύο, ἢ τρεῖς δι' οἰκείαν φιλονεικίαν ἀντιλέγωσι, κρατείτω ἡ τῶν πλειόνων ψῆφος.

ΚΑΝΩΝ Ζʹ.

Ἐπειδὴ συνήθεια κεκράτηκε, καὶ παράδοσις ἀρχαία, ὥστε τὸν ἐν Αἰλίᾳ ἐπίσκοπον τιμᾶσθαι, ἐχέτω τὴν ἀκολουθίαν τῆς τιμῆς· τῇ μητροπόλει σωζομένου τοῦ οἰκείου ἀξιώματος.

ΚΑΝΩΝ Ηʹ.

Περὶ τῶν ὀνομαζόντων μὲν ἑαυτοὺς Καθαρούς ποτε, προσερχομένων δὲ τῇ καθολικῇ καὶ ἀποστολικῇ ἐκκλησίᾳ, ἔδοξε τῇ ἁγίᾳ καὶ μεγάλῃ συνόδῳ, ὥστε χειροθετουμένους αὐτοὺς, μένειν οὕτως ἐν τῷ κλήρῳ. Πρὸ πάντων δὲ τοῦτο ὁμολογῆσαι αὐτοὺς ἐγγράφως προσήκει, ὅτι συνθήσονται καὶ ἀκολουθήσουσι τοῖς τῆς καθολικῆς καὶ ἀποστολικῆς ἐκκλησίας δόγμασι· τουτέστι, καὶ διγάμοις κοινωνεῖν, καὶ τοῖς ἐν τῷ διωγμῷ παραπεπτωκόσιν, ἐφ' ὧν καὶ χρόνος τέτακται, καὶ καιρὸς ὥρισται· ὥστε αὐτοὺς ἀκολουθεῖν ἐν πᾶσι τοῖς δόγμασι τῆς καθολικῆς ἐκκλησίας. Ἔνθα μὲν οὖν πάντες, εἴτε ἐν κώμαις, εἴτε ἐν πόλεσιν, αὐτοὶ μόνοι εὑρίσκοιντο χειροτονηθέντες, οἱ εὑρισκόμενοι ἐν τῷ κλήρῳ, ἔσονται ἐν τῷ αὐτῷ σχήματι. Εἰ δὲ τοῦ τῆς καθολικῆς ἐκκλησίας ἐπισκόπου, ἢ πρεσβυτέρου ὄντος, προσέρχονταί τινες, πρόδηλον, ὡς ὁ μὲν ἐπίσκοπος τῆς ἐκκλησίας ἕξει τὸ ἀξίωμα τοῦ ἐπισκόπου· ὁ δὲ ὀνομαζόμενος παρὰ τοῖς λεγομένοις Καθαροῖς ἐπίσκοπος, τὴν τοῦ πρεσβυτέρου τιμὴν

CANON VI.

Let the ancient customs prevail in Egypt, Lybia, and Pentapolis; so that the Bishop of Alexandria have jurisdiction in all these Provinces, since the like is customary for the Bishop of Rome also. Likewise in Antioch and the other Provinces, let the Churches retain their privileges. And this is to be universally understood, that, if any one be made Bishop without the consent of the Metropolitan, the Great Synod has declared that such a man ought not to be a Bishop. If, however, two or three Bishops shall from natural love of contradiction, oppose the common suffrage of the rest, it being favourable, and according to the Canon of the Church, then let the choice of the majority prevail.

CANON VII.

Since a custom and an ancient tradition have prevailed that the Bishop of Ælia [*i. e.*, Jerusalem] should be honoured, let him, saving its due dignity to the Metropolis [*i. e.*, Cæsarea], have the second place of honour [in the Province].

CANON VIII.

Concerning those who call themselves Cathari, if they come over to the Catholic and Apostolic Church, the Great and Holy Synod decrees that they who are ordained shall continue as they are, in the Clergy. But it is before all things necessary that they should profess in writing that they will observe and follow the decrees of the Catholic and Apostolic Church; in particular that they will communicate with persons who have been twice married, and with those who having lapsed in persecution have had a period [of penance] laid upon them, and a time [of restoration] fixed; and in general that they will follow the decrees of the Catholic Church. Wheresoever, then, whether in villages or in Cities, all of the ordained are found to be of these only, let them remain in the Clergy, and in the same rank in which they are found. But if they come over where there is a Presbyter or Bishop of the Catholic Church, it is manifest that the Bishop of the Church must have the Bishop's dignity; and he who is named Bishop by those who are called Cathari shall have the rank of Pres-

ἕξει· πλὴν εἰ μὴ ἄρα δοκοίη τῷ ἐπισκόπῳ, τῆς τιμῆς τοῦ ὀνόματος αὐτὸν μετέχειν. Εἰ δὲ τοῦτο αὐτῷ μὴ ἀρέσκοι, ἐπινοήσει τόπον ἢ χωρεπισκόπου, ἢ πρεσβυτέρου, ὑπὲρ τοῦ ἐν τῷ κλήρῳ ὅλως δοκεῖν εἶναι· ἵνα μὴ ἐν τῇ πόλει δύο ἐπίσκοποι ὦσιν.

ΚΑΝΩΝ Θʹ.

Εἴ τινες ἀνεξετάστως προήχθησαν πρεσβύτεροι, ἢ ἀνακρινόμενοι ὡμολόγησαν τὰ ἁμαρτήματα αὐτοῖς, καὶ, ὁμολογησάντων αὐτῶν, παρὰ κανόνα κινούμενοι οἱ ἄνθρωποι, τοῖς τοιούτοις χεῖρα ἐπιτεθείκασι, τούτους ὁ κανὼν οὐ προσίεται· τὸ γὰρ ἀνεπίληπτον ἐκδικεῖ ἡ καθολικὴ ἐκκλησία.

ΚΑΝΩΝ Iʹ.

Ὅσοι προεχειρίσθησαν τῶν παραπεπτωκότων, κατ᾿ ἄγνοιαν, ἢ καὶ προειδότων τῶν προχειρισαμένων, τοῦτο οὐ προκρίνει τῷ κανόνι τῷ ἐκκλησιαστικῷ· γνωσθέντες γὰρ, καθαιροῦνται.

ΚΑΝΩΝ IAʹ.

Περὶ τῶν παραβάντων χωρὶς ἀνάγκης, ἢ χωρὶς ἀφαιρέσεως ὑπαρχόντων, ἢ χωρὶς κινδύνου, ἤ τινος τοιούτου, ὃ γέγονεν ἐπὶ τῆς τυραννίδος Λικινίου, ἔδοξε τῇ συνόδῳ, εἰ καὶ ἀνάξιοι ἦσαν φιλανθρωπίας, ὅμως χρηστεύσασθαι εἰς αὐτούς. Ὅσοι οὖν γνησίως μεταμέλονται, τρία ἔτη ἐν ἀκροωμένοις ποιήσουσιν, οἱ πιστοί, καὶ ἑπτὰ ἔτη ὑποπεσοῦνται· δύω δὲ ἔτη χωρὶς προσφορᾶς κοινωνήσουσι τῷ λαῷ τῶν προσευχῶν.

ΚΑΝΩΝ IBʹ.

Οἱ δὲ προσκληθέντες μὲν ὑπὸ τῆς χάριτος, καὶ τὴν πρώτην ὁρμὴν ἐνδειξάμενοι, καὶ ἀποθέμενοι τὰς ζώνας, μετὰ δὲ ταῦτα ἐπὶ τὸν οἰκεῖον ἔμετον ἀναδραμόντες, ὡς κύνες, ὥς τινὰς καὶ ἀργύρια προέσθαι, καὶ βενεφικίοις κατορθῶσαι τὸ ἀναστρατεύσασθαι· οὗτοι δέκα ἔτη ὑποπιπτέτωσαν, μετὰ

byter, unless it shall seem fit to the Bishop to admit him to partake in the honour of the episcopal name. Or, if this should not be satisfactory, then shall the Bishop provide for him a place as Chorepiscopus, or Presbyter, in order that he may be evidently seen to be of the Clergy, and that there may not be two Bishops in the City.

CANON IX.

If any Presbyters have been advanced without examination, or if upon examination they have made confession of crime, and men acting in violation of the Canon have laid hands upon them, notwithstanding their confession, these men the Canon does not admit; for the Catholic Church justifies that [only] which is blameless.

CANON X.

If any who have lapsed have been ordained through the ignorance, or even with the previous knowledge, of the ordainers, this shall not prejudice the Canon of the Church; for when they are discovered they shall be deposed.

CANON XI.

Concerning those who have fallen without compulsion, without the spoiling of their property, without [personal] danger, or the like, as happened during the tyranny of Licinius, the Synod declares that, though they have deserved no clemency, they shall be dealt with mercifully. As many former communicants, therefore, as shall heartily repent, shall pass three years among the hearers; for seven years they shall be prostrators; and for two years they shall communicate with the people in prayers [*i. e.*, as co-standers], but without [being admitted to] the Oblation.

CANON XII.

As many as had been called by grace, and had at first displayed their zeal, but who, having cast aside their military girdles, afterwards returned, like dogs, to their own vomit, (so that some spent money and by means of gifts regained their military stations); let these, after they have passed the

τὸν τῆς τριετοῦς ἀκροάσεως χρόνον. Ἐφ' ἅπασι δὲ τούτοις, προσήκει ἐξετάζειν τὴν προαίρεσιν καὶ τὸ εἶδος τῆς μετανοίας. Ὅσοι μὲν γὰρ φόβῳ, καὶ δάκρυσι, καὶ ὑπομονῇ, καὶ ἀγαθοεργίαις, τὴν ἐπιστροφὴν ἔργῳ, καὶ οὐ σχήματι, ἐπιδείκνυνται, οὗτοι πληρώσαντες τὸν χρόνον τὸν ὡρισμένον τῆς ἀκροάσεως, εἰκότως τῶν εὐχῶν κοινωνήσουσι, μετὰ τοῦ ἐξεῖναι τῷ ἐπισκόπῳ καὶ φιλανθρωπότερόν τι περὶ αὐτῶν βουλεύσασθαι. Ὅσοι δὲ ἀδιαφόρως ἤνεγκαν, καὶ τὸ σχῆμα τοῦ εἰσιέναι εἰς τὴν ἐκκλησίαν ἀρκεῖν ἑαυτοῖς ἡγήσαντο πρὸς τὴν ἐπιστροφήν, ἐξ ἅπαντος πληρούτωσαν τὸν χρόνον.

ΚΑΝΩΝ ΙΓ'.

Περὶ δὲ τῶν ἐξοδευόντων, ὁ παλαιὸς καὶ κανονικὸς νόμος φυλαχθήσεται καὶ νῦν, ὥστε, εἴ τις ἐξοδεύοι, τοῦ τελευταίου καὶ ἀναγκαιοτάτου ἐφοδίου μὴ ἀποστερεῖσθαι. Εἰ δὲ ἀπογνωσθεὶς, καὶ κοινωνίας τυχὼν, πάλιν ἐν τοῖς ζῶσιν ἐξετασθῇ, μετὰ τῶν κοινωνούντων τῆς εὐχῆς μόνης ἔστω. Καθόλου δὲ καὶ περὶ παντὸς οὑτινοσοῦν ἐξοδεύοντος, αἰτοῦντος τοῦ μετασχεῖν εὐχαριστίας, ὁ ἐπίσκοπος μετὰ δοκιμασίας μεταδιδότω τῆς προσφορᾶς.

ΚΑΝΩΝ ΙΔ'.

Περὶ τῶν κατηχουμένων, καὶ παραπεσόντων, ἔδοξε τῇ ἁγίᾳ καὶ μεγάλῃ συνόδῳ, ὥστε, τριῶν ἐτῶν αὐτοὺς ἀκροωμένους μόνον, μετὰ ταῦτα εὔχεσθαι μετὰ τῶν κατηχουμένων.

ΚΑΝΩΝ ΙΕ'.

Διὰ τὸν πολὺν τάραχον, καὶ τὰς στάσεις τὰς γινομένας, ἔδοξε παντάπασι περιαιρεθῆναι τὴν συνήθειαν, τὴν παρὰ τὸν ἀποστολικὸν κανόνα εὑρεθεῖσαν ἔν τισι μέρεσιν, ὥστε ἀπὸ πόλεως εἰς πόλιν μὴ μεταβαίνειν, μήτε ἐπίσκοπον, μήτε πρεσβύτερον, μήτε διάκονον. Εἰ δέ τις, μετὰ τὸν τῆς ἁγίας καὶ μεγάλης συνόδου ὅρον, τοιούτῳ τινὶ ἐπιχειρήσειεν, ἢ ἐπιδοίη ἑαυτὸν πράγματι τοιούτῳ, ἀκυρωθήσεται ἐξ ἅπαντος τὸ κατασκεύασμα, καὶ ἀποκατασταθήσεται τῇ ἐκκλησίᾳ, ἐν ᾗ ὁ ἐπίσκοπος, ἢ ὁ πρεσβύτερος ἐχειροτονήθη.

space of three years as hearers, be for ten years prostrators. But in all these cases it is necessary to examine well into the purpose and appearance of repentance. For as many as give evidence of their conversion by deeds, and not pretence, by fearfulness, and tears, and perseverance, and good works, when they have fulfilled their appointed time as hearers, may properly communicate in prayers [*i. e.*, as co-standers]; and after that the Bishop may determine yet more favourably concerning them. But those who take [the matter] with indifference, and who think the form of entering the Church is sufficient for their conversion, must fulfil the whole time.

CANON XIII.

Concerning the departing, the ancient canonical law is still to be maintained; to wit, that, if any man be at the point of death, he must not be deprived of the last most indispensable provision for the way. But, if any one should be restored to health again who has received the Communion when his life was despaired of, let him remain among those who communicate in prayers only [*i. e.*, as co-standers]. But in general, and in the case of any dying person whatsoever asking to receive the Eucharist, let the Bishop, after examination made, impart to him of the Oblation.

CANON XIV.

Concerning Catechumens who have lapsed, the Holy and Great Synod has decreed that, after they have passed three years only as hearers, they shall pray with the [other] Catechumens.

CANON XV.

On account of the great disturbance and discords that occur, it is decreed that the custom prevailing in certain places, contrary to the [Apostolical] Canon, must by all means be done away; so that neither Bishop, Presbyter, nor Deacon shall pass from City to City. And if any one, after this decree of the Holy and Great Synod, shall attempt any such thing, or continue in any such course, his proceedings shall be utterly void, and he shall be restored to the Church in which he was ordained Bishop or Presbyter.

ΚΑΝΩΝ Ιϛʹ.

Ὅσοι ῥιψοκινδύνως, μήτε τὸν φόβον τοῦ Θεοῦ πρὸ ὀφθαλμῶν ἔχοντες, μήτε τὸν ἐκκλησιαστικὸν κανόνα εἰδότες, ἀναχωρήσουσι τῆς ἰδίας ἐκκλησίας, πρεσβύτεροι ἢ διάκονοι, ἢ ὅλως ἐν τῷ κανόνι ἐξεταζόμενοι, οὗτοι οὐδαμῶς δεκτοὶ ὀφείλουσιν εἶναι ἐν ἑτέρᾳ ἐκκλησίᾳ· ἀλλὰ πᾶσαν αὐτοῖς ἀνάγκην ἐπάγεσθαι χρὴ, ἀναστρέφειν εἰς τὰς ἑαυτῶν παροικίας· ἢ, ἐπιμένοντας, ἀκοινωνήτους εἶναι προσήκει. Εἰ δὲ καὶ τολμήσειέ τις ὑφαρπάσαι τὸν τῷ ἑτέρῳ διαφέροντα, καὶ χειροτονῆσαι ἐν τῇ αὐτοῦ ἐκκλησίᾳ, μὴ συγκατατιθεμένου τοῦ ἰδίου ἐπισκόπου, οὗ ἀνεχώρησεν ὁ ἐν τῷ κανόνι ἐξεταζόμενος, ἄκυρος ἔστω ἡ χειροτονία.

ΚΑΝΩΝ ΙΖʹ.

Ἐπειδὴ πολλοὶ ἐν τῷ κανόνι ἐξεταζόμενοι, τὴν πλεονεξίαν, καὶ τὴν αἰσχροκέρδειαν διώκοντες, ἐπελάθοντο τοῦ θείου γράμματος λέγοντος· τὸ ἀργύριον αὐτοῦ οὐκ ἔδωκεν ἐπὶ τόκῳ· καὶ δανείζοντες, ἑκατοστὰς ἀπαιτοῦσιν· ἐδικαίωσεν ἡ ἁγία καὶ μεγάλη σύνοδος, ὡς εἴ τις εὑρεθείη μετὰ τὸν ὅρον τοῦτον τόκους λαμβάνων, ἐκ μεταχειρίσεως, ἢ ἄλλως μετερχόμενος τὸ πρᾶγμα, ἢ ἡμιολίας ἀπαιτῶν, ἢ ὅλως ἕτερόν τι ἐπινοῶν αἰσχροῦ κέρδους ἕνεκα, καθαιρεθήσεται τοῦ κλήρου, καὶ ἀλλότριος τοῦ κανόνος ἔσται.

ΚΑΝΩΝ ΙΗʹ.

Ἦλθεν εἰς τὴν ἁγίαν καὶ μεγάλην σύνοδον, ὅτι ἔν τισι τόποις καὶ πόλεσι, τοῖς πρεσβυτέροις τὴν εὐχαριστίαν οἱ διάκονοι διδόασιν· ὅπερ οὔτε ὁ κανὼν, οὔτε ἡ συνήθεια παρέδωκε, τοὺς ἐξουσίαν μὴ ἔχοντας προσφέρειν, τοῖς προσφέρουσι διδόναι τὸ σῶμα τοῦ Χριστοῦ. Κακεῖνο δὲ ἐγνωρίσθη, ὅτι ἤδη τινὲς τῶν διακόνων καὶ πρὸ τῶν ἐπισκόπων τῆς εὐχαριστίας ἅπτονται. Ταῦτα οὖν πάντα περιῃρείσθω, καὶ ἐμμενέτωσαν οἱ διάκονοι τοῖς ἰδίοις μέτροις, εἰδότες, ὅτι, τοῦ μὲν ἐπισκόπου ὑπηρέται εἰσὶ, τῶν δέ πρεσβυτέρων ἐλάττους. Λαμβανέτωσαν δὲ κατὰ τὴν τάξιν τὴν εὐχαριστίαν μετὰ τοὺς πρεσβυτέρους, ἢ τοῦ ἐπισκόπου μεταδιδόντος αὐτοῖς, ἢ τοῦ πρεσβυτέρου· Ἀλλὰ μηδὲ καθῆσθαι ἐν μέσῳ τῶν πρεσβυτέρων ἐξέστω τοῖς

CANON XVI.

Neither Presbyters, nor Deacons, nor any others enrolled among the Clergy, who, not having the fear of God before their eyes, nor regarding the Canon of the Church, shall recklessly remove from their own Church, ought by any means to be received by another Church ; but every constraint should be applied to restore them to their own Parishes ; and, if they will not go, they must be suspended from their ministry. And if any [Bishop] shall dare surreptitiously to take and in his own Church ordain a man belonging to another, without the consent of his own proper Bishop, from whom he has seceded, let the ordination be void.

CANON XVII.

Forasmuch as many enrolled among the Clergy, following covetousness and lust of gain, have forgotten the divine Scripture, which says, "He gave not his money upon usury," and in lending money ask the hundredth of the sum [as monthly interest], the Holy and Great Synod thinks it just that if after this decree any one be found to receive usury, whether he accomplish it by secret transaction or otherwise, as by demanding the whole and one half [in kind], or by using any other contrivance whatever for filthy lucre's sake, he shall be deposed from the Clergy and [his name] erased from the list.

CANON XVIII.

It has come to the knowledge of the Holy and Great Synod that, in some Districts and Cities, the Deacons administer the Eucharist to the Presbyters, whereas neither Canon nor custom permits that they who have no right to offer should administer the Body of Christ to them that do offer [It]. And this also has been made known, that certain Deacons now receive the Eucharist even before their Bishops. Let all such practices be utterly done away ; and let the Deacons remain within their own bounds, knowing that they are the ministers of the Bishop and the inferiors of the Presbyters. Let them receive the Eucharist according to their order, after the Presbyters ; and let either the Bishop or the Presbyter administer

διακόνοις· παρὰ κανόνα γὰρ, καὶ παρὰ τάξιν ἐστὶ τὸ γινόμενον. Εἰ δέ τις μὴ θέλοι πειθαρχεῖν καὶ μετὰ τούτους τοὺς ὅρους, πεπαύσθω τῆς διακονίας.

ΚΑΝΩΝ ΙΘ'.

Περὶ τῶν Παυλιανισάντων, εἶτα προσφυγόντων τῇ καθολικῇ ἐκκλησίᾳ, ὅρος ἐκτέθειται ἀναβαπτίζεσθαι αὐτοὺς ἐξάπαντος. Εἰ δέ τινες τῷ παρεληλυθότι χρόνῳ, ἐν τῷ κλήρῳ ἐξητάσθησαν, εἰ μὲν ἄμεμπτοι καὶ ἀνεπίληπτοι φανεῖεν, ἀναβαπτισθέντες, χειροτονείσθωσαν ὑπὸ τοῦ τῆς καθολικῆς ἐκκλησίας ἐπισκόπου. Εἰ δὲ ἡ ἀνάκρισις ἀνεπιτηδείους αὐτοὺς εὑρίσκοι, καθαιρεῖσθαι αὐτοὺς προσήκει. Ὡσαύτως δὲ καὶ περὶ τῶν διακονισσῶν, καὶ ὅλως περὶ τῶν ἐν τῷ κλήρῳ ἐξεταζομένων ὁ αὐτὸς τύπος παραφυλαχθήσεται. Ἐμνήσθημεν δὲ τῶν διακονισσῶν τῶν ἐν τῷ σχήματι ἐξετασθεισῶν, ἐπεὶ μηδὲ χειροθεσίαν τινὰ ἔχουσιν, ὥστε ἐξάπαντος ἐν τοῖς λαϊκοῖς αὐτὰς ἐξετάζεσθαι.*

ΚΑΝΩΝ Κ'.

Ἐπειδή τινές εἰσιν ἐν τῇ κυριακῇ γόνυ κλίνοντες, καὶ ἐν ταῖς τῆς πεντηκοστῆς ἡμέραις· ὑπὲρ τοῦ πάντα ἐν πάσῃ παροικίᾳ ὁμοίως παραφυλάττεσθαι, ἑστῶτας ἔδοξε τῇ ἁγίᾳ συνόδῳ τὰς εὐχὰς ἀποδιδόναι τῷ Θεῷ.

* Others read ἐν τῳ κανόνι, on the Clergy List. There is no difference in the sense; the reference being merely to the customary enrolment of the διακονισσαί on the roll of persons specially recognized by the Church.

to them. Furthermore, let not the Deacons sit among the Presbyters, for that is contrary to Canon and order. And if, after this decree, any one shall refuse to obey, let him be deposed from the Diaconate.

CANON XIX.

Concerning the Paulianists who have returned to the Catholic Church, it has been decreed that they must by all means be rebaptized; and if any of them who in past time have been numbered among their Clergy should be found blameless and without reproach, let them be rebaptized and ordained by the Bishop of the Catholic Church; but if the examination should discover them to be unfit, they ought to be deposed. Likewise in the case of their Deaconesses, and generally in the case of those who have been enrolled among their Clergy, let the same form be observed. And we have considered the Deaconesses who have assumed the habit [of their order], but these, since they have no imposition of hands, are to be numbered only among the laity.

CANON XX.

Forasmuch as there are certain persons who kneel on the Lord's Day and in the days of Pentecost, therefore, to the intent that all things may be uniformly observed in every Parish, it seems good to the Holy Synod that, at these times, all should offer up their prayers standing.

SECOND GENERAL COUNCIL.

CONSTANTINOPLE.

SYMBOLUM CONSTANTINOPOL.

AD EXEMPLAR, QUOD EXTAT IN ACTIS

CHALCEDONENSIS CONCILII.

Πιστεύομεν εἰς ἕνα Θεὸν, Πατέρα, παντοκράτορα, ποιητὴν οὐρανοῦ καὶ γῆς, ὁράτων τε πάντων καὶ ἀοράτων·

Καὶ εἰς ἕνα Κύριον Ἰησοῦν Χριστὸν, τὸν Υἱὸν τοῦ Θεοῦ τὸν μονογενῆ, τὸν ἐκ τοῦ Πατρὸς γεννηθέντα πρὸ πάντων τῶν αἰώνων, φῶς ἐκ φωτὸς, Θεὸν ἀληθινὸν ἐκ Θεοῦ ἀληθινοῦ, γεννηθέντα, οὐ ποιηθέντα, ὁμοούσιον τῷ Πατρί· δι' οὗ τὰ πάντα ἐγένετο· τὸν δι' ἡμᾶς τοὺς ἀνθρώπους, καὶ διὰ τὴν ἡμετέραν σωτηρίαν, κατελθόντα ἐκ τῶν οὐρανῶν, καὶ σαρκωθέντα ἐκ Πνεύματος Ἁγίου καὶ Μαρίας τῆς παρθένου, καὶ ἐνανθρωπήσαντα, σταυρωθέντα τε ὑπὲρ ἡμῶν ἐπὶ Ποντίου Πιλάτου, καὶ παθόντα, καὶ ταφέντα, καὶ ἀναστάντα τῇ τρίτῃ ἡμέρᾳ κατὰ τὰς γραφάς, καὶ ἀνελθόντα εἰς τοὺς οὐρανοὺς, καὶ καθεζόμενον ἐκ δεξιῶν τοῦ Πατρὸς, καὶ πάλιν ἐρχόμενον μετὰ δόξης κρῖναι ζῶντας καὶ νεκρούς· οὗ τῆς βασιλείας οὐκ ἔσται τέλος·

Καὶ εἰς τὸ Πνεῦμα τὸ Ἅγιον, τὸ Κύριον, καὶ τὸ ζωοποιὸν· τὸ ἐκ τοῦ Πατρὸς ἐκπορευόμενον· τὸ σὺν Πατρὶ καὶ Υἱῷ συμπροσκυνούμενον καὶ συνδοξαζόμενον· τὸ λαλῆσαν διὰ τῶν προφητῶν·

Εἰς μίαν ἁγίαν καθολικὴν καὶ ἀποστολικὴν ἐκκλησίαν. Ὁμολογοῦμεν ἓν βάπτισμα εἰς ἄφεσιν ἁμαρτιῶν· προσδοκῶμεν ἀνάστασιν νεκρῶν, καὶ ζωὴν τοῦ μέλλοντος αἰῶνος. Ἀμήν.

THE CONSTANTINOPOLITAN CREED.

AS CONTAINED IN THE ACTS OF THE COUNCIL

OF CHALCEDON.

We believe in one God, the Father, Almighty, Maker of heaven and earth, and of all things visible and invisible:

And in one Lord Jesus Christ, the only begotten Son of God, Begotten of the Father before all worlds, Light of Light, Very God of Very God, Begotten, not made, Being of one substance with the Father; By Whom all things were made; Who, for us men and for our salvation, came down from heaven, And was incarnate of the Holy Ghost and Mary the Virgin, And was made Man, And was crucified for us under Pontius Pilate, And suffered, And was buried, And the third day rose again according to the Scriptures, And ascended into heaven, And sitteth on the right hand of the Father, And cometh again with glory to judge the quick and the dead; Of Whose Kingdom there shall be no end:

And in the Holy Ghost, the Lord, and the Giver of life; Who proceedeth from the Father; Who with the Father and the Son is together worshipped and glorified; Who spake by the prophets:

[And] in One, Holy, Catholic, and Apostolic Church. We acknowledge one Baptism for the remission of sins: We look for the resurrection of the dead, And the life of the world to come. Amen.

CANONES

CONCILII CONSTANTINOPOLITANI GENERALIS.

A.D. 381.

Epistola Synodi ad Theodosium Magnum.

Τῷ εὐσεβεστάτῳ βασιλεῖ Θεοδοσίῳ ἡ ἁγία σύνοδος τῶν ἐπισκόπων τῶν ἐκ διαφόρων ἐπαρχιῶν συνελθόντων ἐν Κωνσταντινουπόλει.

Ἀρχὴ μὲν ἡμῖν τοῦ πρὸς τὴν σὴν εὐσέβειαν γράμματος, εὐχαριστία πρὸς τὸν Θεὸν τὸν ἀναδείξαντα τῆς ὑμετέρας εὐσεβείας τὴν βασιλείαν, ἐπὶ κοινῇ τῶν ἐκκλησιῶν εἰρήνῃ καὶ τῆς ὑγιοῦς πίστεως στηριγμῷ· ἀποδιδόντες δὲ τῷ Θεῷ τὴν ὀφειλομένην εὐχαριστίαν, ἀναγκαίως καὶ τὰ γεγενημένα κατὰ τὴν ἁγίαν σύνοδον πρὸς τὴν σὴν εὐσέβειαν ἀναφέρομεν· καὶ ὅτι συνελθόντες εἰς τὴν Κωνσταντινούπολιν κατὰ τὸ γράμμα τῆς σῆς εὐσεβείας, πρῶτον μὲν ἀνενεωσάμεθα τὴν πρὸς ἀλλήλους ὁμόνοιαν· ἔπειτα δὲ καὶ συντόμους ὅρους ἐξεφωνήσαμεν, τήν τε τῶν πατέρων πίστιν τῶν ἐν Νικαίᾳ κυρώσαντες, καὶ τὰς κατ' αὐτῆς ἐκφυείσας αἱρέσεις ἀναθεματίσαντες. Πρὸς δὲ τούτοις, καὶ ὑπὲρ τῆς εὐταξίας τῶν ἐκκλησιῶν ῥητοὺς κανόνας ὡρίσαμεν· ἅπερ ἅπαντα τῷδε ἡμῶν τῷ γράμματι ὑπετάξαμεν. Δεόμεθα τοίνυν τῆς σῆς εὐσεβείας ἐπικυρωθῆναι τῆς συνόδου τὴν ψῆφον· ἵν' ὥσπερ τοῖς τῆς κλήσεως γράμμασι τὴν ἐκκλησίαν τετίμηκας, οὕτω καὶ τῶν δοξάντων ἐπισφραγίσῃς τὸ τέλος. Ὁ δὲ Κύριος στηρίξῃ σου τὴν βασιλείαν ἐν εἰρήνῃ καὶ δικαιοσύνῃ, καὶ παραπέμψῃ γενεαῖς γενεῶν, καὶ προσθείη τῷ ἐπιγείῳ κράτει καὶ τῆς βασιλείας τῆς ἐπουρανίου τὴν ἀπόλαυσιν. Ἐῤῥωμένον σε, καὶ ἐν πᾶσι τοῖς καλοῖς διαπρέποντα ὁ Θεὸς χαρίσαιτο τῇ οἰκουμένῃ, εὐχαῖς τῶν ἁγίων, τὸν ὡς ἀληθῶς εὐσεβέστατον καὶ θεοφιλέστατον βασιλέα.

CANONS OF CONSTANTINOPLE.

Letter of the Synod to the Emperor Theodosius the Great.

To the most religious Emperor Theodosius, the Holy Synod of Bishops assembled in Constantinople out of different Provinces.

We begin our letter to your Piety with thanks to God, who has established the empire of your Piety for the common peace of the Churches and for the support of the true Faith. And, having rendered due thanks unto God, it is meet that we should lay before your Piety the things which have been done in the Holy Synod. When, then, we had assembled in Constantinople, according to the letter of your Piety, we first of all renewed our unity of heart each with the other, and then we pronounced some concise definitions, ratifying the Faith of the Nicene Fathers, and anathematizing the heresies which have sprung up, contrary thereto. Besides these things, we also framed certain Canons for the better ordering of the Churches, all which we have subjoined to this our letter. Wherefore we beseech your Piety that the decree of the Synod may be ratified, and that, as you have honoured the Church by your letter of citation, so you should set your seal to the conclusion of what has been decreed. May the Lord establish your empire in peace and righteousness, and prolong it from generation to generation; and may He add unto your earthly power fruition of the heavenly kingdom also. May God shew favour to the world, by granting to the prayers of his saints that you may prosper and be eminent in all good things as a most truly pious and religious Emperor.

Τάδε ὥρισαν οἱ ἐν Κωνσταντινουπόλει χάριτι Θεοῦ συνελθόντες ἐπίσκοποι ἐκ διαφόρων ἐπαρχιῶν κατὰ κλῆσιν τοῦ εὐσεβεστάτου βασιλέως Θεοδοσίου.

ΚΑΝΩΝ Α'.

Μὴ ἀθετεῖσθαι τὴν πίστιν τῶν Πατέρων τῶν τριακοσίων δεκαοκτὼ, τῶν ἐν Νικαίᾳ τῆς Βιθυνίας συνελθόντων· ἀλλὰ μένειν ἐκείνην κυρίαν, καὶ ἀναθεματισθῆναι πᾶσαν αἵρεσιν· καὶ ἰδικῶς τὴν τῶν Εὐνομιανῶν, εἴτουν Εὐδοξιανῶν, καὶ τὴν τῶν Ἡμιαρείων, εἴτουν Πνευματομάχων, καὶ τὴν τῶν Σαβελλιανῶν, καὶ τῆν τῶν Μαρκελλιανῶν, καὶ τὴν τῶν Φωτεινιανῶν, καὶ τὴν τῶν Ἀπολλιναριστῶν.

ΚΑΝΩΝ Β'.

Τοὺς ὑπὲρ διοίκησιν ἐπισκόπους ταῖς ὑπερορίοις ἐκκλησίαις μὴ ἐπιέναι, μηδὲ συγχέειν τὰς ἐκκλησίας· ἀλλὰ κατὰ τοὺς κανόνας, τὸν μὲν Ἀλεξανδρείας ἐπίσκοπον, τὰ ἐν Αἰγύπτῳ μόνον οἰκονομεῖν· τοὺς δὲ τῆς Ἀνατολῆς ἐπισκόπους, τὴν Ἀνατολὴν μόνην διοικεῖν· φυλαττομένων τῶν ἐν τοῖς κανόσι τοῖς κατὰ Νίκαιαν πρεσβείων τῇ Ἀντιοχέων ἐκκλησίᾳ· καὶ τοὺς τῆς Ἀσιανῆς διοικήσεως ἐπισκόπους, τὰ κατὰ τὴν Ἀσιανὴν μόνον διοικεῖν· καὶ τοὺς τῆς Ποντικῆς, τὰ τῆς Ποντικῆς μόνον· καὶ τοὺς τῆς Θρᾳκῆς, τὰ τῆς Θρᾳκικῆς μόνον οἰκονομεῖν. Ἀκλήτους δὲ ἐπισκόπους ὑπὲρ διοίκησιν μὴ ἐπιβαίνειν ἐπὶ χειροτονίᾳ, ἤ τισιν ἄλλαις οἰκονομίαις ἐκκλησιαστικαῖς. Φυλαττομένου δὲ τοῦ προγεγραμμένου περὶ τῶν διοικήσεων κανόνος, εὔδηλον ὡς τὰ καθ' ἑκάστην ἐπαρχίαν ἡ τῆς ἐπαρχίας σύνοδος διοικήσει, κατὰ τὰ ἐν Νικαίᾳ ὡρισμένα. Τὰς δὲ ἐν τοῖς βαρβαρικοῖς ἔθνεσι τοῦ Θεοῦ ἐκκλησίας, οἰκονομεῖσθαι χρὴ κατὰ τὴν κρατήσασαν συνήθειαν τῶν πατέρων.

ΚΑΝΩΝ Γ'.

Τὸν μέν τοι Κωνσταντινουπόλεως ἐπίσκοπον ἔχειν τὰ πρεσβεῖα τῆς τιμῆς μετὰ τὸν τῆς Ῥώμης ἐπίσκοπον, διὰ τὸ εἶναι αὐτὴν νέαν Ῥώμην.

The Bishops out of different Provinces assembled by the grace of God in Constantinople, on the summons of the most religious Emperor Theodosius, have decreed as follows:

CANON I.

The Faith of the Three Hundred and Eighteen Fathers assembled at Nicæa in Bithynia shall not be set aside, but shall stand fast. And every heresy shall be anathematized, particularly that of the Eunomians or Eudoxians, and that of the Semi-Arians or Pneumatomachi, and that of the Sabellians, and that of the Marcellians, and that of the Photinians, and that of the Apollinarians.

CANON II.

The Bishops of a Diocese are not to invade Churches lying outside of their bounds, nor bring confusion on the Churches; but let the Bishop of Alexandria, according to the Canons, alone administer the affairs of Egypt; and let the Bishops of the East manage the East only, saving the privileges of the Church in Antioch, which are mentioned in the Canons of Nicæa; and let the Bishops of the Asian Diocese administer the Asian affairs only; and the Pontic Bishops only Pontic matters; and the Thracian Bishops only Thracian affairs. And let not Bishops go beyond their Diocese for ordination or any other ecclesiastical administration, unless they be invited. And the aforesaid Canon concerning Dioceses being observed, it is evident that the Synod of every Province will administer the affairs of that particular Province as was decreed at Nicæa. But the Churches of God in heathen nations must be governed according to the custom which has prevailed among their forefathers.

CANON III.

The Bishop of Constantinople shall have the privilege of rank next after the Bishop of Rome; because Constantinople is New Rome.

ΚΑΝΩΝ Δ'.

Περὶ Μαξίμου τοῦ κυνικοῦ, καὶ τῆς κατ' αὐτὸν ἀταξίας τῆς ἐν Κωνσταντινουπόλει γενομένης, ὥστε μήτε τὸν Μάξιμον ἐπίσκοπον ἢ γενέσθαι, ἢ εἶναι, μήτε τοὺς παρ' αὐτοῦ χειροτονηθέντας, ἐν οἱῳδήποτε βαθμῷ κλήρου· πάντων καὶ τῶν περὶ αὐτὸν, καὶ τῶν παρ' αὐτοῦ γενομένων ἀκυρωθέντων.

ΚΑΝΩΝ Ε'.

Περὶ τοῦ τόμου τῶν δυτικῶν, καὶ τοὺς ἐν Ἀντιοχείᾳ ἀπεδεξάμεθα, τοὺς μίαν ὁμολογοῦντας Πατρὸς καὶ Υἱοῦ καὶ Ἁγίου Πνεύματος Θεότητα.

ΚΑΝΩΝ ϛ'.

Ἐπειδὴ πολλοὶ τὴν ἐκκλησιαστικὴν εὐταξίαν συγχεῖν καὶ ἀνατρέπειν βουλόμενοι, φιλέχθρως καὶ συκοφαντικῶς αἰτίας τινὰς κατὰ τῶν οἰκονομούντων τὰς ἐκκλησίας ὀρθοδόξων ἐπισκόπων συμπλάσσουσιν, οὐδὲν ἕτερον ἢ χραίνειν τὰς τῶν ἱερέων ὑπολήψεις, καὶ ταραχὰς τῶν εἰρηνευόντων λαῶν κατασκευάζειν ἐπιχειροῦντες· τούτου ἕνεκεν ἤρεσε τῇ ἁγίᾳ συνόδῳ τῶν ἐν Κωνσταντινουπόλει συνδραμόντων ἐπισκόπων, μὴ ἀνεξετάστως προσίεσθαι τοὺς κατηγόρους, μηδὲ πᾶσιν ἐπιτρέπειν τὰς κατηγορίας ποιεῖσθαι κατὰ τῶν οἰκονομούντων τὰς ἐκκλησίας, μηδὲ μὴν πάντας ἀποκλείειν. Ἀλλ' εἰ μέν τις οἰκείαν τινὰ μέμψιν, τοῦτ' ἔστιν, ἰδιωτικὴν, ἐπαγάγοι τῷ ἐπισκόπῳ, ὡς πλεονεκτηθεὶς, ἢ ἄλλο τι παρὰ τὸ δίκαιον παρ' αὐτοῦ πεπονθώς, ἐπὶ τῶν τοιούτων κατηγοριῶν μὴ ἐξετάζεσθαι, μήτε πρόσωπον τοῦ κατηγόρου, μήτε τὴν θρησκείαν. Χρὴ γὰρ παντὶ τρόπῳ, τότε συνειδὸς τοῦ ἐπισκόπου ἐλεύθερον εἶναι, καὶ τὸν ἀδικεῖσθαι λέγοντα, οἵας ἂν ᾖ θρησκείας, τῶν δικαίων τυγχάνειν. Εἰ δὲ ἐκκλησιαστικὸν εἴη τὸ ἐπιφερόμενον ἔγκλημα τῷ ἐπισκόπῳ, τότε δοκιμάζεσθαι χρὴ τῶν κατηγορούντων τὰ πρόσωπα· ἵνα πρῶτον μὲν αἱρετικοῖς μὴ ἐξῇ κατηγορίας κατὰ τῶν ὀρθοδόξων ἐπισκόπων ὑπὲρ ἐκκλησιαστικῶν πραγμάτων ποιεῖσθαι. Αἱρετικοὺς δὲ λέγομεν, τούς τε πάλαι τῆς ἐκκλησίας ἀποκηρυχθέντας, καὶ τοὺς μετὰ ταῦτα ὑφ' ἡμῶν ἀναθεματισθέντας· πρὸς δὲ τούτοις,

CANON IV.

Concerning Maximus the Cynic and the disorder which has existed in Constantinople on his account, it is decreed that Maximus is not now and never was a Bishop ; that those who have been ordained by him are in no rank whatever of the Clergy ; and all which has been done by him, or concerning him, has been declared to be of no effect.

CANON V.

In regard to the book cf the Western [Bishops], we receive those in Antioch also who confess the one Deity of FATHER, SON, and HOLY GHOST.

CANON VI.

Forasmuch as many persons, wishing to confuse and overturn the wholesome order of the Church, do contentiously and slanderously fabricate charges against the orthodox Bishops who have the administration of the Churches, intending nothing else than to stain the reputation of the Priests and raise up disturbances amongst the peaceful laity ; therefore it seemed right to the Holy Synod of Bishops assembled together in Constantinople, not to admit accusers without examination; and neither to allow all persons whatsoever to bring accusations against the rulers of the Church, nor, on the other hand, to exclude all. If then, any one shall bring a private complaint against the Bishop, that is, one relating to his own affairs, as, for example, that he has been defrauded, or otherwise unjustly treated by him, in such accusations no examination shall be made, either of the person or of the religion of the accuser ; for it is by all means necessary that the conscience of the Bishop should be free, and that he who says he has been wronged should meet with righteous judgment, of whatever faith he be. But if the charge alleged against the Bishop be that of some ecclesiastical offence, then it is necessary to regard the persons of the prosecutors ; that, in the first place, heretics may not be suffered to bring accusations touching Church affairs against orthodox Bishops. And by heretics we mean both those who were aforetime cast out and those whom we ourselves have since anathematized, and also

καὶ τοὺς τὴν πίστιν μὲν τὴν ὑγιῆ προσποιουμένους ὁμολογεῖν, ἀποσχίσαντας δὲ, καὶ ἀντισυνάγοντας τοῖς κανονικοῖς ἡμῶν ἐπισκόποις. Ἔπειτα δὲ, καὶ εἴ τινες τῶν ἀπὸ τῆς ἐκκλησίας ἐπὶ αἰτίαις τισὶ προκατεγνωσμένοι εἶεν καὶ ἀποβεβλημένοι, ἢ ἀκοινώνητοι, εἴτε ἀπὸ κλήρου, εἴτε ἀπὸ λαϊκοῦ τάγματος, μηδὲ τούτοις ἐξεῖναι κατηγορεῖν ἐπισκόπου, πρὶν ἂν τὸ οἰκεῖον ἔγκλημα πρότερον ἀποδύσωνται. Ὁμοίως δὲ καὶ τοὺς ὑπὸ κατηγορίαν προλαβοῦσαν ὄντας, μὴ πρότερον εἶναι δεκτοὺς εἰς ἐπισκόπου κατηγορίαν, ἢ ἑτέρων κληρικῶν, πρὶν ἂν ἀθώους ἑαυτοὺς τῶν ἐπαχθέντων αὐτοῖς ἀποδείξωσιν ἐγκλημάτων. Εἰ μέν τοι τινὲς μήτε αἱρετικοὶ, μήτε ἀκοινώνητοι εἶεν, μήτε κατεγνωσμένοι, ἢ προκατηγορημένοι ἐπί τισι πλημμελήμασι, λέγοιεν δὲ ἔχειν τινὰ ἐκκλησιαστικὴν κατὰ τοῦ ἐπισκόπου κατηγορίαν, τούτους κελεύει ἡ ἁγία σύνοδος, πρῶτον μὲν ἐπὶ τῶν τῆς ἐπαρχίας πάντων ἐπισκόπων ἐνίστασθαι τὰς κατηγορίας, καὶ ἐπ' αὐτῶν ἐλέγχειν τὰ ἐγκλήματα τοῦ ἐν αἰτίαις τισὶν ἐπισκόπου· εἰ δὲ συμβαίη ἀδυνατῆσαι τοὺς ἐπαρχιώτας πρὸς διόρθωσιν τῶν ἐπιφερομένων ἐγκλημάτων τῷ ἐπισκόπῳ, τότε αὐτοὺς προσιέναι μείζονι συνόδῳ, τῶν τῆς διοικήσεως ἐκείνης ἐπισκόπων, ὑπὲρ τῆς αἰτίας ταύτης συγκαλουμένων· καὶ μὴ πρότερον ἐνίστασθαι τὴν κατηγορίαν, πρὶν ἢ ἐγγράφως αὐτοὺς τὸν ἴσον αὐτοῖς ἐπιτιμήσασθαι κίνδυνον, εἴπερ ἐν τῇ τῶν πραγμάτων ἐξετάσει συκοφαντοῦντες τὸν κατηγορούμενον ἐπίσκοπον ἐλεγχθεῖεν. Εἰ δέ τις καταφρονήσας τῶν κατὰ τὰ προδηλωθέντα δεδογμένων, τολμήσειεν ἢ βασιλικὰς ἐνοχλεῖν ἀκοὰς, ἢ κοσμικῶν ἀρχόντων δικαστήρια, ἢ οἰκουμενικὴν σύνοδον ταράσσειν, πάντας ἀτιμάσας τοὺς τῆς διοικήσεως ἐπισκόπους, τὸν τοιοῦτον τὸ παράπαν εἰς κατηγορίαν μὴ εἶναι δεκτὸν, ὡς καθυβρίσαντα τοὺς κανόνας, καὶ τὴν ἐκκλησιαστικὴν λυμηνάμενον εὐταξίαν.

ΚΑΝΩΝ Ζ'.

Τοὺς προστιθεμένους τῇ ὀρθοδοξίᾳ, καὶ τῇ μερίδι τῶν σωζομένων, ἀπὸ αἱρετικῶν, δεχόμεθα κατὰ τὴν ὑποτεταγμένην ἀκολουθίαν καὶ συνήθειαν. Ἀρειανοὺς μὲν, καὶ Μακεδονιανοὺς, καὶ Σαββατιανοὺς, καὶ Ναυατιανοὺς, τοὺς λέγοντας ἑαυτοὺς Καθαροὺς καὶ Ἀριστεροὺς, καὶ τοὺς Τεσσα-

those professing to hold the true faith who have separated from our canonical Bishops, and set up conventicles in opposition [to them]. Moreover, if there be any who have been condemned for faults and cast out of the Church, or excommunicated, whether from the Clergy or the laity, neither shall it be lawful for these to bring an accusation against the Bishop, until they have cleared away the charge against themselves. In like manner, persons who are under previous accusations are not to be permitted to bring charges against a Bishop or any other Clergyman, until they shall have proved their own innocence of the accusation brought against them. But if any, being neither heretics, nor excommunicate, nor condemned, nor under previous accusation for alleged faults, should declare that they have any ecclesiastical charge against a Bishop, the Holy Synod bids them first to lay their charges before all the Bishops of the Province, and before them to prove the accusations, whatsoever they may be, which they have brought against the Bishop. And if it should come to pass that the Provincials should be unable rightly to settle the charges brought against the Bishop, then the parties must betake themselves to a greater Synod of the Bishops of that Diocese called together for this purpose; and they shall not produce their allegations before they have proposed an equal penalty to be exacted from themselves, if, in the course of the examination, they shall be proved to have slandered the accused Bishop. And if any one, despising what has been decreed concerning these things, shall presume to annoy the ears of the Emperor, or the courts of temporal judges, or, dishonouring all the Bishops of his Province, shall dare to trouble an Œcumenical Synod, such a one shall by no means be admitted as an accuser; forasmuch as he has cast contempt upon the Canons, and brought reproach upon the order of the Church.

CANON VII.

Those of the heretics who come over to orthodoxy, and the part of them that are saved, we receive according to the following customary order: Arians, and Macedonians, and Sabbatians, and Novatians, who call themselves Cathari or Aristeri, and Quarto-decimans or Tetradites, and Apolina-

ρεσκαιδεκατίτας, εἴτουν Τετραδίτας, καὶ Ἀπολλιναριστὰς, δεχόμεθα διδόντας λιβέλλους, καὶ ἀναθεματίζοντας πᾶσαν αἵρεσιν, μὴ φρονοῦσαν, ὡς φρονεῖ ἡ ἁγία τοῦ Θεοῦ καθολικὴ καὶ ἀποστολικὴ ἐκκλησία· καὶ σφραγιζομένους, ἤτοι χριομένους, πρῶτον τῷ ἁγίῳ μύρῳ, τό τε μέτωπον, καὶ τοὺς ὀφθαλμοὺς, καὶ τὰς ῥίνας καὶ τὸ στόμα, καὶ τὰ ὦτα· καὶ σφραγίζοντες αὐτοὺς, λέγομεν· Σφραγὶς δωρεᾶς Πνεύματος Ἁγίου. Εὐνομιανοὺς μέντοι τοὺς εἰς μίαν κατάδυσιν βαπτιζομένους, καὶ Μοντανιστὰς τοὺς ἐνταῦθα λεγομένους Φρύγας, καὶ Σαβελλιανοὺς, τοὺς υἱοπατορίαν διδάσκοντας, καὶ ἑτερά τινα χαλεπὰ ποιοῦντας, καὶ τὰς ἄλλας πάσας αἱρέσεις· (ἐπειδὴ πολλοί εἰσιν ἐνταῦθα, μάλιστα οἱ ἀπὸ τῆς Γαλατῶν χώρας ὁρμώμενοι)· πάντας τοὺς ἀπ' αὐτῶν θέλοντας προστίθεσθαι τῇ ὀρθοδοξίᾳ, ὡς Ἕλληνας δεχόμεθα· καὶ τὴν πρώτην ἡμέραν ποιοῦμεν αὐτοὺς Χριστιανοὺς, τὴν δὲ δευτέραν κατηχουμένους· εἶτα τῇ τρίτῃ ἐξορκίζομεν αὐτοὺς, μετὰ τοῦ ἐμφυσᾷν τρίτον εἰς τὸ πρόσωπον, καὶ εἰς τὰ ὦτα, καὶ οὕτω κατηχοῦμεν αὐτοὺς, καὶ ποιοῦμεν χρονίζειν εἰς τὴν ἐκκλησίαν, καὶ ἀκροᾶσθαι τῶν γραφῶν, καὶ τότε αὐτοὺς βαπτίζομεν.

rians, we receive, upon their giving a written renunciation and anathematizing every heresy which is not likeminded with the Holy, Catholic, and Apostolic Church of God. Thereupon, they are first sealed or anointed with the holy oil upon the forehead, the eyes, the nostrils, the mouth, and the ears ; and when we seal them, we say, "The Seal of the gift of the Holy Ghost." Eunomians, who are baptized with only one immersion, and Montanists, who are here called Phrygians, and Sabellians, who teach the identity of Father and Son, and do sundry other mischievous things, and [the partisans of] all other heresies—for there are many such here, particularly among those who come from the country of the Galatians :—all these, when they desire to come over to orthodoxy, we receive as heathen. The first day we make them Christians ; the second, Catechumens ; on the third, we exorcise them by blowing thrice in their face and ears ; and then we instruct them and oblige them to spend some time in the Church, and to hear the Scriptures ; and then we baptize them.

THIRD GENERAL COUNCIL.

EPHESUS.

CANONES

CONCILII EPHESINI GENERALIS.

A. D. 431.

Epistola Synodica.

Ἡ ἁγία καὶ οἰκουμενικὴ σύνοδος ἡ ἐν Ἐφέσῳ συγκροτηθεῖσα ἐκ θεσπίσματος τῶν εὐσεβεστάτων βασιλέων (Impp. Theodosii et Valentiniani), *τοῖς καθ' ἑκάστην ἐπαρχίαν τε καὶ πόλιν, ἐπισκόποις, πρεσβυτέροις, διακόνοις, καὶ παντὶ τῷ λαῷ.*

Συναχθέντων ἡμῶν κατὰ τὸ εὐσεβὲς γράμμα ἐν τῇ Ἐφεσίων μητροπόλει, ἀπέστησάν τινες ἐξ ἡμῶν, ὄντες τὸν ἀριθμὸν τριάκοντα μικρῷ πρὸς, ἔξαρχον τῆς ἑαυτῶν ἀποστασίας ἐσχηκότες τὸν τῆς Ἀντιοχέων ἐπίσκοπον Ἰωάννην· ὧν καὶ τὰ ὀνόματά ἐστι ταῦτα. Πρῶτος *οὗτος* Ἰωάννης *ὁ* Ἀντιοχείας *τῆς* Συρίας, *καὶ* Ἰωάννης Δαμασκοῦ, Ἀλέξανδρος Ἀπαμείας, Ἀλέξανδρος Ἱεραπόλεως, Ἱμέριος Νικομηδείας, Φριτιλᾶς Ἡρακλείας, Ἑλλάδιος Ταρσοῦ, Μαξιμῖνος Ἀναζάρβου, Θεόδωρος Μαρκιανουπόλεως, Πέτρος Τραϊανουπόλεως, Παῦλος Ἐμίσης, Πολυχρόνιος Ἡρακλειωτῶν *πόλεως*, Εὐθύριος Τυάνων, Μελέτιος Νεοκαισαρείας, Θεοδώρητος Κύρου, Ἀπρίγγιος Καλχηδόνος, Μακάριος Λαοδικείας *τῆς μεγάλης*, Ζῶσυς Ἐσβοῦντος, Σαλούστιος Κωρύκου Κιλικίας, Ἡσύχιος Κασταβάλης Κιλικίας, Οὐαλεντῖνος Μουτλοβλάκης, Εὐστάθιος Παρνασοῦ, Φίλιππος Θεοδοσιανῶν, Δανιήλ *τε, καὶ* Δεξιανὸς, Ἰουλιανός *τε, καὶ* Κύριλλος, Ὀλύμπιός *τε, καὶ* Διογένης, Πολιὸς, Θεοφάνης Φιλαδελφείας, Τραϊανὸς Αὐγούστης, Αὐρήλιος Εἰρηνουπόλεως, Μουσαῖος Ἀράδου, Ἑλλάδιος Πτολεμαΐδος· *οἵ τινες τῆς ἐκκλησιαστικῆς κοινωνίας μηδεμίαν ἔχοντες ἄδειαν ὡς ἐξ αὐθεντίας ἱερατικῆς, εἰς τὸ δύνασθαί τινας ἐκ ταύτης βλάπτειν ἢ ὠφελεῖν, διὰ τὸ καί τινας ἐν αὐτοῖς εἶναι καθῃρημένους, πρὸ πάντων μὲν τὰ* Νεστορίου *καὶ τὰ* Κελεστίου *φρονήματα ἐπιφερόμενοι σαφέστατα ἀπεδείχθησαν, ἐκ τοῦ μὴ ἑλέσθαι μεθ' ἡμῶν* Νεστορίου *καταψηφίσασθαι· οὕς τινας δόγματι κοινῷ ἡ ἁγία σύνοδος πάσης μὲν ἐκκλησιαστικῆς κοινωνίας ἀλλοτρίους ἐποίησε, πᾶσαν δὲ αὐτῶν ἐνέργειαν ἱερατικὴν περιεῖλε, δι' ἧς ἠδύναντο βλάπτειν ἢ ὠφελεῖν τινας.*

CANONS OF EPHESUS.

Encyclical Letter of the Synod.

The Holy and Œcumenical Synod, gathered together in Ephesus by the decree of our most religious Emperors, to the Bishops, Presbyters, Deacons, and all the people in every Province and City :

When we had assembled, according to the religious decree [of the Emperors], in the Metropolis of Ephesus, certain persons, a little more than thirty in number, withdrew from amongst us, having for the leader of their schism John, Bishop of Antioch. Their names are as follows: first, the said John of Antioch in Syria, John of Damascus, Alexander of Apamea, Alexander of Hierapolis, Himerius of Nicomedia, Fritilas of Heraclea, Helladius of Tarsus, Maximin of Anazarbus, Theodore of Marcianopolis, Peter of Trajanopolis, Paul of Emissa, Polychronius of Heracleopolis, Euthyrius of Tyana, Meletius of Neocæsarea, Theodoret of Cyrus, Apringius of Chalcedon, Macarius of Laodicea Magna, Zosys of Esbus, Sallust of Corycus in Cilicia, Hesychius of Castabala in Cilicia, Valentine of Mutloblaca, Eustathius of Parnassus, Philip of Theodosia, and Daniel, and Dexianus, and Julian, and Cyril, and Olympius, and Diogenes, Polius, Theophanes of Philadelphia, Trajan of Augusta, Aurelius of Irenopolis, Mysæus of Aradus, Helladius of Ptolemais. These men, having no privilege of ecclesiastical communion on the ground of a priestly authority, by which they could injure or benefit any persons ; since some of them had already been deposed; and since, from their refusing to join in our decree against Nestorius, it was manifestly evident to all men that they were all promoting the opinions of Nestorius and Celestius ; the Holy Synod, by one common decree, deposed them from all ecclesiastical communion, and deprived them of all their priestly power by which they might injure or profit any persons.

ΚΑΝΩΝ Α'.

Ἐπειδὴ ἐχρῆν καὶ τοὺς ἀπολειφθέντας τῆς ἁγίας συνόδου, καὶ μείναντας κατὰ χώραν ἢ πόλιν, διά τινα αἰτίαν, ἢ ἐκκλησιαστικὴν, ἢ σωματικὴν, μὴ ἀγνοῆσαι τὰ ἐν αὐτῇ τετυπωμένα, γνωρίζομεν τῇ ὑμετέρᾳ ἁγιότητι καὶ ἀγάπῃ, ὅτι περ, εἴ τις μητροπολίτης τῆς ἐπαρχίας, ἀποστατήσας τῆς ἁγίας καὶ οἰκουμενικῆς συνόδου, προσέθετο τῷ τῆς ἀποστασίας συνεδρίῳ, ἢ μετὰ τοῦτο προστεθείη, ἢ τὰ Κελεστίου ἐφρόνησεν, ἢ φρονήσει, οὗτος κατὰ τῶν τῆς ἐπαρχίας ἐπισκόπων διαπράττεσθαί τι οὐδαμῶς δύναται, πάσης ἐκκλησιαστικῆς κοινωνίας ἐντεῦθεν ἤδη ὑπὸ τῆς συνόδου ἐκβεβλημένος, καὶ ἀνενέργητος ὑπάρχων. Ἀλλὰ καὶ αὐτοῖς τοῖς τῆς ἐπαρχίας ἐπισκόποις, καὶ τοῖς πέριξ μητροπολίταις, τοῖς τὰ τῆς ὀρθοδοξίας φρονοῦσιν, ὑποκείσεται εἰς τὸ πάντη καὶ τοῦ βαθμοῦ τῆς ἐπισκοπῆς ἐκβληθῆναι.

ΚΑΝΩΝ Β'.

Εἰ δέ τινες ἐπαρχιῶται ἐπίσκοποι ἀπελείφθησαν τῆς ἁγίας συνόδου, καὶ τῇ ἀποστασίᾳ προσετέθησαν, ἢ προστεθῆναι πειραθεῖεν, ἢ καὶ ὑπογράψαντες τῇ Νεστορίου καθαιρέσει, ἐπαλινδρόμησαν πρὸς τὸ τῆς ἀποστασίας συνέδριον· τούτους πάντη κατὰ τὸ δόξαν τῇ ἁγίᾳ συνόδῳ ἀλλοτρίους εἶναι τῆς ἱερωσύνης, καὶ τοῦ βαθμοῦ ἐκπίπτειν.

ΚΑΝΩΝ Γ'.

Εἰ δέ τινες [καὶ] τῶν ἐν ἑκάστῃ πόλει, ἢ χώρᾳ κληρικῶν, ὑπὸ Νεστορίου, καὶ τῶν σὺν αὐτῷ ὄντων, τῆς ἱερωσύνης ἐκωλύθησαν διὰ τὸ ὀρθῶς φρονεῖν, ἐδικαιώσαμεν καὶ τούτους τὸν ἴδιον ἀπολαβεῖν βαθμόν. Κοινῶς δὲ τοὺς τῇ ὀρθοδόξῳ καὶ οἰκουμενικῇ συνόδῳ συμφρονοῦντας κληρικοὺς, κελεύομεν τοῖς ἀποστατήσασιν, ἢ ἀφισταμένοις ἐπισκόποις, μηδ' ὅλως ὑποκεῖσθαι, κατὰ μηδένα τρόπον.

ΚΑΝΩΝ Δ'.

Εἰ δέ τινες ἀποστατήσαιεν τῶν κληρικῶν, καὶ τολμήσαιεν ἢ κατ' ἰδίαν ἢ δημοσίᾳ, τὰ Νεστορίου, ἢ τὰ Κελεστίου φρονῆσαι, καὶ τούτους εἶναι καθῃρημένους, ὑπὸ τῆς ἁγίας συνόδου δεδικαίωται.

CANON I.

Whereas it is needful that they who were detained from the Holy Synod and remained in their own district or City, for any reason, ecclesiastical or personal, should not be ignorant of the matters which were therein decreed; we, therefore, notify your holiness and love that, if any Metropolitan of a Province, forsaking the Holy and Œcumenical Synod, has joined the assembly of the schismatics, or shall join the same hereafter; or, if he has adopted, or shall hereafter adopt, the doctrines of Celestius, he has no power in any way to do anything in opposition to the Bishops of the Province, since he is already deprived by the Holy Synod, and cast out of all ecclesiastical communion; but he shall himself be subject in all things to the Bishops of the Province and neighbouring orthodox Metropolitans, and shall be degraded from his episcopal rank.

CANON II.

If any provincial Bishops have forsaken the Holy Synod and joined, or attempted to join, the schism; or if, after subscribing the deposition of Nestorius, they have backslidden into the schismatical assembly; these men, according to the decree of the Holy Synod, are to be deposed from the Priesthood and degraded from their rank.

CANON III.

If any of the Clergy in any district or City have been inhibited by Nestorius or his followers from the exercise of the Priesthood, on account of orthodoxy, we have declared it just that these should be restored to their proper rank. And we utterly forbid all the Clergy who adhere to the Orthodox and Œcumenical Synod in any way to submit to the Bishops who have separated or shall hereafter separate.

CANON IV.

If any of the Clergy should fall away, and publicly or privately presume to maintain the doctrines of Nestorius or Celestius, it is declared just by the Holy Synod that these also should be deposed.

ΚΑΝΩΝ Ε'.

Ὅσοι δὲ ἐπὶ ἀτόποις πράξεσι κατεκρίθησαν ὑπὸ τῆς ἁγίας συνόδου, ἢ ὑπὸ τῶν οἰκείων ἐπισκόπων, καὶ τούτοις ἀκανονίστως, κατὰ τὴν ἐν ἅπασιν ἀδιαφορίαν αὐτοῦ, ὁ Νεστόριος, καὶ οἱ τὰ αὐτοῦ φρονοῦντες, ἀποδοῦναι ἐπειράθησαν, ἢ πειραθεῖεν κοινωνίαν, ἢ βαθμὸν, ἀνωφελήτους εἶναι, καὶ μένειν οὐδὲν ἧττον καθῃρημένους ἐδικαιώσαμεν.

ΚΑΝΩΝ ϛ'.

Ὁμοίως δὲ καὶ εἴ τινες βουληθεῖεν, τὰ περὶ ἑκάστου πεπραγμένα ἐν τῇ ἁγίᾳ συνόδῳ, τῇ ἐν Ἐφέσῳ, οἱῳδήποτε τρόπῳ παρασαλεύειν, ἡ ἁγία σύνοδος ὥρισεν, εἰ μὲν ἐπίσκοποι εἶεν, ἢ κληρικοὶ, τοῦ οἰκείου παντελῶς ἀποπίπτειν βαθμοῦ· εἰ δὲ λαϊκοὶ, ἀκοινωνήτους ὑπάρχειν.

Διαλαλία τῆς αὐτῆς ἁγίας συνόδου, ἐκφωνηθεῖσα μετὰ τὸ ἀναγνωσθῆναι τὴν ἔκθεσιν τῶν τριακοσίων δέκα καὶ ὀκτὼ ἁγίων καὶ μακαρίων Πατέρων, τῶν ἐν Νικαίᾳ, καὶ τὸ δυσσεβὲς σύμβολον τὸ ὑπὸ Θεοδώρου τοῦ Μοψουεστίας πλασθὲν, καὶ ὑπὸ Χαρισίου πρεσβυτέρου Φιλαδελφίας ἐπιδοθὲν τῇ αὐτῇ κατὰ Ἔφεσον ἁγίᾳ συνόδῳ.

ΚΑΝΩΝ Ζ'.

Τούτων ἀναγνωσθέντων, ὥρισεν ἡ ἁγία σύνοδος, ἑτέραν πίστιν μηδενὶ ἐξεῖναι προφέρειν, ἤγουν συγγράφειν ἢ συντιθέναι, παρὰ τὴν ὁρισθεῖσαν παρὰ τῶν ἁγίων Πατέρων, τῶν ἐν τῇ Νικαέων συναχθέντων πόλει, σὺν Ἁγίῳ Πνεύματι.

Τοὺς δὲ τολμῶντας ἢ συντιθέναι πίστιν ἑτέραν, ἤγουν προκομίζειν, ἢ προφέρειν τοῖς θέλουσιν ἐπιστρέφειν εἰς ἐπίγνωσιν τῆς ἀληθείας, ἢ ἐξ Ἑλληνισμοῦ, ἢ ἐξ Ἰουδαϊσμοῦ, ἤγουν ἐξ αἱρέσεως οἱασδηποτοῦν· τούτους, εἰ μὲν εἶεν ἐπίσκοποι ἢ κληρικοὶ, ἀλλοτρίους εἶναι τοὺς ἐπισκόπους τῆς ἐπισκοπῆς, καὶ τοὺς κληρικοὺς τοῦ κλήρου· εἰ δὲ λαϊκοὶ εἶεν, ἀναθεματίζεσθαι.

Κατὰ τὸν ἴσον δὲ τρόπον, εἰ φωραθεῖέν τινες, εἴτε ἐπίσκοποι, εἴτε κληρικοὶ, εἴτε λαϊκοὶ, ἢ φρονοῦντες, ἢ διδάσκοντες τὰ ἐν τῇ προκομισθείσῃ ἐκθέσει παρὰ Χαρισίου τοῦ πρεσβυτέρου,

CANON V.

If any have been condemned for evil practices by the Holy Synod, or by their own Bishops; and if, with his usual arrogance, Nestorius (or his followers) has attempted, or shall hereafter attempt, uncanonically to restore such persons to communion and to their former rank, we have declared that they shall not be profited thereby, but shall remain deposed nevertheless.

CANON VI.

Likewise, if any should in any way attempt to set aside the orders in each case made by the Holy Synod at Ephesus, the Holy Synod decrees that, if they be Bishops or Clergymen, they shall absolutely forfeit their rank; and, if laymen, that they shall be excommunicated.

The Decree of the same Holy Synod, pronounced after hearing the Exposition [of the Faith] by the Three Hundred and Eighteen holy and blessed Fathers in the city of Nicæa, and the impious Formula composed by Theodore of Mopsuestia, and given to the same Holy Synod at Ephesus by the Presbyter Charisius, of Philadelphia:

CANON VII.

These things having been read, the Holy Synod decrees that it is unlawful for any man to bring forward, or to write, or to compose a different Faith than that established by the holy and blessed Fathers assembled, with the Holy Ghost, in Nicæa.

But those who shall dare to compose a different Faith, or to produce or offer [any other] to persons desiring to turn to the acknowledgment of the truth, whether from Heathenism or from Judaism, or from any heresy whatsoever, shall be deposed, if they be Bishops or Clergymen; Bishops from the Episcopate and Clergymen from the Clergy; and if they be laymen, they shall be anathematized.

And in like manner, if any, whether Bishops, Clergymen, or laymen, should be discovered to hold or teach the doctrines contained in the Exposition produced by the Presbyter Chari-

περὶ τῆς ἐνανθρωπήσεως τοῦ μονογενοῦς Υἱοῦ τοῦ Θεοῦ, ἤγουν τὰ μιαρὰ καὶ διεστραμμένα τοῦ Νεστορίου δόγματα, ἃ καὶ ὑποτέτακται, ὑποκείσθωσαν τῇ ἀποφάσει τῆς ἁγίας ταύτης καὶ οἰκουμενικῆς συνόδου· ὥστε δηλονότι, τὸν μὲν ἐπίσκοπον, ἀπαλλοτριοῦσθαι τῆς ἐπισκοπῆς, καὶ εἶναι καθῃρημένον· τὸν δὲ κληρικὸν, ὁμοίως ἐκπίπτειν τοῦ κλήρου· εἰ δὲ λαϊκός τις εἴη, καὶ οὗτος ἀναθεματιζέσθω, καθὰ προείρηται.

Ψῆφος τῆς αὐτῆς ἁγίας συνόδου, ἐκφωνηθεῖσα ἐκ προσελεύσεως γενομένης αὐτῇ παρὰ τῶν Κυπρίων ἐπισκόπων:

ΚΑΝΩΝ Η'.

Πρᾶγμα παρὰ τοὺς ἐκκλησιαστικοὺς θεσμοὺς καὶ τοὺς κανόνας τῶν ἁγίων Ἀποστόλων καινοτομούμενον, καὶ τῆς πάντων ἐλευθερίας ἁπτόμενον, προσήγγειλεν ὁ θεοφιλέστατος συνεπίσκοπος Ῥηγῖνος, καὶ οἱ σὺν αὐτῷ θεοφιλέστατοι ἐπίσκοποι τῆς Κυπρίων ἐπαρχίας, Ζήνων καὶ Εὐάγριος· Ὅθεν, ἐπειδὴ τὰ κοινὰ πάθη μείζονος δεῖται τῆς θεραπείας, ὡς καὶ μείζονα τὴν βλάβην φέροντα, καὶ μάλιστα εἰ μηδὲ ἔθος ἀρχαῖον παρηκολούθησεν, ὥστε τὸν ἐπίσκοπον τῆς Ἀντιοχέων πόλεως τὰς ἐν Κύπρῳ ποιεῖσθαι χειροτονίας, καθὰ διὰ τῶν λιβέλλων καὶ τῶν οἰκείων φωνῶν ἐδίδαξαν οἱ εὐλαβέστατοι ἄνδρες, οἱ τὴν πρόσοδον τῇ ἁγίᾳ συνόδῳ ποιησάμενοι, ἕξουσι τὸ ἀνεπηρέαστον καὶ ἀβίαστον οἱ τῶν ἁγίων ἐκκλησιῶν, τῶν κατὰ τὴν Κύπρον, προεστῶτες, κατὰ τοὺς κανόνας τῶν ὁσίων Πατέρων, καὶ τὴν ἀρχαίαν συνήθειαν, δι' ἑαυτῶν τὰς χειροτονίας τῶν εὐλαβεστάτων ἐπισκόπων ποιούμενοι· τὸ δὲ αὐτὸ καὶ ἐπὶ τῶν ἄλλων διοικήσεων, καὶ τῶν ἁπανταχοῦ ἐπαρχιῶν παραφυλαχθήσεται· ὥστε μηδένα τῶν θεοφιλεστάτων ἐπισκόπων ἐπαρχίαν ἑτέραν, οὐκ οὖσαν ἄνωθεν καὶ ἐξ ἀρχῆς ὑπὸ τὴν αὐτοῦ, ἢ γοῦν τῶν πρὸ αὐτοῦ χεῖρα καταλαμβάνειν· ἀλλ' εἰ καί τις κατέλαβε, καὶ ὑφ' ἑαυτὸν πεποίηται, βιασάμενος, ταύτην ἀποδιδόναι· ἵνα μὴ τῶν Πατέρων οἱ κανόνες παραβαίνωνται, μηδὲ ἐν ἱερουργίας προσχήματι, ἐξουσίας τύφος κοσμικῆς παρεισδύηται, μηδὲ λάθωμεν τὴν ἐλευθερίαν κατὰ μικρὸν ἀπολέσαντες, ἣν ἡμῖν ἐδωρήσατο τῷ

sius concerning the Incarnation of the Only-Begotten Son of God, or the abominable and profane doctrines of Nestorius, which have been condemned; they shall be subjected to the sentence of this Holy and Œcumenical Synod. So that, if it be a Bishop, he shall be removed from his Bishopric and degraded from his rank; if it be a Clergyman, he shall likewise forfeit his rank; and if it be a layman, he shall be anathematized, as has been aforesaid.

The Judgment of the same Holy Synod, pronounced on the petition presented to it by the Bishops of Cyprus:

CANON VIII.

Our brother, Bishop Rheginus, the beloved of God, and the beloved of God the Bishops with him, Zeno and Evagrius, of the Province of Cyprus, have reported to us an innovation which has been introduced contrary to the constitutions of the Church and the Canons of the Holy Apostles, and which touches the liberties of all. Wherefore, since injuries affecting all require the more attention, as they cause the greater damage, and particularly when they are transgressions of an ancient custom; and since those excellent men, who have petitioned the Synod, have told us in writing and by word of mouth that the Bishop of Antioch has in this way held ordinations in Cyprus; therefore [we declare that] the Rulers of the Church in Cyprus shall enjoy without dispute or injury, according to ancient custom and the Canons of the blessed Fathers, the right of performing for themselves the ordination of their excellent Bishops. The same rule shall be observed in the other Dioceses and Provinces everywhere, so that none of the most religious Bishops shall assume control of any Province which has not heretofore, from the very beginning, been under his own hand or that of his predecessors. But if any one has violently taken and subjected [a Province], he shall give it up; so that the Canons of the Fathers may not be transgressed; nor the vanities of worldly honour be brought in under pretext of Sacred Office; nor we lose, little by little,

ἰδίῳ αἵματι ὁ Κύριος ἡμῶν Ἰησοῦς Χριστὸς, ὁ πάντων ἀνθρώπων ἐλευθερωτής.

Ἔδοξε τοίνυν τῇ ἁγίᾳ [ταύτῃ] καὶ οἰκουμενικῇ συνόδῳ, σώζεσθαι ἑκάστῃ ἐπαρχίᾳ καθαρὰ καὶ ἀβίαστα τὰ αὐτῇ προσόντα δίκαια ἐξ ἀρχῆς καὶ ἄνωθεν, κατὰ τὸ πάλαι κρατῆσαν ἔθος, ἄδειαν ἔχοντος ἑκάστου μητροπολίτου τὰ ἴσα τῶν πεπραγμένων πρὸς τὸ οἰκεῖον ἀσφαλὲς ἐκλαβεῖν. Εἰ δέ τις μαχόμενον τύπον τοῖς νῦν ὡρισμένοις προκομίσοι, ἄκυρον τοῦτο εἶναι ἔδοξε τῇ ἁγίᾳ πάσῃ καὶ οἰκουμενικῇ συνόδῳ.

and at length forget, the liberty which Our LORD JESUS CHRIST, the Deliverer of all men, hath given us by His own Blood.

Wherefore, this Holy and Œcumenical Synod has decreed that in every Province the rights which heretofore, from the beginning, have belonged to it, shall be preserved to it, according to the old prevailing custom, unchanged and uninjured: every Metropolitan having permission to take, for his own security, a copy of these acts. And if any one shall bring forward a rule contrary to what is here determined this Holy and Œcumenical Synod unanimously decrees that it shall be of no effect.

ΕΠΙΣΤΟΛΗ

ΤΗΣ 'ΑΥΤΗΣ 'ΑΓΙΑΣ ΚΑΙ 'ΟΙΚΟΥΜΕΝΙΚΗΣ ΤΡΙΤΗΣ ΣΥΝΟΔΟΥ, ΠΡΟΣ ΤΗΝ 'ΕΝ ΠΑΜΦΥΛΙΑΙ 'ΕΥΑΓΗ ΣΥΝΟΔΟΝ, ΠΕΡΙ 'ΕΥΣΤΑΘΙΟΥ, ΤΟΥ ΓΕΝΟΜΕΝΟΥ 'ΑΥΤΩΝ ΜΗΤΡΟΠΟΛΙΤΟΥ.

Μετὰ βουλῆς πάντα ποίει, τῆς θεοπνεύστου λεγούσης γραφῆς, χρὴ δὴ μάλιστα τοὺς ἱερᾶσθαι λαχόντας μετὰ πάσης ἀκριβείας τὴν ἐφ' ἅπασι τοῖς πρακτέοις ποιεῖσθαι διάσκεψιν. Διαβιοῦν γὰρ οὕτως ἐθέλουσιν, ἐν καλῷ τῆς ἐλπίδος κεῖσθαί τε τὰ κατ' αὐτοὺς, καί οἷον ἐξ οὐρίας ἐν τοῖς κατ' εὐχὴν ἀποφέρεσθαι συμβαίνει· καὶ πολὺ τό γε εἰκὸς ὁ λόγος ἔχει. 'Αλλ' οἶδεν, ἐσθ' ὅτε, δριμεῖα καὶ ἀφόρητος λύπη, κατασκήψασα νοῦ, καταθολῶσαί τε δεινῶς αὐτὸν, καὶ τῆς τῶν δεόντων ἀποκομίσαι θήρας, ἀναπεῖσαί τε τὸ πεφυκὸς ἀδικεῖν, ὥς τι τῶν ὀνησιφόρων ἰδεῖν. Τοιοῦτόν τι πεπονθότα τεθεάμεθα τὸν εὐλαβέστατον, καὶ θεοσεβέστατον ἐπίσκοπον Εὐστάθιον. Κεχειροτόνηται μὲν γὰρ, ὡς μεμαρτύρηται, κανονικῶς· τεθορυβημένος δὲ, ὥς φησι, παρά τινων, καὶ ἀδοκήτοις περιστάσεσιν ἐμβεβηκὼς, εἶτα ἐκ πολλῆς ἄγαν ἀπραγμοσύνης ἀπειρηκὼς τὴν ἀντίστασιν τῶν ἐπενηνεγμένων αὐτῷ φροντίδων, καίπερ διακρούεσθαι τὰς παρὰ τῶν ἐπιφυομένων αὐτῷ δυσφημίας δυνάμενος, παραιτήσεως, οὐκ ἴσμεν ὅπως, προσεκόμισε βιβλίον. Ἔδει γὰρ, ὡς ἅπαξ ἐγκεχειρισμένον ἱερατικὴν φροντίδα, ταύτης ἔχεσθαι μετ' εὐρωστίας πνευματικῆς, καὶ οἷον ἀνταποδύεσθαι τοῖς πόνοις, καὶ ἱδρῶτα τὸν ἔμμισθον ἐθελοντὶ ὑπομεῖναι. 'Επειδὴ δὲ ἅπαξ ὀλιγώρως ἔχοντα παρέδειξεν ἑαυτὸν, τοῦτο παθὼν ἐξ ἀπραγμοσύνης μᾶλλον,

EPISTLE

OF THE HOLY AND ŒCUMENICAL THIRD COUNCIL TO THE ILLUSTRIOUS COUNCIL IN PAMPHYLIA RESPECTING EUSTATHIUS WHO HAD BEEN THEIR METROPOLITAN.

Forasmuch as the divinely inspired Scripture says, "Do all things with advice," it is especially their duty who have had the priestly ministry allotted to them to examine with all diligence whatever matters are to be transacted. For to those who will so spend their lives, it comes to pass both that they are established in [the enjoyment of] an honest hope concerning what belongs to them, and that they are borne along, as by a favouring breeze, in things that they desire: so that, in truth, the saying [of the Scripture] has much reason [to commend it]. But there are times when bitter and intolerable grief swoops down upon the mind, and has the effect of cruelly beclouding it, so as to carry it away from the pursuit of what is needful, and persuade it to consider that to be of service which is in its [very] nature mischievous. Something of this kind we have seen endured by that most excellent and most religious Bishop Eustathius. For it is in evidence that he has been ordained canonically; but having been much disturbed, as he declares, by certain parties, and having entered upon circumstances he had not foreseen, therefore, though fully able to repel the slanders of his persecutors, he nevertheless, through an extraordinary inexperience of affairs, declined to battle with the difficulties which beset him, and in some way that we know not set forth an act of resignation. Yet it behoved him, when he had been once entrusted with the priestly care, to cling to it with spiritual energy, and, as it were, to strip himself to strive against the troubles and gladly to endure the sweat for which he had bargained. But inasmuch as he proved himself to be deficient in practical capacity, having met with this misfortune rather from

ἢ ὄκνου καὶ ῥᾳθυμίας, κεχειροτόνηκεν ἀναγκαίως ἡ ὑμετέρα θεοσέβεια τὸν εὐλαβέστατον καὶ θεοσεβέστατον ἀδελφὸν ἡμῶν καὶ συνεπίσκοπον Θεύδωρον, φροντιοῦντα τῆς ἐκκλησίας· οὐ γὰρ ἦν ἀκόλουθον χηρεύειν αὐτὴν, καὶ ἐπιστάτου δίχα διατελεῖν τοῦ Σωτῆρος τὰ ποίμνια. Ἐπειδὴ δὲ προσῆλθε κλαίων, οὐ περὶ τῆς πόλεως, οὐδὲ τῆς ἐκκλησίας φιλονεικῶν τῷ μνημονευθέντι θεοσεβεστάτῳ ἐπισκόπῳ Θεοδώρῳ, ἐξαιτῶν δὲ τέως τὴν τοῦ ἐπισκόπου τιμὴν, καὶ κλῆσιν, συνηλγήσαμεν ἅπαντες τῷ πρεσβύτῃ, καὶ κοινὸν εἶναι λογισάμενοι τὸ αὐτοῦ δάκρυον, ἐσπεύδομεν μαθεῖν, εἰ καθαίρεσιν ἔννομον ὑπομεμένηκεν ὁ μνημονευθεὶς, ἢ γοῦν ἐπί τισι τῶν ἀτόπων ἐλήλεγκται παρά τινων καταφλυαρησάντων αὐτοῦ τῆς ὑπολήψεως. Καὶ δὴ ἐμάθομεν πεπρᾶχθαι μὲν τοιοῦτον οὐδὲν, γενέσθαι δὲ μᾶλλον τῷ μνημονευθέντι ἀντὶ ἐγκλήματος τὴν παραίτησιν. Ὅθεν οὐδὲ τῇ ὑμετέρᾳ θεοσεβείᾳ ἐμεμψάμεθα, χειροτονησάσῃ δεόντως εἰς τὸν αὐτοῦ τόπον τὸν μνημονευθέντα εὐλαβέστατον ἐπίσκοπον Θεόδωρον. Ἐπειδὴ δὲ τῇ ἀπραγμοσύνῃ τοῦ ἀνδρὸς οὐ σφόδρα φιλονεικεῖν ἀκόλουθον, ἔδει δὲ μᾶλλον ἐλεῆσαι πρεσβύτην, ἔξω καὶ πόλεως τῆς ἐνεγκούσης αὐτὸν, καὶ πατρῴων ἐνδιαιτημάτων ἐν μακροῖς οὕτω γεγονότα χρόνοις, ἐδικαιώσαμεν, καὶ ὡρίσαμεν, δίχα πάσης ἀντιλογίας, ἔχειν αὐτὸν τό τε τῆς ἐπισκοπῆς ὄνομα, καὶ τὴν τιμὴν, καὶ τὴν κοινωνίαν. Οὕτω μέν τοι, ὥστε μὴ χειροτονεῖν αὐτὸν, μήτε μὴν ἐκκλησίαν καταλαβόντα ἱερουργεῖν ἐξ ἰδίας αὐθεντίας· ἀλλ' ἢ ἄρα συμπαραλαμβανόμενον, εἴτουν ἐπιτρεπόμενον, εἰ τύχοι, παρὰ ἀδελφοῦ, καὶ συνεπισκόπου, κατὰ διάθεσιν, καὶ ἀγάπην τὴν ἐν Χριστῷ. Εἰ δέ τι βουλεύσησθε χρηστότερον ἐπ' αὐτῷ ἢ νῦν, ἢ εἰς τὸ μετὰ ταῦτα, ἀρέσει καὶ τοῦτο τῇ ἁγίᾳ συνόδῳ.

inexperience than from cowardice and sloth, your holiness has of necessity ordained our most excellent and most religious brother and fellow-Bishop, Theodore, as the overseer of the Church; for it was not reasonable that it should remain in widowhood, and that the Saviour's sheep should pass their time without a shepherd. But when he came to us weeping, not contending with the aforenamed most religious Bishop Theodore for his See or Church, but in the meantime seeking only for his rank and title as a Bishop, we all suffered with the old man in his grief, and considering his weeping as our own, we hastened to discover whether the aforenamed [Eustathius] had been subjected to a legal deposition, or whether, forsooth, he had been convicted on any of the absurd charges alleged by certain parties who had poured forth idle gossip against his reputation. And indeed we learned that nothing of such a kind had taken place, but rather that his resignation had been counted against the said Eustathius instead of a [regular] indictment. Wherefore, we did by no means blame your holiness for being compelled to ordain into his place the aforenamed most excellent Bishop Theodore. But forasmuch as it was not seemly to contend much against the unpractical character of the man, while it was rather necessary to have pity on the elder who, at so advanced an age, was now so far away from the city which had given him birth, and from the dwelling-places of his fathers, we have judicially pronounced and decreed without any opposition, that he shall have both the name, and the rank, and the Communion of the Episcopate. On this condition, however, only, that he shall not ordain, and that he shall not take and minister to a Church of his own individual authority; but that [he shall do so only] if taken as an assistant, or when appointed, if it should so chance, by a brother and fellow-Bishop, in accordance with the ordinance and the love which is in Christ. If, however, ye shall determine anything more favourable towards him either now or hereafter, this also will be pleasing to the Holy Synod.

FOURTH GENERAL COUNCIL.

CHALCEDON.

DEFINITIO FIDEI

APUD CONCILIUM

CHALCEDONIUM.

Ἡ ἉΓΙΑ καὶ μεγάλη καὶ οἰκουμενικὴ σύνοδος, ἡ κατὰ Θεοῦ χάριν καὶ θέσπισμα τῶν εὐσεβεστάτων καὶ φιλοχρίστων ἡμῶν βασιλέων Μαρκιανοῦ καὶ Οὐαλεντιανοῦ Αὐγούστων, συναχθεῖσα ἐν τῇ Καλχηδονέων, μητροπόλει τῆς Βιθυνῶν ἐπαρχίας, ἐν τῷ μαρτυρίῳ τῆς ἁγίας καὶ καλλινίκου μάρτυρος Εὐφημίας, ὥρισε τὰ ὑποτεταγμένα.

Ὁ ΚΥΡΙΟΣ ἡμῶν καὶ σωτὴρ Ἰησοῦς Χριστὸς τῆς πίστεως τὴν γνῶσιν τοῖς μαθηταῖς βεβαιῶν, ἔφη· Εἰρήνην τὴν ἐμὴν ἀφίημι ὑμῖν, εἰρήνην τὴν ἐμὴν δίδωμι ὑμίν· ὥστε μηδένα πρὸς τὸν πλησίον διαφωνεῖν ἐν τοῖς δόγμασι τῆς εὐσεβείας, ἀλλ' ἐπίσης ἅπασι τὸ τῆς ἀληθείας ἐπιδείκνυσθαι κήρυγμα. Ἐπειδὴ δὲ οὐ παύεται διὰ τῶν ἑαυτοῦ ζιζανίων ὁ πονηρὸς τοῖς τῆς εὐσεβείας ἐπιφυόμενος σπέρμασι, καί τι καινὸν κατὰ τῆς ἀληθείας ἐφευρίσκων ἀεὶ, διὰ τοῦτο συνήθως ὁ Δεσπότης προνοούμενος τοῦ ἀνθρωπίνου γένους, τὸν εὐσεβῆ τοῦτον καὶ πιστότατον πρὸς ζῆλον ἀνέστησε βασιλέα, καὶ τοὺς ἁπανταχῆ τῆς ἱερωσύνης πρὸς ἑαυτὸν ἀρχηγοὺς συνεκάλεσεν· ὥστε, τῆς χάριτος τοῦ πάντων ἡμῶν δεσπότου Χριστοῦ ἐνεργούσης, πᾶσαν μὲν τοῦ ψεύδους τῶν τοῦ Χριστοῦ προβάτων ἀποσείσασθαι λύμην, τοῖς δὲ τῆς ἀληθείας αὐτὴν καταπιαίνειν βλαστήμασιν. Ὃ δὴ καὶ πεποιήκαμεν, κοινῇ ψήφῳ τὰ τῆς πλάνης ἀπελασαντες δόγματα, τὴν δὲ ἀπλανῆ τῶν Πατέρων ἀνανεωσάμενοι πίστιν, τὸ τῶν τριακοσίων δεκαοκτὼ σύμβολον τοῖς πᾶσι κηρύξαντες, καὶ ὡς οἰκείους τοὺς τοῦτο τὸ σύνθεμα τῆς εὐσεβείας δεξαμένους πατέρας ἐπιγραψάμενοι. Οἵπερ εἰσὶν οἱ μετὰ ταῦτα ἐν τῇ μεγάλῃ Κωνσταντινουπόλει συνελθόντες ρν' καὶ αὐτοὶ τὴν αὐτὴν ἐπισφραγισάμενοι πίστιν. Ὁρίζομεν τοί-

THE DEFINITION OF FAITH,

AGREED UPON AT THE COUNCIL

OF CHALCEDON.

The Holy, Great, and Œcumenical Synod, assembled, by the grace of God and the command of our most Christian and religious Emperors, Marcian and Valentine, at Chalcedon, the Metropolis of the Bithynian Province, in the Martyry of the holy and victorious Martyr Euphemia, has decreed as follows:

Our Lord Jesus Christ, when strengthening the knowledge of the Faith in his disciples, to the end that no one might disagree with his neighbour concerning the doctrines of the Faith, and that the proclamation of the Truth might be set forth equally to all men, said, "My peace I leave with you, my peace I give unto you." But, since the evil one does not desist from sowing tares among the seeds of godliness, but ever invents some new device against the Truth; therefore the Lord, providing, as he ever does, for the human race, has raised up this pious, faithful, and zealous Sovereign, and has called together unto him from all parts the Chief Rulers of the Priesthood; so that, the grace of Christ our common Lord inspiring us, we may cast off every plague of falsehood from the sheep of Christ, and feed them with the tender leaves of truth. And this have we done with one unanimous consent, driving away erroneous doctrines and renewing the unerring Faith of the Fathers, publishing to all men the Formula of the Three Hundred and Eighteen, and to their number adding, as their peers, the Fathers who have received the same summary of religion. Such are the One Hundred and Fifty holy Fathers who afterwards assembled in the great City of

νυν, τὴν τάξιν καὶ τοὺς περὶ τῆς πίστεως ἅπαντας τύπους φυλάττοντες καὶ ἡμεῖς τῆς κατ' Ἔφεσον πάλαι γεγενημένης ἁγίας συνόδου, ἧς ἡγεμόνες οἱ ἁγιώτατοι τὴν μνήμην Κελεστῖνος ὁ τῆς Ῥωμαίων, καὶ Κυρίλλος ὁ τῆς Ἀλεξανδρέων, ἐτύγχανον, προλάμπειν μὲν τῆς ὀρθῆς καὶ ἀμωμήτου πίστεως τὴν ἔκθεσιν τῶν τιη' ἁγίων καὶ μακαρίων πατέρων τῶν ἐν Νικαίᾳ ἐπὶ τοῦ εὐσεβοῦς μνήμης Κωνσταντίνου τοῦ γενομένου βασιλέως συναχθέντων· κρατεῖν δὲ καὶ τὰ παρὰ τῶν ρν' ἁγίων πατέρων ἐν Κωνσταντινουπόλει ὁρισθέντα, πρὸς ἀναίρεσιν μὲν τῶν τότε φυεισῶν αἱρέσεων, βεβαίωσιν δὲ τῆς αὐτῆς καθολικῆς καὶ ἀποστολικῆς ἡμῶν πίστεως·

ΠΙΣΤΕΥΟΜΕΝ κ. τ. λ.

Ἤρκει μὲν οὖν εἰς ἐντελῆ τῆς εὐσεβείας ἐπίγνωσίν τε καὶ βεβαίωσιν τὸ σοφὸν καὶ σωτήριον τοῦτο τῆς θείας χάριτος σύμβολον· περί τε γὰρ τοῦ Πατρὸς καὶ τοῦ Υἱοῦ καὶ τοῦ ἁγίου Πνεύματος ἐκδιδάσκει τὸ τέλειον, καὶ τοῦ Κυρίου τὴν ἐνανθρώπησιν τοῖς πιστῶς δεχομένοις παρίστησιν. Ἀλλ' ἐπειδήπερ οἱ τῆς ἀληθείας ἀθετεῖν ἐπιχειροῦντες τὸ κήρυγμα, διὰ τῶν οἰκείων αἱρέσεων τὰς κενοφωνίας ἀπέτεκον, οἱ μὲν τὸ τῆς δι' ἡμᾶς τοῦ Κυρίου οἰκονομίας μυστήριον παραφθείρειν τολμῶντες, καὶ τὴν Θεοτόκον ἐπὶ τῆς παρθένου φωνὴν ἀπαρνούμενοι· οἱ δὲ σύγχυσιν καὶ κρᾶσιν εἰσάγοντες, καὶ μίαν εἶναι φύσιν τῆς σαρκὸς καὶ τῆς Θεότητος ἀνοήτως ἀναπλάττοντες, καὶ παθητὴν τοῦ μονογενοῦς τὴν θείαν φύσιν τῇ συγχύσει τερατευόμενοι· διὰ τοῦτο πᾶσαν αὐτοῖς ἀποκλεῖσαι κατὰ τῆς ἀληθείας μηχανὴν βουλομένη ἡ παροῦσα νῦν αὕτη ἁγία μεγάλη καὶ οἰκουμενικὴ σύνοδος, τὸ τοῦ κηρύγματος ἄνωθεν ἀσάλευτον ἐκδιδάσκουσα, ὥρισε προηγουμένως, τῶν τριακοσίων δεκαοκτὼ ἁγίων πατέρων τὴν πίστιν μένειν ἀπαρεγχείρητον. Καὶ διὰ μὲν τοὺς τῷ Πνεύματι τῷ Ἁγίῳ μαχομένους, τὴν χρόνοις ὕστερον παρὰ τῶν ἐπὶ τῆς βασιλευούσης πόλεως συνελθόντων ἑκατὸν πεντήκοντα ἁγιων πατέρων περὶ τῆς τοῦ Πνεύματος οὐσίας παραδοθεῖσαν διδασκαλίαν κυροῖ· ἣν ἐκεῖνοι τοῖς πᾶσιν ἐγνώρισαν, οὐκ ὥς τι λεῖπον τοῖς προλαβοῦσιν ἐπ-

Constantinople and ratified the same Faith. Moreover, observing the order and every form relating to the Faith, which was observed by the Holy Synod formerly held in Ephesus, of which Celestine of Rome and Cyril of Alexandria, of holy memory, were the leaders, we do declare that the exposition of the right and blameless Faith made by the Three Hundred and Eighteen holy and blessed Fathers, assembled at Nicæa in the reign of Constantine of pious memory, shall be preëminent: and that those things shall be of force also, which were decreed by the One Hundred and Fifty holy Fathers at Constantinople, for the uprooting of the heresies which had then sprung up, and for the confirmation of the same our Catholic and Apostolic Faith.

WE BELIEVE, &c.

This wise and Salutary Formula of Divine grace sufficed for the perfect acknowledgment and confirmation of religion; for it teaches the perfect [doctrine] concerning FATHER, SON, and HOLY GHOST, and sets forth the Incarnation of the LORD to them that faithfully receive it. But, forasmuch as persons undertaking to make void the preaching of the truth have through their individual heresies given rise to empty babblings; some of them daring to corrupt the mystery of the LORD's incarnation for us and refusing [to use] the name Theotocos in reference to the Virgin, while others, bringing in [the idea of] a confusion and mixture, and idly conceiving that the nature of the flesh and of the Godhead is all one, subtilly maintain that the divine Nature of the Only Begotten is, by mixture, capable of suffering; therefore this present Holy, Great, and Œcumenical Synod, teaching the unaltered truth of the Gospel, which has been held from the beginning, and desiring to exclude every device against the Truth, has at the very outset decreed that the Faith of the Three Hundred and Eighteen Fathers shall not be tampered with. And, on account of them that contend against the HOLY GHOST, it confirms the doctrine afterwards delivered concerning the substance of the SPIRIT by the One Hundred and Fifty holy Fathers who assembled in the imperial City; which doctrine they declared unto all men, not as though they were introducing anything that had been lacking in their predecessors, but in order to explain through

ἄγοντες, ἀλλὰ τὴν περὶ τοῦ Ἁγίου Πνεύματος αὐτῶν ἔννοιαν κατὰ τῶν τὴν αὐτοῦ δεσποτείαν ἀθετεῖν πειρωμένων γραφικαῖς μαρτυρίαις τρανώσαντες. Διὰ δὲ τοὺς τὸ τῆς οἰκονομίας παραφθείρειν ἐπιχειροῦντας μυστήριον, καὶ ψιλὸν ἄνθρωπον εἶναι τὸν ἐκ τῆς ἁγίας τεχθέντα Μαρίας ἀναιδῶς ληρωδοῦντας, τὰς τοῦ μακαρίου Κυρίλλου, τοῦ τῆς Ἀλεξανδρέων ἐκκλησίας γενομένου ποιμένος, συνοδικὰς ἐπιστολὰς πρὸς Νεστόριον καὶ πρὸς τοὺς τῆς ἀνατολῆς, ἁρμοδίους οὔσας ἐδέξατο, εἰς ἔλεγχον μὲν τῆς Νεστορίου φρενοβλαβείας, ἑρμηνείαν δὲ τῶν ἐν εὐσεβεῖ ζήλῳ τοῦ σωτηρίου συμβόλου ποθουντῶν τὴν ἔννοιαν· αἷς καὶ τὴν ἐπιστολὴν τοῦ τῆς μεγίστης καὶ πρεσβυτέρας Ῥώμης προέδρου τοῦ μακαριωτάτου καὶ ἁγιωτάτου ἀρχιεπισκόπου Λέοντος, τὴν γραφεῖσαν πρὸς τὸν ἐν ἁγίοις ἀρχιεπίσκοπον Φλαυιανὸν ἐπ' ἀναιρέσει τῆς Εὐτυχοῦς κακονοίας, ἅτε δὴ τῇ τοῦ μεγάλου Πέτρου ὁμολογίᾳ συμβαίνουσαν, καὶ κοινήν τινα στήλην ὑπάρχουσαν κατὰ τῶν κακοδοξούντων, εἰκότως συνήρμοσε πρὸς τὴν τῶν ὀρθοδόξων δογμάτων βεβαίωσιν. Τοῖς τε γὰρ εἰς υἱῶν δυάδα τὸ τῆς οἰκονομίας διασπᾶν ἐπιχειροῦσι μυστήριον, παρατάττεται· καὶ τοὺς παθητὴν τοῦ μονογενοῦς λέγειν τολμῶντας τὴν Θεότητα, τοῦ τῶν ἱερῶν ἀπωθεῖται συλλόγου· καὶ τοῖς ἐπὶ τῶν δύο φύσεων τοῦ Χριστοῦ κρᾶσιν, ἢ σύγχυσιν ἐπινοοῦσιν ἀνθίσταται· καὶ τοὺς οὐρανίου, ἢ ἑτέρας τινὸς ὑπάρχειν οὐσίας τὴν ἐξ ἡμῶν ληφθεῖσαν αὐτῷ τοῦ δούλου μορφὴν παραπαίοντας ἐξελαύνει· καὶ τοὺς δύο μὲν πρὸ τῆς ἑνώσεως φύσεις τοῦ Κυρίου μυθεύοντας, μίαν δὲ μετὰ τὴν ἕνωσιν ἀναπλάττοντας ἀναθεματίζει· ἑπόμενοι τοίνυν τοῖς ἁγίοις πατράσιν, ἕνα καὶ τὸν αὐτὸν ὁμολογοῦμεν Υἱὸν τὸν Κύριον ἡμῶν Ἰησοῦν Χριστὸν, καὶ συμφώνως ἅπαντες ἐδιδάσκομεν, τέλειον τὸν αὐτὸν ἐν Θεότητι, τέλειον τὸν αὐτὸν ἐν ἀνθρωπότητι, Θεὸν ἀληθῶς, καὶ ἄνθρωπον ἀληθῶς, τὸν αὐτὸν ἐκ ψυχῆς λογικῆς καὶ σώματος, ὁμοούσιον τῷ Πατρὶ κατὰ τὴν Θεότητα, καὶ ὁμοούσιον τὸν αὐτὸν ἡμῖν κατὰ τὴν ἀνθρωπότητα, κατὰ πάντα ὅμοιον ἡμῖν, χωρὶς ἁμαρτίας· πρὸ αἰώνων μὲν ἐκ τοῦ Πατρὸς γεννηθέντα κατὰ τὴν Θεότητα, ἐπ' ἐσχάτων δὲ τῶν ἡμερῶν τὸν αὐτὸν δι' ἡμᾶς καὶ διὰ τὴν ἡμετέραν σωτηρίαν ἐκ Μαρίας τῆς παρθένου τῆς Θεοτόκου κατὰ τὴν ἀνθρωπότητα, ἕνα καὶ τὸν αὐτὸν Χριστὸν, Υἱὸν, Κύριον, μονογενῆ, ἐν δύο φύσεσιν ἀσυγχύτως, ἀτρέπτως, ἀδιαιρέτως, ἀχωρίστως γνωριζόμενον· οὐδαμοῦ τῆς τῶν φύ-

written documents their faith concerning the HOLY GHOST against those who were seeking to destroy His Sovereignty. And, on account of those who have taken in hand to corrupt the mystery of the Incarnation and who shamelessly pretend that He Who was born of the holy Mary was mere man, it receives the synodical letters of the Blessed Cyril, former Pastor of the Church of Alexandria, addressed to Nestorius and the Easterns, judging them suitable for the refutation of the frenzied folly of Nestorius, and for the instruction of those who long with holy ardour for a knowledge of the saving Formula. And, for the confirmation of the orthodox doctrines, it has rightly added to these the letter of the President of the greater and older Rome, the most blessed and holy Archbishop Leo, which was addressed to the saintly Archbishop Flavian for the removal of the false doctrines of Eutyches, judging them to be agreeable to the confession of the great Peter, and as it were a common pillar against misbelievers. For it opposes those who would rend the mystery of the Incarnation into a Duad of Sons; it repels from the assembly of the Saints those who dare to say that the Godhead of the Only Begotten is capable of suffering; it resists those who imagine [that there is] a mixture or confusion of the natures of CHRIST; it drives away those who fancy the form of a servant which was taken by him of us is of an heavenly or some other substance; and it anathematizes those who talk of two natures of our LORD before the union, conceiving that after the union there was only one. We, therefore, following the holy Fathers, confess one and the same SON, our LORD JESUS CHRIST; and we do with one voice teach that He is perfect in Godhead and that He is perfect in Manhood, being truly GOD and truly Man; that He is of a reasonable soul and body, consubstantial with the FATHER as touching the Godhead, and consubstantial with us as touching His manhood, being in all things like us, sin except; that, as touching His Godhead, He was begotten of the FATHER before the worlds; and, as touching His manhood, that in the last days He was for us [men] and for our salvation born of Mary, the Virgin Theotocos, being one and the same CHRIST, SON, LORD, Only Begotten, acknowledged to be in two natures, without confusion, change, division, separation; the distinction of natures being by no means

σεων διαφορᾶς ἀνῃρημένης διὰ τὴν ἕνωσιν, σωζομένης δὲ μᾶλλον τῆς ἰδιότητος ἑκατέρας φύσεως, καὶ εἰς ἓν πρόσωπον καὶ μίαν ὑπόστασιν συντρεχούσης, οὐκ εἰς δύο πρόσωπα μεριζόμενον ἢ διαιρούμενον, ἀλλ' ἕνα καὶ τὸν αὐτὸν Υἱὸν καὶ μονογενῆ, Θεὸν λόγον, Κύριον Ἰησοῦν Χριστόν· καθάπερ ἄνωθεν οἱ προφῆται περὶ αὐτοῦ, καὶ αὐτὸς ἡμᾶς ὁ Κύριος Ἰησοῦς Χριστὸς ἐξεπαίδευσε, καὶ τὸ τῶν πατέρων ἡμῖν παραδέδωκε σύμβολον.

Τούτων τοίνυν μετὰ πάσης πανταχόθεν ἀκριβείας τε καὶ ἐμμελείας παρ' ἡμῶν διατυπωθέντων, ὥρισεν ἡ ἁγία καὶ οἰκουμενικὴ σύνοδος, ἑτέραν πίστιν μηδενὶ ἐξεῖναι προφέρειν, ἤγουν συγγράφειν, ἢ συντιθέναι, ἢ φρονεῖν, ἢ διδάσκειν ἑτέρους. Τοὺς δὲ τολμῶντας ἢ συντιθέναι πίστιν ἑτέραν, ἤγουν προκομίζειν, ἢ διδάσκειν, ἢ παραδιδόναι ἕτερον σύμβολον τοῖς ἐθέλουσιν ἐπιστρέφειν εἰς ἐπίγνωσιν ἀληθείας ἐξ Ἑλληνισμοῦ, ἢ ἐξ Ἰουδαϊσμοῦ, ἤγουν ἐξ αἱρέσεως οἱασδηποτοῦν, τούτους, εἰ μὲν εἶεν ἐπίσκοποι ἢ κληρικοί, ἀλλοτρίους εἶναι τοὺς ἐπισκόπους τῆς ἐπισκοπῆς, καὶ τοὺς κληρικοὺς τοῦ κλήρου· εἰ δὲ μονάζοντες ἢ λαϊκοὶ εἶεν, ἀναθεματίζεσθαι αὐτούς.

ΜΕΤΑ δὲ τὴν ἀνάγνωσιν τοῦ ὅρου πάντες οἱ εὐλαβέστατοι ἐπίσκοποι ἐβόησαν· αὕτη ἡ πίστις τῶν πατέρων. Οἱ μητροπολῖται ἄρτι ὑπογράψωσι· παρόντων αὐτῶν ἀρχόντων, ἄρτι ὑπογράψωσι· τὰ καλῶς ὁρισθέντα ὑπέρθεσιν μὴ δέξηται. Αὕτη ἡ πίστις τῶν ἀποστόλων. Ταύτῃ πάντες στοιχοῦμεν· πάντες οὕτω φρονοῦμεν.

destroyed by their union; but rather, the distinction of each nature being preserved, and concurring in one Person and one Existence; not in somewhat that is parted or divided into two persons; but in one and the same and Only-Begotten Son, God the Word, the Lord Jesus Christ, as the Prophets have from the beginning testified concerning Him, and our Lord Jesus Christ Himself has taught us, and the Creed of the Fathers has delivered to us.

These things, then, having been expressed by us with all possible precision and carefulness, the Holy and Œcumenical Synod decrees that it is not lawful for any man to propose, or compile, or compose, or hold, or teach to others, any different Faith. But those who presume to compose a different Faith, or to propagate, or teach, or deliver a different Formula to persons desirous of turning to the acknowledgment of the Truth from heathenism, or Judaism, or any heresy whatsoever, if they be Bishops or Clergymen, shall be deposed, Bishops from the Episcopate, and Clergymen from the Clergy; and, if they be Monks or laymen, they shall be anathematized.

Now, after the reading of the Definition, all the most religious Bishops cried out: This is the Faith of the Fathers: let the Metropolitans forthwith subscribe it: let them forthwith, in the presence of the rulers, subscribe it: let that which has been well defined have no delay: this is the Faith of the Apostles: by this we all stand: thus we all believe.

C A N O N E S

CHALCEDONENSIS CONCILII GENERALIS.

A. D. 451.

Κανόνες τῶν ἑξακοσίων τριάκοντα ἁγίων καὶ μακαρίων πατέρων τῶν ἐν Χαλκηδόνι συνελθόντων.

ΚΑΝΩΝ Α'.

Τοὺς παρὰ τῶν ἁγίων πατέρων καθ' ἑκάστην σύνοδον ἄχρι τοῦ νῦν ἐκτεθέντας κανόνας κρατεῖν ἐδικαιώσαμεν.

ΚΑΝΩΝ Β'.

Εἴ τις ἐπίσκοπος, ἐπὶ χρήμασι χειροτονίαν ποιήσαιτο, καὶ εἰς πρᾶσιν καταγάγοι τὴν ἄπρατον χάριν, καὶ χειροτονήσοι ἐπὶ χρήμασιν ἐπίσκοπον, ἢ χωρεπίσκοπον, ἢ πρεσβυτέρους, ἢ διακόνους, ἢ ἕτερόν τινα τῶν ἐν τῷ κλήρῳ κατηριθμημένων, ἢ προβάλλοιτο ἐπὶ χρήμασιν οἰκονόμον, ἢ ἔκδικον, ἢ παραμονάριον, ἢ ὅλως τινὰ τοῦ κανόνος, δι' αἰσχροκέρδειαν οἰκείαν, ὁ τοῦτο ἐπιχειρήσας, ἐλεγχθεὶς, κινδυνευέτω περὶ τὸν οἰκεῖον βαθμόν· καὶ ὁ χειροτονούμενος, μηδὲν ἐκ τῆς κατ' ἐμπορίαν ὠφελείσθω χειροτονίας, ἢ προβολῆς· ἀλλ' ἔστω ἀλλότριος τῆς ἀξίας, ἢ τοῦ φροντίσματος, οὗπερ ἐπὶ χρήμασιν ἔτυχεν. Εἰ δέ τις καὶ μεσιτεύων φανείη τοῖς οὕτως αἰσχροῖς καὶ ἀθεμίτοις λήμμασι, καὶ οὗτος, εἰ μὲν κληρικὸς εἴη, τοῦ οἰκείου ἐκπιπτέτω βαθμοῦ· εἰ δὲ λαϊκὸς, ἢ μονάζων, ἀναθεματιζέσθω.

ΚΑΝΩΝ Γ'.

Ἦλθεν εἰς τὴν ἁγίαν σύνοδον, ὅτι τῶν ἐν τῷ κλήρῳ κατειλεγμένων τινὲς, δι' αἰσχροκέρδειαν, ἀλλοτρίων κτημάτων γίνονται μισθωταὶ, καὶ πράγματα κοσμικὰ ἐργολαβοῦσι, τῆς μὲν τοῦ Θεοῦ λειτουργίας καταῤῥᾳθυμοῦντες, τοὺς δὲ τῶν κοσμικῶν ὑποτρέχοντες οἴκους, καὶ οὐσιῶν χειρισμοὺς

CANONS OF CHALCEDON.

CANON I.

We have judged it right that the Canons of the Holy Fathers made in every Synod even until now should remain in force.

CANON II.

If any Bishop should ordain for money, and put to sale a grace which cannot be sold, and for money ordain a Bishop, or Chorepiscopus, or Presbyters, or Deacons, or any other of those who are counted among the Clergy; or if through lust of gain he should nominate for money a Steward, or Advocate, or Bailiff, or any one whatever who is on the roll of the Church, let him who is convicted of this forfeit his own rank; and let him who is ordained be nothing profited by the purchased ordination or promotion; but let him be removed from the charge or dignity he has obtained for money. And if any one should be found negotiating such shameful and unlawful transactions, let him also, if he is a Clergyman, be deposed from his rank, and if he is a layman or Monk, let him be anathematized.

CANON III.

It has come to [the knowledge of] the Holy Synod that certain of those who are enrolled among the Clergy have, through lust of gain, become hirers of other men's possessions, and make contracts pertaining to secular affairs, lightly esteeming the service of God, and that others slip into the houses of secular persons, whose property they undertake through

ἀναδεχόμενοι διὰ φιλαργυρίαν. Ὥρισε τοίνυν ἡ ἁγία καὶ μεγάλη σύνοδος, μηδένα τοῦ λοιποῦ, μὴ ἐπίσκοπον, μὴ κληρικὸν, μὴ μονάζοντα, ἢ μισθοῦσθαι κτήματα, ἢ πραγμάτων ἐπεισάγειν ἑαυτὸν κοσμικαῖς διοικήσεσι· πλὴν εἰ μήπου ἐκ νόμων καλοῖτο εἰς ἀφηλίκων ἀπαραίτητον ἐπιτροπήν· ἢ ὁ τῆς πόλεως ἐπίσκοπος ἐκκλησιαστικῶν ἐπιτρέψοι φροντίζειν πραγμάτων, ἢ ὀρφανῶν, ἢ χηρῶν ἀπρονοήτων, καὶ τῶν προσώπων τῶν μάλιστα τῆς ἐκκλησιαστικῆς δεομένων βοηθείας, διὰ τὸν φόβον τοῦ Θεοῦ. Εἰ δέ τις παραβαίνων τὰ ὡρισμένα τοῦ λοιποῦ ἐπιχειρήσοι, ὁ τοιοῦτος ἐκκλησιαστικοῖς ὑποκείσθω ἐπιτιμίοις.

ΚΑΝΩΝ Δʹ.

Οἱ ἀληθῶς καὶ εἰλικρινῶς τὸν μονήρη μετιόντες βίον, τῆς προσηκούσης ἀξιούσθωσαν τιμῆς. Ἐπειδὴ δέ τινες τῷ μοναχικῷ κεχρημένοι προσχήματι, τάς τε ἐκκλησίας καὶ τὰ πολιτικὰ διαταράσσουσι πράγματα, περιϊόντες ἀδιαφόρως ἐν ταῖς πόλεσιν, οὐ μὴν ἀλλὰ καὶ μοναστήρια ἑαυτοῖς συνιστᾷν ἐπιτηδεύοντες, ἔδοξε, μηδένα μὲν μηδαμοῦ οἰκοδομεῖν, μηδὲ συνιστᾷν μοναστήριον, ἢ εὐκτήριον οἶκον, παρὰ γνώμην τοῦ τῆς πόλεως ἐπισκόπου· τοὺς δὲ καθ' ἑκάστην πόλιν, καὶ χώραν, μονάζοντας, ὑποτετάχθαι τῷ ἐπισκόπῳ, καὶ τὴν ἡσυχίαν ἀσπάζεσθαι, καὶ προσέχειν μόνῃ τῇ νηστείᾳ, καὶ τῇ προσευχῇ, ἐν οἷς τόποις ἀπετάξαντο προσκαρτεροῦντες· μήτε δὲ ἐκκλησιαστικοῖς, μήτε βιωτικοῖς παρενοχλεῖν πράγμασιν, ἢ ἐπικοινωνεῖν, καταλιμπάνοντας τὰ ἴδια μοναστήρια, εἰ μήποτε ἄρα ἐπιτραπεῖεν διὰ χρείαν ἀναγκαίαν ὑπὸ τοῦ τῆς πόλεως ἐπισκόπου· μηδένα δέ προσδέχεσθαι ἐν τοῖς μοναστηρίοις δοῦλον ἐπὶ τῷ μονάσαι, παρὰ γνώμην τοῦ ἰδίου δεσπότου· τὸν δὲ παραβαίνοντα τοῦτον ἡμῶν τὸν ὅρον, ὡρίσαμεν ἀκοινώνητον εἶναι, ἵνα μὴ τὸ ὄνομα τοῦ Θεοῦ βλασφημῆται. Τὸν μέν τοι ἐπίσκοπον τῆς πόλεως, χρὴ τὴν δέουσαν πρόνοιαν ποιεῖσθαι τῶν μοναστηρίων.

ΚΑΝΩΝ Εʹ.

Περὶ τῶν μεταβαινόντων ἀπὸ πόλεως εἰς πόλιν ἐπισκόπων, ἢ κληρικῶν, ἔδοξε τοὺς περὶ τούτων τεθέντας κανόνας παρὰ τῶν ἁγίων πατέρων ἔχειν τὴν ἰσχύν.

covetousness to manage. Wherefore the Great and Holy Synod decrees that henceforth no Bishop, Clergyman, nor Monk shall hire possessions, or engage in business, or occupy himself in worldly engagements, except he shall be called by the law to the unavoidable guardianship of minors; or the Bishop of the City shall commit to him the care of ecclesiastical business, or of unprovided orphans or widows and of persons who stand especially in need of the Church's help, through the fear of God. And if any one shall hereafter transgress these decrees, he shall be subjected to ecclesiastical penalties.

CANON IV.

Let those who truly and sincerely enter the monastic life, be counted worthy of becoming honour; but, forasmuch as certain persons using the pretext of monasticism bring confusion both upon the Church and into political affairs by going about promiscuously in the Cities, seeking only to establish Monasteries for themselves; therefore it is decreed that no Monk shall live anywhere, nor establish a Monastery or an Oratory contrary to the will of the Bishop of the City; and that the Monks in every City and district shall be subject to the Bishop, and embrace a quiet course of life, and give themselves only to fasting and prayer, remaining permanently in the places where they have been settled; and they shall meddle neither in ecclesiastical nor in secular affairs, nor leave their own Monasteries to take part in such; unless, indeed, they should at any time through urgent necessity be appointed thereto by the Bishop of the City. And no slave shall be received into any Monastery to become a Monk against the will of his master. And if any one shall transgress this our judgment, we have decreed that he shall be excommunicated, that the name of God be not blasphemed. But the Bishop of the City must make the needful provision for the Monasteries.

CANON V.

Concerning Bishops or Clergymen who go about from City to City, it is decreed that the Canons enacted by the Holy Fathers shall still retain their force.

ΚΑΝΩΝ ϛʹ.

Μηδένα ἀπολελυμένως χειροτονεῖσθαι, μήτε πρεσβύτερον, μήτε διάκονον, μήτε ὅλως τινὰ τῶν ἐν τῷ ἐκκλησιαστικῷ τάγματι· εἰ μὴ ἰδικῶς ἐν ἐκκλησίᾳ πόλεως, ἢ κώμης, ἢ μαρτυρίῳ, ἢ μοναστηρίῳ, ὁ χειροτονούμενος ἐπικηρύττοιτο. Τοὺς *δὲ ἀπολύτως χειροτονουμένους, ὥρισεν ἡ ἁγία σύνοδος, ἄκυρον ἔχειν τὴν τοιαύτην χειροθεσίαν, καὶ μηδαμοῦ δύνασθαι ἐνεργεῖν ἐφ' ὕβρει τοῦ χειροτονήσαντος.*

ΚΑΝΩΝ Ζʹ.

Τοὺς *ἅπαξ ἐν κλήρῳ τεταγμένους ἢ καὶ μοναστὰς, ὡρίσαμεν μήτε ἐπὶ στρατείαν, μήτε ἐπὶ ἀξίαν κοσμικὴν ἔρχεσθαι· ἢ, τοῦτο τολμῶντας, καὶ μὴ μεταμελουμένους ὥστε ἐπιστρέψαι ἐπὶ τοῦτο, ὃ διὰ* Θεὸν *πρότερον εἵλοντο, ἀναθεματίζεσθαι.*

ΚΑΝΩΝ Ηʹ.

Οἱ *κληρικοὶ τῶν πτωχείων, καὶ μοναστηρίων, καὶ μαρτυρίων, ὑπὸ τὴν ἐξουσίαν τῶν ἐν ἑκάστῃ πόλει ἐπισκόπων, κατὰ τὴν τῶν ἁγίων* Πατέρων *παράδοσιν, διαμενέτωσαν· καὶ μὴ κατὰ αὐθάδειαν ἀφηνιάτωσαν τοῦ ἰδίου ἐπισκόπου.* Οἱ *δὲ τολμῶντες ἀνατρέπειν τὴν τοιαύτην διατύπωσιν, καθ' οἱονδήποτε τρόπον, καὶ μὴ ὑποταττόμενοι τῷ ἰδίῳ ἐπισκόπῳ, εἰ μὲν εἶεν κληρικοὶ, τοῖς τῶν κανόνων ὑποκείσθωσαν ἐπιτιμίοις· εἰ δὲ μονάζοντες, ἢ λαϊκοὶ, ἔστωσαν ἀκοινώνητοι.*

ΚΑΝΩΝ Θʹ.

Εἴ *τις κληρικὸς πρὸς κληρικὸν πρᾶγμα ἔχει, μὴ ἐγκαταλιμπανέτω τὸν οἰκεῖον ἐπίσκοπον, καὶ ἐπὶ κοσμικὰ δικαστήρια μὴ κατατρεχέτω, ἀλλὰ πρότερον τὴν ὑπόθεσιν γυμναζέτω παρὰ τῷ ἰδίῳ ἐπισκόπῳ, ἢ γοῦν, γνώμῃ αὐτοῦ τοῦ ἐπισκόπου, παρ' οἷς ἂν ἀμφότερα τὰ μέρη βούλωνται, τὰ τῆς δίκης συγκροτείσθω· εἰ δέ τις παρὰ ταῦτα ποιήσοι, κανονικοῖς ἐπιτιμίοις ὑποκείσθω.* Εἰ *δὲ καὶ κληρικὸς πρᾶγμα ἔχει πρὸς τὸν ἴδιον, ἢ καὶ πρὸς ἕτερον ἐπίσκοπον παρὰ τῇ συνόδῳ τῆς ἐπαρχίας δικαζέσθω.* Εἰ *δὲ πρὸς τὸν τῆς αὐτῆς ἐπαρχίας μητροπολίτην, ἐπίσκοπος, ἢ κληρικὸς,*

CANON VI.

Neither Presbyter, Deacon, nor any of the ecclesiastical order shall be ordained without a charge, nor unless the person ordained is particularly appointed to a Church in a City or village, or to a Martyry, or to a Monastery. And if any shall be ordained without a charge, the Holy Synod decrees, to the reproach of the ordainer, that such an ordination shall be inoperative, and shall nowhere have effect.

CANON VII.

We have decreed that those who have once been enrolled among the Clergy, or have been made Monks, shall accept neither a military charge nor any secular dignity; and if they shall presume to do so and not repent in such wise as to turn again to that which they had first chosen for the love of God, they shall be anathematized.

CANON VIII.

Let the Clergy of the poor-houses, Monasteries, and Martyries in every City remain under the authority of the Bishops, according to the tradition of the holy Fathers; and let no one arrogantly cast off the rule of his own Bishop; and if any shall contravene this Canon in any way whatever, and will not be subject to their own Bishop, if they be Clergy, let them be subjected to canonical penalties, and if they be Monks or laymen, let them be excommunicated.

CANON IX.

If any Clergyman have a complaint against another Clergyman, he shall not forsake his Bishop and run to secular courts; but let him first try the suit before his own Bishop, or let the matter at issue be submitted to any persons whom parties shall, with the Bishop's consent, select. And if any one shall contravene these decrees, let him be subjected to canonical penalties. And if a Clergyman have a complaint against his own or any other Bishop, let it be decided by the Synod of the Province. And if a Bishop or Clergyman should have a difference with the Metropolitan of the Province, let

ἀμφισβητοίη, καταλαμβανέτω τὸν ἔξαρχον τῆς διοικήσεως, ἢ τὸν τῆς βασιλευούσης Κωνσταντινουπόλεως θρόνον, καὶ ἐπ' αὐτῷ δικαζέσθω.

ΚΑΝΩΝ Ι'.

Μὴ ἐξεῖναι κληρικὸν ἐν δύο πόλεων κατὰ ταυτὸν καταλέγεσθαι ἐκκλησίαις, ἐν ᾗ τε τὴν ἀρχὴν ἐχειροτονήθη, καὶ ἐν ᾗ προσέφυγεν, ὡς μείζονι δῆθεν, διὰ δόξης κενῆς ἐπιθυμίαν. Τοὺς δέ γε τοῦτο ποιοῦντας ἀποκαθίστασθαι τῇ ἰδίᾳ ἐκκλησίᾳ, ἐν ᾗ ἐξ ἀρχῆς ἐχειροτονήθησαν, καὶ ἐκεῖ μόνον λειτουργεῖν. Εἰ μέν τοι ἤδη τις μετετέθη ἐξ ἄλλης εἰς ἄλλην ἐκκλησίαν, μηδὲν τοῖς τῆς προτέρας ἐκκλησίας, ἤτοι τῶν ὑπ' αὐτὴν μαρτυρίων, ἢ πτωχείων, ἢ ξενοδοχείων ἐπικοινωνεῖν πράγμασιν. Τοὺς δέ γε τολμῶντας, μετὰ τὸν ὅρον τῆς μεγάλης καὶ οἰκουμενικῆς ταύτης συνόδου, πράττειν τι τῶν νῦν ἀπηγορευμένων, ὥρισεν ἡ ἁγία σύνοδος ἐκπίπτειν τοῦ ἰδίου βαθμοῦ.

ΚΑΝΩΝ ΙΑ'.

Πάντας τοὺς πένητας καὶ δεομένους ἐπικουρίας, μετὰ δοκιμασίας ἐπιστολίοις, εἴτουν εἰρηνικοῖς ἐκκλησιαστικοῖς μόνοις, ὁδεύειν ὡρίσαμεν, καὶ μὴ συστατικοῖς· διὰ τὸ τὰς συστατικὰς ἐπιστολὰς προσήκειν τοῖς οὖσιν ἐν ὑπολήψει μόνοις παρέχεσθαι προσώποις.

ΚΑΝΩΝ ΙΒ'.

Ἦλθεν εἰς ἡμᾶς, ὥς τινες παρὰ τοὺς ἐκκλησιαστικοὺς θεσμοὺς προσδραμόντες δυναστείαις, διὰ πραγματικῶν τὴν μίαν ἐπαρχίαν εἰς δύο κατέτεμον, ὡς ἐκ τούτου δύο μητροπολίτας εἶναι ἐν τῇ αὐτῇ ἐπαρχίᾳ. Ὥρισε τοίνυν ἡ ἁγία σύνοδος, τοῦ λοιποῦ μηδὲν τοιοῦτο τολμᾶσθαι παρὰ ἐπισκόπου· ἐπεί, τὸν τοιοῦτο ἐπιχειροῦντα ἐκπίπτειν τοῦ ἰδίου βαθμοῦ. Ὅσαι δὲ ἤδη πόλεις διὰ γραμμάτων βασιλικῶν τῷ τῆς μητροπόλεως ἐτιμήθησαν ὀνόματι, μόνης ἀπολαυέτωσαν τῆς τιμῆς, καὶ ὁ τὴν ἐκκλησίαν αὐτῆς διοικῶν ἐπίσκοπος, δηλονότι σωζομένων τῇ κατ' ἀλήθειαν μητροπόλει τῶν οἰκείων δικαίων.

him have recourse to the Exarch of the Diocese, or to the throne of the Imperial City of Constantinople, and there let it be decided.

CANON X.

It shall not be lawful for a Clergyman to be at the same time enrolled in two Churches, that is, in the Church in which he was at first ordained, and in another to which, because it is greater, he has removed from lust of empty honour. And those who do so shall be returned to their own Church in which they were originally ordained, and there only shall they minister. But if any one has heretofore been [lawfully] transferred from one Church to another, he shall not intermeddle with the affairs of his former Church, nor with the Martyries, Almshouses, and Houses of Refuge belonging to it. And if, after the decree of this Great and Œcumenical Synod, any shall dare to do any of the things now forbidden, the Synod decrees that he shall be degraded from his rank.

CANON XI.

We have decreed that the poor and [other] persons needing assistance shall travel, after examination, with letters merely pacifical from the Church, and not with letters commendatory, inasmuch as letters commendatory ought to be given only to persons who are liable to question.

CANON XII.

It has come to our knowledge that certain persons, contrary to the laws of the Church, having had recourse to secular powers, have by means of imperial rescripts divided one Province into two, so that there are consequently two Metropolitans in one Province; therefore the Holy Synod decrees that for the future no such thing shall be attempted by a Bishop, and that whoever shall undertake it shall be degraded from his rank. But the Cities which have already been honored by means of imperial letters with the name of Metropolis, and Bishops in charge of them, shall take the title only, all metropolitan rights being preserved to the true Metropolis.

ΚΑΝΩΝ ΙΓ'.

Ξένους κληρικοὺς καὶ ἀναγνώστας ἐν ἑτέρᾳ πόλει δίχα συστατικῶν γραμμάτων τοῦ ἰδίου ἐπισκόπου, μηδόλως μηδαμοῦ λειτουργεῖν.

ΚΑΝΩΝ ΙΔ'.

Ἐπειδὴ ἔν τισιν ἐπαρχίαις συνκεχώρηται τοῖς ἀναγνώσταις, καὶ ψάλταις, γαμεῖν, ὥρισεν ἡ ἁγία σύνοδος, μὴ ἐξεῖναί τινι αὐτῶν ἑτερόδοξον γυναῖκα λαμβάνειν. Τοὺς δὲ ἤδη ἐκ τοιούτου γάμου παιδοποιήσαντας, εἰ μὲν ἔφθασαν βαπτίσαι τὰ ἐξ αὐτῶν τεχθέντα παρὰ τοῖς αἱρετικοῖς, προσάγειν αὐτὰ τῇ κοινωνίᾳ τῆς καθολικῆς ἐκκλησίας· μὴ βαπτίσαντας δὲ, μὴ δύνασθαι ἔτι βαπτίζειν αὐτὰ παρὰ τοῖς αἱρετικοῖς, μήτε μὴν συνάπτειν πρὸς γάμον αἱρετικῷ, ἢ Ἰουδαίῳ, ἢ Ἕλληνι, εἰ μὴ ἄρα ἐπαγγέλλοιτο μετατίθεσθαι εἰς τὴν ὀρθόδοξον πίστιν τὸ συναπτόμενον πρόσωπον τῷ ὀρθοδόξῳ. Εἰ δέ τις τοῦτον τὸν ὅρον παραβαίη τῆς ἁγίας συνόδου, κανονικῷ ὑποκείσθω ἐπιτιμίῳ.

ΚΑΝΩΝ ΙΕ'.

Διάκονον μὴ χειροτονεῖσθαι γυναῖκα πρὸ ἐτῶν τεσσαράκοντα, καὶ ταύτην μετ' ἀκριβοῦς δοκιμασίας. Εἰ δέ γε δεξαμένη τὴν χειροθεσίαν, καὶ χρόνον τινὰ παραμείνασα τῇ λειτουργίᾳ, ἑαυτὴν ἐπιδῷ γάμῳ, ὑβρίσασα τὴν τοῦ Θεοῦ χάριν, ἡ τοιαύτη ἀναθεματιζέσθω μετὰ τοῦ αὐτῇ συναφθέντος.

ΚΑΝΩΝ Ιϛ'.

Παρθένον ἀναθεῖσαν ἑαυτὴν τῷ δεσπότῃ Θεῷ, ὡσαύτως δὲ καὶ μονάζοντας, μὴ ἐξεῖναι γάμῳ προσομιλεῖν. Εἰ δέ γε εὑρεθεῖεν τοῦτο ποιοῦντες, ἔστωσαν ἀκοινώνητοι. Ὡρίσαμεν δὲ ἔχειν τὴν αὐθεντίαν τῆς ἐπ' αὐτοῖς φιλανθρωπίας τὸν κατὰ τόπον ἐπίσκοπον.

ΚΑΝΩΝ ΙΖ'.

Τὰς καθ' ἑκάστην ἐπαρχίαν ἀγροικικὰς παροικίας ἢ ἐγχωρίους, μένειν ἀπαρασαλεύτους παρὰ τοῖς κατέχουσιν αὐτὰς

CANON XIII.

Clergymen and Readers visiting another City without letters commendatory from their own Bishop, are absolutely prohibited from officiating.

CANON XIV.

Since in certain Provinces it is permitted to the Readers and Singers to marry, the Holy Synod decrees that it shall not be lawful for any of them to take a wife that is heterodox. But those who have already begotten children of such a marriage, if they have already had their children baptized among the heretics, must bring them into the communion of the Catholic Church; but if they have not had them baptized, they may not hereafter baptize them among heretics, nor give them in marriage to a heretic, or a Jew, or a heathen, unless the person marrying the orthodox child shall promise to come over to the orthodox Faith. And if any one shall transgress this decree of the Holy Synod, let him be subjected to canonical punishment.

CANON XV.

A woman shall not be ordained Deaconess under forty years of age, and then only after searching examination. And if, after she has been ordained and has continued for a time to minister, she shall despise the grace of God, and give herself in marriage, she and her husband shall be anathematized.

CANON XVI.

It is unlawful for a Virgin who has dedicated herself to the service of God, and likewise for Monks, to marry; and if they are found to have done this, let them be excommunicated. But we decree that in every place the Bishop shall have the power of indulgence towards them.

CANON XVII.

Outlying or rural Parishes shall in every Province remain to the Bishops who now have jurisdiction over them, particularly

ἐπισκόποις, καὶ μάλιστα εἰ τριακονταετῆ χρόνον ταύτας ἀβιάστως διακατέχοντες ᾠκονόμησαν. Εἰ δὲ ἐντὸς τῶν τριάκοντα ἐτῶν γεγένηταί τις, ἢ γένοιτο περὶ αὐτῶν ἀμφισβήτησις, ἐξεῖναι τοῖς λέγουσιν ἠδικεῖσθαι, περὶ τούτων κινεῖν παρὰ τῇ συνόδῳ τῆς ἐπαρχίας. Εἰ δέ τις ἀδικοῖτο παρὰ τοῦ ἰδίου μητροπολίτου, παρὰ τῷ ἐξάρχῳ τῆς διοικήσεως, ἢ τῷ Κωνσταντινουπόλεως θρόνῳ δικαζέσθω, καθὰ προείρηται. Εἰ δὲ καί τις ἐκ βασιλικῆς ἐξουσίας ἐκαίνισθη πόλις, ἢ αὖθις καινισθείη, τοῖς πολιτικοῖς καὶ δημοσίοις τύποις, καὶ τῶν ἐκκλησιαστικῶν παροικιῶν ἡ τάξις ἀκολουθείτω.

ΚΑΝΩΝ ΙΗ'.

Τὸ τῆς συνωμοσίας ἢ φατρίας ἔγκλημα, καὶ παρὰ τῶν ἔξω νόμων πάντη κεκώλυται, πολλῷ δὴ μᾶλλον ἐν τῇ τοῦ Θεοῦ ἐκκλησίᾳ τοῦτο γίνεσθαι ἀπαγορεύειν προσήκει. Εἴ τινες τοίνυν κληρικοὶ, ἢ μονάζοντες εὑρεθεῖεν συνομνύμενοι, ἢ φατριάζοντες, ἢ κατασκευὰς τυρεύοντες ἐπισκόποις, ἢ συγκληρικοῖς ἐκπιπτέτωσαν πάντη τοῦ οἰκείου βαθμοῦ.

ΚΑΝΩΝ ΙΘ'.

Ἦλθεν εἰς τὰς ἡμετέρας ἀκοὰς, ὡς ἐν ταῖς ἐπαρχίαις αἱ κεκανονισμέναι σύνοδοι τῶν ἐπισκόπων οὐ γίνονται, καὶ ἐκ τούτου πολλὰ παραμελεῖται τῶν διορθώσεως δεομένων ἐκκλησιαστικῶν πραγμάτων. Ὥρισε τοίνυν ἡ ἁγία σύνοδος, κατὰ τοὺς τῶν ἁγίων Πατέρων κανόνας, δὶς τοῦ ἐνιαυτοῦ ἐπὶ τὸ αὐτὸ συντρέχειν καθ' ἑκάστην ἐπαρχίαν τοὺς ἐπισκόπους, ἔνθα ἂν ὁ τῆς μητροπόλεως ἐπίσκοπος δοκιμάσῃ, καὶ διορθοῦν ἕκαστα τὰ ἀνακύπτοντα. Τοὺς δὲ μὴ συνιόντας ἐπισκόπους, ἐνδημοῦντας ταῖς ἑαυτῶν πόλεσι, καὶ ταῦτα ἐν ὑγείᾳ διάγοντας, καὶ πάσης ἀπαραιτήτου καὶ ἀναγκαίας ἀσχολίας ὄντας ἐλευθέρους, ἀδελφικῶς ἐπιπλήττεσθαι.

ΚΑΝΩΝ Κ'.

Κληρικοὺς εἰς ἐκκλησίαν τελοῦντας, καθὼς ἤδη ὡρίσαμεν, μὴ ἐξεῖναι εἰς ἄλλης πόλεως τάττεσθαι ἐκκλησίαν· ἀλλὰ στέργειν ἐκείνην ἐν ᾗ λειτουργεῖν ἐξ ἀρχῆς ἠξιώθησαν, ἐκτὸς ἐκείνων, οἵτινες ἀπολέσαντες τὰς

if the Bishops have peaceably and continuously governed them for the space of thirty years. But if within thirty years there has been, or shall be, any dispute concerning them, it is lawful for those who hold themselves aggrieved to bring their cause before the Synod of the Province. And if any one be wronged by his Metropolitan, let the matter be decided by the Exarch of the Diocese or by the throne of Constantinople, as has been before said. And if any City has been, or shall hereafter be, newly erected by imperial authority, let the arrangement of ecclesiastical Parishes follow the political and municipal forms.

CANON XVIII.

The crime of conspiracy or banding together is utterly prohibited even by the secular law, and much more ought it to be forbidden in the Church of God. Therefore, if any, whether Clergymen or Monks, should be detected in conspiring or banding together, or hatching plots against their Bishops or fellow-clergy, they shall by all means be deposed from their own rank.

CANON XIX.

Whereas it has come to our ears that in the Provinces the Canonical Synods of Bishops are not held, and that on this account many ecclesiastical matters which need regulation are neglected; therefore, according to the Canons of the holy Fathers, the Holy Synod decrees that the Bishops of every Province shall twice in the year assemble together where the Bishop of the Metropolis shall approve, and shall then settle whatever matters may have arisen. And Bishops, who do not attend, but remain in their own Cities, though they are in good health and free from any unavoidable and necessary business, shall receive a brotherly admonition.

CANON XX.

It shall not be lawful, as has been aforesaid, for Clergymen officiating in one Church to be appointed to the Church of another City, but they shall cleave to that in which they were first thought worthy to minister; those, however, being ex-

οἰκείας πατρίδας ἀπὸ ἀνάγκης, εἰς ἄλλην ἐκκλησίαν μετῆλθον. Εἰ δέ τις ἐπίσκοπος μετὰ τὸν ὅρον τοῦτον, ἄλλῳ ἐπισκόπῳ προσήκοντα δέξοιτο κληρικὸν, ἔδοξεν ἀκοινώνητον εἶναι καὶ τὸν δεχθέντα, καὶ τὸν δεξάμενον, ἕως ἂν ὁ μεταστὰς κληρικὸς εἰς τὴν ἰδίαν ἐπανέλθῃ ἐκκλησίαν.

ΚΑΝΩΝ ΚΑ′.

Κληρικοὺς, ἢ λαϊκοὺς, κατηγοροῦντας ἐπισκόπων, ἢ κληρικῶν, ἁπλῶς καὶ ἀδοκιμάστως μὴ προσδέχεσθαι εἰς κατηγορίαν, εἰ μὴ πρότερον ἐξετασθείη αὐτῶν ἡ ὑπόληψις.

ΚΑΝΩΝ ΚΒ′.

Μὴ ἐξεῖναι κληρικοῖς μετὰ θάνατον τοῦ ἰδίου ἐπισκόπου, διαρπάζειν τὰ διαφέροντα αὐτῷ πράγματα, καθὼς καὶ τοῖς πάλαι κανόσιν* ἀπηγόρευται· ἢ τοὺς τοῦτο ποιοῦντας, κινδυνεύειν περὶ τοὺς ἰδίους βαθμούς.

ΚΑΝΩΝ ΚΓ′.

Ἦλθεν εἰς τὰς ἀκοὰς τῆς ἁγίας συνόδου, ὡς κληρικοί τινες καὶ μονάζοντες, μηδὲν ἐγκεχειρισμένοι ὑπὸ τοῦ ἰδίου ἐπισκόπου, ἔστι δ' ὅτε καὶ ἀκοινώνητοι γενόμεμοι παρ' αὐτοῦ, καταλαμβάνοντες τὴν βασιλεύουσαν Κωνσταντινούπολιν, ἐπὶ πολὺ ἐν αὐτῇ διατρίβουσι, ταραχὰς ἐμποιοῦντες, καὶ θορυβοῦντες τὴν ἐκκλησιαστικὴν κατάστασιν, ἀνατρέπουσί τε οἴκους τινῶν. Ὥρισε τοίνυν ἡ ἁγία σύνοδος, τοὺς τοιούτους ὑπομιμνήσκεσθαι μὲν πρότερον διὰ τοῦ ἐκδίκου τῆς κατὰ Κωνσταντινούπολιν ἁγιωτάτης ἐκκλησίας ἐπὶ τὸ ἐξελθεῖν τῆς βασιλευούσης πόλεως· εἰ δὲ τοῖς αὐτοῖς πράγμασιν ἐπιμένοιεν ἀναισχυντοῦντες, καὶ ἄκοντας αὐτοὺς διὰ τοῦ αὐτοῦ ἐκδίκου ἐκβάλλεσθαι, καὶ τοὺς ἰδίους καταλαμβάνειν τόπους.

* The common reading, followed by the Greeks, is καὶ τοῖς παραλαμβάνουσιν, a phrase which is exceedingly obscure, and variously interpreted. I have therefore preferred in this instance to leave the text of the Syntagma and follow that of Beveridge which gives a clear sense, and is not without authority of MSS.

cepted, who have been driven by necessity from their own country, and have therefore taken refuge in another Church. And if, after this decree, any Bishop shall receive a Clergyman belonging to another Bishop, it is decreed that both the receiver and the received shall be suspended until such time as the Clergyman who has removed shall have returned to his own Church.

CANON XXI.

Clergymen and laymen bringing charges against Bishops and Clergymen are not to be received loosely and without examination, as accusers, but their own character shall first be investigated.

CANON XXII.

It is not lawful for Clergymen, after the death of their Bishop, to seize what belongs to him, as has been forbidden even by the ancient Canons; and those who do so shall be in danger of degradation from their own rank.

CANON XXIII.

It has come to the hearing of the Holy Synod that certain Clergymen and Monks, having no authority from their own Bishop, and perhaps, indeed, under sentence of excommunication by him, betake themselves to the imperial City of Constantinople, and remain there for a long time, raising disturbances and troubling the ecclesiastical state, and turning men's houses upside down. Therefore the Holy Synod decrees that such persons be first notified by the Advocate of the most holy Church of Constantinople to depart from the imperial City; and if they shall shamelessly continue in the same practices, that they shall be expelled by the same Advocate even against their will, and [so] return to their own places.

ΚΑΝΩΝ ΚΔʹ.

Τὰ ἅπαξ καθιερωθέντα μοναστήρια, κατὰ γνώμην ἐπισκόπου, μένειν εἰς τὸ διηνεκὲς μοναστήρια, καὶ τὰ ἀνήκοντα αὐτοῖς πράγματα φυλάττεσθαι, καὶ μηκέτι γίνεσθαι ταῦτα κοσμικὰ καταγώγια· τοὺς δὲ συγχωροῦντας τοῦτο γίνεσθαι, ὑποκεῖσθαι τοῖς ἐκ τῶν κανόνων ἐπιτιμίοις.

ΚΑΝΩΝ ΚΕʹ.

Ἐπειδή πέρ τινες τῶν μητροπολιτῶν, ὡς περιηχήθημεν, ἀμελοῦσι τῶν ἐγκεχειρισμένων αὐτοῖς ποιμνίων, καὶ ἀναβάλλονται τὰς χειροτονίας τῶν ἐπισκόπων· ἔδοξε τῇ ἁγίᾳ συνόδῳ, ἐντὸς τριῶν μηνῶν γίνεσθαι τὰς χειροτονίας τῶν ἐπισκόπων, εἰ μήποτε ἄρα ἀπαραίτητος ἀνάγκη παρασκευάσοι ἐπιταθῆναι τὸν τῆς ἀναβολῆς χρόνον. Εἰ δὲ μὴ τοῦτο ποιήσοι, ὑποκεῖσθαι αὐτὸν ἐκκλησιαστικοῖς ἐπιτιμίοις. Τὴν μέν τοι πρόσοδον τῆς χηρευούσης ἐκκλησίας, σώαν παρὰ τῷ οἰκονόμῳ τῆς αὐτῆς ἐκκλησίας φυλάττεσθαι.

ΚΑΝΩΝ Κϛʹ.

Ἐπειδὴ ἔν τισιν ἐκκλησίαις, ὡς περιηχήθημεν, δίχα οἰκονόμων οἱ ἐπίσκοποι τὰ ἐκκλησιαστικὰ χειρίζουσι πράγματα, ἔδοξε πᾶσαν ἐκκλησίαν ἐπίσκοπον ἔχουσαν, καὶ οἰκονόμον ἔχειν ἐκ τοῦ ἰδίου κλήρου, οἰκονομοῦντα τὰ ἐκκλησιαστικὰ κατὰ γνώμην τοῦ ἰδίου ἐπισκόπου· ὥστε μὴ ἀμάρτυρον εἶναι τὴν οἰκονομίαν τῆς ἐκκλησίας, καὶ ἐκ τούτου σκορπίζεσθαι τὰ αὐτῆς πράγματα, καὶ λοιδορίαν τῇ ἱερωσύνῃ προστρίβεσθαι· εἰ δὲ μὴ τοῦτο ποιήσοι, ὑποκεῖσθαι αὐτὸν τοῖς θείοις κανόσιν.

ΚΑΝΩΝ ΚΖʹ.

Τοὺς ἁρπάζοντας γυναῖκας ἐπ᾽ ὀνόματι συνοικεσίου, ἢ συμπράττοντας, ἢ συναιρομένους τοῖς ἁρπάζουσιν, ὥρισεν ἡ ἁγία σύνοδος, εἰ μὲν κληρικοὶ εἶεν, ἐκπίπτειν τοῦ ἰδίου βαθμοῦ· εἰ δὲ λαϊκοί, ἀναθεματίζεσθαι.

CANON XXIV.

Monasteries, which have once been consecrated with the consent of the Bishop, shall remain Monasteries for ever, and the property belonging to them shall be preserved, and they shall never again become secular dwellings. And they who shall permit this to be done shall be subjected to ecclesiastical penalties.

CANON XXV.

Forasmuch as certain of the Metropolitans, as we have heard, neglect the flocks committed to them, and delay the ordinations of the Bishops, the Holy Synod decrees that the ordinations of the Bishops shall take place within three months, unless an inevitable necessity should some time require the term of delay to be prolonged. And if the [Metropolitan] shall not do this, he shall be liable to ecclesiastical penalties. And the income of the widowed Church shall be kept safe by the Steward of the same Church.

CANON XXVI.

Forasmuch as we have heard that in certain Churches the Bishops manage the Church business without Stewards, it is decreed that every Church having a Bishop shall have also a Steward among its own Clergy, who shall manage the Church business under the sanction of his own Bishop ; that so the administration of the Church may not be without a witness ; and that thus the goods of the Church may not be squandered, nor reproach be brought upon the Priesthood ; and if [the Bishop] will not do this, he shall be subjected to the Divine Canons.

CANON XXVII.

The Holy Synod decrees that those who forcibly carry off women, [even] under pretence of marriage, and the aiders or abettors of such ravishers, shall be degraded, if Clergymen, and if laymen, anathematized.

ΨΗΦΟΣ *τῆς αὐτῆς ἁγίας συνόδου, ἐκφωνηθεῖσα χάριν τῶν πρεσβείων τοῦ θρόνου τῆς ἁγιωτάτης ἐκκλησίας Κωνσταντινουπόλεως.*

ΚΑΝΩΝ ΚΗ'.

Πανταχοῦ τοῖς τῶν ἁγίων πατέρων ὅροις ἑπόμενοι, καὶ τὸν ἀρτίως ἀναγνωσθέντα κανόνα τῶν ἑκατὸν πεντήκοντα θεοφιλεστάτων ἐπισκόπων, τῶν συναχθέντων ἐπὶ τοῦ τῆς εὐσεβοῦς μνήμης Μεγάλου Θεοδοσίου, *τοῦ γενομένου βασιλέως ἐν τῇ βασιλίδι* Κωνσταντινουπόλεως Νέᾳ Ῥώμῃ, *γνωρίζοντες, τὰ αὐτὰ καὶ ἡμεῖς ὁρίζομέν τε καὶ ψηφιζόμεθα περὶ τῶν πρεσβείων τῆς ἁγιωτάτης ἐκκλησίας τῆς αὐτῆς* Κωνσταντινουπόλεως Νέας Ῥώμης· *καὶ γὰρ τῷ θρόνῳ τῆς πρεσβυτέρας* Ῥώμης, *διὰ τὸ βασιλεύειν τὴν πόλιν ἐκείνην, οἱ* Πατέρες *εἰκότως ἀποδεδώκασι τὰ πρεσβεῖα.* Καὶ *τῷ αὐτῷ σκοπῷ κινούμενοι οἱ ἑκατὸν πεντήκοντα θεοφιλέστατοι ἐπίσκοποι, τὰ ἴσα πρεσβεῖα ἀπένειμαν τῷ τῆς* Νέας Ῥώμης *ἁγιωτάτῳ θρόνῳ, εὐλόγως κρίναντες, τὴν βασιλείᾳ καὶ συγκλήτῳ τιμηθεῖσαν πόλιν, καὶ τῶν ἴσων ἀπολαύουσαν πρεσβείων τῇ πρεσβυτέρᾳ βασιλίδι* Ῥώμῃ, *καὶ ἐν τοῖς ἐκκλησιαστικοῖς ὡς ἐκείνην μεγαλύνεσθαι πράγμασι, δευτέραν μετ' ἐκείνην ὑπάρχουσαν.* Καὶ *ὥστε τοὺς τῆς* Ποντικῆς, *καὶ τῆς* Ἀσιανῆς, *καὶ τῆς* Θρᾳκικῆς *διοικήσεως μητροπολίτας μόνους, ἔτι δὲ καὶ τοὺς ἐν τοῖς βαρβαρικοῖς ἐπισκόπους τῶν προειρημένων διοικήσεων χειροτονεῖσθαι ὑπὸ τοῦ προειρημένου ἁγιωτάτου θρόνου τῆς κατὰ* Κωνσταντινούπολιν *ἁγιωτάτης ἐκκλησίας· δηλαδὴ ἑκάστου μητροπολίτου τῶν προειρημένων διοικήσεων μετὰ τῶν τῆς ἐπαρχίας ἐπισκόπων χειροτονοῦντος τοὺς τῆς ἐπαρχίας ἐπισκόπους, καθὼς τοῖς θείοις κανόσι διηγόρευται· χειροτονεῖσθαι δὲ, καθὼς εἴρηται, τοὺς μητροπολίτας τῶν προειρημένων διοικήσεων παρὰ τοῦ* Κωνσταντινουπόλεως *ἀρχιεπισκόπου, ψηφισμάτων συμφώνων κατὰ τὸ ἔθος γενομένων, καὶ ἐπ' αὐτὸν ἀναφερομένων.*

ΤΗΣ *αὐτῆς ἁγίας συνόδου ἐκ τῆς πράξεως τῆς περὶ* Φωτίου *ἐπισκόπου* Τύρου *καὶ* Εὐσταθίου *ἐπισκόπου* Βηρύτου.

Οἱ *μεγαλοπρεπέστατοι καὶ ἐνδοξότατοι ἄρχοντες εἶπον.*

Περὶ *τῶν ἐπισκόπων τῶν χειροτονηθέντων μὲν παρὰ* Φωτίου *τοῦ εὐλαβεστάτου ἐπισκόπου, ἀποκινηθέντων δὲ παρὰ* Εὐσταθίου *τοῦ*

Decree of the same Holy Synod published on account of the privileges of the throne of the most holy Church of Constantinople.

CANON XXVIII.

Following in all things the decisions of the holy Fathers, and acknowledging the Canon, which has been just read, of the One Hundred and Fifty most religious Bishops who were assembled in the imperial City of Constantinople, which is New Rome, by the Emperor Theodosius of happy memory, we also do enact and decree the same things concerning the privileges of the most holy Church of New Rome, or Constantinople. For the Fathers rightly granted privileges to the throne of the elder Rome, because that City was the Capital. And the One Hundred and Fifty most religious Bishops, actuated by the same design, gave equal privileges to the most holy throne of New Rome, justly judging that the City which is honoured with the Sovereignty and the Senate, and enjoys equal privileges with the elder imperial Rome, should in ecclesiastical matters also be magnified as she is, and rank next after her; so that, in the Pontic, the Asian, and the Thracian Diocese, the Metropolitans only and such Bishops also of the Dioceses aforesaid as are among the barbarians, should be ordained by the aforesaid most holy throne of the most holy Church of Constantinople ; every Metropolitan of the aforesaid Dioceses, together with the Bishops of his Province, ordaining his own provincial Bishops, as a matter of course, as has been declared by the Divine Canons ; but that, as has been above said, the Metropolitans of the aforesaid Dioceses should be ordained by the Archbishop of Constantinople, the proper elections having been held according to custom and reported to him.

From the Act of the same Holy Synod concerning Photius, Bishop of Tyre, and Eustathius, Bishop of Berytus.

The most illustrious and noble rulers said :

What is determined by the Holy Synod in the matter of the Bishops ordained by the most religious Bishop Photius,

εὐλαβεστάτου ἐπισκόπου, καὶ μετὰ τὴν ἐπισκοπὴν πρεσβυτέρων εἶναι κελευσθέντων, τί παρίσταται τῇ ἁγίᾳ συνόδῳ;

Πασκασῖνος καὶ Λουκήνσιος, οἱ εὐλαβέστατοι ἐπίσκοποι, καὶ Βωνηφάτιος πρεσβύτερος, τοποτηρηταὶ τῆς ἐκκλησίας Ῥώμης εἶπον:

ΚΑΝΩΝ ΚΘʹ.

Ἐπίσκοπον εἰς πρεσβυτέρου βαθμὸν φέρειν, ἱεροσυλία ἐστίν. Εἰ δὲ αἰτία τις δικαία ἐκείνους ἀπὸ τῆς πράξεως τῆς ἐπισκοπῆς ἀποκινεῖ, οὐδὲ πρεσβυτέρου τόπον κατέχειν ὀφείλουσιν. Εἰ δὲ ἐκτός τινος ἐγκλήματος ἀπεκινήθησαν τοῦ ἀξιώματος, πρὸς τὴν τῆς ἐπισκοπῆς ἀξίαν ἐπαναστρέψουσιν.

Ἀνατόλιος, ὁ εὐλαβέστατος ἀρχιεπίσκοπος Κωνσταντινουπόλεως, εἶπεν· Οὗτοι οἱ λεγόμενοι ἀπὸ τῆς ἐπισκοπῆς ἀξίας εἰς τὴν τοῦ πρεσβυτέρου τάξιν κατεληλυθέναι, εἰ μὲν ἀπὸ εὐλόγων τινῶν αἰτιῶν καταδικάζονται, εἰκότως οὐδὲ τῆς πρεσβυτέρου ἐντός ἄξιοι τυγχάνουσιν εἶναι τιμῆς· εἰ δὲ δίχα τινὸς αἰτίας εὐλόγου εἰς τὸν ἥττονα κατεβιβάσθησαν βαθμὸν, δίκαιοι τυγχάνουσιν, εἴγε ἀνεύθυνοι φανεῖεν, τὴν τῆς ἐπισκοπῆς ἐπαναλαβεῖν ἀξίαν τε καὶ ἱερωσύνην.

Πάντες οἱ εὐλαβέστατοι ἐπίσκοποι ἐβόησαν·

Δικαία ἡ κρίσις τῶν πατέρων. Πάντες τὰ αὐτὰ λέγομεν· οἱ πατέρες δικαίως ἐψηφίσαντο· ἡ ψῆφος τῶν ἀρχιεπισκόπων κρατείτω.

Οἱ μεγαλοπρεπέστατοι καὶ ἐνδοξότατοι ἄρχοντες εἶπον·

Τὰ ἀρέσαντα τῇ ἁγίᾳ συνόδῳ εἰς τὸν ἅπαντα χρόνον βέβαια φυλαττέσθω.

ΤΗΣ αὐτῆς ἁγίας συνόδου ἐκ τῆς τετάρτης πράξεως, ἔνθα σκοπεῖται τὸ κεφάλαιον τὸ κατὰ τοὺς ἐπισκόπους Αἰγύπτου·

Οἱ μεγαλοπρεπέστατοι καὶ ἐνδοξότατοι ἄρχοντες, καὶ ἡ ὑπερφυὴς σύγκλητος εἶπον.

ΚΑΝΩΝ Λʹ.

Ἐπειδὴ οἱ εὐλαβέστατοι ἐπίσκοποι τῆς Αἰγύπτου, οὐχ' ὡς μαχόμενοι τῇ καθολικῇ πίστει, ὑπογράψαι τῇ ἐπιστολῇ τοῦ ὁσιωτάτου ἀρχιεπισκόπου Λέοντος ἐπὶ τοῦ παρόντος ἀνεβάλοντο, ἀλλὰ φάσκοντες, ἔθος εἶναι ἐν τῇ Αἰγυπτιακῇ διοικήσει,

but removed by the most religious Bishop Eustathius and ordered to be Presbyters after [having held] the Episcopate?

The most religious Bishops Pascasinus and Lucensius, and the Priest Boniface, representatives of the Church of Rome, said:

CANON XXIX.

It is sacrilege to reduce a Bishop to the rank of a Presbyter; but, if they are for just cause removed from the Episcopate, neither ought they to have the position of a Presbyter; and if they have been displaced without reason, they shall be restored to their episcopal dignity.

And Anatolius, the most religious Archbishop of Constantinople, said: If those who are alleged to have descended from the episcopal dignity to the order of Presbyter, have indeed been condemned for any sufficient causes, neither are they rightly worthy of the honour of a Presbyter. But if they have been forced down into the lower rank without just cause, they are worthy, if they appear guiltless, to receive again both the dignity and Priesthood of the Episcopate.

And all the most religious Bishops said:

The judgment of the Fathers is right. We all say the same. The Fathers have righteously decided. Let the sentence of the Archbishops prevail.

And the most noble and illustrious rulers said:

Let the pleasure of the Holy Synod be established for all time.

From the Fourth Act of the same Holy Synod, having reference to the matter of the Egyptian Bishops.

The most noble and illustrious rulers, and the great Senate, said:

CANON XXX.

Since the most religious Bishops of Egypt have postponed for the present their subscription to the letter of the most holy Archbishop Leo, not because they oppose the Catholic Faith, but because they declare that it is the custom in the Egyptian

παρὰ γνώμην καὶ διατύπωσιν τοῦ ἀρχιεπισκόπου μηδὲν τοιοῦτο ποιεῖν· καὶ ἀξιοῦσιν ἐνδοθῆναι αὐτοῖς ἄχρι τῆς χειροτονίας τοῦ ἐσομένου τῆς τῶν Ἀλεξανδρέων μεγαλοπόλεως ἐπισκόπου· εὔλογον ἡμῖν ἐφάνη καὶ φιλάνθρωπον, ὥστε αὐτοῖς μένουσιν ἐπὶ τοῦ οἰκείου σχήματος ἐν τῇ βασιλευούσῃ πόλει, ἔνδοσιν παρασχεθῆναι, ἄχρις ἂν χειροτονηθῇ ὁ ἀρχιεπίσκοπος τῆς Ἀλεξανδρέων μεγαλοπόλεως.

[Πασκασῖνος ὁ εὐλαβέστατος ἐπίσκοπος τοποτηρητὴς τοῦ ἀποστολικοῦ θρόνου Ῥώμης, εἶπεν·

Εἰ προστάττει ἡ ὑμετέρα ἐξουσία, καὶ κελεύεταί τί ποτε αὐτοῖς παρασχεθῆναι φιλανθρωπίας ἐχόμενον, ἐγγύας δότωσαν, ὅτι οὐκ ἐξέρχωνται ταύτης τῆς πόλεως, ἕως οὗ ἡ Ἀλεξανδρέων πόλις ἐπίσκοπον δέξηται.

Οἱ μεγαλοπρεπέστατοι καὶ ἐνδοξότατοι ἄρχοντες, καὶ ὁ ὑπερφυὴς σύγκλητος εἶπον.

Ἡ τοῦ ὁσιωτάτου Πασκασίνου ψῆφος βέβαια ἔστω·]

Ὅθεν μένοντες ἐπὶ τοῦ οἰκείου σχήματος [οἱ εὐλαβέστατοι ἐπίσκοποι τῶν Αἰγυπτίων], ἢ ἐγγύας παρέξουσιν, εἰ τοῦτο αὐτοῖς δυνατὸν, ἢ ἐξωμοσίᾳ καταπιστευθήσονται.

Diocese to do no such thing without the consent and order of their Archbishop, and ask indulgence until the ordination of the new Bishop of the Metropolis of Alexandria, it seemed to us reasonable and kind that this concession should be made to them, they remaining in their official habit in the imperial city until the Archbishop of the Metropolis of Alexandria shall have been ordained.

[And the most religious Bishop Pascasinus, representative of the apostolic throne of Rome, said :

If your authority suggests and commands that any indulgence be shewn to them, let them give securities that they will not depart from this City until the City of Alexandria receives a Bishop.

And the most noble and illustrious rulers, and the great Senate, said :

Let the sentence of the most holy Pascasinus be confirmed.]

And therefore let [the most religious Bishops of the Egyptians] remain in their official habit, either giving securities, if they can, or being paroled under oath.

CANONS OF PROVINCIAL COUNCILS,

APPROVED AT

CHALCEDON.

ΚΑΝΟΝΕΣ

ΤΗΣ ΕΝ ΑΓΚΥΡᾼ ΣΥΣΤΑΣΗΣ ΣΥΝΟΔΟΥ.

ΚΑΝΩΝ Α'.

Πρεσβυτέρους τοὺς ἐπιθύσαντας, εἶτα ἀναπαλαίσαντας, μήτε ἐκ μεθόδου τινὸς, ἀλλ' ἐξ ἀληθείας, μήτε προκατασκευάσαντας, καὶ ἐπιτηδεύσαντας, καὶ πείσαντας, ἵνα δόξωσι μὲν βασάνοις ὑποβάλλεσθαι, ταύτας δὲ τῷ δοκεῖν καὶ τῷ σχήματι προσαχθῆναι· τούτους ἔδοξε, τῆς μὲν τιμῆς τῆς κατὰ τὴν καθέδραν μετέχειν· προσφέρειν δὲ αὐτοὺς, ἢ ὁμιλεῖν, ἢ ὅλως λειτουργεῖν τι τῶν ἱερατικῶν λειτουργιῶν, μὴ ἐξεῖναι.

ΚΑΝΩΝ Β'.

Διακόνους ὁμοίως θύσαντας, μετὰ δὲ ταῦτα ἀναπαλαίσαντας, τὴν μὲν ἄλλην τιμὴν ἔχειν, πεπαῦσθαι δὲ αὐτοὺς πάσης τῆς ἱερᾶς λειτουργίας, τῆς τε τοῦ ἄρτον ἢ ποτήριον ἀναφέρειν, ἢ κηρύσσειν. Εἰ μέντοι τινὲς τῶν ἐπισκόπων τούτοις συνίδοιεν κάματόν τινα, ἢ ταπείνωσιν πρᾳότητος, καὶ ἐθέλοιεν πλέον τι διδόναι, ἢ ἀφαιρεῖν, ἐπ' αὐτοῖς εἶναι τὴν ἐξουσίαν.

ΚΑΝΩΝ Γ'.

Τοὺς φεύγοντας καὶ συλληφθέντας, ἢ ὑπὸ οἰκείων παραδοθέντας, ἢ ἄλλως τὰ ὑπάρχοντα ἀφαιρεθέντας, ἢ ὑπομείναντας βασάνους, ἢ εἰς δεσμωτήριον ἐμβληθέντας, βοῶντάς τε, ὅτι εἰσὶ Χριστιανοὶ, καὶ περισχισθέντας, ἤ τι εἰς τὰς χεῖρας πρὸς βίαν ἐμβαλλόντων τῶν βιαζομένων ἢ βρῶμά τι πρὸς ἀνάγκην δεξαμένους, ὁμολογοῦντας δὲ διόλου ὅτι εἰσὶ Χριστιανοὶ, καί τὸ πένθος τοῦ συμβάντος ἀεὶ ἐπιδεικνυμένους τῇ πάσῃ καταστολῇ καὶ τῷ σχήματι, καὶ τῇ τοῦ βίου ταπεινότητι, τούτους, ὡς ἔξω ἁμαρτήματος ὄντας,

CANONS OF ANCYRA.

CANON I.

It is decreed that Presbyters who have offered sacrifices and afterwards returned to the conflict, not with hypocrisy, but in sincerity, may retain the honour of their chair; provided they had not used management, arrangement, or persuasion, so as to appear to be subjected to the torture, when it was [in fact] applied only in seeming and pretence. Nevertheless it is not lawful for them to make the Oblation, nor to preach, nor to serve in any ministry whatever of the priestly offices.

CANON II.

It is likewise decreed that Deacons who have sacrificed and afterwards resumed the conflict, shall abstain from every sacred ministry, neither bringing in the bread and the cup, nor making proclamations; yet they may enjoy their other honours. Nevertheless, if any of the Bishops shall observe in them distress of mind and meek humiliation, it shall be lawful to the Bishops to grant more indulgence, or [if otherwise] to take away [what has been granted].

CANON III.

Those who have fled and been apprehended, or have been betrayed by their servants; or otherwise, those who have been despoiled of their goods, or have endured tortures, or have been imprisoned and abused, declaring themselves to be Christians; or who have been forced to receive something which their persecutors violently thrust into their hands, or meat [offered to idols], continually professing that they were Christians; and who, by their whole apparel, and demeanour, and humility of life, always give evidence of grief at what has happened; these persons, inasmuch as they are free from sin

τῆς κοινωνίας μὴ κωλύεσθαι· εἰ δὲ καὶ ἐκωλύθησαν ὑπό τινος, περισσοτέρας ἀκριβείας ἕνεκεν, ἢ καί τινων ἀγνοίᾳ, εὐθὺς προσδεχθῆναι. Τοῦτο δὲ ὁμοίως ἐπί τε τῶν ἐκ τοῦ κλήρου καὶ τῶν ἄλλων λαϊκῶν. Προσεξητάσθη δὲ κἀκεῖνο, εἰ δύνανται καὶ λαϊκοὶ, τῇ αὐτῇ ἀνάγκῃ ὑποπεσόντες, προάγεσθαι εἰς τάξιν· ἔδοξεν οὖν καὶ τούτους, ὡς μηδὲν ἡμαρτηκότας, εἰ καὶ ἡ προλαβοῦσα εὑρίσκοιτο ὀρθὴ τοῦ βίου πολιτεία, προχειρίζεσθαι.

ΚΑΝΩΝ Δ'.

Περὶ τῶν πρὸς βίαν θυσάντων, ἐπὶ δὲ τούτοις καὶ τῶν δειπνησάντων εἰς τὰ εἴδωλα, ὅσοι μὲν ἀπαγόμενοι, καὶ σχήματι φαιδροτέρῳ ἀνῆλθον, καὶ ἐσθῆτι ἐχρήσαντο πολυτελεστέρᾳ, καὶ μετέσχον τοῦ παρασκευασθέντος δείπνου ἀδιαφόρως, ἔδοξεν, ἐνιαυτὸν ἀκροᾶσθαι, ὑποπεσεῖν δὲ τρία ἔτη, εὐχῆς δὲ μόνης κοινωνῆσαι ἔτη δύο, καὶ τότε ἐλθεῖν ἐπὶ τὸ τέλειον.

ΚΑΝΩΝ Ε'.

Ὅσοι δὲ ἀνῆλθον μετὰ ἐσθῆτος πενθικῆς, καὶ ἀναπεσόντες ἔφαγον, μεταξὺ δι' ὅλης τῆς ἀνακλίσεως δακρύοντες, εἰ ἐπλήρωσαν τὸν τῆς ὑποπτώσεως τριετῆ χρόνον, χωρὶς προσφορᾶς δεχθήτωσαν· εἰ δὲ μὴ ἔφαγον, δύο ὑποπεσόντες ἔτη, τῷ τρίτῳ κοινωνησάτωσαν ἔτει χωρὶς προσφορᾶς, ἵνα τὸ τέλειον τῇ τετραετίᾳ λάβωσι. Τοὺς δὲ ἐπισκόπους ἐξουσίαν ἔχειν τὸν τρόπον τῆς ἐπιστροφῆς δοκιμάσαντας, φιλανθρωπεύεσθαι, ἢ πλείονα προστιθέναι χρόνον. Πρὸ πάντων δὲ, καὶ ὁ προάγων βίος, καὶ ὁ μετὰ ταῦτα, ἐξεταζέσθω, καὶ οὕτως ἡ φιλανθρωπία ἐπιμετρείσθω.

ΚΑΝΩΝ ς'.

Περὶ τῶν ἀπειλῇ μόνον εἰξάντων κολάσεων, καὶ ἀφαιρέσεως ὑπαρχόντων, ἢ μετοικίας, καὶ θυσάντων, καὶ μέχρι τοῦ παρόντος καιροῦ μὴ μετανοησάντων, μηδὲ ἐπιστρεψάντων, νῦν δὲ παρὰ τὸν καιρὸν τῆς συνόδου

[in this respect], are not to be repelled from the Communion; and if, through an extreme severity or ignorance of some things, they have been repelled, let them forthwith be readmitted. This shall hold good alike of Clergy and laity. It has also been considered whether laymen who have fallen under the same compulsion may be promoted to the Clergy, and we have decreed that, since they have in no respect been guilty, they may be ordained; provided their past course of life be found to have been upright.

CANON IV.

Concerning those who have been forced to sacrifice, but who, in addition, have partaken of feasts in honour of the idols; as many as were haled away, but afterwards went up with a cheerful countenance, and wore their costliest apparel, and partook with indifference of the feast provided; it is decreed that these be hearers one year, and prostrators three years, and communicants in prayers [*i. e.*, co-standers] two years, and then return to full Communion.

CANON V.

As many, however, as went up in mourning attire and fell down and ate, weeping throughout the whole entertainment; if they have fulfilled the three years as prostrators, let them be received without the Oblation [*i. e.*, as co-standers]; and if they did not eat, let them be prostrators two years, and in the third year let them communicate without the Oblation [*i. e.*, as co-standers]; so that in the fourth year they may receive the full Communion. But the Bishops have the right, after considering the character of their conversion, either to deal with them more leniently, or to extend the time. But, first of all, let their life before and since be thoroughly examined, and let the indulgence be determined accordingly.

CANON VI.

Concerning those who yielded merely upon threat of penalties and of the confiscation of their goods, or of banishment, and sacrificed; and who till this present time have not repented, nor been converted, but who now, at the time of

προσελθόντων, καὶ εἰς διάνοιαν τῆς ἐπιστροφῆς γενομένων, ἔδοξε μέχρι τῆς μεγάλης ἡμέρας εἰς ἀκρόασιν δεχθῆναι, καὶ μετὰ τὴν μεγάλην ἡμέραν ὑποπεσεῖν τρία ἔτη, καὶ μετὰ ἄλλα δύο ἔτη κοινωνῆσαι, χωρὶς προσφορᾶς, καὶ οὕτως ἐλθεῖν ἐπὶ τὸ τέλειον, ὥστε τὴν πᾶσαν ἑξαετίαν πληρῶσαι. Εἰ δέ τινες πρὸ τῆς συνόδου ταύτης ἐδέχθησαν εἰς μετάνοιαν, ἀπ' ἐκείνου τοῦ χρόνου λελογίσθαι αὐτοῖς τὴν ἀρχὴν τῆς ἑξαετίας. Εἰ μέν τοι κίνδυνος καὶ θανάτου προσδοκία ἐκ νόσου, ἢ ἄλλης τινὸς προφάσεως συμβαίη, τούτους ἐπὶ ὅρῳ δεχθῆναι.

ΚΑΝΩΝ Ζ'.

Περὶ τῶν συνεστιαθέντων ἐν ἐθνικῇ ἑορτῇ, ἐν τόπῳ ἀφωρισμένῳ τοῖς ἐθνικοῖς, ἴδια βρώματα ἐπικομισαμένων, καὶ φαγόντων, ἔδοξε διετίαν ὑποπεσόντας δεχθῆναι· τὸ δὲ, εἰ χρὴ μετὰ τῆς προσφορᾶς ἕκαστον, τῶν ἐπισκόπων ἐστὶ δοκιμάσαι, καὶ τὸν ἄλλον βίον ἐφ' ἑκάστου ἐξετάσαι.

ΚΑΝΩΝ Η'.

Οἱ δὲ δεύτερον καὶ τρίτον θύσαντες μετὰ βίας, τετραετίαν ὑποπεσέτωσαν, δύο δὲ ἔτη χωρὶς προσφορᾶς κοινωνησάτωσαν, καὶ τῷ ἑβδόμῳ τελείως δεχθήτωσαν.

ΚΑΝΩΝ Θ'.

Ὅσοι δὲ μὴ μόνον ἀπέστησαν, ἀλλὰ καὶ ἐπανέστησαν, καὶ ἠνάγκασαν ἀδελφοὺς, καὶ αἴτιοι ἐγένοντο τοῦ ἀναγκασθῆναι, οὗτοι ἔτη μὲν τρία, τὸν τῆς ἀκροάσεως δεξάσθωσαν τόπον, ἐν δὲ ἄλλῃ ἑξαετίᾳ τὸν τῆς ὑποπτώσεως· ἄλλον δὲ ἐνιαυτὸν κοινωνησάτωσαν χωρίς προσφορᾶς, ἵνα τὴν δεκαετίαν πληρώσαντες, τοῦ τελείου μετάσχωσιν· ἐν μέν τοι τούτῳ τῷ χρόνῳ, καὶ τὸν ἄλλον αὐτῶν ἐπιτηρεῖσθαι βίον.

this Synod, have conceived a purpose of conversion, it is decreed that they be received as hearers till the Great Day [of Easter], and that after the Great Day they be prostrators for three years, and for two years more communicate without the Oblation [*i. e.*, as co-standers], and then come to the full communion, so as to complete the period of six full years. And if any have been admitted to penance before this Synod, let the beginning of the six years be reckoned to them from that time. Nevertheless, if there should be any danger or prospect of death, whether from disease or any other cause, let them be received, but under limitation [*i. e.*, so long as the danger of death continues].

CANON VII.

Concerning those who have partaken at a heathen feast in a place appointed for heathens, but who have brought and eaten their own meats, it is decreed that they be received after they have been prostrators two years; but whether to the Oblation, every Bishop must determine after he has made examination into the rest of their life.

CANON VIII.

Let those who have twice or thrice sacrificed under compulsion, be prostrators four years, and communicate without the Oblation [*i. e.*, as co-standers] two years, and in the seventh year they shall be received to full Communion.

CANON IX.

As many as have not merely apostatized, but have risen against their brethren and forced them [to apostatize], and have been guilty of their being forced; let these for three years take the place of hearing, and for another term of six years that of prostration, and for another year let them communicate without the Oblation [*i. e.*, as co-standers]; in order that, when they have fulfilled the space of ten years, they may partake of the Communion; but during this time the rest of their life must also be enquired into.

ΚΑΝΩΝ Ι'.

Διάκονοι, ὅσοι καθίστανται, παρ' αὐτὴν τὴν κατάστασιν εἰ ἐμαρτύραντο καὶ ἔφασαν χρῆναι γαμῆσαι, μὴ δυνάμενοι οὕτω μένειν, οὗτοι μετὰ ταῦτα γαμήσαντες, ἔστωσαν ἐν τῇ ὑπηρεσίᾳ, διὰ τὸ ἐπιτραπῆναι αὐτοῖς ὑπὸ τοῦ ἐπισκόπου. Τοῦτο δὲ, εἴ τινες σιωπήσαντες, καὶ καταδεξάμενοι ἐν τῇ χειροτονίᾳ μένειν οὕτω, μετὰ ταῦτα ἦλθον ἐπὶ γάμον, πεπαῦσθαι αὐτοὺς τῆς διακονίας.

ΚΑΝΩΝ ΙΑ'.

Τὰς μνηστευθείσας κόρας, καὶ μετὰ ταῦτα ὑπὸ ἄλλων ἁρπαγείσας, ἔδοξεν ἀποδίδοσθαι τοῖς προμνηστευσαμένοις, εἰ καὶ βίαν ὑπ' αὐτῶν πάθοιεν.

ΚΑΝΩΝ ΙΒ'.

Τοὺς πρὸ τοῦ βαπτίσματος τεθυκότας, καὶ μετὰ ταῦτα βαπτισθέντας, ἔδοξεν εἰς τάξιν προάγεσθαι, ὡς ἀπολουσαμένους.

ΚΑΝΩΝ ΙΓ'.

Χωρεπισκόποις* μὴ ἐξεῖναι πρεσβυτέρους ἢ διακόνους χειροτονεῖν, ἀλλὰ μὴν μηδὲ πρεσβυτέρους πόλεως, χωρὶς τοῦ ἐπιτραπῆναι ὑπὸ τοῦ ἐπισκόπου μετὰ γραμμάτων, ἐν ἑτέρᾳ παροικίᾳ.

ΚΑΝΩΝ ΙΔ'.

Τοὺς ἐν κλήρῳ πρεσβυτέρους ἢ διακόνους ὄντας, ἀπεχομένους κρεῶν, ἔδοξεν ἐφάπτεσθαι, καὶ οὕτως, εἰ βούλοιντο, κρατεῖν ἑαυτῶν· εἰ δὲ μὴ βούλοιντο, ὡς μηδὲ τὰ μετὰ κρεῶν βαλλόμενα λάχανα ἐσθίειν, καὶ εἰ μὴ ὑπείκοιεν τῷ κανόνι, πεπαῦσθαι αὐτοὺς τῆς τάξεως.

* The common reading is χωρεπισκόπους, which makes the Canon wholly unintelligible.

CANON X.

They who have been made Deacons, declaring when they were ordained that they must marry, because they were not able to abide so, and who afterwards have married, shall continue in their ministry, because it was conceded to them by the Bishop. But if any were silent on this matter, undertaking at their ordination to abide [as they were], and afterwards proceeded to marriage, these shall cease from the deaconate.

CANON XI.

It is decreed that virgins who have been betrothed, and who have afterwards been carried off by others, shall be restored to those to whom they had formerly been betrothed, even though they may have suffered violence from the ravisher

CANON XII.

It is decreed that they who have offered sacrifice before their Baptism, and were afterwards baptized, may be promoted to the Clergy, inasmuch as they have washed away [their sins].

CANON XIII.

It is not lawful for Chorepiscopi to ordain Presbyters or Deacons in another Parish, nor, most assuredly, Presbyters of a City, without the commission of the Bishop given in writing.*

CANON XIV.

It is decreed that among the Clergy, Presbyters and Deacons who abstain from flesh shall taste of it, and afterwards, if they shall so please, may abstain. But if they shall refuse, and will not even eat herbs served with flesh, but disobey the Canon, let them be removed from their order.

* This Canon is not easily understood on account of the last three words, ἐν ἑτέρᾳ παροικίᾳ. If, as some have thought, these words are an interpolation, the Canon would prove that with the *written* consent of the Bishop a Chorepiscopus might ordain even a City Presbyter of the Parish to which he himself belonged. If they are part of the original text, as seems to be the case, the Canon shows that in any other Parish than that to which he belonged a Chorepiscopus might ordain even a City Presbyter, provided he had the Bishop's consent in writing; but that in his own Parish the written document was not held to be necessary. In either case the ordaining power of the Chorepiscopi referred to is evident; in other words it is clear that they were true Bishops as to their Orders, though they were not possessed of local jurisdiction.

ΚΑΝΩΝ ΙΕ'.

Περὶ τῶν διαφερόντων τῷ Κυριακῷ, ὅσα ἐπισκόπου μὴ ὄντος πρεσβύτεροι ἐπώλησαν, ἀνακαλεῖσθαι τὸ Κυριακόν. Ἐν δὲ τῇ κρίσει τοῦ ἐπισκόπου εἶναι, εἴπερ προσήκει ἀπολαβεῖν τὴν τιμὴν, εἴτε καὶ μὴ, διὰ τὸ πολλάκις τὴν πρόσοδον τῶν πεπραμένων ἀποδεδωκέναι αὐτοῖς τούτοις πλείονα τὴν τιμήν.

ΚΑΝΩΝ Ιϛ'.

Περὶ τῶν ἀλογευσαμένων, ἢ καὶ ἀλογευομένων, ὅσοι πρὶν εἰκοσαετεῖς γενέσθαι, ἥμαρτον, πέντε καὶ δέκα ἔτεσιν ὑποπεσόντες, κοινωνίας τυγχανέτωσαν τῆς εἰς τὰς προσευχάς· εἶτα ἐν τῇ κοινωνίᾳ διατελέσαντες ἔτη πέντε, τότε καὶ τῆς προσφορᾶς ἐφαπτέσθωσαν. Ἐξεταζέσθω δὲ αὐτῶν καὶ ὁ ἐν τῇ ὑποπτώσει βίος, καὶ οὕτω τυγχανέτωσαν τῆς φιλανθρωπίας. Εἰ δέ τινες κατακόρως ἐν τοῖς ἁμαρτήμασι γεγόνασι, τὴν μακρὰν ἐχέτωσαν ὑπόπτωσιν. Ὅσοι δὲ ὑπερβάντες τὴν ἡλικίαν ταύτην, καὶ γυναῖκας ἔχοντες περιπεπτώκασι τῷ ἁμαρτήματι, πέντε καὶ εἴκοσιν ἔτεσιν ὑποπεσόντες, κοινωνίας τυγχανέτωσαν τῆς εἰς τὰς προσευχάς· εἶτα ἐκτελέσαντες πέντε ἔτη ἐν τῇ κοινωνίᾳ τῶν εὐχῶν, τυγχανέτωσαν τῆς προσφορᾶς. Εἰ δέ τινες καὶ γυναῖκας ἔχοντες, καὶ ὑπερβάντες τὸν πεντηκονταετῆ χρόνον ἥμαρτον, ἐπὶ τῇ ἐξόδῳ τοῦ βίου τυγχανέτωσαν τῆς κοινωνίας.

ΚΑΝΩΝ ΙΖ'.

Τοὺς ἀλογευσαμένους καὶ λεπροὺς ὄντας, ἤτοι λεπρώσαντας, τούτους προσέταξεν ἡ ἁγία σύνοδος, εἰς τοὺς χειμαζομένους εὔχεσθαι.

ΚΑΝΩΝ ΙΗ'.

Εἴ τινες ἐπίσκοποι κατασταθέντες, καὶ μὴ δεχθέντες ὑπὸ τῆς παροικίας ἐκείνης, εἰς ἣν ὠνομάσθησαν, ἑτέραις βούλοιντο παροικίαις ἐπιέναι, καὶ βιάζεσθαι τοὺς καθεστῶτας, καὶ στάσεις κινεῖν κατ' αὐτῶν, τούτους ἀφορίζεσθαι. Ἐὰν μέντοι βούλοιντο εἰς τὸ πρεσβυτέριον καθέζεσθαι, ἔνθα ἦσαν πρότερον πρεσβύτεροι, μὴ ἀποβάλλεσθαι αὐτοὺς τῆς

CANON XV.

Concerning things belonging to the Church, which Presbyters may have sold when there was no Bishop, it is decreed that the Church property shall be reclaimed; and it shall be in the discretion of the Bishop whether it is better to receive the purchase price, or not; for oftentimes the revenue of the things sold might yield them the greater value.

CANON XVI.

Let those who have been or who are guilty of bestial lusts, if they have sinned while under twenty years of age, be prostrators fifteen years, and communicate in prayers [*i. e.*, be co-standers]; then, having passed five years in this Communion, let them be partakers also of the Oblation. But let their life as prostrators be examined, and so let them receive indulgence; and if any have been more insatiable in their crimes, then let their time of prostration be prolonged. And if any who have passed this age and had wives, have fallen into this sin, let them be prostrators twenty-five years, and then communicate in prayers [*i. e.*, as co-standers]; and, after they have been five years in the Communion of prayers, let them partake of the Oblation. And if any married men of more than fifty years of age have so sinned, let them be admitted to Communion only at the point of death.

CANON XVII.

Defilers of themselves with beasts, who are also leprous, that is, who have infected others [with the leprosy of this crime], the holy Synod commands to pray among the Hiemantes.

CANON XVIII.

If any who have been constituted Bishops, but have not been received by the Parish to which they were designated, shall invade other Parishes and wrong the constituted [Bishops] there, stirring up seditions against them, let such persons be suspended. But if they are willing to accept a seat among the Presbyterate, where they formerly were Pres-

τιμῆς· ἐὰν δὲ διαστασιάζωσι πρὸς τοὺς καθεστῶτας ἐκεῖ ἐπισκόπους, ἀφαιρεῖσθαι αὐτοὺς καὶ τὴν τιμὴν τοῦ πρεσβυτερίου. καὶ γίνεσθαι αὐτοὺς ἐκκηρύκτους.

ΚΑΝΩΝ ΙΘ'.

Ὅσοι παρθενίαν ἐπαγγελλόμενοι, ἀθετοῦσι τὴν ἐπαγγελίαν, τὸν τῶν διγάμων ὅρον ἐκπληρούτωσαν. Τὰς μέντοι συνερχομένας παρθένους τισὶν ὡς ἀδελφὰς ἐκωλύσαμεν.

ΚΑΝΩΝ Κ'.

Ἐὰν τινος γυνὴ μοιχευθῇ, ἢ μοιχεύσῃ τις, ἐν ἑπτὰ ἔτεσι δεῖ αὐτὸν τοῦ τελείου τυχεῖν, κατὰ τοὺς βαθμοὺς τοὺς προάγοντας.

ΚΑΝΩΝ ΚΑ'.

Περὶ τῶν γυναικῶν τῶν ἐκπορνευουσῶν καὶ ἀναιρουσῶν τὰ γεννώμενα, καὶ σπουδαζουσῶν φθόρια ποιεῖν, ὁ μὲν πρότερος ὅρος μέχρις ἐξόδου ἐκώλυσε, καὶ τούτῳ συντίθενται. Φιλανθρωπότερον δέ τι εὑρόντες, ὡρίσαμεν δεκαετῆ χρόνον, κατὰ τοὺς βαθμοὺς τοὺς ὡρισμένους πληρῶσαι.

ΚΑΝΩΝ ΚΒ'.

Περὶ ἑκουσίων φόνων, ὑποπιπτέτωσαν μὲν, τοῦ δὲ τελείου ἐν τῷ τέλει τοῦ βίου καταξιούσθωσαν.

ΚΑΝΩΝ ΚΓ'.

Ἐπὶ ἀκουσίων φόνων, ὁ μὲν πρότερος ὅρος ἐν ἑπταετίᾳ κελεύει τοῦ τελείου μετασχεῖν κατὰ τοὺς ὡρισμένους βαθμούς· ὁ δὲ δεύτερος, τὸν πενταετῆ χρόνον πληρῶσαι.

ΚΑΝΩΝ ΚΔ'.

Οἱ καταμαντευόμενοι, καὶ ταῖς συνηθείαις τῶν ἐθνῶν ἐξακολουθοῦντες, ἢ εἰσάγοντές τινας εἰς τοὺς ἑαυτῶν οἴκους ἐπὶ ἀνευρέσει φαρμακειῶν, ἢ καὶ καθάρσει, ὑπὸ τὸν

byters, let them not be deprived of that honour. And if they shall act seditiously against the Bishops constituted there, the honour of the Presbyterate also shall be taken from them and themselves expelled.

CANON XIX.

If any persons who profess Virginity shall disregard their profession, let them fulfil the term of digamists. And, moreover, we prohibit women who are Virgins from living with men as sisters.

CANON XX.

An adulteress or an adulterer shall be restored to full communion after seven years passed in the previous degrees [of penance].

CANON XXI.

Concerning women who commit fornication, and destroy that which they have conceived, or who are employed in making drugs for abortion, the former decree excluded them until the hour of death, and by this they are bound. Nevertheless, being desirous to use somewhat greater lenity, we have ordained that they fulfil ten years [of penance], according to the established degrees.

CANON XXII.

Concerning wilful murderers, let them remain prostrators; but at the end of life let them be indulged with full Communion.

CANON XXIII.

Concerning involuntary homicides, the former decree directs that they be received to full Communion after seven years [of penance], according to the established degrees; but this second, that they fulfil a term of five years.

CANON XXIV.

They who practice divination, and follow the customs of the heathen, or who take men to their houses for the invention of sorceries, or for lustrations, shall fall under the Canon of

κανόνα πιπτέτωσαν τῆς πενταετίας, κατὰ τοὺς βαθμοὺς τοὺς ὡρισμένους, τρία ἔτη ὑποπτώσεως, καὶ δύο ἔτη εὐχῆς, χωρὶς προσφορᾶς.

ΚΑΝΩΝ ΚΕ′.

Μνηστευσάμενός τις κόρην, προσεφθάρη τῇ ἀδελφῇ αὐτῆς, ὡς καὶ ἐπιφορέσαι αὐτήν· ἔγημε δὲ τὴν μνηστὴν μετὰ ταῦτα, ἡ δὲ φθαρεῖσα ἀπήγξατο· οἱ συνειδότες ἐκελεύσθησαν ἐν δεκαετίᾳ δεχθῆναι εἰς τοὺς συνεστῶτας κατὰ τοὺς ὡρισμένους βαθμούς.

five years [penance], according to the established degrees; that is, three years as prostrators, and two years of prayer without the Oblation [*i. e.*, as co-standers].

CANON XXV.

One who had betrothed a maiden, corrupted her sister, so that she conceived. After that he married his betrothed, but she who had been corrupted hanged herself. The parties to this affair were ordered to be received among the co-standers, after ten years [of penance], according to the established degrees.

ΚΑΝΟΝΕΣ

ΤΗΣ ΕΝ ΝΕΟΚΑΙΣΑΡΕΙᾼ ΣΥΝΟΔΟΥ.

ΚΑΝΩΝ Α′.

Πρεσβύτερος ἐὰν γήμῃ, τῆς τάξεως αὐτὸν μετατίθεσθαι· ἐὰν δὲ πορνεύσῃ, ἢ μοιχεύσῃ, ἐξωθεῖσθαι αὐτὸν τέλεον, καὶ ἄγεσθαι εἰς μετάνοιαν.

ΚΑΝΩΝ Β′.

Γυνὴ, ἐὰν γήμηται δύο ἀδελφοῖς, ἐξωθείσθω μέχρι θανάτου· πλὴν ἐν τῷ θανάτῳ διὰ τὴν φιλανθρωπίαν εἰποῦσα, *ὡς ὑγιάνασα λύσει τὸν γάμον, ἕξει τὴν μετάνοιαν.* Ἐὰν *δὲ τελευτήσῃ ἡ γυνὴ ἐν τοιούτῳ γάμῳ οὖσα, ἤτοι ὁ ἀνὴρ, δυσχερὴς τῷ μείναντι ἡ μετάνοια.*

ΚΑΝΩΝ Γ′.

Περὶ *τῶν πλείστοις γάμοις περιπιπτόντων ὁ μὲν χρόνος σαφὴς ὁ ὡρισμένος, ἡ δὲ ἀναστροφὴ καὶ ἡ πίστις αὐτῶν συντέμνει τὸν χρόνον.*

ΚΑΝΩΝ Δ′.

Ἐὰν *πρόθηταί τις, ἐπιθυμήσας γυναικὸς, συγκαθευδῆσαι μετ' αὐτῆς, μὴ ἔλθῃ δὲ εἰς ἔργον αὐτοῦ ἡ ἐνθύμησις, φαίνεται ὅτι ὑπὸ τῆς χάριτος ἐῤῥύσθη.*

ΚΑΝΩΝ Ε′.

Κατηχούμενος, *ἐὰν* εἰσερχόμενος *εἰς* Κυριακὸν, *ἐν τῇ τῶν κατηχουμένων τάξει στήκῃ, οὗτος δὲ ἁμαρτάνῃ, ἐὰν μὲν γόνυ κλίνων, ἀκροάσθω μηκέτι ἁμαρτάνων· ἐὰν δὲ καὶ ἀκροώμενος ἔτι ἁμαρτάνῃ, ἐξωθείσθω.*

CANONS OF NEO-CÆSAREA.

CANON I.

If a Presbyter marry, let him be removed from his Order; but if he commit fornication [being single], or adultery [being married], let him be altogether cast out and brought to penance.

CANON II.

If a woman shall have married two brothers, let her be cast out until her death. Nevertheless, at the hour of death she shall be received to penance, provided she declare that she will break the marriage, if she should recover. But if the woman or her husband die in such a marriage, the penance of the survivor shall be severe.

CANON III.

Concerning those who fall into many marriages, the appointed time of penance is well known; but their amendment and faith shortens the time.

CANON IV.

If any man lusting after a woman purposes to lie with her, and his design does not come to effect, it is evident that he has been saved by grace.

CANON V.

If a Catechumen coming into the Church have taken his place in the order of Catechumens and fall into sin, then let him, if he be a kneeler and forsake his sin, become a hearer; but if he commit sin while he is a hearer, let him be cast out.

ΚΑΝΩΝ ϛ'.

Περὶ κυοφορούσης, ὅτι δεῖ φωτίζεσθαι, ὁπότε βούλεται· οὐδὲν γὰρ ἐν τούτῳ κοινωνεῖ ἡ τίκτουσα τῷ τικτομένῳ· διὰ τὸ ἑκάστου ἰδίαν τὴν προαίρεσιν τὴν ἐπὶ τῇ ὁμολογίᾳ δείκνυσθαι.

ΚΑΝΩΝ Ζ'.

Πρεσβύτερον εἰς γάμους διγαμούντων μὴ ἑστιᾶσθαι· ἐπεὶ μετάνοιαν αἰτοῦντος τοῦ διγάμου, τίς ἔσται ὁ πρεσβύτερος, ὁ διὰ τῆς ἑστιάσεως συγκατατιθέμενος τοῖς γάμοις;

ΚΑΝΩΝ Η'.

Γυνή τινος μοιχευθεῖσα λαϊκοῦ ὄντος, ἐὰν ἐλεγχθῇ φανερῶς, ὁ τοιοῦτος εἰς ὑπηρεσίαν ἐλθεῖν οὐ δύναται. Ἐὰν δὲ καὶ μετὰ τὴν χειροτονίαν μοιχευθῇ, ὀφείλει ἀπολῦσαι αὐτήν· ἐὰν δὲ συζῇ, οὐ δύναται ἔχεσθαι τῆς ἐγχειρισθείσης αὐτῷ ὑπηρεσίας.

ΚΑΝΩΝ Θ'.

Πρεσβύτερος, ἐὰν προημαρτηκὼς σώματι προαχθῇ, καὶ ὁμολογήσῃ, ὅτι ἥμαρτε πρὸ τῆς χειροτονίας, μὴ προσφερέτω, μένων ἐν τοῖς λοιποῖς, διὰ τὴν ἄλλην σπουδήν· τὰ γὰρ λοιπὰ ἁμαρτήματα ἔφασαν οἱ πολλοὶ καὶ τὴν χειροθεσίαν ἀφιέναι. Ἐὰν δὲ αὐτὸς μὴ ὁμολογῇ, ἐλεγχθῆναι δὲ φανερῶς μὴ δυνηθῇ, ἐπ' αὐτῷ ἐκείνῳ ποιεῖσθαι τὴν ἐξουσίαν.

ΚΑΝΩΝ Ι'.

Ὁμοίως καὶ διάκονος, ἐὰν τῷ αὐτῷ ἁμαρτήματι περιπέσῃ, τὴν τοῦ ὑπηρέτου τάξιν ἐχέτω.

ΚΑΝΩΝ ΙΑ'.

Πρεσβύτερος πρὸ τῶν τριάκοντα ἐτῶν μὴ χειροτονείσθω, ἐὰν καὶ πάνυ ᾖ ὁ ἄνθρωπος ἄξιος, ἀλλὰ ἀποτηρείσθω. Ὁ γὰρ Κύριος Ἰησοῦς Χριστὸς ἐν τῷ τριακοστῷ ἔτει ἐβαπτίσθη, καὶ ἤρξατο διδάσκειν.

CANON VI.

Concerning a woman with child, it is determined that she ought to be baptized whensoever she will; for in this the woman communicates nothing to the child, since the bringing forward to profession is evidently the individual [privilege] of every single person.

CANON VII.

A Presbyter shall not be a guest at the nuptials of persons contracting a second marriage; for, if the digamist is worthy of penance, what shall the Presbyter be, who, on account of the feast, sanctions the marriage?

CANON VIII.

If the wife of a layman has committed adultery and been clearly convicted, such [a husband] cannot enter the Ministry; and if she commit adultery after his ordination, he must put her away; but if he retain her, he can have no part in the Ministry committed to him.

CANON IX.

A Presbyter who has been promoted after having committed bodily sin, and who shall confess that he had sinned before his ordination, shall not make the Oblation, though he may remain in his other functions on account of his diligence in other respects; for the majority have affirmed that ordination remits past sins. But if he do not confess and cannot be openly convicted, the decision shall depend upon himself.

CANON X.

Likewise, if a Deacon have fallen into the same sin, let him have the rank of a Sub-deacon.

CANON XI.

Let not a Presbyter be ordained before he is thirty years of age, even though he be in all respects a worthy man, but let him be made to wait. For our LORD JESUS CHRIST was baptized and began to teach in his thirtieth year.

ΚΑΝΩΝ ΙΒ'.

Ἐὰν νοσῶν τις φωτισθῇ, εἰς πρεσβυτέριον ἄγεσθαι οὐ δύναται· οὐκ ἐκ προαιρέσεως γὰρ ἡ πίστις αὐτοῦ, ἀλλ' ἐξ ἀνάγκης· εἰμὴ τάχα διὰ τὴν μετὰ ταῦτα αὐτοῦ σπουδὴν καὶ πίστιν, καὶ διὰ σπάνιν ἀνθρώπων.

ΚΑΝΩΝ ΙΓ'.

Ἐπιχώριοι πρεσβύτεροι ἐν τῷ Κυριακῷ τῆς πόλεως προσφέρειν οὐ δύνανται, παρόντος ἐπισκόπου, ἢ πρεσβυτέρων πόλεως· οὔτε μὴν ἄρτον διδόναι ἐν εὐχῇ, οὐδὲ ποτήριον· ἐὰν δὲ ἀπῶσι, καὶ εἰς εὐχὴν κληθῇ μόνος, δίδωσιν.

ΚΑΝΩΝ ΙΔ'.

Οἱ δὲ χωρεπίσκοποι, εἰσὶ μὲν εἰς τύπον τῶν ἑβδομήκοντα· ὡς δὲ συλλειτουργοί, διὰ τὴν σπουδὴν τὴν εἰς τοὺς πτωχοὺς προσφέρουσι τιμώμενοι.

ΚΑΝΩΝ ΙΕ'.

Διάκονοι ἑπτὰ ὀφείλουσιν εἶναι κατὰ τὸν κανόνα, κἂν πάνυ μεγάλη ᾖ ἡ πόλις· Πεισθείσῃ δὲ ἀπὸ τῆς βίβλου τῶν Πράξεων.

CANON XII.

If any one be baptized when he is sick, forasmuch as his [profession of] faith was not of voluntary purpose, but of necessity, he cannot be promoted to the Presbyterate, unless on account of his subsequent zeal and faithfulness, or because of lack of men.

CANON XIII.

Country Presbyters may not make the Oblation in the Church of the City when the Bishop or Presbyters of the City are present; nor may they give the Bread or the Cup with prayer. If, however, they be absent, and he [*i. e.*, a country Presbyter] alone be called to prayer, he may give them.

CANON XIV.

The Chorepiscopi, however, are indeed after the pattern of the Seventy; nevertheless they offer [*i. e.*, in the City Church and in presence of the Bishop: vid. Can. XIII.], being fellow-servants, honoured on account of their devotion to the poor.

CANON XV.

The Deacons ought to be seven in number, according to the Canon, even if the City be great. Of this you will be persuaded from the Book of Acts.

ΤΗΣ ἘΝ ΓΑΓΓΡᾼ ΣΥΝΟΔΟΥ

ἘΠΙΣΤΟΛΗ ΣΥΝΟΔΙΚΗ.

Κυρίοις τιμιωτάτοις ἐν Ἀρμενίᾳ συλλειτουργοῖς, Εὐσέβιος, Αἰλιανὸς, Εὐγένιος, Ὀλύμπιος, Βιθυνικὸς, Γρηγόριος, Φιλητὸς, Πάππος, Εὐλάλιος, Ὑπάτιος, Προαιρέσιος, Βασίλειος, Βάσσος, οἱ συνελθόντες εἰς τὴν κατὰ Γάγγραν ἁγίαν σύνοδον, ἐν Κυρίῳ χαίρειν.

Ἐπειδὴ συνελθοῦσα ἡ ἁγιωτάτη σύνοδος τῶν ἐπισκόπων ἐν τῇ κατὰ Γάγγραν ἐκκλησίᾳ διά τινας ἐκκλησιαστικὰς χρείας, ζητουμένων καὶ τῶν κατ' Εὐστάθιον, εὕρισκε πολλὰ ἀθέσμως γινόμενα ὑπὸ τούτων αὐτῶν τῶν περὶ Εὐστάθιον, ἀναγκαίως ὥρισε, καὶ πᾶσι φανερὸν ποιῆσαι ἐσπούδασεν, εἰς ἀναίρεσιν τῶν ὑπ' αὐτοῦ κακῶς γινομένων. Καὶ γὰρ ἐκ τοῦ καταμέμφεσθαι αὐτοὺς τὸν γάμον, καὶ ὑποτίθεσθαι, ὅτι οὐδεὶς τῶν ἐν γάμῳ ὄντων ἐλπίδα παρὰ Θεῷ ἔχει, πολλαὶ γυναῖκες ὕπανδροι ἀπατηθεῖσαι, τῶν ἑαυτῶν ἀνδρῶν ἀνεχώρησαν, καὶ ἄνδρες τῶν ἰδίων γυναικῶν· εἶτα ἐν τῷ μεταξὺ μὴ δυνηθεῖσαι ἐγκρατεῖν, ἐμοιχεύθησαν, καὶ διὰ τὴν τοιαύτην ὑπόθεσιν ὠνειδίσθησαν. Εὑρίσκοντο δὲ καὶ ἀναχωρήσεις ἐκ τῶν οἴκων τοῦ Θεοῦ καὶ τῆς ἐκκλησίας ποιούμενοι, καταφρονητικῶς διακείμενοι κατὰ τῆς ἐκκλησίας, καὶ τῶν ἐν τῇ ἐκκλησίᾳ, καὶ ἰδίᾳ συνάξεις ποιούμενοι, καὶ ἐκκλησιάσεις, καὶ διδασκαλίας ἑτέρας, καὶ τὰ ἄλλα κατὰ τῶν ἐκκλησιῶν καὶ τῶν ἐν τῇ ἐκκλησίᾳ, ξένα ἀμφιάσματα ἐπὶ καταπτώσει τῆς κοινότητος τῶν ἀμφιασμάτων συνάγοντες, καρποφορίας τε τὰς ἐκκλησιαστικὰς τὰς ἀνέκαθεν διδομένας τῇ ἐκκλησίᾳ, ἑαυτοῖς καὶ τοῖς σὺν αὐτοῖς, ὡς ἁγίοις, τὰς διαδόσεις ποιούμενοι, καὶ δοῦλοι δεσποτῶν ἀναχωροῦντες, καὶ διὰ τοῦ ξένου ἀμφιάσματος καταφρόνησιν κατὰ τῶν δεσποτῶν ποιούμενοι, καὶ γυναῖκες παρὰ τὸ σύνηθες ἀντὶ ἀμφιασμάτων

SYNODICAL EPISTLE.

COUNCIL OF GANGRA.

Eusebius, Ælian, Eugenius, Olympius, Bithynicus, Gregory, Philetus, Pappus, Eulalius, Hypatius, Proæresius, Basil and Bassus, assembled in the holy Synod at Gangra, to our most honoured lords and fellow-ministers in Armenia, wish health in the Lord.

Forasmuch as the most Holy Synod of Bishops, assembled on account of certain necessary matters of ecclesiastical business in the Church at Gangra, on inquiring also into the matters which concern Eustathius, found that many things had been unlawfully done by these very men who are partisans of Eustathius, it was compelled to make definitions, which it has hastened to make known to all, for the removal of whatever has by him been done amiss. For, from their utter abhorrence of marriage, and from their adoption of the proposition that no one living in a state of marriage has any hope from God, many misguided married women have forsaken their husbands, and husbands their wives: then, afterwards, not being able to contain, they have fallen into adultery; and so, through such a principle as this, have come to shame. They were found, moreover, fomenting separations from the houses of God and of the Church; treating the Church and its members with disdain, and establishing separate meetings and assemblies, and different doctrines and other things in opposition to the Church and its members; wearing strange apparel, to the destruction of the common custom of dress; making distributions, among themselves and their adherents as saints, of the first-fruits of the Church, which have, from the first, been given to the Church; slaves also leaving their masters, and, on account of their own strange apparel, acting insolently towards

γυναικείων ἀνδρικὰ ἀμφιάσματα ἀναλαμβάνουσαι, καὶ ἐκ τούτων οἰόμεναι δικαιοῦσθαι· πολλαὶ δὲ καὶ ἀποκείρονται προφάσει θεοσεβείας τὴν φύσιν τῆς κόμης τῆς γυναικείας· νηστείας τε ἐν Κυριακῇ ποιούμενοι, καὶ τῆς ἁγιότητος τῆς ἐλευθέρας ἡμέρας καταφρονοῦντες, καὶ τῶν νηστειῶν τῶν ἐν ταῖς ἐκκλησίαις τεταγμένων ὑπερφρονοῦντες, καὶ ἐσθίοντες· καί τινες αὐτῶν μεταλήψεις κρεῶν βδελυττόμενοι, καὶ ἐν οἴκοις γεγαμηκότων εὐχὰς ποιεῖσθαι μὴ βουλόμενοι, καὶ γινομένων εὐχῶν καταφρονοῦντες, καὶ πολλάκις προσφορῶν ἐν αὐταῖς ταῖς οἰκίαις τῶν γεγαμηκότων γινομένων μὴ μεταλαμβάνοντες, καὶ πρεσβυτέρων γεγαμηκότων ὑπερφρονοῦντες, καὶ τῶν λειτουργιῶν τῶν ὑπ' αὐτῶν γινομένων μὴ ἁπτόμενοι, καὶ τὰς συνάξεις τῶν μαρτύρων καὶ τῶν ἐκεῖ συνερχομένων καὶ λειτουργούντων καταγινώσκοντες, καὶ πλουσίων δὲ τῶν μὴ πάντων τῶν ὑπαρχόντων ἀναχωρούντων, ὡς ἐλπίδα παρὰ Θεῷ μὴ ἐχόντων· καὶ πολλὰ ἄλλα ἃ ἀριθμῆσαι οὐδεὶς ἂν δυνηθείη. Ἕκαστος γὰρ αὐτῶν, ἐπειδὴ τοῦ κανόνος τοῦ ἐκκλησιαστικοῦ ἐξῆλθεν, ὥσπερ νόμους ἰδιάζοντας ἔσχεν. Οὔτε γὰρ κοινὴ γνώμη αὐτῶν ἁπάντων ἐγένετο· ἀλλ' ἕκαστος, ὅπερ ἂν ἐνεθυμήθη, τοῦτο προσέθηκεν ἐπὶ διαβολῇ τῆς ἐκκλησίας καί ἑαυτοῦ βλάβῃ.

Δι' οὖν ταῦτα ἠναγκάσθη ἡ παραγενομένη ἐν Γάγγραις ἁγία σύνοδος καταψηφίσασθαι αὐτῶν, καὶ ὅρους ἐκθέσθαι, ἐκτὸς αὐτοὺς εἶναι τῆς ἐκκλησίας· εἰ δὲ μεταγνοῖεν, καὶ ἀναθεματίζοιεν ἕκαστον τούτων τῶν κακῶς λεχθέντων, δεκτοὺς αὐτοὺς γίνεσθαι. Καὶ διὰ τοῦτο ἐξέθετο ἡ ἁγία σύνοδος ἕκαστον, ὃ ὀφείλουσιν ἀναθεματίσαντες δεχθῆναι· εἰ δέ τις μὴ πεισθείη τοῖς λεχθεῖσιν, ὡς αἱρετικὸν αὐτὸν ἀναθεματισθῆναι, καὶ εἶναι ἀκοινώνητον καὶ κεχωρισμένον τῆς ἐκκλησίας· καὶ δεήσει τοὺς ἐπισκόπους ἐπὶ πάντων τῶν εὑρισκομένων παρ' αὐτοῖς τοιοῦτον παραφυλάξασθαι.

their masters; women, too, disregarding decent custom, and, instead of womanly apparel, wearing men's clothes, thinking to be justified because of these; while many of them, under a pretext of piety, cut off the growth of hair, which is natural to woman; [and these persons were found] fasting on the Lord's Day, despising the sacredness of that free day, but disdaining and eating on the fasts appointed in the Church; and certain of them abhor the eating of flesh; neither do they tolerate prayers in the houses of married persons, but, on the contrary, despise such prayers when they are made, and often refuse to partake when Oblations are offered in the houses of married persons; contemning married Presbyters, and refusing to touch their ministrations; condemning the Assemblies of the Martyrs and those who gather or minister therein, and the rich also who do not alienate all their wealth, as having nothing to hope from God; and many other things that no one could recount. For every one of them, when he forsook the Canon of the Church, adopted laws that tended as it were to isolation; for neither was there any common judgment among all of them; but whatever any one conceived, that he propounded, to the scandal of the Church, and to his own destruction.

Wherefore, the Holy Synod present in Gangra was compelled, on these accounts, to condemn them, and to set forth definitions declaring them to be cast out of the Church; but that, if they should repent and anathematize every one of these false doctrines, then they should be capable of restoration. And therefore the Holy Synod has particularly set forth everything which they ought to acknowledge when they are received. And if any one will not submit to the said decrees, he shall be anathematized as a heretic, and excommunicated, and cast out of the Church; and it will behove the Bishops to observe a like rule in respect of all who may be found with them.

ΚΑΝΟΝΕΣ

ΤΗΣ ΕΝ ΓΑΓΓΡΑ ΣΥΝΟΔΟΥ.

ΚΑΝΩΝ Α'.

Εἴ τις τὸν γάμον μέμφοιτο, καὶ τὴν καθεύδουσαν μετὰ τοῦ ἀνδρὸς αὐτῆς, οὖσαν πιστὴν καὶ εὐλαβῆ, βδελύσσοιτο ἢ μέμφοιτο, ὡς ἂν μὴ δυναμένην εἰς βασιλείαν εἰσελθεῖν, ἀνάθεμα ἔστω.

ΚΑΝΩΝ Β'.

Εἴ τις ἐσθίοντα κρέα, χωρὶς αἵματος, καὶ εἰδωλοθύτου, καὶ πνικτοῦ, μετ' εὐλαβείας καὶ πίστεως, κατακρίνοι ὡς ἂν διὰ τὸ μεταλαμβάνειν ἐλπίδα μὴ ἔχοντα, ἀνάθεμα ἔστω.

ΚΑΝΩΝ Γ'.

Εἴ τις δοῦλον προφάσει θεοσεβείας διδάσκοι καταφρονεῖν δεσπότου, καὶ ἀναχωρεῖν τῆς ὑπηρεσίας, καὶ μὴ μετ' εὐνοίας καὶ πάσης τιμῆς τῷ ἑαυτοῦ δεσπότῃ ἐξυπηρετεῖσθαι, ἀνάθεμα ἔστω.

ΚΑΝΩΝ Δ'.

Εἴ τις διακρίνοιτο παρὰ πρεσβυτέρου γεγαμηκότος, ὡς μὴ χρῆναι, λειτουργήσαντος αὐτοῦ, προσφορᾶς μεταλαμβάνειν, ἀνάθεμα ἔστω.

ΚΑΝΩΝ Ε'.

Εἴ τις διδάσκοι, τὸν οἶκον τοῦ Θεοῦ εὐκαταφρόνητον εἶναι, καὶ τὰς ἐν αὐτῷ συνάξεις, ἀνάθεμα ἔστω.

CANONS OF GANGRA.

CANON I.

If any one shall condemn marriage, or abominate and condemn a faithful and pious woman who sleeps with her own husband, as though she could not enter into the Kingdom, let him be Anathema.

CANON II.

If any one shall condemn him who with piety and faith eats flesh, which is without blood and has not been offered to idols nor strangled, as though the man were without hope because of his eating, let him be Anathema.

CANON III.

If any one shall teach that a slave may, under pretext of piety, despise his master and withdraw from his service, and that he should not serve his own master with good-will and all honour, let him be Anathema.

CANON IV.

If any one shall declare, concerning a married Presbyter, that it is not lawful to partake of the Oblation when he offers it, let him be Anathema.

CANON V.

If any one shall teach that the House of God and the assemblies held therein are to be despised, let him be Anathema.

ΚΑΝΩΝ ϛʹ.

Εἴ τις παρὰ τὴν ἐκκλησίαν ἰδίᾳ ἐκκλησιάζοι, καὶ καταφρονῶν τῆς ἐκκλησίας, τὰ τῆς ἐκκλησίας ἐθέλοι πράττειν, μὴ συνόντος τοῦ πρεσβυτέρου κατὰ γνώμην τοῦ ἐπισκόπου, ἀνάθεμα ἔστω.

ΚΑΝΩΝ Ζʹ.

Εἴ τις καρποφορίας ἐκκλησιαστικὰς ἐθέλοι λαμβάνειν, ἢ διδόναι ἔξω τῆς ἐκκλησίας παρὰ γνώμην τοῦ ἐπισκόπου, ἢ τοῦ ἐγκεχειρισμένου τὰ τοιαῦτα, καὶ μὴ μετὰ γνώμης αὐτοῦ ἐθέλοι πράττειν, ἀνάθεμα ἔστω.

ΚΑΝΩΝ Ηʹ.

Εἴ τις διδοῖ, ἢ λαμβάνοι καρποφορίαν παρεκτὸς τοῦ ἐπισκόπου, ἢ τοῦ ἐπιτεταγμένου εἰς οἰκονομίαν εὐποιΐας, καὶ ὁ διδοὺς, καὶ ὁ λαμβάνων, ἀνάθεμα ἔστω.

ΚΑΝΩΝ Θʹ.

Εἴ τις παρθενεύοι, ἢ ἐγκρατεύοιτο, ὡς ἂν βδελυκτῶν τῶν γάμων ἀναχωρήσας, καὶ μὴ δι' αὐτὸ τὸ καλὸν καὶ ἅγιον τῆς παρθενίας, ἀνάθεμα ἔστω.

ΚΑΝΩΝ Ιʹ.

Εἴ τις τῶν παρθενευόντων διὰ τὸν Κύριον, κατεπαίροιτο τῶν γεγαμηκότων, ἀνάθεμα ἔστω.

ΚΑΝΩΝ ΙΑʹ.

Εἴ τις καταφρονοίη τῶν ἐκ πίστεως ἀγάπας ποιούντων, καὶ διὰ τιμὴν τοῦ Κυρίου συγκαλούντων τοὺς ἀδελφοὺς, καὶ μὴ ἐθέλοι κοινωνεῖν ταῖς κλήσεσι, διὰ τὸ ἐξευτελίζειν τὸ γινόμενον, ἀνάθεμα ἔστω.

CANON VI.

If any one shall hold private assemblies in opposition to the Church, and, despising the Church, shall presume to perform ecclesiastical acts without the concurrence of the Presbyter and against the judgment of the Bishop, let him be Anathema.

CANON VII.

If any one shall presume to take the fruits offered at the Church, or to give them out of the Church, against the judgment of the Bishop, or the person charged with such things, and shall refuse to act according to his judgment, let him be Anathema.

CANON VIII.

If any one, besides the Bishop or the person appointed for the stewardship of benefactions, shall either give or receive the revenue, let both the giver and the receiver be Anathema.

CANON IX.

If any one shall remain virgin, or observe continence, abstaining from marriage because he abhors it, and not on account of the beauty and holiness of virginity itself, let him be Anathema.

CANON X.

If any one of those who are virgin for the Lord's sake shall insult the married, let him be Anathema.

CANON XI.

If any one shall despise those who out of faith make love-feasts and invite the brethren in honour of the Lord, and shall refuse to accept the invitations because he despises what is done, let him be Anathema.

ΚΑΝΩΝ ΙΒʹ.

Εἴ τις ἀνδρῶν διὰ νομιζομένην ἄσκησιν περιβολαίῳ χρῆται, καὶ ὡς ἂν ἐκ τούτου τὴν δικαιοσύνην ἔχων καταψηφίσοιτο τῶν μετ' εὐλαβείας τοὺς βήρους φορούντων, καὶ τῇ ἄλλῃ κοινῇ καὶ ἐν συνηθείᾳ οὔσῃ ἐσθῆτι κεχρημένων, ἀνάθεμα ἔστω.

ΚΑΝΩΝ ΙΓʹ.

Εἴ τις γυνὴ διὰ νομιζομένην ἄσκησιν μεταβάλλοιτο ἀμφίασμα, καὶ ἀντὶ τοῦ εἰωθότος γυναικείου ἀμφιάσματος ἀνδρῷον ἀναλάβοι, ἀνάθεμα ἔστω.

ΚΑΝΩΝ ΙΔʹ.

Εἴ τις γυνὴ καταλιμπάνοι τὸν ἄνδρα, καὶ ἀναχωρεῖν ἐθέλοι, βδελυττομένη τὸν γάμον, ἀνάθεμα ἔστω.

ΚΑΝΩΝ ΙΕʹ.

Εἴ τις καταλιμπάνοι τὰ ἑαυτοῦ τέκνα, καὶ μὴ τεκνοτροφοῖ, καὶ τὸ ὅσον ἐπ' αὐτῷ πρὸς θεοσέβειαν τὴν προσήκουσαν ἀνάγοι, ἀλλὰ προφάσει τῆς ἀσκήσεως ἀμελοίη, ἀνάθεμα ἔστω.

ΚΑΝΩΝ Ιϛʹ.

Εἴ τινα τέκνα γονέων, μάλιστα πιστῶν, ἀναχωροίη προφάσει θεοσεβείας, καὶ μὴ τὴν καθήκουσαν τιμὴν τοῖς γονεῦσιν ἀπονέμοι, προτιμωμένης δηλονότι παρ' αὐτοῖς τῆς θεοσεβείας, ἀνάθεμα ἔστω.

ΚΑΝΩΝ ΙΖʹ.

Εἴ τις γυναικῶν διὰ νομιζομένην ἄσκησιν ἀποκείροιτο τὰς κόμας, ἃς ἔδωκεν ὁ Θεὸς εἰς ὑπόμνησιν τῆς ὑποταγῆς, ὡς παραλύουσα τὸ πρόσταγμα τῆς ὑποταγῆς, ἀνάθεμα ἔστω.

ΚΑΝΩΝ ΙΗʹ.

Εἴ τις διὰ νομιζομένην ἄσκησιν ἐν τῇ Κυριακῇ νηστεύοι, ἀνάθεμα ἔστω.

ΚΑΝΩΝ ΙΘʹ.

Εἴ τις τῶν ἀσκουμένων, χωρὶς σωματικῆς ἀνάγκης, ὑπερηφανεύοιτο, καὶ τὰς παραδεδομένας νηστείας εἰς τὸ κοινὸν, καὶ φυλασσομένας ὑπὸ τῆς ἐκκλησίας παραλύοι, ὑποικουροῦντος ἐν αὐτῷ τελείου λογισμοῦ, ἀνάθεμα ἔστω.

CANON XII.

If any one, under pretence of asceticism, should wear a [rough] cloak and, as if this gave him righteousness, shall despise those who with piety wear the *Berus* and use other common and customary dress, let him be Anathema.

CANON XIII.

If any woman, under pretence of asceticism, shall change her apparel and, instead of a woman's accustomed clothing, shall put on that of a man, let her be Anathema.

CANON XIV.

If any woman shall forsake her husband, and resolve to depart from him because she abhors marriage, let her be Anathema.

CANON XV.

If any one shall forsake his own children and shall not nurture them, nor so far as in him lies, rear them in becoming piety, but shall neglect them, under pretence of asceticism, let him be Anathema.

CANON XVI.

If, under pretence of religion, any children shall withdraw from their parents, particularly [if the parents are] believers, and shall withhold becoming reverence from their parents, [thus] evidently honouring religion more than them, let them be Anathema.

CANON XVII.

If any woman shall, under pretence of religion, cut off her hair, which God gave her as the reminder of her subjection, let her be Anathema, as one who annuls the ordinance of subjection.

CANON XVIII.

If any one, under pretence of asceticism, shall fast on Sunday, let him be Anathema.

CANON XIX.

If any of the ascetics, without bodily necessity, and having full use of his reason, shall behave with insolence and disregard the fasts commonly prescribed and observed by the Church, let him be Anathema.

ΚΑΝΩΝ Κʹ.

Εἴ τις αἰτιῶτο, ὑπερηφάνῳ διαθέσει κεχρημένος καὶ βδελυσσόμενος, τὰς συνάξεις τῶν μαρτύρων, ἢ τὰς ἐν αὐταῖς γινομένας λειτουργίας, καὶ τὰς μνήμας αὐτῶν, ἀνάθεμα ἔστω.

Ταῦτα δὲ γράφομεν, οὐκ ἐκκόπτοντες τοὺς ἐν τῇ ἐκκλησίᾳ τοῦ Θεοῦ κατὰ τὰς Γραφὰς ἀσκεῖσθαι βουλομένους, ἀλλὰ τοὺς λαμβάνοντας τὴν ὑπόθεσιν τῆς ἀσκήσεως εἰς ὑπερηφανίαν, κατὰ τῶν ἀφελέστερον βιούντων ἐπαιρομένους τε, καὶ παρὰ τὰς Γραφὰς καὶ τοὺς ἐκκλησιαστικοὺς κανόνας καινισμοὺς εἰσάγοντας. Ἡμεῖς τοιγαροῦν, καὶ παρθενίαν μετὰ ταπεινοφροσύνης θαυμάζομεν, καὶ ἐγκράτειαν μετὰ σεμνότητος καὶ θεοσεβείας γινομένην ἀποδεχόμεθα, καὶ ἀναχώρησιν τῶν ἐγκοσμίων πραγμάτων μετὰ ταπεινοφροσύνης ἀγάμεθα, καὶ γάμου συνοίκησιν σεμνὴν τιμῶμεν, καὶ πλοῦτον μετὰ δικαιοσύνης καὶ εὐποιΐας οὐκ ἐξουθενοῦμεν, καὶ λιτότητα καὶ εὐτέλειαν ἀμφιασμάτων δι' ἐπιμέλειαν μόνον τοῦ σώματος ἀπερίεργον ἐπαινοῦμεν· τὰς δὲ ἐκλύτους καὶ τεθρυμμένας ἐν τῇ ἐσθῆτι προόδους ἀποστρεφόμεθα, καὶ τοὺς οἴκους τοῦ Θεοῦ τιμῶμεν, καὶ τὰς συνόδους τὰς ἐπ' αὐτοῖς, ὡς ἁγίας καὶ ἐπωφελεῖς ἀσπαζόμεθα, οὐ συγκλείοντες τὴν εὐσέβειαν ἐν τοῖς οἴκοις, ἀλλὰ πάντα τόπον τὸν ἐπ' ὀνόματι τοῦ Θεοῦ οἰκοδομηθέντα τιμῶντες, καὶ τὴν ἐν αὐτῇ τῇ ἐκκλησίᾳ συνέλευσιν εἰς ὠφέλειαν τοῦ κοινοῦ προσιέμεθα, καὶ τὰς καθ' ὑπερβολὴν εὐποιΐας τῶν ἀδελφῶν, τὰς κατὰ τὰς παραδόσεις διὰ τῆς ἐκκλησίας εἰς τοὺς πτωχοὺς γινομένας, μακαρίζομεν, καὶ πάντα, συνελόντας εἰπεῖν, τὰ παραδοθέντα, ὑπὸ τῶν θείων Γραφῶν καὶ τῶν ἀποστολικῶν παραδόσεων ἐν τῇ ἐκκλησίᾳ γίνεσθαι εὐχόμεθα.

CANON XX.

If any one shall, from a presumptuous disposition, condemn and abhor the assemblies [in honour] of the martyrs, or the services performed therein, and the commemoration of them, let him be Anathema.

These things we write, not to cut off those in the Church of God who wish to lead an ascetic life, according to the Scriptures; but those who carry the pretence of asceticism to superciliousness; both exalting themselves above those who live more simply, and introducing novelties contrary to the Scriptures and the ecclesiastical Canons. We do, assuredly, admire virginity, [attended] by humility; and we have regard for continence, accompanied by godliness and gravity; and we praise a retreat from worldly occupations, [when it is made] with lowliness of mind; [but at the same time] we honour the holy companionship of marriage, and we do not contemn wealth enjoyed with uprightness and beneficence; and we commend plainness and frugality in apparel, [which is worn] only from attention, [and that] not over-fastidious, to the body; but dissolute and effeminate excess in dress we eschew; and we reverence the houses of God and embrace the assemblies held therein as holy and helpful, not confining religion within the houses, but reverencing every place built in the name of God; and we approve of gathering together in the Church itself for the common profit; and we bless the exceeding charities done by the brethren to the poor, according to the traditions of the Church; and, to sum up in a word, we pray that all things which have been delivered by the Holy Scriptures and the Apostolical traditions, may be done throughout the Church.

ΤΗΣ 'ΕΝ 'ΑΝΤΙΟΧΕΙᾼ ΣΥΝΟΔΟΥ

'ΕΠΙΣΤΟΛΗ ΣΥΝΟΔΙΚΗ.

'Η *ἁγία καὶ εἰρηνικωτάτη σύνοδος, ἡ ὑπὸ τοῦ* Θεοῦ *συγκροτηθεῖσα ἐν* 'Αντιοχείᾳ, *ἐξ ἐπαρχίας* Συρίας Κοίλης, Φοινίκης, Παλαιστίνης, 'Αραβίας, Μεσοποταμίας, Κιλικίας, 'Ισαυρίας, *τοῖς κατ' ἐπαρχίαν ὁμοψύχοις καὶ ἁγίοις συλλειτουργοῖς ἐν* Κυρίῳ *χαίρειν.*

'Η *χάρις καὶ ἡ ἀλήθεια* 'Ιησοῦ Χριστοῦ *τοῦ* Κυρίου *καὶ* Σωτῆρος *ἡμῶν, ἐπισκεψαμένη τὴν* 'Αντιοχέων *ἁγίαν ἐκκλησίαν, καὶ κατὰ τὸ αὐτὸ συνάπτουσα μετὰ ὁμονοίας καὶ συμφωνίας καὶ πνεύματος εἰρηνικοῦ, πολλὰ μὲν καὶ ἄλλα κατώρθωσεν, ἐν πᾶσι δὲ καὶ τοῦτο κατορθοῖ ἐξ ὑποβολῆς τοῦ ἁγίου καὶ εἰρηνικοῦ* Πνεύματος. *"Α γὰρ καλῶς ἔχειν ἔδοξε, μετὰ πλείονος σκέψεως καὶ ἐπικρίσεως ὁμοῦ πάντων ἡμῶν τῶν ἐπισκόπων κατὰ τὸ αὐτὸ συγκροτηθέντων ἐπὶ τῆς* 'Αντιοχείας *. ἐκ διαφόρων ἐπαρχιῶν, ἐπὶ τὴν ὑμετέραν γνῶσιν ἀνηνέγκαμεν, πιστεύσαντες τῇ τοῦ* Χριστοῦ *χάριτι, καὶ τῷ τῆς εἰρήνης* 'Αγίῳ Πνεύματι, *ὅτι καῖ αὐτοὶ συμπνεύσητε, ὡς ἂν δυνάμει συνόντες ἡμῖν, καὶ ταις εὐχαῖς συνεργοῦντες, μᾶλλον δὲ ἡνωμένοι ἡμῖν, καὶ τῷ* 'Αγίῳ Πνευματι *συμπαρόντες, τὰ αὐτά τε ἡμῖν συμφωνήσαντες καὶ ὁρισάμενοι, καὶ τὰ ὀρθῶς δόξαντα ἐπισφραγιζόμενοι καὶ βεβαιοῦντες τῇ τοῦ* 'Αγίου Πνεύματος *συμφωνίᾳ.*

Εἰσὶ *δὲ οἱ ὁρισθέντες ἐκκλησιαστικοὶ κανόνες οἱ ὑποτεταγμένοι.*

SYNODICAL EPISTLE.

COUNCIL OF ANTIOCH.

The holy and most peaceful Synod which has been gathered together in Antioch from the Provinces of Cœle-Syria, Phœnicia, Palestine, Arabia, Mesopotamia, Cilicia, and Isauria; to our holy and like-minded fellow Ministers in every Province, wisheth health in the Lord.

The grace and truth of our Lord and Saviour Jesus Christ hath regarded the holy Church of the Antiochians, and, by joining it together with unity of mind and concord and the Spirit of Peace, hath likewise bettered many other things; and in them all this betterment is wrought by the assistance of the holy and peace-giving Spirit. Wherefore, that which, after much examination and investigation, was unanimously agreed upon by us Bishops, who, coming out of various Provinces, have met together in Antioch, we have now brought to your knowledge; trusting in the grace of Christ and in the Holy Spirit of Peace, that ye also will agree with us and stand by us as far as in you lies, striving with us in prayers, and being even more united with us, following the Holy Spirit, uniting in our definitions, and decreeing the same things as we; ye, in the concord which proceedeth of the Holy Spirit, sealing and confirming what has been determined.

Now the Canons of the Church which have been settled are hereto appended.

ΚΑΝΟΝΕΣ

ΤΗΣ ΕΝ ΑΝΤΙΟΧΕΙᾼ ΤΗΣ ΣΥΡΙΑΣ ΣΥΝΟΔΟΥ.

ΚΑΝΩΝ Α'.

Πάντας τοὺς τολμῶντας παραλύειν τὸν ὅρον τῆς ἁγίας καὶ μεγάλης συνόδου τῆς ἐν Νικαίᾳ συγκροτηθείσης ἐπὶ παρουσίᾳ τῆς εὐσεβείας τοῦ θεοφιλεστάτου βασιλέως Κωνσταντίνου, περὶ τῆς ἁγίας ἑορτῆς τοῦ σωτηριώδους Πάσχα, ἀκοινωνήτους καὶ ἀποβλήτους εἶναι τῆς ἐκκλησίας, εἰ ἐπιμένοιεν φιλονεικότερον ἐνιστάμενοι πρὸς τὰ καλῶς δεδογμένα, καὶ ταῦτα εἰρήσθω περὶ τῶν λαϊκῶν. Εἰ δέ τις τῶν προεστώτων τῆς ἐκκλησίας, ἐπίσκοπος, ἢ πρεσβύτερος, ἢ διάκονος, μετὰ τὸν ὅρον τοῦτον τολμήσειεν ἐπὶ διαστροφῇ τῶν λαῶν καὶ ταραχῇ τῶν ἐκκλησιῶν ἰδιάζειν, καὶ μετὰ τῶν Ἰουδαίων ἐπιτελεῖν τὸ Πάσχα· τοῦτον ἡ ἁγία σύνοδος ἐντεῦθεν ἤδη ἀλλότριον ἔκρινε τῆς ἐκκλησίας, ὡς οὐ μόνον ἑαυτῷ ἁμαρτίας ἐπισωρεύοντα, ἀλλὰ πολλοῖς διαφθορᾶς καὶ διαστροφῆς γινόμενον αἴτιον· καὶ οὐ μόνον τοὺς τοιούτους καθαιρεῖ τῆς λειτουργίας, ἀλλὰ καὶ τοὺς τολμῶντας τούτοις κοινωνεῖν μετὰ τὴν καθαίρεσιν. Τοὺς δὲ καθαιρεθέντας ἀποστερεῖσθαι καὶ τῆς ἔξωθεν τιμῆς, ἧς ὁ ἅγιος κανὼν καὶ τὸ τοῦ Θεοῦ ἱερατεῖον μετείληφεν.

ΚΑΝΩΝ Β'.

Πάντας τοὺς εἰσιόντας εἰς τὴν ἐκκλησίαν, καὶ τῶν ἱερῶν Γραφῶν ἀκούοντας, μὴ κοινωνοῦντας δὲ εὐχῆς ἅμα τῷ λαῷ, ἀποστρεφομένους τὴν ἁγίαν μετάληψιν τῆς εὐχαριστίας κατά τινα ἀταξίαν, τούτους ἀποβλήτους γίνεσθαι τῆς ἐκκλησίας, ἕως ἂν ἐξομολογησάμενοι, καὶ δείξαντες καρποὺς μετανοίας, καὶ παρακαλέσαντες, τυχεῖν δυνηθῶσι συγγνώμης· μὴ ἐξεῖναι δὲ κοινωνεῖν τοῖς ἀκοινωνήτοις, μηδὲ

CANONS OF ANTIOCH.

CANON I.

Whosoever shall presume to set aside the decree of the holy and great Synod which was assembled at Nicæa in the presence of the pious and most religious Sovereign Constantine, concerning the holy and salutary feast of Easter, if they shall obstinately persist in opposing what was [then] rightly ordained, let them be excommunicated and cast out; and let this be said concerning the laity. But if any one of those who preside in the Church, whether he be Bishop, Presbyter, or Deacon, shall presume, after this decree, to exercise his own private judgment to the subversion of the people and to the disturbance of the Churches, by observing Easter [at the same time] with the Jews, the holy Synod decrees that he shall thenceforth be an alien from the Church as one who not only heaps sins upon himself, but who is also the cause of destruction and subversion to many; and it deposes not only such persons themselves from their ministry, but those also who after their deposition shall presume to communicate with them. And the deposed shall be deprived even of that external honour, of which the holy Canon [*i. e.*, the Sacerdotal List] and God's priesthood partake.

CANON II.

All who enter the Church and hear the Holy Scriptures, but do not communicate with the people in prayers, or who turn away, with a certain disorder, from the holy partaking of the Eucharist, are to be cast out of the Church, until, after they shall have made confession, and having brought forth the fruits of repentance, and made earnest entreaty, they shall have obtained forgiveness; and it is unlawful to communicate with

κατ' οἴκους συνελθόντας συνεύχεσθαι τοῖς μὴ τῇ ἐκκλησίᾳ συνευχομένοις, μηδὲ ἐν ἑτέρᾳ ἐκκλησίᾳ ὑποδέχεσθαι τοὺς ἐν ἑτέρᾳ ἐκκλησίᾳ μὴ συναγομένους. Εἰ δὲ φανείη τις τῶν ἐπισκόπων, ἢ πρεσβυτέρων, ἢ διακόνων, ἤ τις τοῦ κανόνος τοῖς ἀκοινωνήτοις κοινωνῶν, καὶ τοῦτον ἀκοινώνητον εἶναι, ὡς ἂν συγχέοντα τὸν κανόνα τῆς ἐκκλησίας.

ΚΑΝΩΝ Γ'.

Εἴ τις πρεσβύτερος, ἢ διάκονος, ἢ ὅλως τῶν τοῦ ἱερατείου τις, καταλιπὼν τὴν ἑαυτοῦ παροικίαν, εἰς ἑτέραν ἀπέλθοι, ἔπειτα παντελῶς μεταστὰς, διατρίβειν ἐν ἄλλῃ παροικίᾳ πειρᾶται ἐπὶ πολλῷ χρόνῳ, μηκέτι λειτουργεῖν, εἰ μάλιστα καλοῦντι τῷ ἐπισκόπῳ τῷ ἰδίῳ, καὶ ἐπανελθεῖν εἰς τὴν παροικίαν τὴν ἑαυτοῦ παραινοῦντι, μὴ ὑπακούοι. Εἰ δὲ καὶ ἐπιμένοι τῇ ἀταξίᾳ, παντελῶς αὐτὸν καθαιρεῖσθαι τῆς λειτουργίας, ὡς μηκέτι χώραν ἔχειν ἀποκαταστάσεως. Εἰ δὲ καθαιρεθέντα διὰ ταύτην τὴν αἰτίαν δέχοιτο ἕτερος ἐπίσκοπος, κἀκεῖνον ἐπιτιμίας τυγχάνειν ὑπὸ κοινῆς συνόδου, ὡς παραλύοντα τοὺς θεσμοὺς τοὺς ἐκκλησιαστικούς.

ΚΑΝΩΝ Δ'.

Εἴ τις ἐπίσκοπος ὑπὸ συνόδου καθαιρεθεὶς, ἢ πρεσβύτερος, ἢ διάκονος, ὑπὸ τοῦ ἰδίου ἐπισκόπου, τολμήσειέ τι πρᾶξαι τῆς λειτουργίας, εἴτε ὁ ἐπίσκοπος κατὰ τὴν προάγουσαν συνήθειαν, εἴτε ὁ πρεσβύτερος, εἴτε ὁ διάκονος· μηκέτι ἐξὸν εἶναι αὐτῷ, μηδὲ ἐν ἑτέρᾳ συνόδῳ ἐλπίδα ἀποκαταστάσεως, μήτε ἀπολογίας χώραν ἔχειν, ἀλλὰ καὶ τοὺς κοινωνοῦντας αὐτῷ πάντας ἀποβάλλεσθαι τῆς ἐκκλησίας, καὶ μάλιστα, εἰ μαθόντες τὴν ἀπόφασιν τὴν κατὰ τῶν προειρημένων ἐξενεχθεῖσαν, τολμήσειαν αὐτοῖς κοινωνεῖν.

ΚΑΝΩΝ Ε'.

Εἴ τις πρεσβύτερος, ἢ διάκονος, καταφρονήσας τοῦ ἰδίου ἐπισκόπου, ἀφώρισεν ἑαυτὸν τῆς ἐκκλησίας, καὶ ἰδίᾳ συνήγαγε, καὶ θυσιαστήριον ἔστησε, καὶ, τοῦ ἐπισκόπου προσκα-

excommunicated persons, or to assemble in private houses and pray with those who do not pray in the Church; or to receive in one Church those who do not assemble with another Church. And, if any one of the Bishops, Priests, or Deacons, or any one of the Canon [*i. e.*, the Sacerdotal List] shall be found communicating with excommunicated persons, let him also be excommunicated, as one who brings confusion on the Canon of the Church.

CANON III.

If any Presbyter, or Deacon, or any one whatever belonging to the Priesthood, shall forsake his own Parish, and shall depart, and, having wholly changed his residence, shall set himself to remain for a long time in another Parish, let him no longer officiate; especially if his own Bishop shall summon and urge him to return to his own Parish and he shall disobey. And if he persist in his disorder, let him be wholly deposed from his ministry, so that no further room be left for his restoration. And if another Bishop shall receive a man deposed for this cause, let him be punished by the Common Synod as one who nullifies the laws of the Church.

CANON IV.

If any Bishop who has been deposed by a Synod, or any Presbyter or Deacon who has been deposed by his Bishop, shall presume to execute any part of the ministry, whether it be a Bishop according to his former custom, or a Presbyter, or a Deacon, it shall no longer be lawful for him to have a prospect of restoration, nor an opportunity of making his defence, in another Synod; but they who communicate with him shall all be cast out of the Church, and particularly if they have presumed to communicate with the persons aforementioned, knowing the sentence pronounced against them.

CANON V.

If any Presbyter or Deacon, despising his own Bishop, has separated himself from his Church, and gathered a private assembly, and raised an Altar; and if, when summoned by

λεσαμένου, ἀπειθοίη, καὶ μὴ βούλοιτο αὐτῷ πείθεσθαι, μηδὲ ὑπακούειν καὶ πρῶτον καὶ δεύτερον καλοῦντι, τοῦτον καθαιρεῖσθαι παντελῶς, καὶ μηκέτι θεραπείας τυγχάνειν, μηδὲ δύνασθαι λαμβάνειν τὴν ἑαυτοῦ τιμήν. Εἰ δὲ παραμένοι θορυβῶν καὶ ἀναστατῶν τὴν ἐκκλησίαν, διὰ τῆς ἔξωθεν ἐξουσίας ὡς στασιώδη αὐτὸν ἐπιστρέφεσθαι.

ΚΑΝΩΝ ϛ'.

Εἴ τις ὑπὸ τοῦ ἰδίου ἐπισκόπου ἀκοινώνητος γέγονε, μὴ πρότερον αὐτὸν παρ' ἑτέρων δεχθῆναι, εἰ μὴ ὑπ' αὐτοῦ παραδεχθείη τοῦ ἰδίου ἐπισκόπου, ἢ, συνόδου γενομένης, ἀπαντήσας ἀπολογήσεται, πείσας τε τὴν σύνοδον, καταδέξοιτο ἑτέραν ἀπόφασιν. Ὁ αὐτὸς δὲ ὅρος ἐπὶ λαϊκῶν, καὶ πρεσβυτέρων, καὶ διακόνων, καὶ πάντων τῶν ἐν τῷ κανόνι.

ΚΑΝΩΝ Ζ'.

Μηδένα ἄνευ εἰρηνικῶν δέχεσθαι τῶν ξένων.

ΚΑΝΩΝ Η'.

Μηδὲ πρεσβυτέρους τοὺς ἐν ταῖς χώραις κανονικὰς ἐπιστολὰς διδόναι, ἢ πρὸς μόνους τοὺς γείτονας ἐπισκόπους ἐπιστολὰς ἐκπέμπειν· τοὺς δὲ ἀνεπιλήπτους χωρεπισκόπους διδόναι εἰρηνικάς.

ΚΑΝΩΝ Θ'.

Τοὺς καθ' ἑκάστην ἐπαρχίαν ἐπισκόπους εἰδέναι χρὴ τὸν ἐν τῇ μητροπόλει προεστῶτα ἐπίσκοπον, καὶ τὴν φροντίδα ἀναδέχεσθαι πάσης τῆς ἐπαρχίας, διὰ τὸ ἐν τῇ μητροπόλει πανταχόθεν συντρέχειν πάντας τοὺς τὰ πράγματα ἔχοντας. Ὅθεν ἔδοξε καὶ τῇ τιμῇ προηγεῖσθαι αὐτὸν, μηδέν τε πράττειν περιττὸν τοὺς λοιποὺς ἐπισκόπους ἄνευ αὐτοῦ, κατὰ τὸν ἀρχαῖον κρατήσαντα ἐκ τῶν Πατέρων ἡμῶν κανόνα· ἢ ταῦτα μόνα, ὅσα τῇ ἑκάστου ἐπιβάλλει παροικίᾳ, καὶ ταῖς ὑπ' αὐτὴν χώραις. Ἕκαστον γὰρ ἐπίσκοπον ἐξουσίαν ἔχειν τῆς ἑαυτοῦ παροικίας, διοικεῖν τε κατὰ τὴν ἑκάστῳ ἐπιβάλλουσαν εὐλάβειαν, καὶ πρόνοιαν ποιεῖσθαι πάσης τῆς χώρας τῆς ὑπὸ τὴν ἑαυτοῦ πόλιν· ὡς καὶ χειροτονεῖν πρεσβυτέρους

his Bishop, he shall refuse to be persuaded and will not obey, even though [his Bishop] summon him a first and a second time, let such a one be wholly deposed and have no further remedy, neither be capable of regaining his rank. And if he persist in troubling and disturbing the Church, let him be corrected, as a seditious person, by the civil power.

CANON VI.

If any one has been excommunicated by his own Bishop, let him not be received by others until he has either been restored by his own Bishop, or until, when a Synod is held, he shall have appeared and made his defence, and, having convinced the Synod, shall have received a different sentence. And let this decree apply to the laity, and to Presbyters and Deacons, and all who are in the Canon [*i. e.*, on the Sacerdotal List].

CANON VII.

No stranger shall be received without letters pacifical.

CANON VIII.

Let not country Presbyters give letters canonical, or let them send such letters only to the neighbouring Bishops. But the Chorepiscopi of good report may give letters pacifical.

CANON IX.

It behoves the Bishops in every Province to acknowledge the Bishop who presides in the Metropolis, and who has to take thought for the whole Province; because all men of business come together from every quarter to the Metropolis. Wherefore it is decreed that he have precedence in rank, and that the other Bishops do nothing extraordinary without him, (according to the ancient Canon which prevailed from [the times of] our Fathers) or such things only as pertain to their own particular Parishes and the districts subject to them. For each Bishop has authority over his own Parish, both to manage it with the piety which is incumbent on every one, and to make provision for the whole district which is depend-

καὶ διακόνους, καὶ μετὰ κρίσεως ἕκαστα διαλαμβάνειν· περαιτέρω δὲ μηδὲν πράττειν ἐπιχειρεῖν, δίχα τοῦ τῆς μητροπόλεως ἐπισκόπου, μηδὲ αὐτὸν ἄνευ τῆς τῶν λοιπῶν γνώμης.

ΚΑΝΩΝ Ι'.

Τοὺς ἐν ταῖς κώμαις, ἢ ταῖς χώραις, ἢ τοὺς καλουμένους χωρεπισκόπους, εἰ καὶ χειροθεσίαν εἶεν ἐπισκόπου εἰληφότες, ἔδοξε τῇ ἁγίᾳ συνόδῳ εἰδέναι τὰ ἑαυτῶν μέτρα, καὶ διοικεῖν τὰς ὑποκειμένας αὐτοῖς ἐκκλησίας, καὶ τῇ τούτων ἀρκεῖσθαι φροντίδι καὶ κηδεμονίᾳ, καθιστᾷν δὲ ἀναγνώστας, καὶ ὑποδιακόνους, καὶ ἐφορκιστὰς, καὶ τῇ τούτων ἀρκεῖσθαι προαγωγῇ· μήτε δὲ πρεσβύτερον, μήτε διάκονον χειροτονεῖν τολμᾷν δίχα τοῦ ἐν τῇ πόλει ἐπισκόπου, ᾗ ὑπόκεινται αὐτός τε καὶ ἡ χώρα. Εἰ δὲ τολμήσειέ τις παραβῆναι τὰ ὁρισθέντα, καθαιρεῖσθαι αὐτὸν καὶ ἧς μετέχει τιμῆς. Χωρεπίσκοπον δὲ γίνεσθαι ὑπὸ τοῦ τῆς πόλεως, ᾗ ὑπόκειται, ἐπισκόπου.

ΚΑΝΩΝ ΙΑ'.

Εἴ τις ἐπίσκοπος, ἢ πρεσβύτερος, ἢ ὅλως τοῦ κανόνος, ἄνευ γνώμης καὶ γραμμάτων τῶν ἐν τῇ ἐπαρχίᾳ ἐπισκόπων, καὶ μάλιστα τοῦ κατὰ τὴν μητρόπολιν, ὁρμήσειε πρὸς βασιλέα ἀπελθεῖν, τοῦτον ἀποκηρύττεσθαι, καὶ ἀπόβλητον γίνεσθαι, οὐ μόνον τῆς κοινωνίας, ἀλλὰ καὶ τῆς ἀξίας, ἧς μετέχων τυγχάνει· ὡς παρενοχλεῖν τολμῶντα τὰς τοῦ θεοφιλεστάτου βασιλέως ἡμῶν ἀκοὰς, παρὰ τὸν θεσμὸν τῆς ἐκκλησίας. Εἰ δὲ ἀναγκαία καλοίη χρεία πρὸς βασιλέα ὁρμᾷν, τοῦτο πράττειν μετὰ σκέψεως καὶ γνώμης τοῦ κατὰ τὴν μητρόπολιν τῆς ἐπαρχίας ἐπισκόπου καὶ τῶν ἐν αὐτῇ, τοῖς τε τούτων γράμμασιν ἐφοδιάζεσθαι.

ΚΑΝΩΝ ΙΒ'.

Εἴ τις ὑπὸ τοῦ ἰδίου ἐπισκόπου καθαιρεθεὶς πρεσβύτερος, ἢ διάκονος, ἢ καὶ ἐπίσκοπος ὑπὸ συνόδου, ἐνοχλῆσαι τολμήσειε τὰς βασιλέως ἀκοάς, δέον ἐπὶ μείζονα ἐπισκόπων σύνοδον

ent on his City; to ordain Presbyters and Deacons; and to settle everything with judgment. But let him undertake nothing further without the Bishop of the Metropolis; neither [let] the latter [do anything] without the consent of the others.

CANON X.

The Holy Synod decrees that persons in villages and districts, or who are called Chorepiscopi, even though they may have received a Bishop's Ordination, shall regard their own limits and manage the Churches subject to them, and be content with the care and administration of these; but they may ordain Readers, Sub-Deacons, and Exorcists, and shall be content with promoting these. But [such a one] shall not presume to ordain either a Presbyter or a Deacon, without the Bishop of the City to which he and his district are subject. And if he shall dare to transgress [these] decrees, he shall be deposed from the rank which he enjoys. And a Chorepiscopus is to be made by the Bishop of the City to which he is subject.

CANON XI.

If any Bishop, or Presbyter, or any one whatever of the Canon [*i. e.*, the Sacerdotal List] shall presume to betake himself to the Emperor without the consent and letters of the Bishops of the Province, and particularly of the Bishop of the Metropolis, such a one shall be publicly deposed and cast out, not only from Communion, but also from the rank which he happens to have; inasmuch as he dares to trouble the ears of our most religious Sovereign, contrary to the law of the Church. But, if necessary business shall require any one to go to the Emperor, let him do it with the advice and consent of the Metropolitan Bishop and other [Bishops] in the Province, and let him undertake his journey with letters from them.

CANON XII.

If any Presbyter, or Deacon, deposed by his own Bishop, or any Bishop deposed by a Synod, shall dare to trouble the ears of the Emperor, when it is his duty to submit his cause

τρέπεσθαι, καὶ, ἃ νομίζει δίκαια ἔχειν, προσαναφέρειν πλείοσιν ἐπισκόποις, καὶ τὴν παρ' αὐτῶν ἐξέτασίν τε καὶ ἐπίκρισιν ἐκδέχεσθαι, ὁ δὲ, τούτων ὀλιγωρήσας ἐνοχλήσειε τῷ βασιλεῖ· καὶ τοῦτον μηδεμιᾶς συγγνώμης ἀξιοῦσθαι, μηδὲ χώραν ἀπολογίας ἔχειν, μηδ' ἐλπίδα μελλούσης ἀποκαταστάσεως προσδοκᾷν.

ΚΑΝΩΝ ΙΓ'.

Μηδένα ἐπίσκοπον τολμᾷν ἀφ' ἑτέρας ἐπαρχίας εἰς ἑτέραν μεταβαίνειν, καὶ χειροτονεῖν ἐν ἐκκλησίᾳ τινὰς εἰς προαγωγὴν λειτουργίας, μηδὲ εἰ συνεπάγοιτο ἑαυτῷ ἑτέρους, εἰ μὴ παρακληθεὶς ἀφίκοιτο διὰ γραμμάτων τοῦ τε μητροπολίτου καὶ τῶν σὺν αὐτῷ ἐπισκόπων, ὧν εἰς τὴν χώραν παρέρχοιτο. Εἰ δὲ μηδενὸς καλοῦντος ἀπέλθοι ἀτάκτως ἐπὶ χειροθεσίᾳ τινῶν, καὶ καταστάσει τῶν ἐκκλησιαστικῶν πραγμάτων, μὴ προσηκόντων αὐτῷ, ἄκυρα μὲν τὰ ὑπ' αὐτοῦ πραττόμενα τυγχάνειν, καὶ αὐτὸν δὲ ὑπέχειν τῆς ἀταξίας αὐτοῦ, καὶ τῆς παραλόγου ἐπιχειρήσεως τὴν προσήκουσαν δίκην, καθῃρημένον ἐντεῦθεν ἤδη ὑπὸ τῆς ἁγίας συνόδου.

ΚΑΝΩΝ ΙΔ'.

Εἴ τις ἐπίσκοπος ἐπί τισιν ἐγκλήμασι κρίνοιτο, ἔπειτα συμβαίη περὶ αὐτοῦ διαφωνεῖν τοὺς ἐν τῇ ἐπαρχίᾳ ἐπισκόπους, τῶν μὲν ἀθῶον τὸν κρινόμενον ἀποφαινόντων, τῶν δὲ, ἔνοχον· ὑπὲρ ἀπαλλαγῆς πάσης ἀμφισβητήσεως, ἔδοξε τῇ ἁγίᾳ συνόδῳ, τὸν τῆς μητροπόλεως ἐπίσκοπον ἀπὸ τῆς πλησιοχώρου ἐπαρχίας μετακαλεῖσθαι ἑτέρους τινὰς, τοὺς ἐπικρινοῦντας, καὶ τὴν ἀμφισβήτησιν διαλύσοντας, τοῦ βεβαιῶσαι σὺν τοῖς τῆς ἐπαρχίας τὸ παριστάμενον.

ΚΑΝΩΝ ΙΕ'.

Εἴ τις ἐπίσκοπος, ἐπί τισιν ἐγκλήμασι κατηγορηθεὶς, κριθείη ὑπὸ πάντων τῶν ἐν τῇ ἐπαρχίᾳ ἐπισκόπων, πάντές τε σύμφωνοι μίαν κατ' αὐτοῦ ἐξενέγκοιεν ψῆφον, τοῦτον μηκέτι παρ' ἑτέροις δικάζεσθαι, ἀλλὰ μένειν βεβαίαν τὴν σύμφωνον τῶν ἐπὶ τῆς ἐπαρχίας ἐπισκόπων ἀπόφασιν.

to a greater Synod of Bishops, and to refer to more Bishops the things which he thinks right, and to abide by the examination and decision made by them; if, despising these, he shall trouble the Emperor, he shall be entitled to no pardon, neither shall he have an opportunity of defence, nor any hope of future restoration.

CANON XIII.

No Bishop shall presume to pass from one Province to another, and ordain persons to the dignity of the Ministry in the Church, not even should he have others with him, unless he should go at the written invitation of the Metropolitan and Bishops into whose country he goes. But if he should, without invitation, proceed irregularly to the ordination of any, or to the regulation of ecclesiastical affairs which do not concern him, the things done by him shall be disallowed, and he himself shall suffer the due punishment of his irregularity and his unreasonable undertaking, by being forthwith deposed by the Holy Synod.

CANON XIV.

If a Bishop shall be tried on any accusations, and it should then happen that the Bishops of the Province disagree concerning him, some pronouncing the accused innocent, and others [pronouncing him] guilty; for the settlement of all dispute, the Holy Synod decrees that the Metropolitan call on some others of the neighbouring Province, who shall add their judgment and resolve the dispute, and thus, with those of the Province, confirm what is determined.

CANON XV.

If any Bishop, lying under any accusation, shall be judged by all the Bishops in his Province, and all shall unanimously deliver the same verdict concerning him, he shall not be again judged by others, but the unanimous sentence of the Bishops of the Province shall remain established.

ΚΑΝΩΝ Ιϛʹ.

Εἴ τις ἐπίσκοπος σχολάζων, ἐπὶ σχολάζουσαν ἐκκλησίαν ἑαυτὸν ἐπιῤῥίψας, ὑφαρπάζοι τὸν θρόνον δίχα συνόδου τελείας, τοῦτον ἀπόβλητον εἶναι, κἂν εἰ πᾶς ὁ λαὸς, ὃν ὑφήρπασεν, ἕλοιτο αὐτόν. Τελείαν δὲ ἐκείνην εἶναι σύνοδον, ᾗ συμπάρεστι καὶ ὁ τῆς μητροπόλεως.

ΚΑΝΩΝ ΙΖʹ.

Εἴ τις ἐπίσκοπος χειροθεσίαν ἐπισκόπου λαβὼν, καὶ ὁρισθεὶς προεστάναι λαοῦ, μὴ καταδέξοιτο τὴν λειτουργίαν, μηδὲ πείθοιτο ἀπιέναι εἰς τὴν ἐγχειρισθεῖσαν αὐτῷ ἐκκλησίαν, τοῦτον εἶναι ἀκοινώνητον, ἕς τ' ἂν ἀναγκασθεὶς καταδέξοιτο, ἢ ὁρίσοι τι περὶ αὐτοῦ ἡ τελεία σύνοδος τῶν κατὰ τὴν ἐπαρχίαν ἐπισκόπων.

ΚΑΝΩΝ ΙΗʹ.

Εἴ τις ἐπίσκοπος χειροτονηθεὶς εἰς παροικίαν, μὴ ἀπέλθῃ εἰς ἣν ἐχειροτονήθη, οὐ παρὰ τὴν ἑαυτοῦ αἰτίαν, ἀλλ' ἤτοι διὰ τὴν τοῦ λαοῦ παραίτησιν, ἢ δι' ἑτέραν αἰτίαν οὐκ ἐξ αὐτοῦ γενομένην, τοῦτον μετέχειν τῆς τιμῆς καὶ τῆς λειτουργίας, μόνον μηδὲν παρενοχλοῦντα τοῖς πράγμασι τῆς ἐκκλησίας, ἔνθα ἂν συνάγοιτο· ἐκδέχεσθαι δὲ τοῦτον, ὃ ἂν ἡ τῆς ἐπαρχίας τελεία σύνοδος κρίνασα τὸ παριστάμενον ὁρίσῃ.

ΚΑΝΩΝ ΙΘʹ.

Ἐπίσκοπον μὴ χειροτονεῖσθαι δίχα συνόδου καὶ παρουσίας τοῦ ἐν τῇ μητροπόλει τῆς ἐπαρχίας· τούτου δὲ παρόντος ἐξάπαντος, βέλτιον μὲν συνεῖναι αὐτῷ πάντας τοὺς ἐν τῇ ἐπαρχίᾳ συλλειτουργοὺς, οὓς καὶ προσήκει δι' ἐπιστολῆς τὸν ἐν τῇ μητροπόλει συγκαλεῖν. Καὶ εἰ μὲν ἀπαντοῖεν οἱ πάντες, βέλτιον· εἰ δὲ δυσχερὲς τοῦτο εἴη, τούς γε πλείους ἐξάπαντος παρεῖναι δεῖ, ἢ διὰ γραμμάτων ὁμοψήφους γενέσθαι, καὶ οὕτω μετὰ τῆς τῶν πλειόνων ἤτοι παρουσίας, ἢ ψήφου, γίνεσθαι τὴν κατάστασιν· εἰ δὲ ἄλλως παρὰ τὰ ὡρισμένα γίγνοιτο, μηδὲν ἰσχύειν τὴν χειροτονίαν. Εἰ δὲ κατὰ τὸν ὡρισμένον κανόνα γίγνοιτο ἡ κατάστασις, ἀντιλέγοιεν δέ τινες δι' οἰκείαν φιλονεικίαν, κρατεῖν τὴν τῶν πλειόνων ψῆφον.

CANON XVI.

If any Bishop without a See shall throw himself upon a vacant church and seize its throne, without a full Synod, he shall be cast out, even if all the people over whom he has usurped jurisdiction should elect him. And that shall be [accounted] a full Synod, in which the Metropolitan is present.

CANON XVII.

If any Bishop, having received the ordination of a Bishop, and having been appointed to preside over a people, shall not accept his ministry, and will not be persuaded to proceed to the Church entrusted to him, he shall be suspended, until he shall have been constrained to accept it, or until a full Synod of the Bishops of the Province shall have determined concerning him.

CANON XVIII.

If any Bishop ordained to a Parish shall not proceed to the Parish to which he has been ordained, not through any fault of his own, but either because of the rejection of the people, or for some other reason not arising from himself, let him enjoy his rank and ministry; only he shall not disturb the affairs of the Church which he joins; and he shall abide whatever the full Synod of the Province shall determine, after judging the case.

CANON XIX.

A Bishop shall not be ordained without a Synod and the presence of the Metropolitan of the Province. And when he is present, it is by all means better that all his brethren in the Ministry of the Province should assemble together with him; and these the Metropolitan ought to invite by letter. And it were better that all should meet; but if this be difficult, it is by all means necessary that a majority should be present or take part, by letter, in the election, and that thus the appointment should be made in the presence, or with the consent, of the majority; but if it should be done contrary to these decrees, the ordination shall be of no force. And if the appointment shall be made according to the prescribed Canon, and any should object through natural love of contradiction, the decision of the majority shall prevail.

ΚΑΝΩΝ Κʹ.

Διὰ τὰς ἐκκλησιαστικὰς χρείας, καὶ τὰς τῶν ἀμφισβητουμένων διαλύσεις, καλῶς ἔχειν ἔδοξε συνόδους καθ' ἑκάστην ἐπαρχίαν τῶν ἐπισκόπων γίνεσθαι δεύτερον τοῦ ἔτους· ἅπαξ μὲν μετὰ τὴν τρίτην ἑβδομάδα τῆς ἑορτῆς τοῦ Πάσχα, ὥστε τῇ τετάρτῃ ἑβδομάδι τῆς Πεντηκοστῆς ἐπιτελεῖσθαι τὴν σύνοδον, ὑπομιμνήσκοντος τοὺς ἐπαρχιώτας τοῦ ἐν τῇ μητροπόλει· τὴν δὲ δευτέραν σύνοδον γίνεσθαι εἰδοῖς ὀκτωβρίαις, ἥτις ἐστὶ δεκάτη Ὑπερβερεταίου· ὥστε ἐν αὐταῖς ταύταις ταῖς συνόδοις προσιέναι πρεσβυτέρους, καὶ διακόνους, καὶ πάντας τοὺς ἠδικεῖσθαι νομίζοντας, καὶ παρὰ τῆς συνόδου ἐπικρίσεως τυγχάνειν. Μὴ ἐξεῖναι δέ τινας καθ' ἑαυτοὺς συνόδους ποιεῖσθαι, ἄνευ τῶν πεπιστευμένων τὰς μητροπόλεις.

ΚΑΝΩΝ ΚΑʹ.

Ἐπίσκοπον ἀπὸ παροικίας ἑτέρας εἰς ἑτέραν μὴ μεθίστασθαι, μήτε αὐθαιρέτως ἐπιῤῥίπτοντα ἑαυτὸν, μήτε ὑπὸ λαῶν ἐκβιαζόμενον, μήτε ὑπὸ ἐπισκόπων ἀναγκαζόμενον· μένειν δὲ εἰς ἣν ἐκληρώθη ὑπὸ τοῦ Θεοῦ ἐξ ἀρχῆς ἐκκλησίαν, καὶ μὴ μεθίστασθαι αὐτῆς, κατὰ τὸν ἤδη πρότερον περὶ τούτου ἐξενεχθέντα ὅρον.

ΚΑΝΩΝ ΚΒʹ.

Ἐπίσκοπον μὴ ἐπιβαίνειν ἀλλοτρίᾳ πόλει τῇ μὴ ὑποκειμένῃ αὐτῷ, μηδὲ χώρᾳ τῇ αὐτῷ μὴ διαφερούσῃ, ἐπὶ χειροτονίᾳ τινὸς, μηδὲ καθιστᾶν πρεσβυτέρους ἢ διακόνους εἰς τόπους ἑτέρῳ ἐπισκόπῳ ὑποκειμένους, εἰ μὴ ἄρα μετὰ γνώμης τοῦ οἰκείου τῆς χώρας ἐπισκόπου. Εἰ δὲ τολμήσειέ τις τοιοῦτον, ἄκυρον εἶναι τὴν χειροθεσίαν, καὶ αὐτὸν ἐπιτιμίας ὑπὸ τῆς συνόδου τυγχάνειν.

ΚΑΝΩΝ ΚΓʹ.

Ἐπίσκοπον μὴ ἐξεῖναι ἀντ' αὐτοῦ καθιστᾶν ἕτερον ἑαυτοῦ διάδοχον, κἂν πρὸς τῇ τελευτῇ τοῦ βίου τυγχάνῃ· εἰ δέ τι τοιοῦτον γίγνοιτο, ἄκυρον εἶναι τὴν κατάστασιν. Φυλάττεσθαι δὲ τὸν θεσμὸν τὸν ἐκκλησιαστικὸν περιέχοντα, μὴ

CANON XX.

With a view to the business of the Church and the settlement of disputes, it is decreed to be well that Synods of the Bishops, (to which the Metropolitan shall summon the Provincials), should be held in every Province twice a year; one after the third week of the feast of Easter, so that the Synod may be ended in the fourth week of the Pentecost; and the second on the Ides of October which is the tenth day of the month Hyperberetæus; so that, to these Synods, Presbyters and Deacons, and all who think themselves unjustly dealt with, may resort and obtain the judgment of the Synod. But it shall be unlawful for any to hold Synods by themselves, without the persons entrusted with the Metropolitan Sees.

CANON XXI.

A Bishop may not be translated from one Parish to another, either intruding himself [thereinto] of his own choice, or under compulsion by the people, or by constraint of the Bishops; but he shall remain in the Church to which he was allotted by God from the beginning, and shall not be translated from it, according to the decree formerly passed on the subject.

CANON XXII.

A Bishop may not enter a City [which belongs] to another, and is not subject to himself, nor may he enter into a district which does not belong to him, either to ordain any one, or to appoint Presbyters or Deacons to places within the jurisdiction of another Bishop, unless with the consent of the proper Bishop of the place. And if any one shall presume to do any such thing, the ordination shall be void, and he himself shall be punished by the Synod.

CANON XXIII.

It shall not be lawful for a Bishop, even at the close of life, to appoint another as successor to himself; and if any such thing should be done, the appointment shall be void. And the ecclesiastical law must be observed, that a Bishop must

δεῖν ἄλλως γίνεσθαι ἐπίσκοπον, ἢ μετὰ συνόδου καὶ ἐπικρίσεως ἐπισκόπων, τῶν μετὰ τὴν κοίμησιν τοῦ ἀναπαυσαμένου τὴν ἐξουσίαν ἐχόντων τοῦ προάγεσθαι τὸν ἄξιον.

ΚΑΝΩΝ ΚΔ'.

Τὰ τῆς ἐκκλησίας τῇ ἐκκλησίᾳ καλῶς ἔχειν φυλάττεσθαι δεῖ μετὰ πάσης ἐπιμελείας, καὶ ἀγαθῆς συνειδήσεως, καὶ πίστεως τῆς εἰς τὸν πάντων ἔφορον καὶ κριτὴν Θεόν. Ἃ καὶ διοικεῖσθαι προσήκει μετὰ κρίσεως καὶ ἐξουσίας τοῦ ἐπισκόπου, τοῦ πεπιστευμένου πάντα τὸν λαὸν, καὶ τὰς ψυχὰς τῶν συναγομένων. Φανερὰ δὲ εἶναι τὰ διαφέροντα τῇ ἐκκλησίᾳ, μετὰ γνώσεως τῶν περὶ αὐτὸν πρεσβυτέρων καὶ διακόνων, ὥστε τούτους εἰδέναι καὶ μὴ ἀγνοεῖν, τίνα ποτὲ τὰ ἴδιά ἐστι τῆς ἐκκλησίας, ὥστε μηδὲν αὐτοὺς λανθάνειν· ἵν' εἰ συμβαίη τὸν ἐπίσκοπον μεταλλάττειν τὸν βίον, φανερῶν ὄντων τῶν διαφερόντων τῇ ἐκκλησίᾳ πραγμάτων, μήτε αὐτὰ διαπίπτειν καὶ ἀπόλλυσθαι, μήτε τὰ ἴδια τοῦ ἐπισκόπου ἐνοχλεῖσθαι, προφάσει τῶν ἐκκλησιαστικῶν πραγμάτων. Δίκαιον γὰρ καὶ ἀρεστὸν παρά τε Θεῷ καὶ ἀνθρώποις, τὰ ἴδια τοῦ ἐπισκόπου, οἷς ἂν αὐτὸς βούληται, καταλιμπάνεσθαι· τὰ μέντοι τῆς ἐκκλησίας αὐτῇ φυλάττεσθαι· καὶ μήτε τὴν ἐκκλησίαν ὑπομένειν τινὰ ζημίαν, μήτε τὸν ἐπίσκοπον προφάσει τῆς ἐκκλησίας δημεύεσθαι, ἢ καὶ εἰς πράγματα ἐμπίπτειν τοὺς αὐτῷ διαφέροντας, μετὰ τοῦ καὶ αὐτὸν μετὰ θάνατον δυσφημίᾳ περιβάλλεσθαι.

ΚΑΝΩΝ ΚΕ'.

Ἐπίσκοπον ἔχειν τῶν τῆς ἐκκλησίας πραγμάτων ἐξουσίαν, ὥστε αὐτὰ διοικεῖν εἰς πάντας τοὺς δεομένους, μετὰ πάσης εὐλαβείας καὶ φόβου Θεοῦ· μεταλαμβάνειν δὲ καὶ αὐτὸν τῶν δεόντων, εἴγε δέοιτο, εἰς τὰς ἀναγκαίας αὐτοῦ χρείας, καὶ τῶν παρ' αὐτῷ ἐπιξενουμένων ἀδελφῶν, ὡς κατὰ μηδένα τρόπον αὐτοὺς στερεῖσθαι, κατὰ τὸν θεῖον Ἀπόστολον, λέγοντα· Ἔχοντες διατροφὰς καὶ σκεπάσματα, τούτοις ἀρκεσθησόμεθα· εἰ δὲ μὴ τούτοις ἀρκοῖτο, μεταβάλλοι δὲ τὰ πράγματα εἰς οἰκείας αὐτοῦ χρείας, καὶ τοὺς πόρους τῆς ἐκκλησίας, ἢ τοὺς τῶν ἀγρῶν καρποὺς, μὴ μετὰ γνώμης τῶν πρεσβυτέρων ἢ τῶν

not be constituted otherwise than with a Synod and with the judgement of the Bishops, who, after the decease of a former Bishop, have the authority to promote the man who is worthy.

CANON XXIV.

It is right that what belongs to the Church be preserved with all care to the Church, with a good conscience and fidelity to God, the Inspector and Judge of all. And these things ought to be administered under the judgement and authority of the Bishop, who is entrusted with the whole people and with the souls of the congregation. And whatever belongs to the Church should be plainly distinguished, with the knowledge of the Presbyters and Deacons about him; so that these may know assuredly what things are the property of the Church, and that nothing be concealed from them : in order that, when the Bishop may happen to depart this life, the property belonging to the Church may be well known, and not be embezzled nor lost, and in order that the private property of the Bishop may not be disturbed on a pretence that it is [part] of the ecclesiastical goods. For it is right and well-pleasing to God and man that the private property of the Bishop be bequeathed to whomsoever he will, but that for the Church be kept whatever belongs to the Church; so that neither the Church may suffer loss, nor the Bishop be injured for the sake of the Church, nor those who belong to him fall after him into lawsuits, and himself, after his death, be brought under reproach.

CANON XXV.

Let the Bishop have power over the funds of the Church, so as to dispense them with all piety and in the fear of God to all who need. And if there be occasion, let him take what he requires for his own necessary uses and those of his brethren sojourning with him, so that they may in no way lack, according to the divine Apostle, who says, "Having food and raiment, let us therewith be content." And if he shall not be content with these, but shall apply the funds to his own private uses, and not manage the revenues of the Church, or the fruits of his lands, with the consent of the Presbyters and

διακόνων χειρίζοι, ἀλλ' οἰκείοις αὐτοῦ καὶ συγγενέσιν, ἢ ἀδελφοῖς, ἢ υἱοῖς παράσχοιτο τὴν ἐξουσίαν, ὥστε διὰ τῶν τοιούτων λεληθότως βλάπτεσθαι τοὺς λόγους τῆς ἐκκλησίας, τοῦτον εὐθύνας παρέχειν τῇ συνόδῳ τῆς ἐπαρχίας. Εἰ δὲ καὶ ἄλλως διαβάλλοιτο ὁ ἐπίσκοπος, ἢ οἱ σὺν αὐτῷ πρεσβύτεροι, ὡς τὰ τῇ ἐκκλησίᾳ διαφέροντα, ἤτοι ἐξ ἀγρῶν, ἢ καὶ ἐξ ἑτέρας προφάσεως ἐκκλησιαστικῆς, εἰς ἑαυτοὺς ἀποφερόμενοι, ὡς θλίβεσθαι μὲν τοὺς πένητας, διαβολὴν δὲ καὶ δυσφημίαν προστρίβεσθαι τῷ τε λόγῳ καὶ τοῖς οὕτω διοικοῦσι, καὶ τούτους διορθώσεως τυγχάνειν, τὸ πρέπον δοκιμαζούσης τῆς ἁγίας συνόδου.

Deacons, but shall give the authority to his own domestics and kinsmen, brothers, or sons, so that the accounts of the Church are secretly injured, he himself shall submit to an investigation by the Synod of the Province. And if in any other way the Bishop or his Presbyters shall be accused of appropriating to themselves what belongs to the Church, (whether from lands or any other ecclesiastical resources), so that the poor are oppressed, and accusation and infamy are brought upon the account and on those who so administer it, let them also be subject to correction, the holy Synod determining what is right.

ΚΑΝΟΝΕΣ

ΤΗΣ ΕΝ ΛΑΟΔΙΚΕΙᾼ ΤΗΣ ΚΑΠΑΤΙΑΝΗΣ

ΦΡΥΓΙΑΣ ΣΥΓΚΡΟΤΗΘΕΙΣΗΣ ΣΥΝΟΔΟΥ.

ΚΑΝΩΝ Α'.

Περὶ τοῦ δεῖν κατὰ τὸν ἐκκλησιαστικὸν κανόνα, τοὺς ἐλευθέρως καὶ νομίμως συναφθέντας δευτέροις γάμοις, μὴ λαθρογαμίαν ποιήσαντας, ὀλίγου χρόνου παρελθόντος, καὶ σχολάσαντας ταῖς προσευχαῖς καὶ νηστείαις, κατὰ συγγνώμην ἀποδίδοσθαι αὐτοῖς τὴν κοινωνίαν ὡρίσαμεν.

ΚΑΝΩΝ Β'.

Περὶ τοῦ τοὺς ἐξαμαρτάνοντας ἐν διαφόροις πταίσμασι, καὶ προσκαρτεροῦντας τῇ προσευχῇ τῆς ἐξομολογήσεως καὶ μετανοίας, καὶ τὴν ἀποστροφὴν τῶν κακῶν τελείαν ποιουμένους, κατὰ τὴν ἀναλογίαν τοῦ πταίσματος, καιροῦ μετανοίας δοθέντος τοῖς τοιούτοις, διὰ τοὺς οἰκτιρμοὺς καὶ τὴν ἀγαθότητα τοῦ Θεοῦ προσάγεσθαι τῇ κοινωνίᾳ.

ΚΑΝΩΝ Γ'.

Περὶ τοῦ μὴ δεῖν προσφάτως φωτισθέντα προσάγεσθαι ἐν τάγματι ἱερατικῷ.

ΚΑΝΩΝ Δ'.

Περὶ τοῦ μὴ δεῖν ἱερατικοὺς δανείζειν, καὶ τόκους, καὶ τὰς λεγομένας ἡμιολίας λαμβάνειν.

ΚΑΝΩΝ Ε'.

Περὶ τοῦ μὴ δεῖν τὰς χειροτονίας ἐπὶ παρουσίᾳ ἀκροωμένων γίνεσθαι.

CANONS OF LAODICEA.

CANON I.

We declare it to be right, according to the ecclesiastical Canon, that the Holy Communion should by indulgence be given to those who have freely and lawfully joined in second marriages, but have not made a clandestine marriage ; a short space having elapsed, which is to be spent by them in prayer and fasting.

CANON II.

They who have sinned in divers particulars, if they apply themselves to the prayer of confession and penitence, and are wholly converted from their faults, shall be brought to Communion, through the mercy and goodness of God, after a time of penance appointed to them, in proportion to the nature of their offence.

CANON III.

He who has been recently baptized ought not to be promoted to the Sacerdotal Order.

CANON IV.

They who are of the Sacerdotal Order ought not to lend and receive usury, nor what is called Hemioliæ [*i. e.*, the whole and one-half in kind].

CANON V.

Elections* are not to be held in the presence of Hearers.

* Χειροτονία in this Canon, as in the Synodical Epistle of Nicæa, is interpreted as above, both by Balsamon and by Zonaras. If, however, it has its usual force of *ordination*, as Aristenas maintains, the reference is to the low tone of voice in which the prayer of ordination was uttered.

ΚΑΝΩΝ ς′.

Περὶ τοῦ μὴ συγχωρεῖν τοῖς αἱρετικοῖς εἰσιέναι εἰς τὸν οἶκον τοῦ Θεοῦ, ἐπιμένοντας τῇ αἱρέσει.

ΚΑΝΩΝ Ζ′.

Περὶ τοῦ τοὺς ἐκ τῶν αἱρέσεων, τουτέστι Ναυατιανῶν, ἤτοι Φωτεινιανῶν, ἢ Τεσσαρεσκαιδεκατιτῶν, ἐπιστρεφομένους, εἴτε κατηχουμένους, εἴτε πιστοὺς τοὺς παρ' ἐκείνοις, μὴ προσδέχεσθαι, πρὶν ἀναθεματίσωσι πᾶσαν αἵρεσιν, ἐξαιρέτως δὲ ἐν ᾗ κατείχοντο· καὶ τότε λοιπὸν τοὺς λεγομένους παρ' αὐτοῖς πιστοὺς, ἐκμανθάνοντας τὰ τῆς πίστεως σύμβολα, χρισθέντας τε τῷ ἁγίῳ χρίσματι, οὕτω κοινωνεῖν τῶν μυστηρίων τῶν ἁγίων.

ΚΑΝΩΝ Η′.

Περὶ τοῦ τοὺς ἀπὸ τῆς αἱρέσεως τῶν λεγομένων Φρυγῶν ἐπιστρέφοντας, εἰ καὶ ἐν κλήρῳ νομιζομένῳ παρ' αὐτοῖς τυγχάνοιεν, εἰ καὶ μέγιστοι λέγοιντο, τοὺς τοιούτους μετὰ πάσης ἐπιμελείας, κατηχεῖσθαί τε καὶ βαπτίζεσθαι ὑπὸ τῶν τῆς ἐκκλησίας ἐπισκόπων τε καὶ πρεσβυτέρων.

ΚΑΝΩΝ Θ′.

Περὶ τοῦ μὴ συγχωρεῖν εἰς τὰ κοιμητήρια, ἢ εἰς τὰ λεγόμενα μαρτύρια πάντων τῶν αἱρετικῶν ἀπιέναι τοὺς τῆς ἐκκλησίας, εὐχῆς ἢ θεραπείας ἕνεκα· ἀλλὰ τοὺς τοιούτους, ἐὰν ὦσι πιστοὶ, ἀκοινωνήτους γίνεσθαι μέχρι τινός. Μετανοοῦντας δὲ, καὶ ἐξομολογουμένους ἐσφάλθαι, παραδέχεσθαι.

ΚΑΝΩΝ Ι′.

Περὶ τοῦ μὴ δεῖν τοὺς τῆς ἐκκλησίας ἀδιαφόρως πρὸς γάμου κοινωνίαν συνάπτειν τὰ ἑαυτῶν παιδία αἱρετικοῖς.

ΚΑΝΩΝ ΙΑ′.

Περὶ τοῦ μὴ δεῖν τὰς λεγομένας πρεσβύτιδας, ἤτοι προκαθημένας, ἐν τῇ ἐκκλησίᾳ καθίστασθαι.

CANON VI.

It is not permitted to heretics to enter the house of God while they continue in heresy.

CANON VII.

Persons converted from heresies, that is, of the Novatians, Photinians, and Quartodecimans, whether they were Catechumens or Communicants among them, shall not be received until they shall have anathematized every heresy, and particularly that in which they were enthralled; and afterwards those who among them were called Communicants, having thoroughly learned the Symbols of the Faith, and having been anointed with the holy Chrism, shall so communicate in the holy Mysteries.

CANON VIII.

Persons converted from the heresy of those who are called Phrygians, even should they be among what is with them reputed as the Clergy, and even should they be called the very chief, are with all care to be both instructed and baptized by the Bishops and Presbyters of the Church.

CANON IX.

The members of the Church are not to meet in the Cemeteries, nor attend the so-called Martyries, of any of the heretics, for prayer or service; but such as so do, if they be Communicants, shall be excommunicated for a time. But if they shall repent and confess that they have sinned, they shall be received.

CANON X.

The members of the Church shall not indiscriminately marry their children to heretics.

CANON XI.

Presbyteresses, as they are called, or female Presidents, are not to be appointed in the Church.

ΚΑΝΩΝ ΙΒʹ.

Περὶ τοῦ τοὺς ἐπισκόπους κρίσει τῶν μητροπολιτῶν καὶ τῶν πέριξ ἐπισκόπων καθίστασθαι εἰς τὴν ἐκκλησιαστικὴν ἀρχὴν, ὄντας ἐκ πολλοῦ δεδοκιμασμένους ἔν τε τῷ λόγῳ τῆς πίστεως, καὶ τῇ τοῦ εὐθέος βίου πολιτείᾳ.

ΚΑΝΩΝ ΙΓʹ.

Περὶ τοῦ μὴ τοῖς ὄχλοις ἐπιτρέπειν τὰς ἐκλογὰς ποιεῖσθαι τῶν μελλόντων καθίστασθαι εἰς ἱερατεῖον.

ΚΑΝΩΝ ΙΔʹ.

Περὶ τοῦ μὴ τὰ ἅγια, εἰς λόγον εὐλογιῶν, κατὰ τὴν ἑορτὴν τοῦ Πάσχα, *εἰς ἑτέρας παροικίας διαπέμπεσθαι.*

ΚΑΝΩΝ ΙΕʹ.

Περὶ τοῦ μὴ δεῖν πλὴν τῶν κανονικῶν ψαλτῶν, τῶν ἐπὶ τὸν ἄμβωνα ἀναβαινόντων, καὶ ἀπὸ διφθέρας ψαλλόντων, ἑτέρους τινὰς ψάλλειν ἐν ἐκκλησίᾳ.

ΚΑΝΩΝ Ιϛʹ.

Περὶ τοῦ ἐν σαββάτῳ εὐαγγέλια μετὰ ἑτέρων Γραφῶν *ἀναγινώσκεσθαι.*

ΚΑΝΩΝ ΙΖʹ.

Περὶ τοῦ μὴ δεῖν ἐπισυνάπτειν ἐν ταῖς συνάξεσι τοὺς ψαλμοὺς, ἀλλὰ διὰ μέσου καθ' ἕκαστον ψαλμὸν γίνεσθαι ἀνάγνωσιν.

ΚΑΝΩΝ ΙΗʹ.

Περὶ τοῦ τὴν αὐτὴν λειτουργίαν τῶν εὐχῶν πάντοτε καὶ ἐν ταῖς ἐννάταις, καὶ ἐν ταῖς ἑσπέραις ὀφείλειν γίνεσθαι.

ΚΑΝΩΝ ΙΘʹ.

Περὶ τοῦ δεῖν ἰδίᾳ πρῶτον, μετὰ τὰς ὁμιλίας τῶν ἐπισκόπων, καὶ τῶν κατηχουμένων εὐχὴν ἐπιτελεῖσθαι· καὶ μετὰ τὸ ἐξελθεῖν τοὺς κατηχουμένους, τῶν ἐν μετανοίᾳ

CANON XII.

Bishops are to be appointed to the ecclesiastical government by the judgment of the Metropolitans and [other] neighbouring Bishops, after having been long proved both in the foundation of their faith and in the conversation of an honest life.

CANON XIII.

The election of those who are to be appointed to the Priesthood is not to be committed to the multitude.

CANON XIV.

The holy [Gifts] are not to be sent into other Parishes at the feast of Easter by way of Eulogiæ.

CANON XV.

No others shall sing in the Church, save only the canonical Singers, who go up into the Ambo and sing from a book.

CANON XVI.

The Gospels are to be read on the Sabbath Day, with the other Scriptures.

CANON XVII.

The Psalms are not to be joined together in the congregations, but a lesson shall intervene after every Psalm.

CANON XVIII.

The same Office of Prayers is to be said both at Nones and at Vespers.

CANON XIX.

After the sermons of the Bishops, the prayer for the Catechumens is to be made first by itself; and, after the Catechumens have gone out, the prayer for those who are under

τὴν εὐχὴν γίνεσθαι· καὶ τούτων προσελθόντων ὑπὸ χεῖρα καὶ ὑποχωρησάντων, οὕτω τῶν πιστῶν τὰς εὐχὰς γίνεσθαι τρεῖς, μίαν μὲν τὴν πρώτην διὰ σιωπῆς, τὴν δὲ δευτέραν καὶ τρίτην διὰ προσφωνήσεως πληροῦσθαι· εἶθ' οὕτω τὴν εἰρήνην δίδοσθαι· καὶ μετὰ τὸ τοὺς πρεσβυτέρους δοῦναι τῷ ἐπισκόπῳ τὴν εἰρήνην, τότε τοὺς λαϊκοὺς τὴν εἰρήνην διδόναι, καὶ οὕτω τὴν ἁγίαν προσφορὰν ἐπιτελεῖσθαι· καὶ μόνοις ἐξὸν εἶναι τοῖς ἱερατικοῖς εἰσιέναι εἰς τὸ θυσιαστήριον, καὶ κοινωνεῖν.

ΚΑΝΩΝ Κ'.

Ὅτι οὐ δεῖ διάκονον ἔμπροσθεν πρεσβυτέρου καθέζεσθαι, ἀλλὰ μετὰ κελεύσεως τοῦ πρεσβυτέρου καθέζεσθαι. Ὁμοίως δὲ ἔχειν τιμὴν καὶ τοὺς διακόνους ὑπὸ τῶν ὑπηρετῶν καὶ πάντων τῶν κληρικῶν.

ΚΑΝΩΝ ΚΑ'.

Ὅτι οὐ δεῖ ὑπηρέτας ἔχειν χώραν ἐν τῷ διακονικῷ, καὶ ἅπτεσθαι τῶν ἱερῶν σκευῶν.

ΚΑΝΩΝ ΚΒ'.

Ὅτι οὐ δεῖ ὑπηρέτην ὠράριον φορεῖν, οὐδὲ τὰς θύρας ἐγκαταλιμπάνειν.

ΚΑΝΩΝ ΚΓ'.

Ὅτι οὐ δεῖ ἀναγνώστας, ἢ ψάλτας ὠράριον φορεῖν, καὶ οὕτως ἀναγινώσκειν, ἢ ψάλλειν.

ΚΑΝΩΝ ΚΔ'.

Ὅτι οὐ δεῖ ἱερατικοὺς ἀπὸ πρεσβυτέρων ἕως διακόνων, καὶ ἑξῆς τῆς ἐκκλησιαστικῆς τάξεως ἕως ὑπηρετῶν, ἢ ἀναγνωστῶν, ἢ ψαλτῶν, ἢ ἐφορκιστῶν, ἢ θυρωρῶν, ἢ τοῦ τάγματος τῶν ἀσκητῶν, εἰς καπηλεῖον εἰσιέναι.

ΚΑΝΩΝ ΚΕ'.

Ὅτι οὐ δεῖ ὑπηρέτην ἄρτον διδόναι, οὐδὲ ποτήριον εὐλογεῖν.

penance; and, after these have passed under the hand [of the Bishop] and departed, there should then be offered the three prayers of the Faithful, the first to be with silence, the second and third to be completed with acclamation [or response], and then [the kiss of] peace is to be given. And, after the Presbyters have given [the kiss of] peace to the Bishop, then the laity are to give it, and so the Holy Oblation is to be completed. And it is lawful to the Priesthood alone to go to the Altar and [there] communicate.

CANON XX.

It is not right for a Deacon to seat himself in the presence of a Presbyter, unless he be bidden by the Presbyter to sit down. Likewise the Deacons shall have worship of the Sub-Deacons and all the Clergy.

CANON XXI.

The Subdeacons have no right to a place in the Deacon's Room, nor to touch the Sacred vessels.

CANON XXII.

The Sub-deacon has no right to wear an Orarium [*i. e.*, Stole], nor to leave the doors.

CANON XXIII.

The Readers and Singers have no right to wear an Orarium, and to read or sing thus [habited].

CANON XXIV.

No one of the Priesthood, from Presbyters to Deacons, and so on in the ecclesiastical order to Sub-deacons, or Readers, or Singers, or Exorcists, or Door-keepers, or any of the order of the Ascetics, ought to enter a tavern.

CANON XXV.

A Sub-deacon must not give the Bread, nor bless the Cup.

ΚΑΝΟΝ Κϛʹ.

Ὅτι οὐ δεῖ ἐφορκίζειν τοὺς μὴ προαχθέντας ὑπὸ ἐπισκόπων, μήτε ἐν ταῖς ἐκκλησίαις, μήτε ἐν ταῖς οἰκίαις.

ΚΑΝΩΝ ΚΖʹ.

Ὅτι οὐ δεῖ ἱερατικοὺς, ἢ κληρικοὺς, ἢ λαϊκοὺς, καλουμένους εἰς ἀγάπην, μέρη αἴρειν, διὰ τὸ τὴν ὕβριν τῇ τάξει προστρίβεσθαι τῇ ἐκκλησιαστικῇ.

ΚΑΝΩΝ ΚΗʹ.

Ὅτι οὐ δεῖ ἐν τοῖς Κυριακοῖς, ἢ ἐν ταῖς ἐκκλησίαις, τὰς λεγομένας ἀγάπας ποιεῖν, καὶ ἐν τῷ οἴκῳ τοῦ Θεοῦ ἐσθίειν, καὶ ἀκούβιτα στρωννύειν.

ΚΑΝΩΝ ΚΘʹ.

Ὅτι οὐ δεῖ Χριστιανοὺς ἰουδαΐζειν καὶ ἐν τῷ σαββάτῳ σχολάζειν, ἀλλ' ἐργάζεσθαι αὐτοὺς ἐν τῇ αὐτῇ ἡμέρᾳ· τὴν δὲ Κυριακὴν προτιμῶντας, εἴγε δύναιντο, σχολάζειν ὡς Χριστιανοί. Εἰ δὲ εὑρεθεῖεν Ἰουδαϊσταὶ, ἔστωσαν ἀνάθεμα παρὰ Χριστῷ.

ΚΑΝΩΝ Λʹ.

Ὅτι οὐ δεῖ ἱερατικοὺς, ἢ κληρικοὺς, ἢ ἀσκητὰς, ἐν βαλανείῳ μετὰ γυναικῶν ἀπολούεσθαι, μηδὲ πάντα Χριστιανὸν, ἢ λαϊκόν· αὕτη γὰρ πρώτη κατάγνωσις παρὰ τοῖς ἔθνεσιν.

ΚΑΝΩΝ ΛΑʹ.

Ὅτι οὐ δεῖ πρὸς πάντας αἱρετικοὺς ἐπιγαμίας ποιεῖν, ἢ διδόναι υἱοὺς, ἢ θυγατέρας, ἀλλὰ μᾶλλον λαμβάνειν, εἴγε ἐπαγγέλλοιντο Χριστιανοὶ γίνεσθαι.

ΚΑΝΩΝ ΛΒʹ.

Ὅτι οὐ δεῖ αἱρετικῶν εὐλογίας λαμβάνειν, αἵτινές εἰσιν ἀλογίαι μᾶλλον, ἢ εὐλογίαι.

CANON XXVI.

They who have not been promoted [as Exorcists] by the Bishops, ought not to exorcise, either in Churches or in [private] houses.

CANON XXVII.

Neither they of the Priesthood, nor Clergymen, nor laymen, who are invited to a love feast, may take away their portions, for this is to cast reproach on the ecclesiastical order.

CANON XXVIII.

It is not permitted to hold love feasts, as they are called, in the Lord's Houses, or in Church assemblies, nor to eat and to spread couches in the House of the Lord.

CANON XXIX.

Christians must not judaize by resting on the Sabbath, but must work on that day, rather honouring the Lord's Day; and, if they can, resting then as Christians. But if any shall be found to be Judaizers, let them be Anathema from Christ.

CANON XXX.

None of the Priesthood, nor Clergymen, nor Ascetics, nor any Christian or layman, shall wash in a bath with women; for this is a chief [cause of] condemnation, [even] among the heathen.

CANON XXXI.

It is not lawful to make marriages with all [sorts of] heretics, nor to give our sons and daughters to them; but rather to receive them, if they promise to become Christians.

CANON XXXII.

It is unlawful to receive the Eulogiæ of heretics, for they are rather *Alogiæ* [*i. e.*, follies], than Eulogiæ [*i. e.* blessings].

ΚΑΝΩΝ ΛΓ'.

Ὅτι οὐ δεῖ αἱρετικοῖς, ἢ σχισματικοῖς συνεύχεσθαι.

ΚΑΝΩΝ ΛΔ'.

Ὅτι οὐ δεῖ πάντα Χριστιανὸν ἐγκαταλείπειν μάρτυρας Χριστοῦ, καὶ ἀπιέναι πρὸς τοὺς ψευδομάρτυρας, τουτέστιν αἱρετικῶν, ἢ αὐτοὺς πρὸς τοὺς προειρημένους αἱρετικοὺς γενομένους· οὗτοι γὰρ ἀλλότριοι τοῦ Θεοῦ τυγχάνουσιν. Ἔστωσαν οὖν ἀνάθεμα οἱ ἀπερχόμενοι πρὸς αὐτούς.

ΚΑΝΩΝ ΛΕ'.

Ὅτι οὐ δεῖ Χριστιανοὺς ἐγκαταλείπειν τὴν ἐκκλησίαν τοῦ Θεοῦ, καὶ ἀπιέναι, καὶ ἀγγέλους ὀνομάζειν, καὶ συνάξεις ποιεῖν, ἅπερ ἀπηγόρευται. Εἴ τις οὖν εὑρεθῇ ταύτῃ τῇ κεκρυμμένῃ εἰδωλολατρείᾳ σχολάζων, ἔστω ἀνάθεμα, ὅτι ἐγκατέλιπε τὸν Κύριον ἡμῶν Ἰησοῦν Χριστὸν, τὸν Υἱὸν τοῦ Θεοῦ, καὶ εἰδωλολατρείᾳ προσῆλθεν.

ΚΑΝΩΝ Λϛ'.

Ὅτι οὐ δεῖ ἱερατικοὺς ἢ κληρικοὺς, μάγους ἢ ἐπαοιδοὺς εἶναι, ἢ μαθηματικοὺς, ἢ ἀστρολόγους, ἢ ποιεῖν τὰ λεγόμενα φυλακτήρια, ἅτινά ἐστι δεσμωτήρια τῶν ψυχῶν αὐτῶν. Τοὺς δὲ φοροῦντας, ῥίπτεσθαι ἐκ τῆς ἐκκλησίας ἐκελεύσαμεν.

ΚΑΝΩΝ ΛΖ'.

Ὅτι οὐ δεῖ παρὰ τῶν Ἰουδαίων, ἢ αἱρετικῶν, τὰ πεμπόμενα ἑορταστικὰ λαμβάνειν, μηδὲ συνεορτάζειν αὐτοῖς.

ΚΑΝΩΝ ΛΗ'.

Ὅτι οὐ δεῖ παρὰ τῶν Ἰουδαίων ἄζυμα λαμβάνειν, ἢ κοινωνεῖν ταῖς ἀσεβείαις αὐτῶν.

ΚΑΝΩΝ ΛΘ'.

Ὅτι οὐ δεῖ τοῖς ἔθνεσι συνεορτάζειν, καὶ κοινωνεῖν τῇ ἀθεότητι αὐτῶν.

CANON XXXIII.

It is unlawful to join in prayers with heretics or schismatics.

CANON XXXIV.

No Christian ought to forsake the Martyrs of CHRIST, and resort to false martyrs; that is, to those of the heretics, or those who have been themselves accounted heretics; for they are aliens from GOD. Let those, therefore, who go after them, be Anathema.

CANON XXXV.

Christians must not forsake the Church of GOD, and go away and invoke angels and gather assemblies; which things are forbidden. If, therefore, any one shall be found engaged in this covert idolatry, let him be Anathema; for he has forsaken our LORD JESUS CHRIST, the SON of GOD, and has become a proselyte to idolatry.

CANON XXXVI.

They who are of the Priesthood, or of the Clergy, shall not be Magicians, nor Enchanters, nor Mathematicians, nor Astrologers; nor shall they make what are called Phylacteries, which are chains for their own souls. And those who wear such, we command to be cast out of the Church.

CANON XXXVII.

It is not lawful to receive portions sent from the feasts of Jews or heretics, nor to feast together with them.

CANON XXXVIII.

It is not lawful to receive unleavened bread from the Jews, nor to be partakers of their impiety.

CANON XXXIX.

It is not lawful to feast together with the heathen, and to be partakers of their godlessness.

ΚΑΝΩΝ Μ'.

Ὅτι οὐ δεῖ ἐπισκόπους καλουμένους εἰς σύνοδον καταφρονεῖν, ἀλλ' ἀπιέναι, καὶ διδάσκειν, ἢ διδάσκεσθαι, εἰς κατόρθωσιν τῆς ἐκκλησίας καὶ τῶν λοιπῶν. Εἰ δὲ καταφρονήσειεν ὁ τοιοῦτος, ἑαυτὸν αἰτιάσεται, παρεκτὸς εἰ μὴ δι' ἀνωμαλίαν ἀπολιμπάνοιτο.

ΚΑΝΩΝ ΜΑ'.

Ὅτι οὐ δεῖ ἱερατικὸν ἢ κληρικὸν ἄνευ κελεύσεως ἐπισκόπου ὁδεύειν.

ΚΑΝΩΝ ΜΒ'.

Ὅτι οὐ δεῖ ἱερατικοὺς ἢ κληρικοὺς ἄνευ κανονικῶν γραμμάτων ὁδεύειν.

ΚΑΝΩΝ ΜΓ'.

Ὅτι οὐ δεῖ ὑπηρέτας, κἂν βραχὺ, τὰς θύρας ἐγκαταλείπειν, καὶ τῇ εὐχῇ σχολάζειν.

ΚΑΝΩΝ ΜΔ'.

Ὅτι οὐ δεῖ γυναῖκας ἐν τῷ θυσιαστηρίῳ εἰσέρχεσθαι.

ΚΑΝΩΝ ΜΕ'.

Ὅτι οὐ δεῖ μετὰ δύο ἑβδομάδας τῆς Τεσσαρακοστῆς δέχεσθαι εἰς τὸ φώτισμα.

ΚΑΝΩΝ Μϛ'.

Ὅτι δεῖ τοὺς φωτιζομένους τὴν πίστιν ἐκμανθάνειν, καὶ τῇ πέμπτῃ τῆς ἑβδομάδος ἀπαγγέλλειν τῷ ἐπισκόπῳ ἢ τοῖς πρεσβυτέροις.

ΚΑΝΩΝ ΜΖ'.

Ὅτι δεῖ τοὺς ἐν νόσῳ παραλαμβάνοντας τὸ φώτισμα, καὶ εἶτα ἀναστάντας, ἐκμανθάνειν τὴν πίστιν, καὶ γινώσκειν, ὅτι θείας δωρεᾶς κατηξιώθησαν.

CANON XL.

Bishops called to a Synod must not be guilty of contempt, but must attend, and either teach, or be taught, for the reformation of the Church and others. And if such an one shall be guilty of contempt, he will condemn himself, unless he be detained by ill health.

CANON XLI.

None of the Priesthood nor of the Clergy may go on a journey, without permission of the Bishop.

CANON XLII.

None of the Priesthood nor of the Clergy may travel without letters canonical.

CANON XLIII.

The Sub-deacons may not leave the doors, to engage in the prayer, even for a short time.

CANON XLIV.

Women may not go in to the Altar [*i. e.*, into the Sanctuary].

CANON XLV.

[Candidates] for Baptism are not to be received after the second week in Lent.

CANON XLVI.

They who are to be baptized must learn the Creed by heart, and recite it to the Bishop, or to the Presbyters, on the fifth of the Great Week [*i. e.*, on Maundy Thursday].

CANON XLVII.

They who are baptized in sickness and afterwards recover, must learn the Creed by heart, and know that they have been vouchsafed the Divine gifts.

ΚΑΝΩΝ ΜΗ'.

Ὅτι δεῖ τοὺς φωτιζομένους μετὰ τὸ βάπτισμα χρίεσθαι χρίσματι ἐπουρανίῳ, καὶ μετόχους εἶναι τῆς βασιλείας τοῦ Χριστοῦ.

ΚΑΝΩΝ ΜΘ'.

Ὅτι οὐ δεῖ ἐν τῇ Τεσσαρακοστῇ ἄρτον προσφέρειν, εἰ μὴ ἐν σαββάτῳ καὶ Κυριακῇ μόνον.

ΚΑΝΩΝ Ν'.

Ὅτι οὐ δεῖ ἐν τῇ Τεσσαρακοστῇ τῇ ὑστέρᾳ ἑβδομάδι τὴν πέμπτην λύειν, καὶ ὅλην τὴν Τεσσαρακοστὴν ἀτιμάζειν· ἀλλὰ δεῖ πᾶσαν τὴν Τεσσαρακοστὴν νηστεύειν ξηροφαγοῦντας.

ΚΑΝΩΝ ΝΑ'.

Ὅτι οὐ δεῖ ἐν τῇ Τεσσαρακοστῇ μαρτύρων γενέθλια ἐπιτελεῖν, ἀλλὰ τῶν ἁγίων μαρτύρων μνήμας ποιεῖν ἐν τοῖς σαββάτοις καὶ ταῖς Κυριακαῖς.

ΚΑΝΩΝ ΝΒ'.

Ὅτι οὐ δεῖ ἐν τῇ Τεσσαρακοστῇ γάμους ἢ γενέθλια ἐπιτελεῖν.

ΚΑΝΩΝ ΝΓ'.

Ὅτι οὐ δεῖ Χριστιανοὺς εἰς γάμους ἀπερχομένους, βαλλίζειν ἢ ὀρχεῖσθαι, ἀλλὰ σεμνῶς δειπνεῖν ἢ ἀριστᾷν, ὡς πρέπει Χριστιανοῖς.

ΚΑΝΩΝ ΝΔ'.

Ὅτι οὐ δεῖ ἱερατικοὺς ἢ κληρικούς τινας θεωρίας θεωρεῖν ἐν γάμοις, ἢ δείπνοις, ἀλλὰ, πρὸ τοῦ εἰσέρχεσθαι τοὺς θυμελικοὺς, ἐγείρεσθαι αὐτοὺς καὶ ἀναχωρεῖν.

CANON XLVIII.

They who are baptized must after Baptism be anointed with the heavenly Chrism, and be partakers of the Kingdom of God [*i. e.*, must be confirmed and brought to the Holy Eucharist].

CANON XLIX.

There must be no Oblation of Bread in Lent, except on the Sabbath Day and on the Lord's Day only.

CANON L.

The fast must not be broken on the fifth day of the last week in Lent [*i. e.*, on Maundy Thursday], and the whole of Lent be dishonoured; but it is necessary to fast during all the Lenten season by eating only dry meats.

CANON LI.

The nativities of Martyrs are not to be celebrated in Lent, but commemorations of the holy Martyrs are to be made on Sabbath days and Sundays.

CANON LII.

Marriages and birthday feasts are not to be celebrated in Lent.

CANON LIII.

Christians, when they attend at weddings, must not join in wanton dances, but modestly sup or dine, as is becoming to Christians.

CANON LIV.

Members of the Priesthood and of the Clergy must not witness the plays at weddings or banquets; but, before the players enter, they must rise and depart.

ΚΑΝΩΝ ΝΕ'.

Ὅτι οὐ δεῖ ἱερατικοὺς ἢ κληρικοὺς ἐκ συμβολῆς συμπόσια ἐπιτελεῖν, ἀλλ' οὐδὲ λαϊκούς.

ΚΑΝΩΝ Νϛ'.

Ὅτι οὐ δεῖ πρεσβυτέρους πρὸ τῆς εἰσόδου τοῦ ἐπισκόπου εἰσιέναι καὶ καθέζεσθαι ἐν τῷ βήματι, ἀλλὰ μετὰ τοῦ ἐπισκόπου εἰσιέναι· πλὴν εἰ μὴ ἀνωμαλοίη ἢ ἀποδημοῖ ὁ ἐπίσκοπος.

ΚΑΝΩΝ ΝΖ'.

Ὅτι οὐ δεῖ ἐν ταῖς κώμαις καὶ ἐν ταῖς χώραις καθίστασθαι ἐπισκόπους, ἀλλὰ περιοδευτάς· τοὺς μέν τοι ἤδη προκατασταθέντας, μηδὲν πράττειν ἄνευ γνώμης τοῦ ἐπισκόπου τοῦ ἐν τῇ πόλει· ὡσαύτως δὲ καὶ τοὺς πρεσβυτέρους μηδὲν πράττειν ἄνευ τῆς γνώμης τοῦ ἐπισκόπου.

ΚΑΝΩΝ ΝΗ'.

Ὅτι οὐ δεῖ ἐν τοῖς οἴκοις προσφορὰν γίνεσθαι παρὰ ἐπισκόπων ἢ πρεσβυτέρων.

ΚΑΝΩΝ ΝΘ'.

Ὅτι οὐ δεῖ ἰδιωτικοὺς ψαλμοὺς λέγεσθαι ἐν τῇ ἐκκλησίᾳ, οὐδὲ ἀκανόνιστα βιβλία, ἀλλὰ μόνα τὰ κανονικὰ τῆς Παλαιᾶς *καὶ* Καινῆς Διαθήκης.

ΚΑΝΩΝ Ξ'.

Ὅσα δεῖ βιβλία ἀναγινώσκεσθαι τῆς Παλαιᾶς Διαθήκης· *ά.* Γένεσις *κόσμου· β'.* Ἔξοδος *ἐξ* Αἰγύπτου· *γ'.* Λευϊτικόν· *δ'.* Ἀριθμοί· *ε'.* Δευτερονόμιον· *ϛ'.* Ἰησοῦς τοῦ Ναυῆ· *ζ'.* Κριταί· Ῥούθ· *η'.* Ἐσθήρ· *θ'.* Βασιλειῶν *πρώτη καὶ δευτέρα· ι'.* Βασιλειῶν *τρίτη καὶ τετάρτη· ια'.* Παραλειπομένων *πρῶτον καὶ δεύτερον· ιβ'.* Ἔσδρας *πρῶτον καὶ δεύτερον· ιγ'.* Βίβλος Ψαλμῶν *ρν'. ιδ'.* Παροιμίαι Σολομῶντος· *ιε'.* Ἐκκλησιαστής· *ιϛ'.* Ἆσμα ᾀσμάτων· *ιζ'.* Ἰώβ· *ιη'.* Δωδεκαπρόφητον· *ιθ'.* Ἡσαΐας· *κ'.* Ἱερεμίας, *καὶ* Βαροὺχ, Θρῆνοι *καὶ* ἐπιστολαί· *κα'.* Ἰεζεκιήλ· *κβ'.* Δανιήλ·

CANON LV.

Neither members of the Priesthood nor of the Clergy, nor yet laymen, may form clubs for drinking entertainments.

CANON LVI.

Presbyters may not enter and take their seats in the Bema before the entrance of the Bishop; but they must enter after the Bishop, unless he be sick or absent.

CANON LVII.

Bishops must not be appointed in villages or country districts, but itinerant [visitors only]: and those who have been already appointed, must do nothing without the consent of the City Bishop. Presbyters, in like manner, must do nothing without the consent of the Bishop.

CANON LVIII.

The Oblation must not be made by Bishops or Presbyters in any private houses.

CANON LIX.

Private Psalms and uncanonical books must not be read in the Church, but only the Canonical Books of the Old and New Testament.

CANON LX.

These Books of the Old Testament are appointed to be read: 1, Genesis of the world; 2, The Exodus from Egypt; 3, Leviticus; 4, Numbers; 5, Deuteronomy; 6, Joshua, the son of Nun; 7, Judges, Ruth; 8, Esther; 9, Kings, First and Second; 10, Kings, Third and Fourth; 11, Paralipomena, First and Second; 12, Ezra, First and Second; 13, One Hundred and Fifty Psalms; 14, Proverbs of Solomon; 15, Ecclesiastes; 16, Song of Songs; 17, Job; 18, The Twelve Prophets; 19, Isaiah; 20, Jeremiah, and Baruch, Lamentations, and Epistles; 21, Ezekiel; 22, Daniel.

Τὰ δὲ τῆς Καινῆς Διαθήκης ταῦτα· Εὐαγγέλια τέσσαρα, κατὰ Ματθαῖον, κατὰ Μάρκον, κατὰ Λουκᾶν, κατὰ Ἰωάννην· Πράξεις Ἀποστόλων· Ἐπιστολαὶ καθολικαὶ ἑπτὰ, Ἰακώβου μία, Πέτρου δύο, Ἰωάννου τρεῖς, Ἰούδα μία· Ἐπιστολαὶ Παύλου δεκατέσσαρες· πρὸς Ῥωμαίους μία, πρὸς Κορινθίους δύο, πρὸς Γαλάτας μία, πρὸς Ἐφεσίους μία, πρὸς Φιλιππησίους μία, πρὸς Κολοσσαεῖς μία, πρὸς Θεσσαλονικεῖς δύο, πρὸς Ἑβραίους μία, πρὸς Τιμόθεον δύο, πρὸς Τίτον μία, καὶ πρὸς Φιλήμονα μία.

And these are the Books of the New Testament: Four Gospels, according to Matthew, according to Mark, according to Luke, according to John; Acts of the Apostles; Seven Catholic Epistles, One of James, Two of Peter, Three of John, one of Jude; Fourteen Epistles of Paul, One to the Romans, Two to the Corinthians, One to the Galatians, One to the Ephesians, One to the Philippians, One to the Colossians, Two to the Thessalonians, One to the Hebrews, Two to Timothy, One to Titus, and One to Philemon.

DIGEST.

DIGEST.

ABORTION.—Women who use, or prepare drugs for, abortion, are to fulfil ten years of penance (Anc. XXI).

ABSTINENCE.—Clergymen are forbidden to abstain from marriage, flesh, or wine, except for discipline (Ap. Can. LI); and particularly, to abstain from flesh and wine on festival days, except for discipline (Ap. Can. LIII); but after tasting flesh once, they may abstain from it (Anc. XIV).

ACCOUNTS.—A Bishop charged with malversation in the accounts of the Church, is to be tried by the Provincial Synod (Ant. XXV).

ACCUSATION.—An accusation of fornication, adultery, or any other forbidden act, brought against a Communicant, if proved, disqualifies him for ordination (Ap. Can. LXI). Persons who are themselves under accusation, are disqualified from bringing charges of ecclesiastical offences against a Clergyman (Const. VI). See also *Accusers.*

ACCUSERS.—I. Of a Metropolitan.—

Accusers of a Metropolitan must lay their charges before the Exarch of the Diocese, or before the Throne of Constantinople (Chal. IX, XVII).

II. Of a Bishop.—

Accusers of a Bishop must be trustworthy persons (Ap. Can. LXXIV): they must not themselves be under discipline, nor even under accusation of offences (Const. VI); and they must be examined as to character (Chal. XXI).

Heretics are not to be received as accusers of a Bishop (Ap. Can. LXXV). Neither heretics, nor schismatics, may bring accusations of ecclesiastical offences against a Bishop (Const. VI); but those who complain of personal wrong done to them by the Bishop, may be of any religion (Const. VI).

A single Communicant cannot be received as the accuser of a Bishop (Ap. Can. LXXV), especially if he brings a charge of any sensual sin (Nic. II).

ACCUSERS.—Of a Bishop.—*Continued.*

Accusers of a Bishop are to bring their complaint before the Provincial Synod (Const. VI, Chal. IX), especially if the charge be that of malversation in the accounts of the Church (Ant. XXV); and if they resort to the Civil Power or an Œcumenical Synod, they are not to be received as accusers (Const. VI).

False accusers of a Bishop are to suffer the same penalty to which he would have been liable, had the charge been proved (Const. VI).

III. Of a Priest.—

A Priest is not to be convicted of any sensual sin, on the evidence of a single witness (Nic. II).

Those who are themselves under accusation, are not to be received as accusers of a Priest (Const. VI).

Accusers of a Priest are to be examined as to character (Chal. XXI).

IV. Of a Deacon or the Minor Clergy.—

Those who are themselves under accusation, are not to be received as accusers of a Clergyman of any rank (Const. VI).

Accusers of a Clergyman are to be examined as to character (Chal. XXI).

See also *Accusation.*

ACTRESS.—Marriage with an actress is a disqualification for ordination (Ap. Can. XVIII).

ACTS OF THE APOSTLES.—The Book of Acts is referred to, as of authority, in Neo Cæs. XV: it is also included in the lists of canonical books, in Ap. Can. LXXXV, Laod. LX.

ADDRESS.—To the Emperor: vid. *Petition.*

ADMONITION.—Schismatics are to be admonished before punishment (Ap. Can. XXXI, Ant. V).

A Bishop who neglects, without reasonable cause, to attend a Provincial Synod, is to be admonished (Chal. XIX).

ADULTERY.—If a layman commit adultery, he cannot be ordained (Ap. Can. LXI): nor can he be ordained if his wife has committed adultery (Neo Cæs. VIII).

A Priest who commits adultery is to be punished by complete excommunication (Neo Cæs. I).

If the wife of a Clergyman commit adultery, he must put her away, or cease from his ministry (Neo Cæs. VIII).

An adulterer, or an adulteress, must fulfil seven years of penance (Anc. XX).

ADVOCATE.—Bishops are forbidden to nominate Advocates, for money (Chal. II).

The Advocate of the Church of Constantinople is to expel from the City Clergymen and Monks who go there and create disturbances (Chal. XXIII).

ÆLIA.—The Bishop of Ælia is to rank next to the Metropolitan (Nic. VII).

AGAPÆ.—Vid. *Lovefeasts.*

AGAPETÆ.—Agapetæ are forbidden to reside with Clergymen (Nic. III), or with men of any class (Anc. XIX).

AGE.—A Priest is not to be ordained before he is thirty years of age (Neo Cæs. XI); nor a Deaconess before she is forty (Chal. XV).

AGENT.—Clergymen and Monks are forbidden to act as agents of laymen (Chal. III).

ALEXANDRIA.—The Church of Alexandria is to retain its ancient and customary prerogatives (Nic. VI).

The Bishop of Alexandria is to have jurisdiction in Egypt, Lybia, and Pentapolis (Nic. VI); he is to have jurisdiction in Egypt (Const. II); he is entitled, by ancient custom, to be consulted by the Bishops of Egypt, before their signing even acts which they approve (Chal. XXX).

ALIENATION.—The Bishops are forbidden to alienate Church property (Ap. Can. XXXVIII).

ALMONER.—Priests and Deacons are to act as their Bishop's almoners (Ap. Can. XLI).

ALMSHOUSES.—Almshouses are not to be meddled with by Clergy who have left them, and gone into another Parish (Chal. X).

ALTAR.—Nothing is to be offered at the Altar, except new ears of grain and clusters of grapes (Ap. Can. III, IV).

A Priest is forbidden to raise a separate Altar (Ap. Can. XXXI; Ant. V); also a Deacon (Ant. V).

The Priesthood alone may communicate at the Altar (Laod. XIX).

Women are forbidden to go into the Altar (Laod. XLIV).

AMBO.—Singers are to sing in the Ambo (Laod. XV).

AMULETS.—Vid. *Phylacteries.*

ANATHEMA.—The penalty of Anathema is pronounced on Clergymen and Monks who accept civil or military office (Chal. VII).

And on Monks who negotiate Simony (Chal. II); or

Who compose or use any other than the Nicene Creed (Chal. Encyc.):

ANATHEMA.—*Continued.*

And on a Deaconess who marries, and her husband (Chal. XV):

And on Ascetics who abhor marriage (Gang. I); or reject the Oblation when offered by a married Priest (Gang. IV); or who, being virgin, insult the married (Gang. X); or who abhor eaters of flesh (Gang. II); or despise lovefeasts (Gang. XI); or who attempt to withdraw slaves from their masters' service, under pretext of religion (Gang. III); or who despise the Church and Church Assemblies (Gang. V); or abhor the services in honour of the Martyrs (Gang. XX); or who perform ecclesiastical acts without the concurrence of the Bishop and Priest (Gang. VI); or who misappropriate the Fruits of the Church (Gang. VII, VIII); or who forsake or neglect their children (Gang. XV); or forsake their parents (Gang. XVI); or who fast on Sunday, under pretence of religion (Gang. XVIII); or disregard the fasts of the Church (Gang. XIX).

And on women who forsake their husbands, from abhorrence of marriage (Gang. XIV); or who cut off their hair, under pretence of religion (Gang. XVII).

And on laymen who profess the heresies of Nestorius or Theodore of Mopsuestia (Eph. VII); or who compose or use any other than the Nicene Creed (Eph. VII, Chal. Encyc.); or who marry Deaconesses (Chal. XV); or who ravish, under pretence of Marriage (Chal. XXVII); or who negotiate Simony (Chal. II); or who judaize, by resting on the Sabbath (Laod. XXIX).

And on Christians, who honour heretic martyrs (Laod. XXXIV); or invoke Angels (Laod. XXXV).

Anathema against heresies in general (Const. I).

Heretics must anathematize all heresies, and particularly their own, before reconciliation (Const. VII, Laod. VII).

ANCIENT CUSTOM.—Vid. *Custom.*

ANCYRA.—The Canons of the Council of Ancyra are confirmed by Chal. I.

ANGELS.—Christians are forbidden to invoke Angels (Laod. XXXV).

ANIMALS.—Animals are forbidden to be offered at the Altar (Ap. Can. III).

ANOINTING.—Vid. *Chrism.*

ANOMEANS.—Vid. *Eunomians.*

ANTIOCH.—The Canons of the Council of Antioch are confirmed by Chal. I.

The doctrine of the Trinity is accepted by the Church in Antioch (Const. V).

The Church of Antioch is to retain its ancient and customary prerogatives (Nic. VI, Const. II).

The Bishop of Antioch has no jurisdiction in Cyprus (Eph. VIII).

APOLLINARIANS.—The heresy of the Apollinarians anathematized (Const. I).

Apollinarians are admitted to the Catholic Church, by Chrism, after renunciation of their heresies (Const. VII).

APOSTATE.—Vid. *Lapsed.*

APOSTOLICAL CANONS.—Vid. *Canons.*

TRADITION.—Vid. *Tradition.*

The Throne of Rome is spoken of as Apostolic (Chal. XXX).

APPAREL.—Vid. *Dress.*

APPEAL.—OF A BISHOP.

A Bishop cannot appeal against the unanimous sentence of his Comprovincials (Ant. XV).

An appeal by a Bishop or his accusers, is to be from the Pròvincial to the Diocesan Synod (Const. VI).

If a Bishop appeal to the Emperor, against a sentence of deposition, he cannot be restored, nor can his cause be reheard by a Synod (Ant. XII).

See also *Defence.*

—OF A PRIEST, DEACON, OR MINOR CLERGYMAN.

Appeals of the Clergy, from their Bishops, are to be made to the Provincial Synod (Nic. V, Ant. XX); if made to the Emperor, the appellant cannot be restored, nor can his cause be reheard, by a Synod (Ant. XII).

See also *Defence.*

—OF A LAYMAN.

A layman may appeal, from the sentence of his Bishop, to the Provincial Synod (Nic. V, Ant. XX).

See also *Defence.*

APPOINTMENT.—The appointment of Presbyteresses, or female Presidents, is forbidden (Laod. XI).

See also *Bishop.*

APPROPRIATION.—Bishops are forbidden to appropriate ecclesiastical property to themselves or their relations (Ap. Can. XXXVIII, Ant. XXV).

APPROPRIATION.—*Continued.*

Priests are forbidden to appropriate ecclesiastical property to themselves (Ant. XXV).

The appropriation, to private purposes, of wax or oil of the Church, is forbidden (Ap. Can. LXXII); also of consecrated vessels (Ap. Can. LXIII); also of the First Fruits (Gang. VII, VIII).

The appropriation, to secular purposes, of Monasteries or their property, is forbidden (Chal. XXIV).

ARBITRATOR.—Vid. *Referee.*

ARCHBISHOP.—Vid. *Exarch.*

ARIANS.—The heresy of the Arians is anathematized (Const. I).

Arians are admitted to the Catholic Church, by Chrism, after renunciation of their heresies (Const. VII).

ARISTERI.—Vid. *Cathari.*

ARMY.—Bishops, Priests, and Deacons, are forbidden to serve in the army (Ap. Can. LXXXIII, Chal. VII); also the Minor Clergy, and Monks (Chal. VII).

ASCETICS.—Ascetics must observe the fasts of the Church (Gang. XIX).

Ascetics are forbidden to enter a tavern (Laod. XXIV); or to wash in a bath with women (Laod. XXX).

ASCETICISM.—True Asceticism commended (Gang. XXI).

False Asceticism is condemned in various instances as follows:

In a Bishop, Priest, or Deacon, who divorces his wife, under pretext of religion (Ap. Can. V), or who abstains from marriage because he abhors it (Ap. Can. LI, Gang. IX); and in those who condemn marriage (Gang. I); or who refuse the Oblation when offered by a married Priest (Gang. IV); and in women who forsake their husbands from abhorrence of marriage (Gang. XIV),

And in a Bishop, Priest, or Deacon, who abstains from flesh and wine, on festival days, because he abhors them (Ap. Can. LIII); and in those who, in general, abstain from flesh and wine because they abhor them (Ap. Can. LI); or who condemn persons who eat flesh (Gang. II); or

Who despise lovefeasts (Gang. XI); and

In those who fast on Sunday (Gang. XVIII); or who do not observe the fasts of the Church (Gang. XIX); and

In those who despise persons who wear the customary dress (Gang. XII); and in women who assume the dress of men (Gang. XIII), or who cut off their hair (Gang. XVII).

ASCETICISM—*Continued.*

And in those who despise Church Assemblies (Gang. V); or who abhor the services in honour of the Martyrs (Gang. XX);

And in parents who forsake their children (Gang. XV); or children who forsake their parents (Gang. XVI).

ASIA.—The Metropolitans of the Asian Diocese are to be elected according to custom, and are to be ordained by the Patriarch of Constantinople (Chal. XXVIII).

Their jurisdiction is limited to their own Diocese (Const. II), within which they are to ordain the Bishops (Chal. XXVIII).

ASSEMBLIES.—Schismatical and separated assemblies are forbidden (Ap. Can. XXXI, Gang. VI, Ant. II, V, Laod. XXXV).

Those who despise Church Assemblies are to be anathematized (Gang. V); also those who abhor the Assemblies in honour of the Martyrs (Gang. XX).

Assembling in Church, for public worship, is commended (Gang. XXI).

ASTROLOGERS.—Astrologers are to fulfil five years of penance (Anc. XXIV).

Clergymen are forbidden to be astrologers (Laod. XXXVI).

ATTENDANCE.—Attendance at Provincial Synods is enjoined on Bishops (Chal. XIX, Laod. XL).

AUNT.—The aunt of a Clergyman may reside with him (Nic. III).

AUTUMN.—Provincial Synods are to be held about Autumn (Nic. V).

BAILIFF.—No Bishop is to ordain a Bailiff for money (Chal. II).

No Clergyman or Monk is to act as bailiff to a layman (Chal. III).

BANISHMENT.—Clergymen and Monks, going to Constantinople and causing disturbances there, are to be banished from the city (Chal. XXIII).

BANQUETS.—Clergymen are forbidden to attend plays at banquets (Laod. LIV).

BAPTISM.—Baptism washes away all sins (Anc. XII).

Baptism is to be performed according to the Catholic formula (Ap. Can. XLIX), and by trine-immersion (Ap. Can. L); it must not be into the LORD's death (Ap. Can. L); it is to be followed by Chrism and the Eucharist (Laod. XLVIII).

Bishops and Priests are forbidden to refuse to baptize one who has been polluted by the impious (Ap. Can. XLVII).

BAPTISM—*Continued.*

A pregnant woman may be baptized whenever she will (Neo-Cæs. VI).

Children of a Reader or Singer, by a heretic wife, must be baptized in the Catholic Church (Chal. XIV).

Candidates for Baptism are forbidden to be received after the second week in Lent (Laod. XLV); they must learn the Creed by heart, and recite it to the Bishop on Maundy Thursday (Laod. XLVI).

Clinic Baptism is, generally, a disqualification for Priests' orders (Neo-Cæs. XII). Those who have received clinic Baptism, if afterwards restored to health, must learn the Creed by heart (Laod. XLVII).

A heathen who is converted and baptized, may be ordained (Anc. XII).

Bishops and Priests are forbidden to admit the Baptism of heretics (Ap. Can. XLVI); Baptism by heretics is declared void (Ap. Can. LXVIII); the Baptism of Eunomians, by one immersion, is declared void (Const. VII); the Baptism of Phrygians and Sabellians is void (Const. VII).

Bishops and Priests are forbidden to rebaptize those who have true Baptism (Ap. Can. XLVII); Paulianists must be rebaptized upon reconciliation (Nic. XIX), and also Phrygians (Laod. VIII, Const. VII), and Eunomians, and Sabellians, and all other heretics, with certain exceptions (Const. VII).

BARBARIANS.—Castration, by Barbarians, does not disqualify a man for being ordained (Nic. I).

BATHING.—Bathing with women is forbidden to men of every class (Laod. XXX).

BEASTS.—Communicants are forbidden to eat the flesh of animals slain by beasts (Ap. Can. LXIII).

BEMA.—Priests are forbidden to enter the Bema before their Bishops (Laod. LVI).

Vid. also *Sanctuary.*

BENEFACTIONS.—The Steward of Benefactions is to have charge of the First Fruits (Gang. VIII).

BENEFICENCE.—Beneficence in the enjoyment of wealth is commended (Gang. XXI).

BEQUEST.—A Bishop is not allowed to bequeath his See to heirs (Ap. Can. LXXVI).

BERUS.—Ascetics who despise those who wear the *berus*, are anathematized (Gang. XII).

BESTIALITY.—Persons who are guilty of bestial lusts, are to fulfil a term of penance, varying from twenty to thirty years, according to circumstances; and in some cases they are to be admitted to Communion only at the point of death (Anc. XVI).

Those who are themselves guilty, and who have corrupted others, are to pray amongst the Hyemantes (Anc. XVII).

BETROTHED.—One who ravishes a virgin who is not betrothed, must marry her (Ap. Can. LXVII); the ravisher of a betrothed virgin must restore her to the man to whom she is betrothed (Anc. XI).

BIRDS.—Birds are forbidden to be offered at the Altar (Ap. Can. III).

BIRTHDAYS.—Birthdays are forbidden to be observed in Lent (Laod. LII).

BISHOP.—I. Disqualifications for the Office of a Bishop.

A person to be ordained Bishop, must not, after Baptism, have been twice married, nor have had a concubine (Ap. Can. XVII); he must not have married a widow, a divorced woman, a harlot, a slave, or an actress (Ap. Can. XVIII); he must not have married two sisters, nor a niece (Ap. Can. XIX).

He must not have committed adultery, fornication, or any other forbidden act (Ap. Can. LXI). One whose wife has committed adultery cannot be ordained (Neo-Cæs. VIII).

He must not have castrated himself (Ap. Can. XXII, Nic. I); but if castrated by force or persecution, or if born an eunuch, he may be ordained (Ap. Can. XXI, Nic. I); also if castrated for surgical purposes (Nic. I); and if castrated by force, or for surgical purposes, after ordination, he may remain among the Clergy (Nic. I).

He must not be totally deaf or blind (Ap. Can. LXXVIII), but partial lameness or blindness is not a disqualification (Ap. Can. LXXVII).

He must not be possessed of a devil, but if dispossessed, and worthy, he may be made a Bishop (Ap. Can. LXXIX).

One whose ordination would injure the Church, must not be made a Bishop (Ap. Can. LXXVIII).

A Neophyte, or a person suddenly converted from a dishonourable life, must not be immediately made a Bishop (Ap. Can. LXXX, Nic. II, Laod. III); but former profession of heathenism is not, in itself, a disqualification (Anc. XII).

A slave cannot be ordained, unless manumitted by his master (Ap. Can. LXXXII).

BISHOP. — Disqualifications for the Office of a Bishop.— *Continued.*

One who has lapsed cannot be ordained (Nic. X); but those who have been steadfast throughout the persecutions, though forced to seem otherwise, may be ordained (Anc. III).

A Bishop must not be ordained without a charge (Chal. VI).

A Bishop must not be appointed in a village or country district (Laod. LVII).

—II. Of the Election of a Bishop.

A Bishop is not to be elected during the lifetime of his predecessor (Ant. XXIII).

He is not to be elected until after long probation, both of faith and life (Laod. XII).

He is not to be elected by the multitude (Laod. XIII).

He is to be elected by all the Bishops of the Province, assembled together, if possible; otherwise, the suffrage and consent of those who are absent, is to be given in writing (Nic. IV, Ant. XIX); he is to be elected by the Provincial Synod (Ant. XXIII); by the Metropolitan and Provincial Bishops (Laod. XII).

He is to be elected by a majority of votes, in case of factious opposition (Nic. VI, Ant. XIX).

His election is to be ratified by the Metropolitan (Nic. IV, VI).

A Bishop without a See, unless elected by a full Synod, cannot occupy a vacant See, even by unanimous suffrage of the people (Ant. XVI).

—III. Of the Ordination of a Bishop.

A Bishop must be ordained by two or three Bishops (Ap. Can. I); he must be ordained by at least three Bishops (Nic. IV), and with the consent of the majority of the Bishops of the Province (Nic. IV, VI, Ant. XIX).

He must be ordained to his See within three months of its becoming vacant (Chal. XXV).

—IV. Of the Jurisdiction of a Bishop.

A Bishop's jurisdiction is confined to his own Parish (Ap. Can. XXXIV, XXXV, Ant. IX). Two Bishops cannot have jurisdiction in one City (Nic. VIII).

A Bishop already exercising jurisdiction over outlying Parishes, is to retain it (Chal. XVII).

A Bishop has control over Monks within his Parish (Chal. IV); also over the Clergy of Poor-houses, Monasteries, and Martyries (Chal. VIII); also over Ecclesiastical Property

BISHOP—IV. OF THE JURISDICTION OF A BISHOP.—*Continued.*

(Ap. Can. XXXVIII, Ant. XXIV), and the moneys of the Church (Ap. Can. XLI, Ant. XXV), and the offerings (Gang. VII, VIII).

A Bishop is to be consulted in all matters, by Priests within his jurisdiction, before they act (Ap. Can. XXXIX, Laod. LVII), and by Deacons (Ap. Can. XXXIX). Bishops and itinerant visitors, appointed in country districts, are to do nothing without the consent of the City Bishop (Laod. LVII). A Clergyman must obtain his Bishop's permission before travelling (Laod. XLI). A Monastery, or an Oratory, cannot be established in a Bishop's Parish, without his consent (Chal. IV, XXIV), nor can ecclesiastical acts be performed, by private persons, against his will (Gang. VI); nor can referees, in disputes between Clergymen, be appointed without his consent (Chal. IX); nor can a petition be presented to the Emperor, by a Clergyman, without his consent (Ant. XI).

A Bishop may authorize a Chorepiscopus to ordain Priests or Deacons beyond his own district (Ant. X); or even in a City (Anc. XIII); he may authorize another Bishop to act within his Parish (Ant. XXI); he may grant to a reconciled Bishop of the Cathari, who is within his jurisdiction, authority to retain his Episcopal title (Nic. VIII).

A Bishop who suspends or excommunicates a person, can alone readmit him (Ap. Can. XXXII, Nic. V).

A Bishop may grant indulgence to the lapsed, who have fallen a second time (Nic. XII); and to lapsed Deacons, who have been restored (Anc. II); and to the lapsed who have fallen with extenuating circumstances (Anc. V, VII).

And to Monks and dedicated Virgins, excommunicated for marrying (Chal. XVI); and to persons who have fallen into many marriages (Neo-Cæs. III).

And to persons under penance for bestial lusts (Anc. XVI).

A Bishop convicted of anything contrary to religion or morals, is not entitled to the obedience of his Clergy (Ap. Can. XV).

—V. OF THE DUTIES OF A BISHOP.

A Bishop is to ordain Priests, Deacons, and Minor Clergymen (Ap. Can. II); he is to ordain Priests and Deacons within his own Parish and districts (Ant. IX); he is to ordain Chorepiscopi, Priests, and Deacons (Ant. X); and to appoint Exorcists (Laod. XXVI).

He must appoint a Steward of his See (Chal. XXVI).

BISHOP.—V. Of the Duties of a Bishop.—*Continued.*

Offerings, not made at the Altar, are to be taken to the house of the Bishop and Priest, and to be shared by them with the other Clergy (Ap. Can. IV). A Bishop is to designate all Church property to the Priests and Deacons (Ant. XXIV); and to manage the revenues of the Church with their approval (Ant. XXV).

He is to relieve the poor, from the funds of the Church (Ant. XXV), through the Priests and Deacons (Ap. Can. XLI); and to supply necessaries to Clergymen in need (Ap. Can. LIX); he is to practice hospitality at the expense of the Church (Ap. Can. XLI); to entertain foreign Clergymen, bringing letters commendatory (Ap. Can. XXXIII); and to make needful provision for Monasteries within his Parish (Chal. IV).

He is to reclaim Church Property, which had been sold during the vacancy of his See, and to decide how it shall be reclaimed (Anc. XV).

He is to appoint Clergymen and Monks, for the transaction of necessary business, and for the guardianship of Widows and Orphans (Chal. III).

He is to settle disputes between Clergymen (Chal. IX).

He is to attend Synods twice a year, for examination concerning doctrines of religion, and the settlement of ecclesiastical disputes (Ap. Can. XXXVII, Ant. XX); for revising episcopal sentences (Nic. V, Ant. XX); and for the regulation of ecclesiastical affairs (Chal. XIX); and if he do not attend, he is to be admonished, unless prevented by unavoidable business (Chal. XIX), or ill health (Chal. XIX, Laod. XL).

He is to admonish schismatics three times before punishment (Ap. Can. XXXI); to admonish schismatical Clergymen three times before deposing them (Ant. V); he should summon a Clergyman, who leaves his own Parish, to return, before punishing him (Ap. Can. XV, Ant. III).

He is to baptize persons who have been polluted by the impious (Ap. Can. XLVII); to baptize according to the Catholic formula (Ap. Can. XLIX); and by trine-immersion (Ap. Can. L); he is to instruct and baptize reconciled Phrygians (Laod. VIII); and to hear candidates for Baptism recite the Creed (Laod. XLVI).

He is to examine the dying before administering the Eucharist (Nic. XIII); to administer the Eucharist to Priests and Deacons (Nic. XVIII); and he must partake himself, or give reasons for refusing (Ap. Can. VIII).

BISHOP.—Of the Duties of a Bishop.—*Continued.*

He is to commence Divine Service with a Sermon, and, at its close, to give the Kiss of Peace to the Priests and full Communicants (Laod. XIX).

He is to receive penitents (Ap. Can. LII).

He is to fast during Lent, and on Wednesdays and Fridays, unless prevented by bodily weakness (Ap. Can. LXIX).

He is to keep his own property distinct from that of the Church (Ap. Can. XL, Ant. XXIV); and to provide for his wife, children, and other relatives, out of the former (Ap. Can. XL); if his relatives are poor, he is to relieve them like the rest of the poor (Ap. Can. XXXVIII).

He is to find a place, as Chorepiscopus or Priest, for a reconciled Bishop of the Cathari, who is within his jurisdiction (Nic. VIII).

—VI. Of the Privileges of a Bishop.

A Bishop is to receive his share of offerings not made at the Altar (Ap. Can. IV); he is to be supported from the funds of the Church (Ap. Can. XLI, Ant. XXV); he is not to be at personal expense in the practice of hospitality (Ap. Can. XLI); when in need, he is to be supplied with necessaries (Ap. Can. LIX).

He may bequeath his property to whom he will (Ap. Can. XL, Ant. XXIV); at his death, his property is not to be seized for the Church (Chal. XXII).

If he has been degraded to the rank of a Priest, he is to be either altogether deposed, or restored to his former rank (Chal. XXIX). A Bishop displaced by Nestorius or his followers, is to be restored (Eph. III).

A Bishop who has not been received by his Parish, may retain his rank (Ap. Can. XXXVI); and, if he pleases, resume his position as Priest (Anc. XVIII).

A Bishop may consent in writing, to the ordination of a Bishop, if personal attendance is difficult (Nic. IV, Ant. XIX).

It is his privilege to communicate at the Altar (Laod. XIX).

Clergymen are forbidden to insult their Bishop (Ap. Can. LV); Priests are forbidden to enter the Bema before the Bishop (Laod. LVI); Country Priests are forbidden to officiate, in a City Church, in the presence of a Bishop (Neo-Cæs. XIII); but Chorepiscopi may do so (Neo-Cæs. XIV).

A Deacon is the helper of his Bishop (Nic. XVIII).

A Bishop who has been steadfast throughout the persecutions, though forced to seem otherwise, is entitled to all his former privileges (Anc. III).

BISHOP.—VI. Of the Privileges of a Bishop.—*Continued.*

A Bishop who has a complaint against his Metropolitan, may lay it before the Exarch of the Diocese, or the throne of Constantinople (Chal. IX, XVII).

Vid. also "*Bishop.—IV. Of the Jurisdiction of a Bishop.*"

—VII. Of Things Forbidden to a Bishop.

A Bishop is forbidden to divorce his wife, under pretext of religion (Ap. Can. V); or to marry after ordination (Ap. Can. XXVI); or to abstain from marriage, except for discipline (Ap. Can. LI); or to have any woman dwelling with him, except such relations, or other persons, as are beyond suspicion (Nic. III); or to wash in a bath with women (Laod. XXX).

He is forbidden to engage in worldly business (Ap. Can. VI, LXXXI), unless he be called by law to the guardianship of minors (Chal. III); he is forbidden to serve in the army (Ap. Can. LXXXIII); or to accept military or civil office (Chal. VII); or to exact usury (Ap. Can. XLIV, Nic. XVII, Laod. IV); or to become security (Ap. Can. XX).

He is forbidden to read false and heretical books in Church, as Scripture (Ap. Can. LX); or to compose, or use, any other than the Nicene Creed (Eph. VII, Chal. Encyc.); or to join in prayer with heretics (Ap. Can. XLV, Laod. XXXIII); or to employ them as Clergymen (Ap. Can. XLV); or to admit the Baptism, or Sacrifice, of heretics (Ap. Can. XLVI); or to receive the Eulogiæ of heretics (Laod. XXXII); or to attend the Cemeteries, or Martyries, of heretics (Laod. IX); or to marry his children to heretics (Laod. XXXI); or to observe, or receive gifts from, festivals of heretics (Laod. XXXVII); to enter a synagogue of Jews or heretics, for prayer (Ap. Can. LXIV); or to celebrate Easter before the Vernal Equinox, as the Jews do (Ap. Can. VII, Nic. Encyc., Ant. I); or to observe, or receive gifts from, Jewish fasts or festivals (Ap. Can. LXX, Laod. XXXVII); or to receive unleavened bread from the Jews (Ap. Can. LXX, Laod. XXXVIII); or to feast with the heathen (Laod. XXXIX); or to join in prayer with schismatics (Ant. II, Laod. XXXIII); or to adhere to the maintainers of conventicles (Ap. Can. XXXI).

He is forbidden to submit to the jurisdiction of Nestorius and his partisans (Eph. III).

He is forbidden to communicate with the excommunicated (Ap. Can. X, Ant. II); or with a Bishop who has obtained his Church through secular rulers (Ap. Can. XXX); or with

BISHOP.—V. OF THINGS FORBIDDEN TO A BISHOP.—*Continued.*

a Clergyman who is deposed for celebrating Easter before the Vernal Equinox (Ant. I); or with a Clergyman who, after deposition, meddles with his former ministry (Ant. IV); or to join in prayer with a deposed Clergyman (Ap. Can. XI).

He is forbidden to receive, in their clerical capacity, Clergymen who are suspended or deposed for leaving their own Parishes (Ap. Can. XVI, Ant. III); or to restore a Priest or Deacon, properly suspended by another Bishop, unless the latter die (Ap. Can. XXXII, Nic. V); or to receive and ordain one who has seceded from another Bishop (Nic. XVI); or to receive a Clergyman of another Bishop (Chal. XX); or to receive persons excommunicated by another Bishop, unless restored by him (Ap. Can. XII, Ant. VI).

He is forbidden to leave his own Parish and enter another, except under special circumstances, and by special request (Ap. Can. XIV); or unless he is driven by necessity from his own country (Chal. XX); he is forbidden to do so without any exception (Nic. XV, Chal. V, Ant. XXI); and if he do so, his extra-parochial acts are declared void (Nic. XV); he is forbidden to act beyond his own Parish (Ap. Can. XXIV, XXXV, Nic. XV, Ant. XXII); without a written invitation from the Metropolitan and provincial Bishops of the Province into which he goes (Ant. XIII); or to act beyond his own Diocese without invitation (Const. II).

He is forbidden to do anything of great moment without the consent of his presiding Bishop (Ap. Can. XXXIV), Metropolitan (Ant. IX); or to address the Emperor without the consent of his Metropolitan and Com-provincials (Ant. XI). A Bishop appointed in a village, or country district, is to do nothing without the consent of the City Bishop (Laod. LVII).

He is forbidden to carry off wax or oil from the Church (Ap. Can. LXXII); or to appropriate consecrated vessels to private purposes (Ap. Can. LXXIII); or to appropriate ecclesiastical property to himself or his relatives (Ap. Can. XXXVIII); or to employ his own domestics, or relatives, in the administration of Church funds (Ant. XXV).

He is forbidden to offer anything at the Altar except new ears of grain, or clusters of grapes (Ap. Can. III).

He is forbidden to celebrate Easter before the Vernal Equinox (Ap. Can. VII, Nic. Encyc., Ant. I).

He is forbidden to rebaptize one who has true Baptism, or to refuse to baptize one who has been polluted by the impious (Ap. Can. XLVII).

BISHOP.—V. OF THINGS FORBIDDEN TO A BISHOP.—*Continued.*

He is forbidden to make the Oblation in a private house (Laod. LVIII).

He is forbidden to receive a second ordination, unless the first was void (Ap. Can. LXVIII).

He is forbidden to commit simony (Ap. Can. XXIX, Chal. II); or to negotiate simoniacal contracts (Chal. II); or to obtain his Church through secular rulers (Ap. Can. XXX); or to seize a vacant See (Ant. XVI).

He is forbidden to ordain a relative to the Episcopate from personal motives, or to bequeath his See to heirs (Ap. Can. LXXVI); or to appoint his successor (Ant. XXIII).

He is forbidden to ordain a neophyte, without a time of probation (Nic. II).

He is forbidden to abstain from flesh or wine, except for discipline (Ap. Can. LI), especially on festival days (Ap. Can. LIII); he is forbidden to eat flesh with the blood, or of animals which have been slain by beasts, or have died a natural death (Ap. Can. LXIII), or to fast on Sunday, or on any Sabbath except Easter Even (Ap. Can. LXVI); or to join in forming drinking clubs (Laod. LV); or to eat in a tavern, except on a journey (Ap. Can. LIV).

If invited to a lovefeast, he is forbidden to take away his portion (Laod. XXVII); he is forbidden to attend plays at weddings and banquets (Laod. LIV).

He is forbidden to castrate himself (Ap. Can. XXIII, Nic. I).

He is forbidden to strike backsliders or unbelievers (Ap. Can. XXVII).

If deposed, he is forbidden to touch his former ministry (Ap. Can. XXVIII, Ant. IV).

He is forbidden to insult a Priest or Deacon (Ap. Can. LVI); or to insult the Emperor, or a magistrate (Ap. Can. LXXXIV); or to mock the infirm (Ap. Can. LVII).

He is forbidden to neglect his duties (Ap. Can. LVIII).

He is forbidden to deny his office (Ap. Can. LXII).

He is forbidden to misuse his power of Excommunication (Nic. V).

He is forbidden to obtain an Imperial Rescript for dividing a Province (Chal. XII).

A Bishop who has not been received by his Parish, is forbidden to assume authority elsewhere (Anc. XVIII, Ant. XVIII).

He is forbidden to practice magic, enchantment, mathematics, or astrology; or to make, or wear, phylacteries (Laod. XXXVI).

BISHOP.—VIII. Of the Trial of a Bishop.

Accusers of a Bishop must be trustworthy (Ap. Can. (LXXIV); they must not themselves be under accusation of, nor condemnation for, offences; nor under sentence of Excommunication (Const. VI); they must be examined as to character (Chal. XXI).

Heretics are not to be received as accusers of a Bishop (Ap. Can. LXXV); neither heretics nor schismatics may bring accusations, of ecclesiastical offences, against a Bishop (Const. VI), but those who complain of personal wrong, done to them by the Bishop, may be of any religion (Const. VI).

A single communicant cannot be received as the accuser of a Bishop (Ap. Can. LXXV); especially if the charge be that of any sensual sin (Nic. II).

False accusers of a Bishop are to suffer the penalty to which he would have been liable, had the charge been proved (Const. VI).

A Bishop accused of offences, is to be summoned by the Bishops (Ap. Can. LXXIV); he is to be summoned a second, and a third time, if necessary; and if he fail to appear on the third summons, he is to be tried in his absence (Ap. Can. LXXIV); he is to be tried by the Provincial or Diocesan Synod, not by the civil courts, or an Œcumenical Synod (Const. VI); he is to be tried by the Provincial Synod (Chal. IX, Ant. XVII).

A Bishop misappropriating Church Funds, is to be judged by the Synod (Ant. XXV).

If the Provincial Bishops cannot agree to a verdict, on the trial of a Bishop, the Metropolitan is to call in some of the Bishops of the neighboring Provinces, to rehear the case (Ant. XIV).

A Bishop who appeals to the Emperor, instead of to a Synod, against a sentence of deposition, cannot be restored; nor can his cause be reheard by a Synod (Ant. XII); a Bishop cannot appeal against the unanimous sentence of his Com-provincials (Ant. XV).

Vid. also *Accusers*.

—IX. Penalties to be inflicted on a Bishop. Vid. *Suspension of a Bishop*, *Deposition of a Bishop*, *Degradation*, *Excommunication*, *Anathema*, and *Metropolitan*.

—X. General Regulations as to a Bishop.

A Bishop is not to be received from abroad, without commendatory letters; nor, even if he bring such letters, without examination (Ap. Can. XXXIII).

BISHOP.—X. General Regulations as to a Bishop.—*Continued.*

A Bishop who refuses to enter upon his ministry, is to be suspended (Ap. Can. XXXVI, Ant. XVII); and judged by the Synod (Ant. XVII).

One Bishop of each Nation is to be acknowledged as chief (Ap. Can. XXXIV). The Bishop of the Metropolis is to be acknowledged as the head of the Bishops of the Province (Ant. IX).

A Bishop deposed for celebrating Easter before the Vernal Equinox, is to be deprived of the external honour due to the Priesthood (Ant. I).

If the wife of a Bishop commit adultery, he must divorce her, or desist from his ministry (Neo-Cæs. VIII).

A Bishop of the Cathari, reconciled to the Catholic Church, retains his orders, and his rank amongst other reconciled Clergy, but ranks as a Priest if within the jurisdiction of a Catholic Bishop, unless the latter give him permission to use the episcopal title (Nic. VIII); he is entitled to employment as Chorepiscopus, or Priest, if within the jurisdiction of a Catholic Bishop (Nic. VIII).

A Bishop of the Paulianists, reconciled to the Catholic Church, is, if worthy, to be ordained, and, if unworthy, to be deposed (Nic. XIX).

A Bishop of the Phrygians, seeking reconciliation to the Catholic Church, is to be instructed and baptized before admission (Laod. VIII).

BISHOPS.—The Bishops of each country, are to acknowledge one of their body as chief (Ap. Can. XXXIV). The Bishops of each Province, are to acknowledge the Bishop of the Metropolis as their head (Ant. IX).

The Bishops are to hold Synods twice a year, for mutual examination concerning the doctrines of religion, and for the settlement of ecclesiastical disputes (Ap. Can. XXXVII, Ant. XX); for revising Episcopal sentences (Nic. V, Ant. XX); and for the regulation of ecclesiastical affairs (Chal. XIX).

The Bishops must summon three times, if necessary, a Bishop accused of offences; and if he fail to appear on the third summons, they must try him in his absence (Ap. Can. LXXIV).

All the Bishops of a Province, should, if possible, meet for the appointment of a Bishop; but those who cannot attend, may vote in writing (Nic. IV, Ant. XIX); and a majority must consent to the appointment, either personally, or by letter (Nic. VI, Ant. XIX). The Metropolitan and Provin-

BISHOPS.—*Continued.*

cial Bishops of a Province, must concur in the appointment of a Bishop (Laod XII).

The Metropolitan and Provincial Bishops of a Province, must consent, before a Clergyman can address the Emperor (Ant. XI).

They may jointly give, to a Bishop of another Province, a written invitation to ordain for them (Ant. XIII).

A Bishop is forbidden to leave his own Parish and enter another, except at the request of several Bishops (Ap. Can. XIV).

A Metropolitan, falling into the heresies of Nestorius or Celestius, or joining the schismatical assembly at Ephesus, is to be subject to his own Bishops, and the neighbouring orthodox Metropolitans (Eph. Encyc., Can. I).

The Bishops of one Province may take part in the trial of a Bishop of another Province, if the proper Bishops cannot agree (Ant. XIV).

Bishops are described as belonging to the Priesthood (Const. VI, Eph. II, Chal. XXVI).

For regulations as to the Bishops of particular Sees, vid. *Alexandria*, *Antioch*, *Asia*, *Constantinople*, *Cyprus*, *Egypt*, *the East*, *Jerusalem*, *Lybia*, *Pentapolis*, *Pontus*, *Rome*, *Thrace*.

BLEMISH.—A bodily blemish is not a disqualification for the Episcopate (Ap. Can. LXXVII).

BLIND.—Clergy and laity are forbidden to mock the blind (Ap. Can. LVII).

BLINDNESS.—Total blindness is a disqualification for the Episcopate (Ap. Can. LXXVIII), but partial blindness is not (Ap. Can. LXXVII).

BLOOD.—Flesh with blood, is forbidden to be eaten (Ap. Can. LXIII, Gang. II).

BODILY SIN.—Vid. *Sin.*

BLEMISH.—Vid. *Blemish.*

BONIFACE.—A Priest called Boniface, was present at the Council of Chalcedon, as one of the legates of Rome (Chal. Introduction to Can. XXIX),

BOOK.—The book of the Western Bishops is approved by the Church of Antioch (Const. V).

Singers are to sing from a book (Laod. XV).

BOOKS.—Spurious and heretical books are forbidden to be read publicly in Church (Ap. Can. LX); uncanonical books are forbidden to be read in Church (Laod. LIX).

For lists of Canonical Books, see Ap. Can. LXXXV, Laod. LX.

BREAD.—Communicants are forbidden to receive unleavened bread from the Jews (Ap. Can. LXX, Laod. XXXVIII).

Lapsed Deacons, who have been restored, are forbidden to bring in the Bread (Anc. II); country Priests are forbidden to offer the Bread, unless in the absence of the Bishops and city Priests (Neo-Cæs. XIII); Sub-deacons are forbidden to give the Bread (Laod. XXV).

There is to be no Oblation of Bread in Lent, except on Sabbaths and Sundays (Laod. XLIX).

BROTHER-IN-LAW.—A woman who has married two brothers, is to be cast out until the hour of death (Neo-Cæs. II).

BROTHERS.—Bishops are forbidden to ordain their own brothers to the Episcopate from personal motives (Ap. Can. LXXVI); or to employ them in the management of Church Funds (Ant. XXV).

BUSINESS.—Bishops and Priests are forbidden to engage in worldly business (Ap. Can. VI, LXXXI, Chal. III); also Deacons (Ap. Can. VI, Chal. III), and Monks (Chal. III, IV); but either Clergymen or Monks may accept the guardianship of minors, if called upon by the law to do so (Chal. III). Clergymen are forbidden to engage in ecclesiastical business, except by direction of their Bishops (Chal. III); and also Monks (Chal. III, IV).

Unavoidable business, is a sufficient excuse, to a Bishop, for not attending a Provincial Synod (Chal. XIX).

CAKES.—Communicants are forbidden to receive unleavened cakes from Jewish feasts (Ap. Can. LXX).

CALUMNY.—Those who bring false and calumnious accusations against a Bishop, are to suffer the penalty to which he would have been liable, had the charges been proved (Const. VI).

CANDIDATES.—Candidates for Baptism are not to be received after the second week in Lent (Laod. XLV); they must learn the Creed by heart, and recite it to the Bishop on Maundy Thursday (Laod. XLVI).

CANON.—Vid. *List.*

CANONICAL BOOKS.—Vid. *Books.*

LETTERS.—Vid. *Letters.*

CANONS.—The Canons of Nicæa are confirmed by Const. I; the Canons of Nicæa, Constantinople, Ephesus, Ancyra, Neo-Cæsarea, Gangra, Antioch, and Laodicea, are confirmed by Chal. I; the third Canon of Constantinople is confirmed by Chal. XXVIII; the decision of the Council of Nicæa, as to the time for celebrating Easter, is confirmed by Ant. I.

CASTRATION.—Castration by force, or persecution, is not a disqualification for the Episcopate (Ap. Can. XXI); castration by force, or for surgical purposes, is not a disqualification for Ordination (Nic. I); but self-castration is a disqualification for Orders (Ap. Can. XXII, Nic. I).

Self-castration is punishable, in Clergymen, by deposition (Ap. Can. XXIII, Nic. I); and in laymen, by suspension for three years (Ap. Can. XXIV).

CATECHISING.—Catechising is enjoined on Bishops and Priests (Ap. Can. LVIII).

CATECHUMEN.—A catechumen cannot be made a Bishop or Priest (Laod. III), without a time of probation (Ap. Can. LXXX, Nic. II).

The Mass of the Catechumens, is to follow the Bishop's sermon (Laod. XIX); the Catechumens are to leave the Church before the prayer for penitents (Laod. XIX).

Lapsed Catechumens are to pass three years as hearers (Nic. XIV); if a Catechumen fall into sin, whilst he is a Kneeler, he may be admitted to penance; but if he sin when he is a Hearer, he is to be cast out (Neo-Cæs. V).

CATHARI.—Cathari, seeking reconciliation to the Catholic Church, must promise, in writing, to observe its decrees, and particularly, to communicate with digamists, and with the lapsed who have been admitted to penance (Nic. VIII).

The Clergy of the Cathari, reconciled to the Catholic Church, retain their Orders, and their respective ranks, *inter se*; but a Bishop of the Cathari, if within the jurisdiction of a Catholic Bishop, is to rank as a Priest, unless the latter should give him permission to use the episcopal title; and he is entitled to a place as Chorepiscopus, or Priest, if within the jurisdiction of a Catholic Bishop (Nic. VIII).

Cathari are admitted to the Catholic Church by Chrism, after renunciation of their heresies (Const. VII, Laod. VII).

CELESTIUS.—A Metropolitan, professing the heresies of Celestius, is to be deposed and excommunicated, and to be under the control of his own Bishops and the neighbouring orthodox Metropolitans (Eph. Encyc., Can. I); a Provincial Bishop, for the same cause, is to be deposed (Eph. Encyc., Can. II); and also a Priest, Deacon, or Minor Clergyman (Eph. Encyc., Can. IV).

The heresies of Celestius are anathematized (Eph. VII).

CELIBACY.—None of the Clergy, except Readers and Singers, may marry after ordination (Ap. Can. XXVI); but Deacons may marry, if, at their ordination, they have declared an inten-

CELIBACY—*Continued.*

tion to do so (Anc. X). A Priest who marries is to be deposed (Neo-Cæs. I); a Deaconess who marries is to be anathematized (Chal. XV); a Monk, or dedicated Virgin, who marries, is to be excommunicated (Chal. XVI). Those who break their vows of celibacy, are to fulfil the penance of digamists (Anc. XIX).

CEMETERIES.—Communicants are forbidden to assemble in the Cemeteries, or attend the Martyries, of heretics (Laod. IX).

CENSURE.—ECCLESIASTICAL.—Vid. *Anathema*, *Deposition*, *Degradation*, *Excommunication*, *Expulsion*, and *Suspension.*

CENTESIMÆ.—Vid. *Usury.*

CHARGE.—No Clergyman is to be ordained without a charge (Chal. VI).

CHARGES.—BROUGHT AGAINST CLERGYMEN.—Vid. *Accusers*, *Bishop*, *Priest*, *Deacon*, and *Clergy*, *Minor.*

CHARISIUS.—A Priest of Philadelphia, named Charisius, produced the creed of Theodore of Mopsuestia to the Council of Ephesus (Eph. VII, and Introduction to the same Canon).

CHARITY.—The traditions of the Church inculcate charity (Gang. XXI).

CHARMS.—Vid. *Phylacteries.*

CHILDREN.—The children of a Bishop are to be provided for out of his private property (Ap. Can. XL).

Children of a Reader or Singer, by a heretic wife, must be brought into communion with the Catholic Church (Chal. XIV); they are not to be given in marriage to heretics, unless such heretics promise to become Christians (Chal. XIV); nor are children of communicants to be given in marriage to heretics (Laod. X), unless such heretics are converted to Christianity (Laod. XXXI).

Parents who forsake, or neglect, their children, are anathematized (Gang. XV); and also children who forsake their parents (Gang. XVI).

CHOREPISCOPUS.—A Chorepiscopus is to be ordained by the Bishop of the City (Ant. X).

He is to ordain Readers, Sub-deacons, and Exorcists, within his own district (Ant. X); he is not to ordain Priests, beyond his own Parish, without the Bishop's written consent (Anc. XIII); nor is he to ordain Priests or Deacons, at all, without his Bishop; nor, in any way, to act officially beyond his own district (Ant. X).

CHOREPISCOPUS—*Continued.*

He may offer the Oblation in a City Church, in the presence of the Bishop (Neo-Cæs. XIV).

He may give Letters Pacifical (Ant. VIII).

He is forbidden to commit Simony (Chal. II).

A Bishop of the Cathari, reconciled to the Catholic Church, is entitled to employment as a Chorepiscopus, or Priest (Nic. VIII).

CHRISM.—Chrism is declared to be the Seal of the Gift of the HOLY GHOST (Const. VII).

Certain heretics are admitted to the Catholic Church by Chrism, after renunciation of their heresies Const. VII, Laod. VII).

For the ceremony of anointing, in this case, see Const. VII.

Chrism is to follow Baptism (Laod. XLVIII).

CHRISTIANS.—Christians are forbidden to take oil into, or light lamps in a heathen temple, or a Jewish synagogue (Ap. Can. LXXI); or to judaize, by resting on the Sabbath (Laod. XXIX); or to honour martyrs of heretics (Laod. XXXIV); or to forsake the Church, and invoke Angels and gather assemblies (Laod. XXXV).

They are forbidden to wash in a bath with women (Laod. XXX); or to join in wanton dances at weddings (Laod. LIII).

Reconciled heretics are to be first received as Christians (Const. VII).

Christians are distinguished from laymen (Laod. XXX).

CHURCH.—Assembling in Church is commended (Gang. XXI); those who despise the Church are to be anathematized (Gang. V); also those who misappropriate the Fruits offered at the Church (Gang. VII, VIII).

Confusion in the Church is forbidden (Ap. Can. IX, Ant. II).

Heretical and spurious books are forbidden to be read in Church (Ap. Can. LX); also private psalms, and uncanonical books (Laod. LIX).

None but canonical Singers are to sing in Church (Laod. XV); none but duly appointed Exorcists are to exorcise either in Churches or private houses (Laod. XXVI); country Priests are forbidden to officiate in a City Church, in the presence of the Bishop and City Priests (Neo-Cæs. XIII); but Chorepiscopi may do so (Neo-Cæs. XIV).

Eating and sleeping in Church are forbidden (Laod. XXVIII).

Heretics are forbidden to enter the Church (Laod. VI).

Bishops are forbidden to obtain their Churches through secular rulers (Ap. Can. XXX).

CHURCH—*Continued.*

Appointment to a Church is necessary for ordination (Chal. VI).

A Church having a Bishop, is to have also a Steward amongst its Clergy (Chal. XXVI).

For regulations as to Clergymen leaving their Churches, vid. *Parish.*

PROPERTY.—Vid. *Property, Ecclesiastical.*

CHURCHES.—The Churches, in all the Provinces, are to retain their ancient and customary prerogatives (Nic. VI).

CITY.—A Bishop's jurisdiction is limited to his own City and districts (Ap. Can. XXXV, Ant. XXII); he is to have charge of his own City (Ant. IX); Monasteries are to be dependent upon the Bishop of the City (Chal. IV); Bishops appointed in villages, or country districts, are to do nothing without the consent of the Bishop of the City (Laod. LVII); Chorepiscopi are forbidden to ordain City Priests, without the Bishop's written consent (Anc. XIII); country Priests are forbidden to make the Oblation in a City Church, in the presence of the Bishops and City Priests (Neo-Cæs. XIII); but Chorepiscopi may do so (Neo-Cæs. XIV).

Those who are excommunicated in one City are not to be received in another (Ap. Can. XII).

In a new or rebuilt City, the Ecclesiastical Districts are to follow the political and municipal arrangement (Chal. XVII).

The number of Deacons in a City is to be seven (Neo-Cæs. XV).

A City rejecting a Bishop, Priest, or Deacon, is to be punished by the suspension of its Clergy (Ap. Can. XXXVI); a City rejecting its Bishop is to be judged by the Synod (Ant. XVIII).

For regulations as to Clergymen leaving their Cities, vid. *Parish.*

CIVIL POWER.—Charges against a Bishop are not to be brought before the civil power (Const. VI).

Bishops are forbidden to obtain their Churches from the civil power (Ap. Can. XXX); or to obtain the division of Provinces by the civil power (Chal. XII).

The civil power is to treat contumacious persistence in schism as sedition (Ant. V).

OFFICE.—Clergymen and Monks are forbidden to accept any civil office (Chal. VII).

CLERGY, MINOR.—I. DISQUALIFICATIONS FOR THE OFFICE.—

A man to be ordained, must not, after Baptism, have been

CLERGY, MINOR.—I. Disqualifications for the Office.—*Continued.*

twice married, nor have had a concubine (Ap. Can. XVII); he must not have married a widow, a divorced woman, a harlot, a slave, or an actress (Ap. Can. XVIII); he must not have married two sisters, or a niece (Ap. Can. XIX).

He must not have committed adultery, fornication, or any other forbidden act (Ap. Can. LXI); one whose wife has committed adultery cannot be ordained (Neo-Cæs. VIII).

He must not have castrated himself (Ap. Can. XXII, Nic. I); but if castrated by force, or for surgical purposes, he may be ordained; and if so castrated after ordination, he may remain among the Clergy (Nic. I).

He must not be possessed of a devil (Ap. Can. LXXIX): but if dispossessed, and worthy, he may be ordained (Ap. Can. LXXIX).

A slave, unless manumitted by his master, cannot be ordained (Ap. Can. LXXXII).

One who has lapsed cannot be ordained (Nic. X); but those who have been steadfast throughout the persecutions, though forced to seem otherwise, may be ordained (Anc. III).

A Neophyte must not be ordained (Laod. III); but former profession of heathenism is not, in itself, a disqualification for ordination (Anc. XII).

No Clergyman may be ordained without a charge (Chal. VI).

—II. Of the Ordination of the Minor Clergy.—

A Minor Clergyman is to be ordained by a Bishop (Ap. Can. II); Readers, Sub-deacons, and Exorcists may be ordained by a Chorepiscopus (Ant. X).

A Minor Clergyman is not to be ordained in another Church, after leaving his own (Nic. XVI).

—III. Of their Duties.—

The Minor Clergy are to partake, when the Oblation is made, or to give reasons for refusing (Ap. Can. VIII); they are to fast during Lent, and on Wednesdays and Fridays, unless prevented by bodily weakness (Ap. Can. LXIX).

The Minor Clergy of Poorhouses, Monasteries, and Martyries, are to remain subject to the Bishop of the Parish (Chal. VIII).

—IV.—Of their Rights and Privileges.—

The Minor Clergy are to receive a share of offerings not made at the Altar (Ap. Can. IV); when in need, they are to be supplied with necessaries (Ap. Can. LIX).

CLERGY, MINOR.—IV. Of their Rights and Privileges.—*Continued.*

If displaced by heretics or schismatics, they are to be restored (Eph. III).

They owe no obedience to a Bishop convicted of anything contrary to religion or morals (Ap. Can. XXXI).

They have a right of appeal to the Provincial Synod against a sentence of their Bishop (Ant. VI, XX).

A Minor Clergyman, having a complaint against another Clergyman, may lay it before his Bishop; or if the complaint be against a Bishop, he may lay it before the Provincial Synod (Chal. IX); if he have a complaint against a Metropolitan, he may lay it before the Exarch of the Diocese or the Throne of Constantinople (Chal. IX, XVII).

A Minor Clergyman, who has been steadfast throughout the persecutions, though forced to seem otherwise, is entitled to all his former privileges (Anc. III).

—V. Things Forbidden to the Minor Clergy.—

The Minor Clergy are forbidden to read false and heretical books in Church, as Scripture (Ap. Can. LX); or to compose, or use, any other than the Nicene Creed (Eph. VII, Chal. Encyc.); or to join in prayer with heretics (Laod. XXXIII); or to attend the Cemeteries or Martyries of heretics (Laod. IX); or to marry their children to heretics (Laod. X, XXXI); or to observe, or receive gifts from, festivals of heretics (Laod. XXXVII); or to enter a synagogue of Jews or heretics for prayer (Ap. Can. LXIV); or to observe, or receive gifts from, Jewish fasts or festivals (Ap. Can. LXX, Laod. XXXVII); or to receive unleavened bread from the Jews (Laod. XXXVIII); or to feast with the heathen (Laod. XXXIX); or to join in prayer with schismatics (Ant. II, Laod. XXXIII); or to adhere to the maintainers of conventicles (Ap. Can. XXXI).

They are forbidden to submit to the jurisdiction of Nestorius or his partisans (Eph. III).

They are forbidden to communicate with the excommunicated (Ap. Can. X, Ant. II); or with a Clergyman who is deposed for celebrating Easter before the Vernal Equinox (Ant. I); or with a Bishop who has obtained his Church through secular rulers (Ap. Can. XXX); or with a Clergyman who, after deposition, meddles with his former ministry (Ant. IV); or to join in prayer with a deposed Clergyman (Ap. Can. XI).

They are forbidden to remove from their own Parishes (Nic. XVI, Chal. V, XX), without the Bishop's consent (Ap.

CLERGY, MINOR.—V. THINGS FORBIDDEN.—*Continued.*

Can. XV, Ant. III); or unless driven by necessity from their own country (Chal. XX); and if they do so, they cannot officiate (Ap. Can. XV, Nic. XV, XVI); nor be received by another Church (Nic. XVI); they are forbidden to be enrolled in two Churches (Chal. X); and if lawfully transferred to another Church, they are forbidden to meddle with the affairs of their former ministry (Chal. X).

None of the Clergy, except Readers and Singers, may marry after ordination (Ap. Can. XXVI); the Clergy are forbidden to abstain from marriage, except for discipline (Ap. Can. LI); or to have any women dwelling with them, except such relations or other persons as are beyond suspicion (Nic. III); or to wash in a bath with women (Laod. XXX.)

They are forbidden to carry off wax or oil from the Church (Ap. Can. LXXII); or to appropriate consecrated vessels to private purposes (Ap. Can. LXXIII).

They are forbidden to seize their Bishop's property on his death (Chal. XXII).

They are forbidden to transact worldly business, unless called by law to the guardianship of minors (Chal. III); or to accept military or civil office (Chal. VII); or to meddle with ecclesiastical business, except by direction of the Bishop (Chal. III); or to become security (Ap. Can. XX); or to exact usury (Nic. XVII, Laod. IV).

They are forbidden to officiate in another City, without letters commendatory (Chal. XIII); or to travel without the Bishop's consent (Laod. XLI); or without Letters Canonical (Laod. XLII); or to address the Emperor, without the consent of the Metropolitan and Provincial Bishops (Ant. XI).

They are forbidden to commit Simony, or negotiate simoniacal contracts (Chal. II).

They are forbidden to castrate themselves (Ap. Can. XXIII, Nic. I).

They are forbidden to abstain from flesh or wine, except for discipline (Ap. Can. LI); they are forbidden to eat flesh with the blood, or of animals which have been slain by beasts, or have died a natural death (Ap. Can. LXIII); or to fast on Sunday, or on any Sabbath, except Easter Even (Ap. Can. LXVI); or to join in forming drinking clubs (Laod. LV); or to eat in a tavern, except on a journey (Ap. Can. LIV); or to enter a tavern (Laod. XXIV).

If invited to a Lovefeast, they are forbidden to take away their portions (Laod. XXVII).

CLERGY, MINOR.—V. THINGS FORBIDDEN.—*Continued.*

They are forbidden to attend plays at weddings and banquets (Laod. LIV).

They are forbidden to insult a Bishop (Ap. Can. LV); or a Priest, or Deacon (Ap. Can. LVI); or the Emperor, or a Magistrate (Ap. Can. LXXXIV); or to mock the infirm (Ap. Can. LVII).

They are forbidden to sit in the presence of a Deacon, without his permission (Laod. XX).

They are forbidden to practise magic, enchantment, mathematics, or astrology, or to make or wear phylacteries (Laod. XXXVI).

If a Minor Clergyman have a complaint against another Clergyman, he is forbidden to forsake his own Bishop and run to secular courts (Chal. IX).

—VI. OF THE TRIAL OF THE MINOR CLERGY.—

Accusers of a Clergyman are to be examined as to character (Chal. XXI).

A Minor Clergyman cannot be convicted of any offence on the evidence of those who are themselves under accusation (Const. VI).

—VII. FOR THE PENALTIES TO BE INFLICTED ON THE MINOR CLERGY, vid. *Suspension of the Minor Clergy, Deposition of the Minor Clergy, Excommunication, and Anathema.*

—VIII. GENERAL REGULATIONS AS TO THE MINOR CLERGY.—

A Minor Clergyman, if suspended, or deposed, for leaving his Parish, cannot be received as a Clergyman (Ap. Can. XVI, Ant. III); nor, if suspended, or excommunicated, in one City, can he be received in another, without letters commendatory (Ap. Can. XII); if excommunicated by his Bishop, he cannot be restored by another Bishop (Nic. V); nor can he be received by others, unless restored by his Bishop, or unless the sentence is reversed by a Synod (Ant. VI).

The restoration of deposed Clergymen by Nestorius or his followers, is declared void (Eph. V).

Heretics cannot be employed as Clergymen in the Catholic Church (Ap. Can. XLV).

A Clergyman who adheres to the maintainers of conventicles, is to be admonished three times, by his Bishop, before punishment (Ap. Can. XXXI).

A Clergyman who is excommunicated, cannot bring accusations against a Bishop (Const. VI); a Minor Clergyman, bringing accusations against a Clergyman, is to be examined as to character (Chal. XXI).

CLERGY, MINOR.—VIII. GENERAL REGULATIONS AS TO THE MINOR CLERGY.—*Continued.*

A Clergyman deposed for celebrating Easter before the Vernal Equinox, is to be deprived of the external honour due to the Clergy (Ant. I).

A Clergyman going to Constantinople, and raising disturbances there, is to be expelled from the City (Chal. XXIII).

If the wife of a Clergyman commit adultery, he must divorce her, or desist from his ministry (Neo-Cæs. VIII).

Minor Clergy of the Cathari, reconciled to the Catholic Church, retain their orders, and their rank amongst other reconciled Clergy (Nic. VIII).

Minor Clergy of the Paulianists, reconciled to the Catholic Church, are, if worthy, to be ordained, and, if unworthy, to be deposed (Nic. XIX).

Minor Clergy of the Phrygians, seeking reconciliation to the Catholic Church, are to be instructed and baptized before admission (Laod. VIII).

Minor Clergy ordained by Maximus the Cynic, are declared not to be Clergymen (Const. IV).

CLERGY.—Denial of one's Clergy is punishable by deposition (Ap. Can. LXII).

Bishops and Priests are forbidden to neglect their Clergy (Ap. Can. LVIII).

Every Church that has a Bishop, is to have also a Steward amongst its Clergy (Chal. XXVI).

CLINIC BAPTISM.—Clinic Baptism is generally a disqualification for Priests' orders (Neo-Cæs. XII); those who have received clinic Baptism, if afterwards restored to health, must learn the Creed by heart (Laod. XLVII).

CLOAK.—Anathema on those who wear a rough cloak, and despise persons who use the *berus*, and other customary dress (Gang. XII).

CLOTHING.—Vid. *Dress.*

CLUBS.—Communicants of every class are forbidden to join in forming clubs for drinking entertainments (Laod. LV).

CLUSTERS OF GRAPES.—See *Grapes.*

COHABITATION, CLANDESTINE.—A digamist, who has been guilty of clandestine cohabitation, cannot be readmitted to communion under Laod. I.

COMMEMORATION.—Anathema on those who despise the commemorations of the Martyrs (Gang. XX); in Lent, commemorations of the Martyrs are to be made only on Sabbaths and

COMMEMORATION—*Continued.*

Sundays (Laod. LI); the commemoration of Martyrs of heretics is forbidden to Christians (Laod. XXXIV).

COMMENDATORY LETTERS.—Vid. *Letters.*

COMMUNICANTS.—Vid. *Laymen.*

In Divine Service, the prayers for full communicants are to follow the prayers for penitents (Laod. XIX).

COMMUNION, HOLY.—I. OF FULL COMMUNICANTS.—

Communicants are to remain in Church for Communion, as well as for the reading of Scripture (Ap. Can. IX, Ant. II).

—II. OF THE READMISSION OF OFFENDERS TO COMMUNION.—

Communion is permitted to those who remained steadfast throughout the persecutions, though forced to appear otherwise (Anc. III).

Penitents are to be admitted to communion after penance proportioned to the nature of their offences (Laod. II); this rule is applied in the case of persons who are guilty of bestial lusts (Anc. XVI).

The lapsed may be readmitted to communion after a term of penance varying, according to circumstances, from two to thirteen years (Nic. XI, XII, XIV, Anc. IV, V, VI, VII, VIII, IX). A lapsed Priest, readmitted to communion, is not permitted to officiate (Anc. I); nor a lapsed Deacon, unless by indulgence of his Bishop (Anc. II).

Digamists may be admitted to communion (Nic. VIII), after a short period of prayer and fasting (Laod. I); those who contract many marriages may be readmitted to communion after a term of penance which is mentioned as being well known (Neo-Cæs. III).

An adulterer or an adulteress may be readmitted to communion after seven years of penance (Anc. XX); women causing, or preparing drugs for, abortion, after ten years (Anc. XXI); involuntary homicides, after five years (Anc. XXIII); and diviners, sorcerers, and astrologers, after five years (Anc. XXIV).

A certain case of seduction is mentioned as having entailed ten years of penance on the parties before they were received as co-standers (Anc. XXV).

Communion is not in any case to be refused to the dying, but it must not be administered to them until after examination (Nic. XIII); the first part of this rule is applied to married men, over fifty years of age, who are guilty of bestial lusts (Anc. XVI); and to wilful murderers (Anc. XXII); and to a woman who has married two brothers (Neo-Cæs. II);

COMMUNION.—II. Of the Readmission of Offenders to Communion.—*Continued.*

but if any of the lapsed have been readmitted to Communion at the point of death, this gives them no privilege in case of their recovery (Anc. VI).

Communion in prayers only, and without the Oblation, is the last degree of penance (Nic. XI, XII, XIII, Anc. IV, V, VI, VIII, IX, XVI, XXIV).

—III. Of the Admission of Heretics to Communion.—

The Cathari may be admitted to Communion, upon their promising to observe the decrees and discipline of the Catholic Church (Nic. VIII); they are admitted by Chrism (Const. VII); Paulianists, by Baptism (Nic. XIX); Arians, Macedonians, Sabbatians, Quartodecimans, and Apollinarians, by Chrism, after renouncing and anathematizing all heresies (Const. VII); Eunomians, Phrygians, Sabellians, and all other heretics, are received as heathen, and are exorcised, instructed, and baptized (Const. VII); Novatians (Cathari), Photinians, and Quartodecimans are admitted by Chrism after having renounced all heresies, and having learned the Symbols of the Faith (Laod. VII); Phrygians are to be instructed and baptized before admission (Laod. VIII).

—IV. General Regulations.—

Communion is not to be granted to foreign Clergymen without examination, nor if the result of such examination should be unsatisfactory (Ap. Can. XXXIII); communion is not to be granted to one possessed of a devil (Ap. Can. LXXIX).

Communion is to follow Baptism and Chrism (Laod. XLVIII).

Communion with the excommunicated is forbidden (Ap. Can. X, Ant. II).

None but the Priesthood may communicate at the Altar (Laod. XIX).

Vid. also *Eucharist*, *Oblation*, *Suspension from Communion*, and *Lay Communion*.

COMPLAINT.—A complaint of a personal wrong done by a Bishop, may be brought by a person of any religion (Const. VI).

COMPULSION.—The lapsed, who have fallen without compulsion, are to fulfil twelve years of penance (Nic. XI).

CONCUBINE.—One who, after Baptism, has had a concubine, cannot be ordained (Ap. Can. XVII).

CONCUPISCENCE.—Concupiscence is not to be regarded as actual sin (Neo-Cæs. IV).

CONFESSION.—A crime discovered by confession, is a disqualification for ordination as Priest (Nic. IX). A Priest who makes confession of bodily sin, is forbidden to offer the Oblation (Neo-Cæs. IX).

CONFIRMATION.—Vid. *Chrism.*

Of Canons and Creed.—Vid. *Canon, Creed.*

CONFUSION.—Confusion in the Church is forbidden (Ap. Can. IX, Ant. II).

CONGREGATION.—Priests are forbidden to gather separate congregations (Ap. Can. XXXI, Ant. V); also Deacons (Ant. V).

CONSANGUINITY.—For regulations as to marriages within the prohibited degrees of consanguinity, vid. *Marriage.*

CONSECRATION.—Consecrated vessels are forbidden to be appropriated to private purposes (Ap. Can. LXXIII); the Subdeacons are forbidden to touch them (Laod. XXI).

Monasteries, once consecrated, are forbidden to be used as secular dwellings (Chal. XXIV).

CONSENT.—Neither the Metropolitan, nor the Provincial Bishops of a Province, may act alone without the concurrent consent of both (Ap. Can. XXXIV, Ant. IX); a Clergyman cannot address the Emperor, without the consent of the Metropolitan and Provincial Bishops (Ant. XI); Bishops are to be elected with the consent of the Metropolitan and a majority of the Provincial Bishops of the Province (Nic. IV, VI, Ant. XIX).

Priests and Deacons are forbidden to act without the consent of their Bishop (Ap. Can. XXXIX, Laod. LVII); a Bishop cannot act beyond his own jurisdiction, without the consent of the Bishop having jurisdiction (Ap. Can. XXXV). The consent of the Bishop is required to the appointment of referees in disputes between Clergymen (Chal. IX); also to the establishment of a Monastery or Oratory (Chal. IV, XXIV); also to the performance of ecclesiastical acts (Gang. VI); also to the appropriation of Fruits offered at the Church (Gang., VII, VIII). Chorepiscopi are forbidden to ordain Priests and Deacons beyond their own districts, without the Bishop's consent (Anc. XIII). Clergymen are forbidden to travel without the Bishop's consent (Laod. XLI). Bishops appointed in country villages, itinerant visitors and Priests, are forbidden to act without the consent of the Bishop of the City (Laod. LVII).

Bishops must manage the revenues of the Church with the consent of their Priests and Deacons (Ant. XXV).

CONSENT—*Continued.*

The consent of the master must be obtained, before a slave can be ordained (Ap. Can. LXXXII); or received as a Monk (Chal. IV).

CONSPIRACY.—Clergymen and Monks, conspiring against their Bishop and fellow Clergymen, are to be deposed (Chal. XVIII).

CONSTANTINOPLE.—The Canons of Constantinople are confirmed (Chal. I); the Third Canon is expressly confirmed (Chal. XXVIII).

The Bishop of Constantinople is to rank next after the Bishop of Rome (Const. III); this precedence is declared, by the Council of Chalcedon, to have been rightly conceded by the Fathers of Constantinople, because that City is a seat of government and an imperial residence (Chal. XXVIII); the Bishop of Constantinople may hear accusations brought against any Metropolitan (Chal. IX, XVII); he is to ordain the Metropolitans of Pontus, Asia, and Thrace (Chal. XXVIII).

The disturbances in Constantinople, occasioned by Maximus the Cynic, are mentioned (Const. IV); Clergymen and Monks going to Constantinople and raising disturbances there, are to be expelled from the City (Chal. XXIII).

For regulations as to the creed of Nicæa and Constantinople, see *Creed.*

CONTINENCE.—Those who observe continence from abhorrence of marriage are anathematized (Gang. IX); continence for its own sake is commended (Gang. IX, XXI).

CONTINUOUS POSSESSION.—Vid. *Uninterrupted Possession.*

CONTRACTS.—The negotiators of simoniacal contracts, are, if Clergymen, to be deposed; and, if laymen or Monks, to be anathematized (Chal. II).

Clergymen and Monks are forbidden to make contracts relating to secular affairs (Chal. III).

CONVENTICLES.—MAINTAINING OF.—Vid. *Schism.*

CONVERT.—One who is recently converted from heathenism, is not to be made a Bishop (Ap. Can. LXXX, Nic. II); nor a Priest (Nic. II); nor a Clergyman of any rank (Laod. III); but former profession of heathenism is not in itself a disqualification for ordination (Anc. XI).

A converted heathen, Jew, or heretic, may marry the child of a Reader or Singer (Chal, XIV); a converted heretic may marry the child of a Communicant (Laod. XXXI).

CO-STANDERS.—The lapsed, and other offenders, after passing a certain time, first as Hearers, and secondly as Prostrators, are to be received as Communicants in Prayers, or Co-standers, that being the last degree of Penance (Nic. XI, XII, XIII, Anc. IV, V, VI, VIII, IX, XVI, XXIV, XXV).

COUNCIL.—See *Synod.*

COUNTRY PRIESTS are forbidden to serve in a City, unless in the absence of the Bishop and City Priests (Neo-Cæs. XIII); they are forbidden to send Letters Canonical except to the neighbouring Bishops (Ant. VIII).

DISTRICTS are not to have independent Bishops; and such Bishops, if already appointed, are not to act without the consent of the City Bishop (Laod. LVII).

COURTS.—Charges against a Bishop cannot be brought before the secular courts (Const. VI); nor can disputes between Clergymen (Chal. IX).

CREED.—The Creed of Nicæa is confirmed (Const. I); the Nicene and Constantinopolitan Creed is confirmed by Chal. Encyc.; it is to be the only Declaration of Faith demanded of converts from heathenism, Judaism, or heresy; and the composition of any other Creed is stringently forbidden (Eph. VII, Chal. Encyc.); it is to be recited before Baptism (Laod. XLVI); it is to be learned by heart, by those who have received Clinic Baptism, and are afterwards restored to health (Laod. XLVII; and certain classes of heretics are required to learn the Symbols of the Faith before reconciliation to the Catholic Church (Laod. VII).

CRIME.—Conviction of crime is a disqualification for ordination (Ap. Can. LXI); confession of crime is a disqualification for ordination as Priest (Nic. IX).

CUP.—Lapsed Deacons, who have been restored, are forbidden to bring in the Cup (Anc. II); country Priests are forbidden to offer the Cup in a City Church, unless in the absence of the Bishop and City Priests (Neo-Cæs. XIII); a Sub-deacon is not permitted to bless the Cup (Laod. XXV).

CUSTOM.—The prerogatives of all Churches are to be retained according to ancient custom (Nic. VI); ancient custom is to be observed and to regulate Diocesan rights (Eph. VIII); Churches in heathen nations are to be governed according to ancient custom (Const. II).

The ancient customs are to continue in Egypt, Libya, and Pentapolis (Nic. VI); and in the election of the Metropolitans of Pontus, Asia, and Thrace (Chal. XXVIII); ancient custom entitles the Bishop of Jerusalem to rank next his

CUSTOM—*Continued.*

Metropolitan (Nic. VII); the ancient custom of Egypt, by which the Bishops were bound not to sign even acts which they approved, without the consent of their Metropolitan, was respected in practice at Chalcedon (Chal. XXX).

The custom of the removal of Clergy is declared uncanonical (Nic. XV).

Those who follow the customs of the heathen are to be received to Communion after five years of Penance (Anc. XXIV).

CYNIC, MAXIMUS THE—Ordinations by Maximus the Cynic, and also his own ordination as Bishop, are declared void (Const. IV).

CYPRUS.—The Bishops of Cyprus are not within the jurisdiction of the Bishop of Antioch (Eph. VIII).

DANCES.—Communicants are forbidden to join in wanton dances at weddings (Laod. LIII).

DANGER.—Personal danger is an extenuating circumstance in case of lapse (Nic. XI).

DEACON.—I. Of the Disqualifications for the Office of a Deacon.—

A person, to be ordained Deacon, must not, after Baptism, have been twice married, nor have had a concubine (Ap. Can. XVII); he must not have married a widow, a divorced woman, a harlot, a slave, or an actress (Ap. Can. XVIII); he must not have married two sisters, or a niece (Ap. Can. XIX).

He must not have committed adultery, fornication, or any other forbidden act (Ap. Can. LXI); one whose wife has committed adultery cannot be ordained (Neo-Cæs. VIII);

He must not have castrated himself (Ap. Can. XXII, Nic. I); but if castrated by force, or for surgical purposes, he may be ordained; and if so castrated after Ordination, he may remain amongst the Clergy (Nic. I).

He must not be possessed of a devil (Ap. Can. LXXIX); but if dispossessed, and worthy, he may be ordained (Ap. Can. LXXIX).

A slave cannot be ordained, unless manumitted by his master (Ap. Can. LXXXII).

One who has lapsed, cannot be ordained (Nic. X); and if he lapse after ordination, and is subsequently restored, he cannot officiate, except by indulgence of the Bishop (Anc. II); but those who have been steadfast throughout the persecutions, though forced to seem otherwise, may be ordained (Anc. III).

DEACON.—I. OF THE DISQUALIFICATIONS FOR THE OFFICE OF A DEACON.—*Continued.*

A neophyte must not be made a Deacon (Laod. III); but former profession of heathenism is not in itself a disqualification for a Deacon's Orders (Anc. XII).

A Deacon is not to be ordained without a charge (Chal. VI).

—II. OF THE ELECTION OF A DEACON.—

A Deacon is not to be elected by the multitude (Laod. XIII).

—III. OF THE ORDINATION OF A DEACON.—

A Deacon is to be ordained by a Bishop (Ap. Can. II); he is to be ordained by the Bishop of the Parish (Ant. IX); he is not to be ordained by a Chorepiscopus, beyond his own Parish, without the Bishop's consent (Anc. XIII); he is not to be ordained by a Chorepiscopus without the Bishop (Ant. X); he is not to be ordained by a Bishop beyond his jurisdiction (Ant. XXII).

He is not to be ordained in another Church, after leaving his own (Nic. XVI).

—IV. OF THE DUTIES OF A DEACON.—

A Deacon is to partake, when the Oblation is made, or to give reasons for refusing (Ap. Can. VIII); he is to receive the Eucharist from a Bishop or Priest, not to administer to either (Nic. XVIII).

He is to act as his Bishop's Almoner (Ap. Can. XLI); and to supply necessaries to Clergy in need (Ap. Can. LIX); and to join with the Bishop in the administration of Church Funds (Ant. XXV).

He is to fast during Lent, and on Wednesdays and Fridays, unless prevented by bodily weakness (Ap. Can. LXIX).

He is his Bishop's helper, and the inferior of the Priest (Nic. XVIII); the Deacons of Poorhouses, Monasteries, and Martyries, are to remain subject to their Bishop (Chal. VIII).

—V. OF THE PRIVILEGES OF A DEACON.—

A Deacon is to receive his share of Offerings, not made at the Altar (Ap. Can. IV); when in need, he is to be supplied with necessaries (Ap. Can. LIX).

Clergymen are forbidden to insult a Deacon (Ap. Can. LVI); Sub deacons, and other Minor Clergy, are forbidden to sit in the presence of a Deacon, without his permission (Laod. XX).

DEACON.—V. Of the Privileges of a Deacon.—*Continued.*

A Deacon, who has declared, at his ordination, that he cannot contain, may marry (Anc. X).

A Deacon has the right of appeal to a Provincial Synod, against a sentence of his Bishop (Nic. V, Ant. VI, XII, XX).

A Deacon, having a complaint against another Clergyman, may lay it before his Bishop, and if he have a complaint against a Bishop, he may lay it before the Provincial Synod (Chal. IX); if he have a complaint against a Metropolitan, he may lay it before the Exarch of the Diocese, or the Throne of Constantinople (Chal. IX, XVII).

A Deacon displaced by heretics or schismatics, is to be restored (Eph. III).

A Deacon owes no obedience to a Bishop convicted of anything contrary to religion or morals (Ap. Can. XXXI).

A Deacon who has been steadfast throughout the persecutions, though forced to seem otherwise, is entitled to all his former privileges (Anc. III).

Deacons are to be informed, by their Bishops, which is, and which is not Church property (Ant. XXIV).

A Deacon may communicate at the Altar (Laod. XIX).

—VI. Things Forbidden to a Deacon.—

A Deacon is forbidden to divorce his wife, under pretext of religion (Ap. Can. V); or to marry after ordination (Ap. Can. XXVI); unless, when ordained, he has declared that he cannot contain (Anc. X); he is forbidden to abstain from marriage, except for discipline (Ap. Can. LI); or to have any woman dwelling with him, except such relations, or other persons, as are beyond suspicion (Nic. III); or to wash in a bath with women (Laod. XXX).

He is forbidden to engage in worldly business (Ap. Can. VI); unless called by law to the guardianship of minors (Chal. III); he is forbidden to meddle with ecclesiastical business, except by direction of his Bishop (Chal. III); he is forbidden to serve in the army (Ap. Can. LXXXIII); or to accept military or civil office (Chal. VII); he is forbidden to become security (Ap. Can XX); or to exact usury (Ap. Can. XLIV, Nic. XVII, Laod. IV).

He is forbidden to read false and heretical books in Church, as Scripture (Ap. Can. LX); or to compose, or use, any other than the Nicene Creed (Eph. VII, Chal. Encyc.); or to join in prayer with heretics (Ap. Can. XLV, Laod. XXXIII); or to employ them as Clergymen (Ap. Can. XLV); or to admit the Baptism or Sacrifice of heretics (Ap. Can.

DEACON.—VI. THINGS FORBIDDEN TO A DEACON.—*Continued.*

XLVI); or to receive the Eulogiæ of heretics (Laod. XXXII); or to attend the Cemeteries or Martyries of heretics (Laod. IX); or to marry his children to heretics (Laod. X, XXXI); or to observe, or receive gifts from, festivals of heretics (Laod. XXXVII); or to enter a synagogue of Jews or heretics, for prayer (Ap. Can. LXIV); or to celebrate Easter before the Vernal Equinox, as the Jews do (Ap. Can. VII, Nic. Encyc., Ant. I); or to observe, or receive gifts from, Jewish fasts or festivals (Ap. Can. LXX, Laod. XXXVII); or to receive unleavened bread from the Jews (Ap. Can. LXX, Laod. XXXVIII); or to feast with the heathen (Laod. XXXIX); or to join in prayer with schismatics (Ant. II, Laod. XXXIII); or to adhere to the maintainers of conventicles (Ap. Can. XXXI).

He is forbidden to submit to the jurisdiction of Nestorius or his partisans (Eph. III).

He is forbidden to gather a separate congregation, and raise another Altar (Ap. Can. XXXI, Ant. V).

He is forbidden to communicate with the excommunicated (Ap. Can. X, Ant. II); or with a Bishop who has obtained his Church through secular rulers (Ap. Can. XXX); or with a Clergyman who is deposed for celebrating Easter before the Vernal Equinox (Ant. I); or with a Clergyman who, after deposition, meddles with his former ministry (Ant. IV); or to join in prayer with a deposed Clergyman (Ap. Can. XI).

He is forbidden to remove from his own Parish (Nic. XV, Chal. V, XX); without his Bishop's consent (Ap. Can. XV, Ant. III); or unless he is driven by necessity from his own country (Chal. XX); and if he do so, he cannot act officially (Ap. Can. XV, Nic. XV, XVI, Ant. III); nor be received by another Church (Nic. XVI); he is forbidden to be enrolled in two Churches; and if lawfully transferred to another Church, he is forbidden to meddle with the affairs of his former ministry (Chal. X).

He is forbidden to act without the consent of his Bishop (Ap. Can. XXXIX); or to address the Emperor, without the consent of the Metropolitan and Provincial Bishops (Ant. XI); or to officiate in another City, without Letters Commendatory from his own Bishop (Chal. XIII); or to travel without his Bishop's consent (Laod. XLI); or without Letters Canonical (Laod. XLII).

He is forbidden to carry off wax or oil from the Church (Ap. Can. LXXII); or to appropriate consecrated vessels to private purposes (Ap. Can. LXXIII).

DEACON.—VI. Things Forbidden to a Deacon.—*Continued.*

He is forbidden to seize his Bishop's property, on his death (Chal. XXII).

He is forbidden to receive the Eucharist before the Bishop or Priest, or to administer It to a Priest; and he has no right to offer at all (Nic. XVIII).

If deposed, he is forbidden to touch his former ministry (Ap. Can. XXVIII, Ant. IV).

He is forbidden to commit simony (Ap. Can. XXIX, Chal. II); or to negotiate simoniacal contracts (Chal. II).

He is forbidden to receive a second ordination, unless the first was void (Ap. Can. LXVIII).

He is forbidden to gather a separate congregation, and raise another Altar (Ap. Can. XXXI).

He is forbidden to abstain from flesh or wine, except for discipline (Ap. Can. LI); especially on festival days (Ap. Can. LIII); but after tasting flesh once, he may abstain if he wishes (Anc. XIV); he is forbidden to eat flesh with the blood, or of animals which have been slain by beasts, or have died a natural death (Ap. Can. LXIII); or to fast on Sunday, or on any Sabbath except Easter Even (Ap. Can. LXVI); or to join in forming drinking clubs (Laod. LV); or to eat in a tavern, except on a journey (Ap. Can. LIV); or to enter a tavern (Laod. XXIV).

If invited to a Lovefeast, he is forbidden to take away his portion (Laod. XXVII); he is forbidden to attend plays at weddings and banquets (Laod. LIV).

He is forbidden to castrate himself (Ap. Can. XXIII, Nic. I).

He is forbidden to strike backsliders or unbelievers (Ap. Can. XXVII).

He is forbidden to insult a Bishop (Ap. Can. LV); or a Priest, or Deacon (Ap. Can. LVI); or the Emperor, or a magistrate (Ap. Can. LXXXIV); or to mock the infirm (Ap. Can. LVII).

He is forbidden to deny his office (Ap. Can. LXII).

He is forbidden to sit amongst the Priests (Nic. XVIII); or to sit in the presence of a Priest, without his permission (Laod. XX).

He is forbidden to practice magic, enchantment, mathematics, or astrology, or to make, or wear, phylacteries (Laod. XXXVI).

If he have a complaint against another Clergyman, he is forbidden to forsake his own Bishop, and run to secular courts (Chal. IX).

DEACON.—VII. Of the Trial of a Deacon.—

A Deacon cannot be convicted of any offence on the evidence of those who are themselves under accusation (Const. VI); his accusers are to be examined as to character (Chal. XXI).

A Deacon appealing to the Emperor, instead of to a Synod, against a sentence of deposition, cannot be restored, nor can his cause be reheard, by a Synod (Ant. XII).

—VIII. Penalties to be Inflicted on a Deacon.—Vid. *Suspension of a Deacon*, *Deposition of a Deacon*, *Excommunication*, and *Anathema*.

—IX. General Regulations as to a Deacon.—

A Deacon who is suspended or excommunicated, by his Bishop, cannot be restored by any other Bishop (Ap. Can. XXXII, Nic. V), unless the Bishop who suspended him should die (Ap. Can. XXXII); nor can he be received by others, unless restored by his Bishop, or unless the sentence is reversed by a Synod (Ant. VI); nor if suspended or excommunicated in one City, can he be received in another, without Letters Commendatory (Ap. Can. XII); nor if suspended or deposed, for leaving his own Parish, can he be received as a Clergyman (Ap. Can. XVI, Ant. III).

A Deacon is not to be received from abroad, without Commendatory Letters, nor without examination, even if he bring them (Ap. Can. XXXIII).

A heretic cannot be employed as a Deacon in the Catholic Church (Ap. Can. XLV).

A Deacon who is guilty of maintaining conventicles, is to be admonished three times, by his Bishop, before punishment (Ap. Can. XXXI, Ant. V).

The restoration, by Nestorius or his followers, of a deposed Deacon, is declared void (Eph. V).

An excommunicated Deacon cannot bring accusations against a Bishop (Const. VI); a Deacon bringing charges against a Clergyman, is to be examined as to character (Chal. XXI).

A lapsed Deacon,. if restored, is entitled to his former honours, but he cannot officiate, except by indulgence of his Bishop (Anc. II).

A Deacon going to Constantinople, and causing disturbances there, is to be expelled from the City (Chal. XXIII).

A Deacon deposed for celebrating Easter before the Vernal Equinox, is to be deprived of the external honour due to the Priesthood (Ant. I).

DEACON.—IX. GENERAL REGULATIONS.—*Continued.*

A Deacon who abstains from flesh, must taste it at least once (Anc. XIV).

A Deacon who commits bodily sin, is to rank as a Subdeacon (Neo-Cæs. X).

If the wife of a Deacon commit adultery, he must divorce her, or desist from his ministry (Neo-Cæs. VIII).

There should be seven Deacons in a City, of whatever size it may be (Neo-Cæs. XV).

A Deacon of the Cathari, reconciled to the Catholic Church, retains his orders, and his rank amongst other reconciled Clergymen (Nic. VIII).

A Deacon of the Paulianists, reconciled to the Catholic Church, is, if worthy, to be ordained, and if unworthy, to be deposed (Nic. XIX).

A Deacon ordained by Maximus the Cynic, is declared not to be a Clergyman (Const. IV).

A Deacon of the Phrygians, seeking reconciliation to the Catholic Church, is to be instructed and baptized, before admission (Laod. VIII).

DEACONESS.—A Deaconess is not to be ordained under forty years of age, nor without examination; and she is forbidden to marry (Chal. XV).

A Deaconess of the Paulianists, reconciled to the Catholic Church, is, if worthy, to be ordained; but Paulianist Deaconesses, who appear in the habit of that order, are to be numbered among the laity (Nic. XIX).

DEAF.—Clergymen and laymen are forbidden to mock the deaf (Ap. Can. LVII).

DEAFNESS.—Total deafness is a disqualification for the Episcopate (Ap. Can. LXXVII).

DEBTORS.—Clergymen are forbidden to exact usury from debtors (Ap. Can. XLIV, Nic. XVII, Laod. IV).

DECEASED WIFE'S SISTER.—Vid. *Sister-in-Law.*
HUSBAND'S BROTHER.—Vid. *Sister-in-Law.*

DECREES.—The Cathari must promise to obey the Decrees of the Catholic Church, before being received into it (Nic. VIII).

DEDICATED VIRGIN.—Dedicated Virgins are forbidden to marry (Chal. XVI); if they commit fornication, they are to fulfil the penance of digamists (Anc. XIX).

DEFENCE.—A deposed Clergyman, who meddles with his former ministry, is not allowed to make a new defence before the Synod (Ant. IV); nor can a Clergyman who appeals to the

DEFENCE—*Continued.*

Emperor, instead of to a Synod, make any further defence before the Synod (Ant. XII); a Bishop, who is deposed by the unanimous sentence of his Provincial Synod, cannot make any further defence (Ant. XV); nor a Priest or Deacon, who is deposed for leaving his Parish (Ant. III); or for the contumacious maintaining of conventicles (Ant. V).

DEGRADATION.—The degradation of a Bishop to the rank of a Priest, is declared to be sacrilege (Chal. XXIX).

DEGREES OF PENANCE.—See *Penance.*

DELAY.—Delay by a Metropolitan, in the ordination of a Bishop, is condemned (Chal. XXV).

DEPOSED CLERGYMAN.—Clergymen are forbidden to join in prayer with a deposed Clergyman (Ap. Can. XI); Bishops are forbidden to receive Clergymen who are deposed for leaving their own Parishes (Ap. Can. XVI, Ant. III).

A deposed Bishop, Priest, or Deacon, is forbidden to touch his former ministry (Ap. Can. XXVIII, Ant. IV).

A deposed Clergyman cannot be restored by Nestorius or his partisans (Eph. V).

A deposed Clergyman, who appeals to the Emperor, instead of to a Synod, cannot be restored, nor can his cause be reheard, by a Synod (Ant. XII).

DEPOSITION.—OF A METROPOLITAN.—

The penalty of deposition is pronounced against a Metropolitan, who joins the schismatical assembly of Bishops at Ephesus, or who falls into the heresies of Nestorius and Celestius (Eph. Encyc. and Can. I); or who unnecessarily delays the ordination of a Bishop (Chal. XXV).

—OF A BISHOP.—

The penalty of deposition is pronounced against a Bishop who offers anything at the Altar, except new ears of grain and clusters of grapes (Ap. Can. III).

Or who engages in worldly business (Ap. Can. VI, LXXXI, Chal. III); or serves in the army (Ap. Can. LXXXIII); or becomes security (Ap. Can. XX); or exacts usury (Ap. Can. XLIV, Nic. XVII).

Or who celebrates Easter before the Vernal Equinox, as the Jews do (Ap. Can. VII, Ant. I); or professes the heresies of Nestorius and Celestius (Eph. Encyc., Can. II, Can. VII), or of Theodore of Mopsuestia (Eph. VII); or reads heretical and spurious books in Church, as Scripture (Ap. Can. LX); or composes, or uses, any other than the Nicene Creed (Eph. VII, Chal. Encyc.); or enters a synagogue of Jews or here-

DEPOSITION.—Of a Bishop.—*Continued.*

tics to pray (Ap. Can. LXIV); or observes or receives gifts from Jewish fasts or festivals (Ap. Can. LXX); or admits the Baptism or Sacrifice of heretics (Ap. Can. XLVI); or employs them as Clergymen (Ap. Can. XLV).

Or who joins the schismatical assembly of Bishops at Ephesus (Eph. II).

Or who joins in prayer with a deposed Clergyman (Ap. Can. XI); or receives him as a Clergyman (Ant. III); or communicates with a Clergyman who is deposed for celebrating Easter before the Vernal Equinox (Ant. I).

Or who commits simony (Ap. Can. XXIX, Chal. II); or negotiates simoniacal contracts (Chal. II); or obtains his Church through secular rulers (Ap. Can. XXX).

Or who holds ordinations beyond his own jurisdiction (Ap. Can. XXXV); or acts, without invitation, beyond his own Province (Ant. XIII).

Or who rebaptizes one who has true Baptism (Ap. Can. XLVII); or refuses to baptize one who has been polluted by the impious (Ap. Can. XLVII); or does not baptize according to the Catholic formula (Ap. Can. XLIX); or does not baptize by trine-immersion (Ap. Can. L).

Or who refuses to receive Penitents (Ap. Can. LII).

Or who persists in neglect of his duties (Ap. Can. LVIII); or persists in refusing to relieve Clergymen in need (Ap. Can. LIX); or refuses to appoint a Steward (Chal. XXVI).

Or who denies his clerical position (Ap. Can. LXII).

Or who has been ordained after lapse (Nic. X).

Or who receives, or grants, a second ordination, unless the first is void (Ap. Can. LXVIII).

Or who disobeys the Canons of the lawful Synod of Ephesus (Eph. VI).

Or who obtains an imperial rescript for dividing a Province (Chal. XII).

Or who allows Monasteries to be used for secular purposes, or appropriates their property (Chal. XXIV).

Or who seizes on a vacant See, without a full Synod (Ant. XVI).

Or who persists in divorcing his wife, under pretext of religion (Ap. Can. V); or abstains from marriage because he abhors it (Ap. Can. LI); or refuses to divorce an adulterous wife (Neo-Cæs. VIII).

Or who castrates himself (Ap. Can. XXIII, Nic. I).

Or who commits fornication, perjury, or theft (Ap. Can. XXV); or commits manslaughter (Ap. Can. LXV); or is

DEPOSITION.—Of a Bishop.—*Continued.*

guilty of any sensual sin (Nic. II); or ravishes a woman, under pretence of marriage (Chal. XXVII).

Or who is given to dice, or drunkenness (Ap. Can. XLII); or who strikes backsliders or unbelievers (Ap. Can. XXVI).

Or who abstains from flesh and wine because he abhors them (Ap. Can. LI); especially if he so abstain on festival days (Ap. Can. LIII); or who eats flesh with the blood, or of animals which have been slain by beasts, or have died a natural death (Ap. Can. LXIII); or who fasts on Sunday, or on any Sabbath except Easter Even (Ap. Can. LXVI); or neglects to fast during Lent, and on Wednesdays and Fridays, unless prevented by bodily weakness (Ap. Can. LXIX).

Or who insults the Emperor or a magistrate (Ap. Can. LXXXIV).

Or who resorts to secular courts, against another Clergyman (Chal. IX).

Or who, retaining the seat, as Priest, which he held before his ordination as Bishop, stirs up sedition against the constituted Bishop (Anc. XVIII).

Or who petitions the Emperor, without the consent of his Metropolitan and Com-provincials (Ant. XI).

Deposition from the Episcopate involves loss of all clerical rank (Chal. XXIX).

A Bishop of the Paulianists, reconciled to the Catholic Church, is, if unworthy, to be deposed (Nic. XIX).

—Of a Chorepiscopus.—

The penalty of deposition is pronounced against a Chorepiscopus who commits simony (Chal. II).

Or who ordains Priests, or Deacons, without his Bishop (Ant. X).

—Of a Priest.—

The penalty of deposition is pronounced against a Priest who offers anything at the Altar, except new ears of grain and clusters of grapes (Ap. Can. III).

Or who engages in worldly business (Ap. Can. VI, LXXXI, Chal. III); or serves in the army (Ap. Can. LXXXIII); or becomes security (Ap. Can. XX); or exacts usury (Ap. Can. XLIV, Nic. XVII).

Or who celebrates Easter before the Vernal Equinox, as the Jews do (Ap. Can. VII, Ant. I); or professes the heresies of Nestorius and Celestius (Eph. Encyc., Can. IV, Can. VII); or of Theodore of Mopsuestia (Eph. VII); or reads heretical and spurious books, in Church, as Scripture (Ap. Can. LX); or composes, or uses, any other than the Nicene

DEPOSITION.—Of a Priest.—*Continued.*

Creed (Eph. VII, Chal. Encyc.); or enters a synagogue of Jews or heretics, to pray (Ap. Can. LXIV); or observes, or receives gifts from, Jewish fasts or festivals (Ap. Can. LXX); or admits the Baptism or Sacrifice of heretics (Ap. Can. XLVI); or employs heretics as Clergymen (Ap. Can. XLV).

Or who joins in prayer with a deposed Clergyman (Ap. Can. XI); or communicates with a Clergyman who is deposed for celebrating Easter before the Vernal Equinox (Ant. I); or with a Bishop who has obtained his Church through secular rulers (Ap. Can. XXX).

Or who separates himself from the Church (Ap. Can. XXXI, Ant. V); or adheres to those who do so (Ap. Can. XXXI).

Or who commits simony (Ap. Can. XXIX, Chal. II); or negotiates simoniacal contracts (Chal. II).

Or who receives irregular and uncanonical ordination (Ap. Can. XXXV); or receives a second ordination, unless the first was void (Ap. Can. LXVIII); or who has been ordained without examination, or after confession of crimes (Nic. IX); or after lapse (Nic. X).

Or who denies his clerical position (Ap. Can. LXII).

Or who rebaptizes one who has true Baptism, or refuses to baptize one who has been polluted by the impious (Ap. Can. XLVII); or does not baptize according to the Catholic formula (Ap. Can. XLIX); or does not baptize by trine-immersion (Ap. Can. L).

Or who refuses to receive penitents (Ap. Can. LII).

Or who persists in neglecting his duties (Ap. Can. LVIII); or persists in refusing to relieve Clergymen in need (Ap. Can. LIX).

Or who disobeys the Canons of the lawful Synod of Ephesus (Eph. VI); or disobeys his Bishop (Chal. VIII); or leaves his Parish and refuses to return on his Bishop's summons (Ant. III).

Or who seizes the property of a Bishop on his death (Chal. XXII); or who allows Monasteries to be used as secular dwellings, or appropriates their property (Chal. XXIV).

Or who, after being transferred to another Church, meddles with the affairs of his former ministry (Chal. X).

Or who persists in divorcing his wife under pretext of religion (Ap. Can. V); or refuses to divorce an adulterous wife (Neo-Cæs. VIII); or who abstains from marriage because he abhors it (Ap. Can. LI); or who marries (Neo-Cæs. I).

DEPOSITION.—Of a Priest.—*Continued.*

Or who castrates himself (Ap. Can. XXIII, Nic. I).

Or who commits fornication, perjury, or theft (Ap. Can. XXV); or commits manslaughter (Ap. Can. LXV); or is guilty of any sensual sin (Nic. II); or ravishes a woman, under pretence of marriage (Chal. XXVII).

Or who is given to dicing or drunkenness (Ap. Can. XLII).

Or who strikes backsliders or unbelievers (Ap. Can. XXVII).

Or who abstains from flesh and wine because he abhors them (Ap. Can. LI); especially if he so abstain on Festival Days (Ap. Can. LIII); or refuses to taste flesh, or to eat herbs served therewith (Anc. XIV); or who eats flesh with the blood, or of animals which have been slain by beasts, or have died a natural death (Ap. Can. LXIII); or who fasts on Sunday, or on any Sabbath except Easter Even (Ap. Can. LXVI); or neglects to fast during Lent, and on Wednesdays and Fridays, unless prevented by bodily weakness (Ap. Can. LXIX).

Or who insults his Bishop (Ap. Can. LV); or insults the Emperor, or a Magistrate (Ap. Can. LXXXIV).

Or who resorts to secular courts, against another Clergyman (Chal. IX).

Or who petitions the Emperor, without the consent of the Metropolitan and Provincial Bishops (Ant. XI).

Or who joins in a conspiracy against his Bishop and fellow Clergyman (Chal. XVIII); or who, having received a Bishop's Orders, but retaining the seat, as Priest, which he had previously held, stirs up sedition against the constituted Bishop (Anc. XVIII).

A Priest of the Paulianists, reconciled to the Catholic Church, is, if unworthy, to be deposed (Nic. XIX).

—Of a Deacon.—

The penalty of deposition is pronounced against a Deacon who engages in worldly business (Ap. Can. VI, Chal. III); or serves in the army (Ap. Can. LXXXIII); or becomes security (Ap. Can. XX); or exacts usury (Ap. Can. XLIV, Nic. XVII).

Or who celebrates Easter before the Vernal Equinox, as the Jews do (Ap. Can. VII, Ant. I); or professes the heresies of Nestorius and Celestius (Eph. Encyc., Can. IV, Can. VII); or of Theodore of Mopsuestia (Eph. VII); or reads heretical and spurious books, in Church, as Scripture (Ap. Can. LX);

DEPOSITION.—Of a Deacon.—*Continued.*

or composes, or uses, any other than the Nicene Creed (Eph. VII, Chal. Encyc.); or enters a synagogue of Jews or heretics, to pray (Ap. Can. LXIV); or observes, or receives gifts from, Jewish fasts or festivals (Ap. Can. LXX); or employs heretics as Clergymen (Ap. Can. XLV).

Or who joins in prayer with a deposed Clergyman (Ap. Can. XI); or communicates with a Clergyman who is deposed for celebrating Easter before the Vernal Equinox (Ant. I); or with a Bishop who has obtained his Church through secular rulers (Ap. Can. XXX).

Or who separates himself from the Church (Ap. Can. XXXI, Ant. V); or adheres to those who do so (Ap. Can. XXXI).

Or who commits simony (Ap. Can. XXIX, Chal. II); or negociates simoniacal contracts (Chal. II).

Or who receives irregular and uncanonical ordination (Ap. Can. XXXV); or receives a second ordination, unless the first was void (Ap. Can. LXVIII); or who has been ordained after lapse (Nic. X).

Or who denies his clerical position (Ap. Can. LXII).

Or who persists in refusing to relieve Clergymen in need (Ap. Can. LIX).

Or who disobeys the Canons of the lawful Synod of Ephesus (Eph. VI); or disobeys his Bishop (Chal. VIII); or leaves his Parish, and refuses to return on his Bishop's summons (Ant. III).

Or who seizes the property of a Bishop, on his death (Chal. XXII); or who allows Monasteries to be used as secular dwellings, or appropriates their property (Chal. XXIV).

Or who, after being transferred to another Church, meddles with the affairs of his former ministry (Chal. X).

Or who administers the Eucharist to a Priest, or receives it before the Bishop or Priest (Nic. XVIII).

Or who persists in divorcing his wife, under pretext of religion (Ap. Can. V); or refuses to divorce an adulterous wife (Neo-Cæs. VIII); or abstains from marriage because he abhors it (Ap. Can. LI); or marries after being ordained, without having, at his ordination, declared a purpose to marry (Anc. X).

Or who castrates himself (Ap. Can. XXIII, Nic. I).

Or who commits fornication, perjury, or theft (Ap. Can. XXV); or commits manslaughter (Ap. Can. LXV); or ravishes a woman, under pretence of marriage (Chal. XXVII).

Or who is given to dicing or drunkenness (Ap. Can. XLII).

DEPOSITION.—OF A DEACON.—*Continued.*

Or who strikes backsliders or unbelievers (Ap. Can. XXVII).

Or who abstains from flesh and wine because he abhors them (Ap. Can. LI); especially if he so abstain on Festival Days (Ap. Can. LIII); or who refuses to taste flesh, or to eat herbs served therewith (Anc. XIV); or who eats flesh with the blood, or of animals which have been slain by beasts, or have died a natural death (Ap. Can. LXIII); or who fasts on Sunday, or on any Sabbath except Easter Even (Ap. Can. LXVI); or neglects to fast during Lent, and on Wednesdays and Fridays, unless prevented by bodily weakness (Ap. Can. LXIX).

Or who insults his Bishop (Ap. Can. LV); or insults the Emperor, or a Magistrate (Ap. Can. LXXXIV).

Or who resorts to secular courts, against another Clergyman (Chal. IX).

Or who petitions the Emperor, without the consent of the Metropolitan and Provincial Bishops (Ant. XI).

Or who joins in a conspiracy against his Bishop and fellow Clergymen (Chal. XVIII).

A Deacon of the Paulianists, reconciled to the Catholic Church, is, if unworthy, to be deposed (Nic. XIX).

—OF THE MINOR CLERGY.—

The penalty of deposition is pronounced against those of the Minor Clergy who engage in worldly business (Chal. III); or become security (Ap. Can. XX); or exact usury (Nic. XVII).

Or who profess the heresies of Nestorius and Celestius (Eph. Encyc., Can. IV); or of Theodore of Mopsuestia (Eph. VII); or who read heretical and spurious books, in Church, as Scripture (Ap. Can. LX); or compose, or use, any other than the Nicene Creed (Eph. VII, Chal. Encyc.); or enter a synagogue of Jews or heretics, to pray (Ap. Can. LXIV); or observe, or receive gifts from, Jewish fasts or festivals (Ap. Can. LXX).

Or who join in prayer with a deposed Clergyman (Ap. Can. XI); or communicate with a Clergyman who is deposed for celebrating Easter before the Vernal Equinox (Ant. I); or with a Bishop who has obtained his Church through secular rulers (Ap. Can. XXX).

Or who adhere to the maintainers of conventicles (Ap. Can. XXXI).

Or who commit simony, or negotiate simoniacal contracts (Chal. II).

DEPOSITION.—Of the Minor Clergy.—*Continued.*

Or who receive irregular and uncanonical ordination (Ap. Can. XXXV); or have been ordained after lapse (Nic. X).

Or who deny their clerical position (Ap. Can. LXII).

Or who disobey the Canons of the lawful Synod of Ephesus (Eph. VI); or disobey their Bishops (Chal. VIII).

Or who seize the property of a Bishop, on his death (Chal. XXII); or who use Monasteries as secular dwellings, or appropriate their property (Chal. XXIV).

Or who, after being transferred to another Church, meddle with the affairs of their former ministry (Chal. X).

Or who abstain from marriage because they abhor it (Ap. Can. LI); or refuse to divorce wives who commit adultery (Neo-Cæs. VIII).

Or who castrate themselves (Ap. Can. XXIII, Nic. I).

Or who commit fornication, perjury, or theft (Ap. Can. XXV); or commit manslaughter (Ap. Can. LXV); or ravish, under pretence of marriage (Chal. XXVII).

Or who abstain from flesh and wine from abhorrence of them (Ap. Can. LI); or who eat flesh with the blood, or of animals which have been slain by beasts, or have died a natural death (Ap. Can. LXIII), or who fast on Sunday, or on any Sabbath except Easter Even (Ap. Can. LXVI); or neglect to fast during Lent, and on Wednesdays and Fridays, unless prevented by bodily weakness (Ap. Can. LXIX).

Or who insult their Bishops (Ap. Can. LV); or insult the Emperor or a Magistrate (Ap. Can. LXXXIV).

Or who resort to secular courts, against other Clergymen (Chal. IX).

Or who petition the Emperor, without the consent of the Metropolitan and Provincial Bishops (Ant. XI).

Or who join in conspiracies against their Bishops and fellow Clergymen (Chal. XVIII).

Minor Clergy of the Paulianists, reconciled to the Catholic Church, are, if unworthy, to be deposed (Nic. XIX).

—Of a Reader or Singer.—

A Reader, or Singer, who intermarries with, or gives his children in marriage to, heretics, or who baptizes his children amongst heretics, is to be deposed (Chal. XIV).

—Of a Steward, Advocate, or Bailiff.—

A Steward, Advocate, or Bailiff, who commits simony, or negotiates simoniacal contracts, is to be deposed (Chal. II).

DEPRIVATION.—Deprivations by Nestorius or his followers are declared void (Eph. III).

DEVIL.—A man possessed by a devil, is excluded from the ministry, and from the congregation, until he is dispossessed (Ap. Can. LXXIX).

DIACONICUM.—A Sub-deacon is forbidden to enter the Diaconicum (Laod XXI).

DICE.—Dice are forbidden to Bishops, Priests, and Deacons (Ap. Can. XLII); also to Sub-deacons, Readers, Singers, and Laymen (Ap. Can. XLIII).

DIGAMISTS.—A digamist may be admitted to communion (Nic. VIII) after a short period of prayer and fasting (Laod. I); he is declared to be worthy of penance (Neo-Cæs. VII).

A digamist cannot be ordained (Ap. Can. XVII).

A Priest is not allowed to attend, as guest, the marriage of a digamist (Neo-Cæs. VII).

Those who profess Virginity, if they disregard their professions, are to do the same penance as digamists (Anc. XIX).

The Cathari, who are reconciled to the Catholic Church, must promise to communicate with digamists (Nic. VIII).

DIGNITY, SECULAR.—Clergymen and Monks are forbidden to accept secular dignity (Chal. VII).

DIOCESE.—A Diocese of the Church might include more than one civil Diocese within its jurisdiction (Chal. XVIII); and the ancient customary rights of Dioceses are to be maintained (Eph. VIII); but Bishops are forbidden to bring confusion on the Churches, by officiating beyond their own Dioceses (Const. II). See also *Exarch*, *Diocesan Synod*, *Appeal*, *Province*, *Alexandria*, *Antioch*, *Constantinople*, *Cyprus*, *Rome.*

DISCIPLINE.—Abstinence from marriage, flesh, or wine, for Discipline, is permitted (Ap. Can. LI, LIII.).

The Cathari, before reconciliation to the Catholic Church, must promise conformity to its Discipline (Nic. VIII).

DISHONOURABLE LIFE.—A man who is just converted from a dishonourable life, must not be immediately made a Bishop (Ap. Can. LXXX).

DISOBEDIENCE.—Disobedience to his Bishop, of a Clergyman, who refuses to return to his Parish when summoned to do so, is punishable by suspension (Ap. Can. XV, Ant. III); and, if persisted in, by deposition (Ant. III); disobedience of Clergymen to their Bishops, is punishable by deposition, and of Monks or laymen, by excommunication (Chal. VIII); disobedience of a Priest to his Bishop is punishable by deposition (Anc. XVIII).

Disobedience to the third Canon of Nicæa, is at the peril

DISOBEDIENCE—*Continued.*

of a man's Orders (Nic. III); disobedience to the Canons of the lawful Synod of Ephesus, is punishable in Clergymen by deposition, and in laymen by excommunication (Eph. VI).

DISPENSATION.—Vid. *Indulgence.*

DISPUTES.—Disputes with a Metropolitan are to be decided by the Exarch of the Diocese, or by the Throne of Constantinople (Chal. XVII).

Disputes as to a Bishop's jurisdiction over outlying Parishes, are to be decided by the Provincial Synod (Chal. XVII).

Disputes between Clergymen are to be decided by the Bishop, or by referees appointed with his consent (Chal. IX).

Ecclesiastical disputes are to be settled by the Provincial Synod (Ap. Can. XXXVII, Ant. XX).

DISQUALIFICATIONS.—For Ordination.—

One who, after Baptism, has been twice married, or has had a concubine, cannot be ordained (Ap. Can. XVII); nor one who has married a widow, a divorced woman, a harlot, a slave, or an actress (Ap. Can. XVIII); nor one who has married two sisters or a niece (Ap. Can. XIX).

Nor one who has castrated himself (Ap. Can. XXII, Nic. I); but castration by force, or for surgical purposes, is not a disqualification (Nic. I).

A husband, whose wife commits adultery, cannot be ordained (Neo-Cæs. VIII).

One who has committed fornication, adultery, or any other forbidden act, cannot be ordained (Ap. Can. LXI).

Nor one who is possessed of a devil, until he is dispossessed (Ap. Can. LXXIX).

Nor a slave, unless the master manumit him (Ap. Can. LXXXII).

Nor one who has lapsed (Nic. X); but those who have remained steadfast throughout the persecutions, though forced to seem otherwise, are not disqualified (Anc. IV).

A recent convert from heathenism cannot be ordained (Laod. III); but former profession of heathenism is not, in itself, a disqualification (Anc. XII); nor is former profession of the Paulianist heresy (Nic. XIX).

One who has left his own Church, cannot be ordained in another Church (Nic. XVI).

A Clergyman cannot be ordained without a charge (Chal. VI).

DISQUALIFICATIONS.—For Ordination.—*Continued.*

One who is already canonically ordained, cannot receive a second Ordination (Ap. Can. LXVIII).

—For the Episcopate.—

A eunuch, if made by force or persecution, or so born, is not disqualified for the Episcopate (Ap. Can. XXI).

Total deafness or blindness is a disqualification for the Episcopate (Ap. Can. LXXVIII); but partial blindness or lameness is not (Ap. Can. LXXVII).

One whose Ordination would injure the Church, cannot be made a Bishop (Ap. Can. LXXVIII).

A Bishop cannot ordain a relative, to the Episcopate, from personal motives (Ap. Can. LXXVI).

Recent conversion from heathenism or a dishonourable life, is a disqualification for the Episcopate (Ap. Can. LXXX, Nic. II); a Bishop cannot be ordained until after long probation both of faith and life (Laod. XII).

—For the Presbyterate.—

A Priest cannot be ordained without examination, nor after confession of crimes (Nic. IX); bodily sin in a Priest disqualifies him for making the Oblation (Neo-Cæs. IX); but the married state does not (Gang. IV).

Lapse disqualifies a Priest for performing any of his duties, even after he is restored (Anc. I).

Clinic Baptism is, generally, a disqualification for the Presbyterate (Neo-Cæs. XIII).

Recent conversion from heathenism, is a disqualification for the Presbyterate (Nic. II).

One who is under thirty years of age, is disqualified for Ordination as a Priest (Neo-Cæs. XI).

—In General.—

Lapse disqualifies a Priest for performing any of his duties, even after he is restored, unless his Bishop grant him indulgence (Anc. II).

A Deaconess cannot be ordained under forty years of age, or without examination (Chal. XV).

A slave is disqualified for being received as a Monk (Chal. IV).

One who is possessed of a devil, is disqualified for admission to the congregation, until he is dispossessed (Ap. Can. LXXIX).

Heretics, single communicants, maintainers of conventicles, and persons who are themselves under accusation, or are excommunicated, are disqualified for bringing accusations of

DISQUALIFICATIONS.—IN GENERAL.—*Continued.*

ecclesiastical offences against a Bishop (Ap. Can. LXXV, Const. VI); also persons who are under accusation are disqualified for bringing such charges against any Clergyman (Const. VI).

DISTRICTS.—The jurisdiction of a Bishop is limited to his own Parish and Districts (Ap. Can. XXXIV, Ant. IX); it is limited to his own City and Districts (Ap. Can. XXXV, Ant. XXII).

Chorepiscopi are forbidden to act beyond their own Districts, within which they are to ordain Readers, Sub-deacons, and Exorcists (Ant. X).

Country Districts are not to have independent Bishops, but those already appointed are to consult the City Bishop before acting (Laod. LVII).

In a new or rebuilt City, the Ecclesiastical Districts are to follow the political and municipal arrangements (Chal. XVII).

DISTURBANCES IN CONSTANTINOPLE.—The disturbances in Constantinople, occasioned by Maximus the Cynic, are mentioned (Const. IV); Clergymen and Monks, going to Constantinople and causing disturbances there, are to be expelled from the City (Chal. XXIII).

DIVINE SERVICE.—Vid. *Service.*

DIVINERS.—Diviners are to fulfil five years of penance (Anc. XXIV).

DIVISION OF PROVINCES.—Bishops are forbidden to obtain imperial rescripts for dividing Provinces (Chal. XII).

DIVORCE.—A Bishop, Priest, or Deacon, is forbidden to divorce his wife under pretext of religion (Ap. Can. V); but if she commits adultery, he must divorce her, or desist from his ministry (Neo-Cæs. VIII).

A layman is forbidden to divorce his wife and take another (Ap. Can. XLVIII).

DIVORCED WOMAN.—Marriage with a divorced woman is a disqualification for ordination (Ap. Can. XVIII); and is forbidden to laymen (Ap. Can. XLVIII).

DOCTRINE.—The purity of Doctrine is to be guarded by Synods (Ap. Can. XXXVII).

—OF THE TRINITY.—Vid. *Trinity.*

DOMESTICS.—Bishops are forbidden to employ their own domestics in the management of Church Funds (Ant. XXV).

DOORKEEPER.—A Doorkeeper is forbidden to enter a tavern (Laod. XXIV).

DOORS.—The Sub-deacon is forbidden to leave the doors (Laod. XXII, XLIII).

DRESS.—Anathema on one who wears a rough cloak, and despises those who use the *berus*, and other customary dress (Gang. XII); also on a woman who assumes the dress of a man, under pretence of asceticism (Gang. XIII).

Plainness in dress is commended, and dissolute excess, and over-fastidiousness, condemned (Gang. XXI).

DRINKING CLUBS.—Communicants, of every class, are forbidden to join in forming clubs for drinking entertainments (Laod. LV).

DRUGS.—Women who prepare drugs for causing abortion, are to fulfil ten years of penance (Anc. XXI).

DRUNKENNESS.—Drunkenness in a Bishop, Priest, or Deacon, is punishable by deposition (Ap. Can. XLII); and in a Sub-deacon, Reader, Singer, or Layman, by suspension (Ap. Can. XLIII).

DWELLINGS, SECULAR.—Monasteries, once consecrated with the Bishop's consent, are forbidden to be used as secular dwellings (Chal. XXIV).

DYING.—The dying are entitled, in all cases, to receive the Oblation, after being examined by the Bishop (Nic. XIII).

The lapsed, who have been admitted to penance, if in danger of death, are to be received to full communion, so long as the danger continues (Anc. VI).

A married man, of over fifty years of age, who is guilty of bestial lust, is to be admitted to communion only at the point of death (Anc. XVI); also a wilful murderer (Anc. XXII); also a woman who marries two brothers (Neo-Cæs. II).

EAST, THE.—The jurisdiction of the Bishops of the East is confined to their own Diocese (Const. II).

The identity of the doctrine of the TRINITY in East and West is declared (Const. V).

EASTER.—Clergymen are forbidden to celebrate Easter before the Vernal Equinox, as the Jews do (Ap. Can. VII, Nic. Encyc., Ant. I).

Fasting is permitted on Easter Even (Ap. Can. LXVI).

Provincial Synods are to be held in the third week of Easter (Ant. XX).

Eulogiæ are forbidden to be sent from one Parish to another at Easter (Laod. XIV).

EATING.—Eating in Church is forbidden (Laod. XXVIII).

ECCLESIASTICAL BUSINESS.—Clergymen are forbidden to engage in ecclesiastical business except by direction of their Bishops (Chal. III); Monks are under the same restriction (Chal. III, IV).

—CENSURE.—Vid. *Suspension*, *Deposition*, *Degradation*, *Expulsion*, *Excommunication*, and *Anathema*.

—DISTRICTS.—Ecclesiastical Districts in a new or rebuilt City, are to follow the political and municipal arrangement (Chal. XVII).

—OFFENCES.—Heretics, maintainers of conventicles, and persons who are themselves under accusation, or are excommunicated, are disqualified for bringing accusations of ecclesiastical offences against a Bishop (Const. VI); also persons who are under accusation, are disqualified for bringing such charges against any Clergyman (Const. VI).

—PROPERTY.—Vid. *Property, Ecclesiastical.*

EGYPT.—The Bishop of Alexandria is to have jurisdiction in Egypt (Nic. VI, Const. II).

The Bishops of Egypt are bound, by ancient custom, not to sign even acts which they approve, without the consent of their Archbishop; and this custom was respected in practice at Chalcedon (Chal. XXX).

ELECTION.—The election of the Metropolitans of Pontus, Asia, and Thrace, is to be according to custom (Chal. XXVIII).

—OF A BISHOP.—Vid. *Bishop.*

—OF A PRIEST.—Vid. *Priest.*

—OF A DEACON.—Vid. *Deacon.*

Elections are forbidden to be held in the presence of the Hearers (Laod. V).

EMASCULATION.—Vid. *Castration.*

EMPEROR, THE.—Communicants are forbidden to insult the Emperor (Ap. Can. LXXXIV).

Charges against a Bishop are not to be brought before the Emperor (Const. VI).

Bishops and Priests are forbidden to address the Emperor, without the consent and letters of the Metropolitan and Provincial Bishops (Ant. XI).

A Clergyman appealing to the Emperor, instead of to a Synod, against a sentence of deposition, cannot be restored, nor can his cause be reheard, by a Synod (Ant. XII).

ENCHANTERS.—Clergymen are forbidden to be enchanters (Laod. XXXVI).

ENTREATY.—Offenders are not to be admitted to penance, without earnest entreaty (Ant. II).

EPHESUS.—The Canons of Ephesus are confirmed by Chal. I.

EPISCOPATE.—Bishops are forbidden to raise their relatives to the Episcopate from personal motives (Ap. Can. LXXVI); or to bequeath his Episcopal office to heirs (Ap. Can. LXXVI).

Deposition from the Episcopate involves loss of all clerical rank (Chal. XXIX).

For the disqualifications for the Episcopate, vid. *Disqualification*, *Bishop*.

EQUINOX, VERNAL.—Easter is not to be celebrated before the Vernal Equinox (Ap. Can. VII, Nic. Encyc., Ant. I).

EUCHARIST.—The word *Eucharist* is used in the Canons only three times—Nic. XIII, XVIII, Ant. II; and, in these instances, it is used in reference to the Holy Gifts. In the Apostolical Canons, the celebration of the Eucharist is called the Sacrifice (θυσία) (Ap. Can. III, XLVI). The word for *Holy Communion* or *Eucharist* commonly used in the Canons is Oblation (προσφορά), which see.

EUDOXIANS.—The heresy of the Eudoxians is anathematized (Const. I).

EULOGIÆ.—Eulogiæ are forbidden to be sent from one Parish to another at Easter (Laod. XIV). Clergymen are forbidden to receive the Eulogiæ of heretics (Laod. XXXII).

EUNOMIANS.—The heresy of the Eunomians is anathematized (Const. I); Eunomians who come over to orthodoxy are to be received as heathen (Const. VII).

EUNUCH.—A Eunuch, if made by force or persecution, or so born, may be made a Bishop (Ap. Can. XXI); if so made by force or for surgical purposes, he may be ordained (Nic. I).

EVIDENCE.—For regulations as to evidence, on the trial of a Clergyman, see *Bishop*, *Priest*, *Deacon*, *Clergy*, *Minor*.

EXAMINATION.—Examination is to be made of candidates for Priests' Orders (Nic. IX); and of Deaconesses before ordination (Chal. XV); and of Clergy of the Paulianists, who are reconciled to the Catholic Church, before ordination (Nic. XIX).

Examination is not to be made of those who bring personal accusations against a Bishop (Const. VI); but those who bring charges of ecclesiastical offences must be examined (Const. VI, Chal. XXI).

Examination is to be made of Clergymen received from abroad, before they are admitted to communion (Ap. Can. XXXIII).

EXAMINATION—*Continued.*

Examination is to be made into the lives of the lapsed, who desire restoration to the Catholic Church (Anc. II, III, V, VII, IX); and into the lives of those who are under penance for bestial lusts (Anc. XVI).

Examination is to be made of the dying, before administering the Eucharist (Nic. XIII).

Examination is to be made of the poor, before giving them Letters Pacifical (Chal. XI).

Mutual examination, concerning the doctrines of religion, is one of the objects of Synods (Ap. Can. XXXVII).

EXARCH.—Complaints against a Metropolitan are to be laid before the Exarch of the Diocese, or the Throne of Constantinople (Chal. IX, XVII).

Exarchs may not acquire or usurp jurisdiction contrary to ancient custom (Eph. VIII).

The Exarch, or Archbishop, of Alexandria was entitled, by ancient custom, to be consulted by the Bishops of Egypt before they signed even acts which they approved (Chal. XXX).

Se also *Alexandria*, *Antioch*, *Constantinople*, *Cyprus*, *Pontus*, *Rome*, *Thrace*.

EXCESS.—Dissolute and effeminate excess in dress is condemned (Gang. XXI).

EXCOMMUNICATED PERSONS.—Communicants are forbidden to join with an excommunicated person in prayer (Ap. Can. X); or to communicate with him (Ant. II); those who are excommunicated in one City, are not to be received in another, without Letters Commendatory (Ap. Can. XII); they are not to be received at all, until restored to communion (Ant. VI).

A person who is excommunicated by one Bishop, is not to be restored by another (Nic. V).

Persons under sentence of excommunication, cannot bring accusations of ecclesiastical offences, against a Bishop (Const. VI).

EXCOMMUNICATION.—OF A METROPOLITAN.—

A Metropolitan, who professes the heresies of Nestorius and Celestius, is to be excommunicated (Eph. Encyc., Can. I).

—OF A BISHOP.—

The penalty of excommunication is pronounced against a Bishop who, after deposition, meddles with his former ministry (Ap. Can. XXVIII, Ant. IV); or who communicates with one who does so (Ant. IV); or communicates with the

EXCOMMUNICATION.—OF A BISHOP.—*Continued.*

excommunicated (Ant. II); or with a Bishop who has obtained his Church through secular rulers (Ap. Can. XXX).

Or who commits simony (Ap. Can. XXIX); or obtains his Church through secular rulers (Ap. Can. XXX).

Or who denies the name of Christ (Ap. Can. LXII).

Or who abstains from marriage, flesh, and wine, because he abhors them (Ap. Can. LI).

Or who petitions the Emperor, without the consent of the Metropolitan and Provincial Bishops (Ant. XI).

A Bishop deposed for fornication, perjury, or theft, is not to be excommunicated (Ap. Can. XXV).

—OF A PRIEST.—

The penalty of excommunication is pronounced against a Priest who, after deposition, meddles with his former ministry (Ap. Can. XXVIII, Ant. IV); or who communicates with one who does so (Ant. IV); or communicates with the excommunicated (Ant. II); or with a Bishop who has obtained his Church through secular rulers (Ap. Can. XXX).

Or who commits simony (Ap. Can. XXIX).

Or who denies the name of Christ (Ap. Can. LXII).

Or who petitions the Emperor, without the consent of the Metropolitan and Provincial Bishops (Ant. XI).

Or who abstains from marriage, flesh, and wine, because he abhors them (Ap. Can. LI).

Or who commits fornication or adultery (Neo-Cæs. I).

A Priest deposed for fornication, perjury, or theft, is not to be excommunicated (Ap. Can. XXV).

—OF A DEACON.—

The penalty of excommunication is pronounced against a Deacon who, after deposition, meddles with his former ministry (Ap. Can. XXVII, Ant. IV); or who communicates with one who does so (Ant. IV); or communicates with the excommunicated (Ant. II); or with a Bishop who has obtained his Church through secular rulers (Ap. Can. XXX).

Or who commits simony (Ap. Can. XXIX).

Or who denies the name of Christ (Ap. Can. LXII).

Or who petitions the Emperor, without the consent of the Metropolitan and Provincial Bishops (Ant. XI).

Or who abstains from marriage, flesh, and wine, because he abhors them (Ap. Can. LI).

A Deacon deposed for fornication, perjury, or theft, is not to be excommunicated (Ap. Can. XXV).

EXCOMMUNICATION.—OF THE MINOR CLERGY.—

The penalty of excommunication is pronounced against those of the Minor Clergy who communicate with a Bishop who has obtained his Church through secular rulers (Ap. Can. XXX); or with a Bishop, Priest, or Deacon, who, after deposition, meddles with his former ministry (Ant. IV); or with the excommunicated (Ant. II).

Or who denies the Name of CHRIST (Ap. Can. LXII).

Or who petitions the Emperor, without the consent of the Metropolitan and Provincial Bishops (Ant. XI).

Or who abstains from marriage, flesh, and wine, because he abhors them (Ap. Can. LI).

—OF A MONK.—

The penalty of excommunication is pronounced against a Monk who engages in worldly business (Chal. III, IV); or who permits Monasteries to be used as secular dwellings, or appropriates their property (Chal. XXIV).

Or who will not remain permanently at his Monastery, and subject to his Bishop (Chal. IV, VIII).

Or who marries (Chal. XVI).

—OF A DEDICATED VIRGIN.—

A dedicated Virgin, who marries, is to be excommunicated (Chal. XVI).

—OF THE LAITY.—

The penalty of excommunication is pronounced against those of the laity who disobey the decrees of the lawful Synod of Ephesus (Eph. VI); or who disobey their Bishops (Chal. VIII).

Or who celebrate Easter before the Vernal Equinox, as the Jews do (Ant. I).

Or who permit Monasteries to be used as secular dwellings, or appropriate their property (Chal. XXIV).

Or who communicate with a Bishop, Priest, or Deacon, who, after deposition, meddles with his former ministry (Ant. IV).

Or who are guilty of bestial lusts (Anc. XVI).

Or who wear phylacteries (Laod. XXXVI).

A woman who marries two brothers is to be excommunicated (Neo-Cæs. II).

-OF A CATECHUMEN.—

A Catechumen who falls into sin whilst he is a Hearer, is to be excommunicated (Neo-Cæs. V).

EXCOMMUNICATION—GENERAL REGULATIONS.—

Excommunication is to be for sufficient reason (Nic. V).

A Bishop's sentence of excommunication may be reversed by a Provincial Synod (Nic. V, Ant. VI).

Vid. also *Anathema.*

EXORCISM.—For the ceremony of exorcism, in the case of certain classes of reconciled heretics, and for an enumeration of those classes, see Const. VII.

EXORCIST.—An Exorcist may be ordained by a Chorepiscopus (Ant. X); he must be promoted by the Bishop, or he cannot act officially (Laod. XXVI).

An Exorcist is forbidden to enter a tavern (Laod. XXIV).

EXPULSION.—A Monk, who joins in a conspiracy against his Bishop or the Clergy, is to be expelled from his order (Chal. XVIII).

Clergymen and Monks going to Constantinople, and causing disturbances there, are to be expelled from the City (Chal. XXIII).

A Bishop who, retaining the seat, as Priest, which he held before his ordination as Bishop, stirs up sedition against the constituted Bishop, is to be expelled (Anc. XVIII).

A Bishop who seizes on a vacant See, without a full Synod, is to be expelled (Ant. XVI).

FAITH, SYMBOLS OF THE.—Vid. *Creed.*

FAITHFUL, THE.—Vid. *Laymen.*

FALSE ASCETICISM.—Vid. *Asceticism.*

FASTIDIOUSNESS.—Fastidiousness in dress is condemned (Gang. XXI).

FASTING.—Communicants are forbidden to fast on Sunday (Ap. Can. LXVI, Gang. XVIII); or on any Sabbath except Easter Even (Ap. Can. LXVI); or to fast with the Jews (Ap. Can. LXX).

Communicants are required to fast during Lent (Ap. Can. LXIX, Laod. L); and on Wednesdays and Fridays (Ap. Can. LXIX); and persons who disregard the fasts appointed by the Church, are anathematized (Gang. XIX).

Fasting is enjoined on Monks (Chal. IV).

A digamist may be admitted to communion, after a short period of prayer and fasting (Laod. I); those who have been guilty of many sins, may be admitted to penance, if they apply themselves to prayer, with fasting and penitence (Laod. II).

FATHER.—A father who forsakes or neglects his children, is anathematized (Gang. XV).

FEASTS.—Vid. *Festivals.*

FEMALE PRESIDENTS (*i. e.*, Presbyters).—Female Presidents are forbidden to be appointed (Laod. XI).

FESTIVALS.—Communicants are forbidden to observe, or receive gifts from, festivals of Jews (Ap. Can. LXX, Laod. XXXVII, XXXVIII); or of heretics (Laod. XXXVII); or heathen (Laod. XXXIX); or to take oil into, or light lamps in a temple of the heathen, or a synagogue of the Jews at their festivals (Ap. Can. LXXI).

A Bishop, Priest, or Deacon, who abstains from flesh and wine on festival days, because he abhors them, is to be deposed (Ap. Can. LIII).

Clergymen are forbidden to attend plays at festivals (Laod. LIV).

FIRST-FRUITS.—The first-fruits are not to be offered at the Altar, except new ears of grain, and clusters of grapes (Ap. Can. III); all other first-fruits are to be taken to the house of the Bishop and Priest, and to be shared by them with the other Clergy (Ap. Can. IV); persons who misappropriate the first-fruits of the Church, are to be anathematized (Gang. VII, VIII).

FLESH.—Abhorrence of flesh is a blasphemous slander of GOD's work, and is punishable by excommunication (Ap. Can. LI); and a Bishop, Priest, or Deacon, who abstains from flesh on festival days because he abhors it, is to be deposed (Ap. Can. LIII); Priests and Deacons who abstain from flesh, are to taste it at least once, and if they refuse to do so, or to eat herbs served with flesh, they are to be deposed (Anc. XIV); those who condemn the use of flesh, are anathematized (Gang. II).

Flesh containing blood, is forbidden to be eaten (Ap. Can. LXIII, Gang. II); also the flesh of animals that have been slain by beasts, or have died a natural death (Ap. Can. LXII); or have been strangled (Gang. II); also flesh offered to idols (Gang. II).

FOREIGNER.—Foreign Clergymen are forbidden to be received without Letters Commendatory (Ap. Can. XXXIII). Foreigners are not to be received without Letters Pacifical (Ant. VII).

FORMULA.—Baptism is to be performed according to the Catholic formula; for which see Ap. Can. XLIX.

FORNICATION.—Fornication, in a Clergyman, is punishable by deposition (Ap. Can. XXV); in a Priest, by complete excommunication (Neo-Cæs. I).

Professed Virgins, guilty of fornication, are to fulfil the penance of digamists (Anc. XIX).

A layman, convicted of fornication, cannot be ordained (Ap. Can. LXI).

FRIDAY.—Fasting is ordained on Fridays (Ap. Can. LXIX).

FRUGALITY.—Frugality is commended (Gang. XXI).

FRUITS.—Vid. *First-fruits.*

FUNDS OF THE CHURCH.—Vid. *Moneys.*

GALATIANS.—The numerous heresies arising amongst the Galatians are mentioned (Const. VII).

GAMBLING.—Gambling is forbidden to the Clergy and laity (Ap. Can. XLII, XLIII).

GANGRA.—The Canons of Gangra are confirmed by Chal. I.

GIFTS.—Clergymen and laymen are forbidden to receive gifts from feasts of Jews (Ap. Can. LXX, Laod. XXXVII, XXXVIII); or of heretics (Laod. XXXVII).

The Holy Gifts are forbidden to be sent at Easter as Eulogiæ (Laod. XIV).

GODLINESS.—Godliness is commended (Gang. XXI).

GOSPEL.—The Gospel is to be read on the Sabbath (Laod. XVI).

GRAIN.—New ears of grain may be offered at the Altar (Ap. Can. III).

GRAPES.—Clusters of grapes may be offered at the Altar (Ap. Can. III).

GRAVITY.—Gravity is commended (Gang. XXI).

GUARDIANSHIP.—Clergymen and Monks may undertake the guardianship of widows, orphans, and minors (Chal. III).

GUEST.—The expenses of a Bishop's guests are to be borne by the Church (Ap. Can. XLI, Ant. XXV).

A Priest is forbidden to be a guest at the marriage of a digamist (Neo-Cæs. VII).

HABIT.—The habit customarily worn by Deaconesses of the Paulianists is mentioned (Nic. XIX).

HAIR.—A woman's hair is the token of her subjection; and if she cut it off, she is to be Anathema (Gang. XVII).

HALT.—The Clergy and laity are forbidden to mock the halt (Ap. Can. LVII).

HANDS, IMPOSITION OF.—Paulianist Deaconesses, enrolled as far as the dress, had no Imposition of Hands (Nic. XIX).

HANDS, IMPOSITION OF.—*Continued.*

Persons under penance, are to receive Imposition of Hands from the Bishop, before leaving the Church (Laod. XIX).

HARLOT.—Marriage with a harlot is a disqualification for ordination (Ap. Can. XVIII).

HEARERS.—A Catechumen, falling into sin whilst he is a Hearer, is to be cast out (Neo-Cæs. V).

Hearers are not to be present at elections (Laod. V).

Vid. also *Penance.*

HEATHEN.—A convert from heathenism, must not be immediately made a Bishop (Ap. Can. LXXX, Nic. II), or Priest (Nic. II); but former profession of heathenism does not, of itself, disqualify a man for being ordained (Anc. XII).

Communicants are forbidden to feast with the heathen (Laod. XXXIX); Readers and Singers are forbidden to give their children in marriage amongst the heathen (Chal. XIV).

Lapse, from fear of heathens, is punishable, in Clergymen, by complete excommunication (Ap. Can. LXII).

Christians are forbidden to take oil into, or light lamps in a temple of the heathen, at their festivals (Ap. Can. LXXI).

Churches, in heathen nations, are to be governed according to custom (Const. II).

Persons who follow the customs of the heathen, are to fulfil five years of penance (Anc. XXIV).

HEIRS. A Bishop cannot bequeath his See to heirs (Ap. Can. LXXVI).

HEMIOLIÆ.—Clergymen are forbidden to receive hemioliæ (Nic. XVII, Laod. IV).

HERBS.—A Priest or Deacon, who refuses to eat herbs served with flesh, is to be deposed (Anc. XIV).

HERESIES.—Heresies in general are anathematized (Const. I).

Vid. also *Heretics.*

HERETICAL BOOKS.—Heretical and spurious books are forbidden to be read publicly, in Church, as Scripture (Ap. Can. LX).

HERETICS.—Bishops, Priests, and Deacons, are forbidden to join in prayer with heretics, or to employ them as Clergymen (Ap. Can. XLV); or to admit the Baptism or Sacrifice of heretics (Ap. Can. XLVI); Communicants are forbidden to join in prayer with heretics (Laod. XXXIII); or to enter a synagogue of heretics to pray (Ap. Can. LXIV); or to assemble in the Cemeteries, or attend the Martyries, of heretics (Laod. IX); or to honour the martyrs of heretics (Laod. XXXIV);

HERETICS—*Continued.*

or to observe, or receive gifts from, the festivals of heretics (Laod. XXXVII); or to give their children in marriage to heretics (Laod. X); unless they promise to become Christians (Laod. XXXI); Readers and Singers are forbidden to intermarry with, or give their children in marriage to, or baptize them amongst heretics (Chal. XIV); Clergymen are forbidden to receive the Eulogiæ of heretics (Laod. XXXII).

Lapse, from fear of heretics, is punishable, in Clergymen, by complete excommunication (Ap. Can. LXII).

Heretics are not allowed to enter the Church, whilst they remain in heresy (Laod. VI).

Heretics cannot be received as accusers of a Bishop (Ap. Can. LXXV); they may bring accusations of personal wrong, but not of ecclesiastical offence against a Bishop (Const. VI); and for this purpose, maintainers of conventicles are classed with heretics (Const. VI).

Ordinations by heretics are void (Ap. Can. LXVIII); deprivations by Nestorius, or by the partisans of his heresy, are declared to be void (Eph. III).

Heretics must renounce and anathematize all heresies, and especially their own, before reconciliation to the Catholic Church (Const. VII, Laod. VII). Cathari, seeking reconciliation to the Catholic Church, must promise, in writing, to obey its decrees (Nic. VIII). Phrygians must be instructed and baptized before admission (Laod. VIII). Certain heretics must learn by heart the Symbols of the Faith, before being received (Laod. VII). Certain classes of heretics are admitted to the Catholic Church by Chrism, others are received as heathen; for an enumeration of these classes, and an account of the forms and ceremonies used in each case, see Const. VII.

HETERODOX.—Vid. *Heretic.*

HIRING,—The hiring of property for profit is forbidden to Clergymen and Monks (Chal. III).

HOLY.—GIFTS.—Vid. *Gifts*

MYSTERIES.—Vid. *Mysteries.*

OBLATION.—Vid. *Oblation.*

HOMICIDE.—Involuntary homicides are to fulfil five years of penance (Anc. XXIII); wilful homicides are to remain prostrators for life, receiving communion only at their death (Anc. XXII).

HONEY.—Honey is forbidden to be offered at the Altar (Ap. Can. III).

HOSPITALITY.—Hospitality to foreign Clergymen is commended (Ap. Can. XXXIII).

Hospitality is to be maintained at the expense of the Church (Ap. Can. XLI, Ant. XXV).

HOUSE, PRIVATE.—Communicants are forbidden to join in prayer with an excommunicated person, even in a private house (Ap. Can. X).

None but duly-appointed Exorcists, may exorcise, either in a Church, or a private house (Laod. XXVI).

The Oblation is not to be made in a private house (Laod. LVIII).

HOUSES OF REFUGE.—Clergymen, who have been lawfully transferred to another Parish, are forbidden to meddle with the Houses of Refuge of their former ministry (Chal. X).

HUMILITY.—Humility is commended (Gang. XXI).

HUSBAND.—The husband of a Deaconess who marries, is to be anathematized (Chal. XV).

A woman who marries the brother of a deceased husband, is to be cast out till her death; and if she or her husband should die in the unlawful marriage, penance cannot readily be allowed to the survivor (Neo-Cæs. II).

The husband of an adulteress cannot be ordained (Neo-Cæs. VIII).

A woman who forsakes her husband, from abhorrence of marriage, is to be anathematized (Gang. XIV).

HYEMANTES.—Persons who are guilty of bestial lusts and who have corrupted others, are to pray among the Hiemantes (Anc. XVII).

HYPERBORETÆUS.—Vid. *October.*

IDES OF OCTOBER.—Provincial Synods are to be held on the Ides of October (Ant. XX).

IDOLATRY.—The Invocation of Angels is covert idolatry (Laod. XXXV).

IDOLS.—Flesh that has been offered to idols, is forbidden to be eaten (Gang. II).

ILLNESS.—Illness is a sufficient excuse, to a Bishop, for not attending a Provincial Synod (Chal. XIX).

IMMERSION.—Baptism must be by trine-immersion (Ap. Can. L); the baptism of the Eunomians, by one immersion, is void (Const. VII).

IMPERIAL RESCRIPT.—Vid. *Rescript.*

IMPOSITION OF HANDS.—Vid. *Hands.*

INCARNATION, THE.—The heresies of Theodore of Mopsuestia, respecting the Incarnation of CHRIST, are anathematized (Eph. VII).

INCENSE.—Incense may be offered at the Holy Oblation (Ap. Can. III).

INCOME OF THE CHURCH.—Vid. *Revenue.*

INDULGENCE.—Provincial Synods may grant indulgence to persons under sentence of excommunication (Nic. V).

Bishops may grant indulgence to Monks, and dedicated Virgins, who are excommunicated for marrying (Chal. XVI); and to the lapsed (Nic. XII, Anc. II, V, VII); and to persons who are under penance for bestial lusts (Anc. XVI); and to those who contract many marriages (Neo-Cæs. III); but a Bishop may, if necessary, take away indulgence, already granted to a lapsed Deacon, who has been restored (Anc. II).

INFIRM.—Clergy and laity are forbidden to mock the infirm (Ap. Can. LVII).

INHERITANCE.—The right to a See cannot be acquired by inheritance (Ap. Can. LXXVI).

INITIATION.—Vid. *Baptism.*

INN.—Clergymen are forbidden to eat in an inn, except on a journey (Ap. Can. LIV); Clergymen and Monks are forbidden to enter an inn (Laod. XXIV).

INSOLENCE.—Insolence, of a Clergyman to his Bishop, is punishable by deposition (Ap. Can. LV); insolence of a Clergyman to a Priest or Deacon, is punishable by suspension (Ap. Can. LVI); insolence to the Emperor or a Magistrate, is punishable, in Clergymen, by deposition, and in laymen by suspension (Ap. Can. LXXXIV); insolence of Virgins to the married, is punishable by anathema (Gang. X).

INSTRUCTION.—Instruction of converted heathen is required before Baptism (Const. VII); also of certain classes of reconciled heretics (Const. VII, Laod. VII, VIII).

INVESTIGATION.—An investigation is to be made, by the Provincial Synod, into the accounts of a Bishop, who is charged with dishonesty (Ant. XXV).

INVITATION.—Bishops are forbidden to act officially beyond their Provinces, without invitation (Const. II, Ant. XIII); an invitation by the Metropolitan, and Provincial Bishops of a Province, to a Bishop of another Province, to act within their jurisdiction, must be in writing (Ant. XIII); as also should be the invitation of a Metropolitan to his Provincial Bishops to attend a Provincial Synod (Ant. XIX).

INVOCATION OF ANGELS.—The Invocation of Angels is declared to be covert idolatry (Laod. XXXV).

INVOLUNTARY HOMICIDE.—Vid. *Homicide.*

ITINERANT VISITORS.—Vid. *Visitors.*

JERUSALEM.—The Bishop of Jerusalem is entitled to rank next to the Metropolitan of Cæsarea (Nic. VII).

JEWS.—Communicants are forbidden to observe, or receive gifts from, fasts or festivals of Jews (Ap. Can. LXX, Laod. XXXVII); or to receive unleavened bread from them (Ap. Can. LXX, Laod. XXXVIII); Clergymen are forbidden to celebrate Easter with the Jews (Ap. Can. VII, Ant. I); Readers and Singers are forbidden to give their children in marriage to Jews (Chal. XIV); Clergymen and laymen are forbidden to enter a synagogue of Jews to pray (Ap. Can. LXIV); Christians are forbidden to take oil into, or light lamps in a synagogue of Jews, at their festivals (Ap. Can. LXXI).

Lapse, from fear of Jews, is punishable in Clergymen by complete excommunication (Ap. Can. LXII).

JOURNEY.—Vid. *Travelling.*

JUDAISERS.—Judaisers, who rest on the Sabbath, are anathematized (Laod. XXIX).

JUDGMENT.—If a Bishop, who is charged with offences, should refuse to obey the summons of the Bishops, they may give judgment in his absence (Ap. Can. LXXIV).

—PRIVATE.—Private judgment is forbidden to be maintained, against the decision of the Church as to the time of celebrating Easter (Ant. I).

JURISDICTION.—The Bishop of Egypt has jurisdiction over Egypt, Libya, and Pentapolis (Nic. VI).

The jurisdiction of the Bishop of Rome is founded on custom (Nic. VI).

The jurisdiction of the Bishops of Egypt, the East, Asia, Pontus, and Thrace, is confined to their own Dioceses (Const. II).

—OF PROVINCIAL SYNODS.—Vid. *Synods.*

—OF A BISHOP.—Vid. *Bishop.*

KINSMEN OF A BISHOP.—The kinsmen of a Bishop are to be provided for out of his private property (Ap. Can. XL, Ant. XXIV); if in need, they are to be relieved like the rest of the poor (Ap. Can. XXXVIII).

A Bishop is forbidden to ordain his own kinsmen to the Episcopate, from personal motives (Ap. Can. LXXVI); or to

KINSMEN OF A BISHOP—*Continued.*

employ them in the management of the Church Funds (Ant. XXV).

KISS OF PEACE.—The Kiss of Peace is to follow prayers for full Communicants, in Divine Service (Laod. XIX).

KNEELER.—A Catechumen, who falls into sin whilst he is a Kneeler, may be admitted to penance (Neo-Cæs. V).

KNEELING.—Kneeling for prayers, on Sunday, and during Whitsuntide, is forbidden (Nic. XX).

LAME.—Clergymen and laymen are forbidden to mock the lame (Ap. Can. LVII).

A man who is partially lame, may, if worthy, be made a Bishop (Ap. Can. LXXVII).

LAMPS.—Christians are forbidden to light lamps in a synagogue of the Jews, at their festivals (Ap. Can. LXXI).

LAODICEA.—The Canons of Laodicea are confirmed by Chal. I.

LAPSED, THE.—Lapsed Clergymen are punishable by complete excommunication (Ap. Can. LXII); a lapsed Priest, if restored, may retain his title, but is not allowed to officiate (Anc. I); the same rule applies to lapsed Deacons; but the Bishop may, if he thinks fit, grant them further indulgence (Anc. II).

The lapsed, who have fallen in persecution, may be admitted to penance and communion (Nic. VIII); the lapsed who have fallen without compulsion, are to fulfil twelve years of penance (Nic. XI); those who yielded merely upon threats, are to fulfil six years of penance (Anc. VI); those who submitted to force with indifference, are to fulfil a term of five years (Anc. IV); and those who submitted to force with mourning, are to be prostrators three years, if they partook of the feast provided; and if not, they are to be prostrators two years, and the third year co-standers (Anc. V); those who brought and ate their own meats at heathen feasts, are to be prostrators two years (Anc. VII); those who have fallen a second time, are to be hearers three years, and prostrators ten years (Nic. XII); those who sacrificed two or three times, under compulsion, are to fulfil six years of penance (Anc. VII); those who forced their brethren to apostatize, are to fulfil ten years of penance (Anc. IX); lapsed Catechumens are to fulfil three years of penance (Nic. XIV); those who are under penance for lapse, may be allowed the Sacrament, if in danger of death (Anc. VI).

The lapsed, if afterwards ordained, are to be deposed (Nic. X).

LAWSUITS.—Lawsuits, as to the ownership of property in the possession of a Bishop at the time of his death, are to be prevented, by his keeping his private property distinct from that of the Church (Ap. Can. XL, Ant. XXIV).

LAYMEN.—I. OF THE DUTIES OF LAYMEN.—

Laymen are to remain in Church for prayers and the Holy Communion, as well as for the reading of Scripture (Ap. Can. IX, Ant. II); they are to fast during Lent, and on Wednesdays and Fridays, unless prevented by bodily weakness (Ap. Can. LXIX); they are to remain subject to their Bishops (Chal. VIII); they are to give the Kiss of Peace to the Bishop, after the Priests have done so (Laod. XIX).

—II. OF THE PRIVILEGES OF LAYMEN.—

Bishops, Priests, and Deacons, are forbidden to strike laymen who sin (Ap. Can. XXVII); Bishops and Priests are forbidden to neglect the laity (Ap. Can. LVIII).

Laymen who have been steadfast through the persecutions, though forced to seem otherwise, are entitled to all their former rights, and may, if worthy, be ordained (Anc. III).

A layman has a right of Appeal to a Provincial Synod, against a sentence of his Bishop (Ant. VI, XX).

—III. THINGS FORBIDDEN TO LAYMEN.—

They are forbidden to compose, or use, any other than the Nicene Creed (Eph. VII); or to join in prayer with heretics (Laod. XXXIII); or to assemble in the Cemeteries, or attend the Martyries, of heretics (Laod. IX); or to observe, or receive gifts from, festivals of heretics (Laod. XXXVII); or to marry their children to heretics (Laod. X, XXXI); or to enter a synagogue of Jews or heretics to pray (Ap. Can. LXIV); or to observe, or receive gifts from, Jewish fasts or festivals (Ap. Can. LXX, Laod. XXXVII); or to receive unleavened bread from the Jews (Ap. Can. LXX, Laod. XXXVIII); or to feast with the heathen (Laod. XXXIX); or to join in prayer with schismatics (Laod. XXXIII); or to adhere to the maintainers of conventicles (Ap. Can. XXXI).

They are forbidden to communicate with the excommunicated (Ap. Can. X, Ant. II); or with a Clergyman who, after deposition, meddles with his former ministry (Ant. IV).

They are forbidden to fast on Sunday, or on any Sabbath except Easter Even (Ap. Can. LXVI); or to judaize, by resting on the Sabbath (Laod. XXIX).

They are forbidden to marry after obtaining a divorce, or to marry a divorced woman (Ap. Can. XLVIII); or to

LAYMEN.—Things Forbidden to Laymen.—*Continued.*

abstain from marriage, except for discipline (Ap. Can. LI).

They are forbidden to wash in a bath with women (Laod. XXX).

They are forbidden to castrate themselves (Ap. Can. XXIV).

They are forbidden to abstain from flesh and wine, except for discipline (Ap. Can. LI); or to eat flesh with the blood thereof, or the flesh of animals which have been slain by beasts, or have died a natural death (Ap. Can. LXIII); or to join in forming drinking clubs (Laod. LV).

If invited to a lovefeast, they are forbidden to take away their portions (Laod. XXVII); they are forbidden to join in wanton dances at weddings (Laod. LIII).

They are forbidden to mock the infirm (Ap. Can. LVII); or to insult the Emperor or a Magistrate (Ap. Can. LXXXIV).

They are forbidden to carry off wax or oil from the Church (Ap. Can. LXXII); or to appropriate consecrated vessels to private purposes (Ap. Can. LXXIII).

They are forbidden to negotiate simoniacal contracts (Chal. II).

They are forbidden to communicate at the Altar (Laod. XIX).

—IV. For the penalties to be inflicted on a layman, see *Suspension*, *Excommunication*, and *Anathema*.

—V. General Regulations.—

Laymen who are suspended or excommunicated, in one City, are forbidden to be received in another, without Letters Commendatory (Ap. Can. XII); if excommunicated by their Bishops, they cannot be received by others, unless restored by the Bishop, or unless the sentence is reversed by a Synod (Ant. VI); nor can they be restored by any other than the Bishop who excommunicates them (Nic. V).

A single Communicant cannot be received as the accuser of a Bishop (Ap. Can. LXXV); nor can one who is excommunicated, or who is under accusation for alleged faults, bring charges of ecclesiastical offences against a Bishop; nor can those who are themselves under accusation, bring such charges against any Clergyman (Const. VI); but any one may bring a charge of personal injury done to him by a Bishop; accusers of a Bishop are to be examined as to character (Chal. XXI).

LAYMEN.—V. GENERAL REGULATIONS.—*Continued.*

Laymen who adhere to the maintainers of conventicles, are to be admonished three times before excommunication (Ap. Can. XXXI).

A Deaconess of the Paulianists, who has assumed the habit of that order, if reconciled to the Catholic Church, is to be received amongst the laity (Nic. XIX).

A layman is not to be received from abroad without Letters Pacifical (Ant. VII).

A layman who is possessed of a devil, is to be suspended (Ap. Can. LXXIX).

Prayers for full Communicants (lay) are to follow prayers for those under penance, in Divine Service (Laod. XIX).

For the disqualifications which prevent the ordination of a layman, see *Disqualifications.*

Vid. also *Lay Communion.*

By Laod. XXX, laymen are distinguished from Christians. For regulations as to the latter, see *Christians.*

LAY COMMUNION.—A Priest who is deposed, for leaving his Parish without his Bishop's consent, may be admitted to Lay Communion (Ap. Can. XV); also one who is deposed for denying his clerical position (Ap. Can. LXII).

LEGATES OF ROME.—Vid. *Rome.*

LENT.—Both Clergy and laity are to fast during Lent, unless prevented by bodily weakness (Ap. Can. LXIX); the whole of Lent is to be fasted, by eating only dry meats (Laod. L).

There is to be no Oblation of Bread in Lent, except on Sabbaths and Sundays (Laod. XLIX); the Nativities of Martyrs are not to be celebrated in Lent, but commemorations of the Martyrs are to be made on Sabbaths and Sundays (Laod. LI).

Marriages and birthdays are not to be celebrated in Lent (Laod. LII).

The second week in Lent is the last for receiving candidates for Baptism (Laod. XLV).

Provincial Synods are to be held before Lent (Nic. V).

LEO, SAINT.—The letter of Leo, Archbishop of Rome, is approved by Chal. Encyc. and Can. XXX.

LESSON.—A Lesson is to come after every Psalm in Divine Service (Laod. XVII).

LETTER.—A Letter of Summons to attend the ordination of a Bishop, is to be sent by the Metropolitan to his Provincial Bishops (Ant. XIX).

Vid. also *Tome.*

LETTERS CANONICAL.—Country Priests are forbidden to send Letters Canonical, except to the neighbouring Bishops (Ant. VIII).

Clergymen are forbidden to travel without Letters Canonical (Laod. XLII).

—COMMENDATORY.—Strangers are not to be received without Letters Commendatory (Ap. Can. XII, XXXIII); Clergymen and Readers are forbidden to officiate in another City without Letters Commendatory (Chal. XIII).

Letters Commendatory are not to be given to the poor, but only to persons who are liable to question (Chal. XI).

A Clergyman must obtain the letters of the Metropolitan and Provincial Bishops, before he can petition the Emperor (Ant. XI).

—PACIFICAL.—Strangers are not to be received without Letters Pacifical (Ant. VII).

Letters Pacifical are to be given to the poor after examination (Chal. XI).

A Chorepiscopus may give Letters Pacifical (Ant. VIII).

LIBERTIES.—The liberties of Churches are not to be invaded, even by Exarchs (Eph. VIII).

LICINIUS.—The persecutions under Licinius are mentioned (Nic. XI).

LIMITATION.—The time within which a Bishop's jurisdiction over outlying Provinces can be questioned, is limited to thirty years from the date when such jurisdiction was first acquired (Chal. XVII).

The lapsed, who are admitted to penance, if in danger of death, may be received to communion under limitation (Anc. VI).

LIST.—The Canon, Sacerdotal List, or Roll of the Church, is mentioned in Ap. Can. VIII, XVII, XVIII, LI, LXIII, LXX, Nic. XVII, Chal. II, Ant. I, II, VI, XI.

For lists of Canonical books, see Ap. Can. LXXXV, Laod. LX.

LORD'S DAY.—Vid. *Sunday.*

LORD'S SUPPER.—Vid. *Oblation.*

LOVEFEASTS.—Those who despise Lovefeasts, are to be anathematized (Gang. XI).

Persons who attend Lovefeasts, are forbidden to take away their portions (Laod. XXVII).

Lovefeasts are not to be held in Church (Laod. XXVIII).

LOWLINESS OF MIND—Lowliness of mind is commended (Gang. XXI).

LUCENSIUS.—A Bishop named Lucensius was present at Chalcedon, as one of the Legates of Rome (Chal., Introduction to Can. XXIX).

LUSTRATIONS.—Persons who practice lustrations are to fulfil five years of penance (Anc. XXIV).

LUST.—The penance of those who are guilty of bestial lusts, varies, from a term of fifteen years to complete excommunication, according to circumstances (Anc. XVI); those who have been guilty themselves and have corrupted others, are to pray amongst the Hyemantes (Anc. XVII).

Vid. also *Concupiscence.*

LIBYA.—The Bishop of Alexandria is to have jurisdiction in Libya (Nic. VI).

MACEDONIANS.—Macedonians are admitted to the Catholic Church by Chrism, after renunciation of their heresies (Const. VII).

MAGICIANS.—Magicians are to fulfil five years of penance (Anc. XXIV); Clergymen are forbidden to be magicians (Laod. XXXVI).

MAGISTRATE.—Communicants are forbidden to insult a Magistrate (Ap. Can. LXXXIV).

MAJORITY.—The election of a Bishop is to be by a majority of the Bishops of the Province, in case of factious opposition (Nic. VI, Ant. XIX).

MALICE.—Bishops must not excommunicate persons through malice (Nic. V).

MALVERSATION.—The Provincial Synod is to investigate the accounts of a Bishop who is charged with malversation (Ant. XXV).

MANSLAUGHTER.—A Clergyman, who commits manslaughter, is to be deposed, and a layman to be suspended (Ap. Can. LXV).

MANUMISSION.—Manumission is necessary before a slave can be ordained (Ap. Can. LXXXII).

MARCELLIANS.—The heresy of the Marcellians is anathematized (Const. I).

MARRIAGE.—Marriage is forbidden to the Clergy after ordination, except to Readers and Singers (Ap. Can. XXVI); it is forbidden to Priests (Neo-Cæs. I); but the married state does not disqualify a Priest for offering the Oblation (Gang. IV); marriage is forbidden to Deacons, unless they have been ordained after declaring that they cannot contain (Anc. X); marriage is forbidden to Deaconesses (Chal. XV); and to Monks and dedicated Virgins (Chal. XVI).

MARRIAGE—*Continued.*

Abhorrence of marriage is a blasphemous slander of GOD'S work, and is punishable by complete excommunication (Ap. Can. LI); those who abhor and condemn marriage, are anathematized (Gang. I); also those who abstain from marriage because they abhor it (Gang. IX); also women who forsake their husbands from abhorrence of marriage (Gang. XIV).

Marriage is commended (Gang. XXI).

Readers and Singers are forbidden to intermarry with, or to give their children in marriage to, heretics (Chal. XIV); communicants are forbidden to give their children in marriage to heretics (Laod. X, XXXI), unless they promise to become Christians (Laod. XXXI).

A second marriage, by a man who has divorced his first wife, is forbidden; also marriage with a divorced woman (Ap. Can. XLVIII); also the marriage of a woman with her deceased husband's brother (Neo-Cæs. II).

A second marriage after Baptism disqualifies a man for being ordained (Ap. Can. XVII); also marriage with a widow, a divorced woman, a harlot, a slave, or an actress (Ap. Can. XVIII); also marriage with a deceased wife's sister, or a niece (Ap. Can. XIX).

Persons who have been twice married, are permitted to communicate (Nic. VIII, Laod. I), after a short term of penance (Laod. I); a Priest is forbidden to be a guest at the nuptials of a man contracting a second marriage (Neo-Cæs. VII); those who contract many marriages, may be admitted to communion after penance (Neo-Cæs. III).

One who ravishes a virgin not betrothed, must marry her (Ap. Can. LXVII). Ravishing, under pretence of marriage, is punishable in Clergymen by deposition, and in laymen by excommunication (Chal. XXVII).

Marriages are forbidden to be celebrated in Lent (Laod. LII).

Vid. also *Weddings.*

MARRIED, THE.—Persons who maintain Virginity are forbidden to insult the married (Gang. X).

MARTYRIES.—The Clergy of Martyries are to be subject to the Bishop of the Parish (Chal. VIII).

A Clergyman, who is lawfully transferred to another Parish, is forbidden to meddle with the Martyries of his former ministry (Chal. X).

Communicants are forbidden to attend the Martyries of heretics (Laod. IX).

MARTYRIES—*Continued.*

Appointment to a Martyry is a sufficient title for a Clergyman (Chal. VI).

MARTYRS.—Persons who abhor services in honour of the Martyrs, are anathematized (Gang. XX, and Synodical Epistle); the Martyrs of CHRIST are to be honoured (Laod. XXXIV); the Nativities of Martyrs are not to be celebrated during Lent, but commemorations of the Martyrs are to be made on Sabbaths and Sundays (Laod. LI).

Christians are forbidden to honour the Martyrs of heretics (Laod. XXXIV).

MASS OF THE CATECHUMENS.—The Mass of the Catechumens is to follow the Bishop's Sermon in Divine Service (Laod. XIX).

MASTER.—A slave cannot be ordained, against the will of his master (Ap. Can. LXXXII); nor can he be received as a Monk (Chal. IV); those who attempt to withdraw slaves from their masters' service, are anathematized (Gang. III).

MATHEMATICS.—Clergymen are forbidden to be mathematics (Laod. XXXVI).

MAUNDY THURSDAY.—Candidates for Baptism must recite the Creed to the Bishop, on Maundy Thursday (Laod. XLVI); the fast is not to be broken on Maundy Thursday so as to dishonour the whole of Lent (Laod. L).

MAXIMUS THE CYNIC.—The disturbances in Constantinople, occasioned by Maximus the Cynic, are mentioned, and it is declared that he is not a Bishop, and that those who are ordained by him are not Clergymen (Const. IV).

MEAT.—Vid. *Flesh.*

MEATS.—Only dry meats are allowed during Lent (Laod. L).

Those who have eaten their own meats at heathen feasts, are to be Prostrators two years (Anc. VII).

METROPOLIS.—The Metropolis is to have its due dignity assured (Nic. VII).

The erection of a new Metropolis in a Province, is forbidden; and Cities already uncanonically raised by the civil power to the Metropolitan rank, are to have the title only of Metropolis, and not the jurisdiction (Chal. XII).

METROPOLITAN.—One Bishop in each country is to be recognized as chief (Ap. Can. XXXIV); the Bishops of each Province are to recognize the Bishop of the Metropolis as their head (Ant. IX); there is to be only one Metropolitan in a Province (Chal. XII).

METROPOLITAN—*Continued.*

A Metropolitan is not to act without the consent of his Provincial Bishops (Ap. Can. XXXIV, Ant. IX); he is to be consulted by his Bishops, before they do anything of great moment (Ap. Can. XXXIV, Ant. IX); he is to have charge of the whole Province (Ant. IX); his consent is necessary to the election of a Bishop (Nic. IV, VI); he must be personally present at the ordination of a Bishop (Ant. XIX); he and his Provincial Bishops must concur in the appointment of a Bishop (Laod. XII); a Synod at which the Metropolitan is not present, is not to be considered a full Synod (Ant. XVI, XX); he must consent before a petition can be presented to the Emperor (Ant. XI); he may, on the trial of a Bishop, call in some of the Bishops of the neighbouring Provinces, if his own Bishops cannot agree (Ant. XIV); he and his Provincial Bishops may jointly give, to a Bishop of another Province, a written invitation to ordain for them (Ant. XIII).

The Metropolitan is to appoint the place of meeting of Provincial Synods (Chal. XIX); he is to ordain a Bishop to a See within three months of its becoming vacant (Chal. XXV); he is to invite his Provincial Bishops, by letter, to assist at the ordination of a Bishop (Ant. XIX).

The Metropolitan is to have precedence in rank, within his own Province (Ant. IX); Metropolitan rights unlawfully divided, are reserved to the true Metropolis (Chal. XII); each Metropolitan is entitled to a copy of the Canons of Ephesus (Eph. VIII).

Complaints against a Metropolitan, are to be brought before the Exarch of the Diocese, or the Throne of Constantinople (Chal. IX, XVII).

A Metropolitan who professes the heresies of Nestorius and Celestius, is to be deposed and excommunicated, and to be subject to the control of his own Bishops and the neighbouring orthodox Metropolitans (Eph. Encyc., and Can. I).

MILITARY SERVICE.—Military service is forbidden to Bishops, Priests, and Deacons (Ap. Can. LXXXIII); it is forbidden to Clergymen of all ranks, and to Monks (Chal. VII).

MILK.—Milk is forbidden to be offered at the Altar (Ap. Can. III).

MINISTRY.—A Bishop, Priest, or Deacon, is forbidden, after deposition, to touch his former ministry (Ap. Can. XXVIII, Ant. IV).

A Bishop who will not enter upon his ministry, is to be suspended (Ap. Can. XXXVI, Ant. XVII), and judged by the Synod (Ant. XVII); a Priest or Deacon, who will not

MONEYS.—The moneys of the Church are to be under the control of the Bishops (Ap. Can. XLI, Ant. XXV), acting with the consent of the Priests and Deacons (Ant. XXV); and are to be used for the support of the Bishop and his guests, and of the poor (Ap. Can. XLI, Ant. XXV).

MONKS.—A slave cannot be made a Monk, without the consent of his master; and no Monastery, or Oratory, can be established anywhere without the consent of the Bishop of the Parish (Chal. IV).

Monks are to remain permanently at their Monasteries, and to give themselves to fasting and prayer (Chal. IV); they are to be subject to the Bishop of the Parish (Chal. IV, VIII).

Monks are forbidden to engage in secular business (Chal. III, IV); unless called by the law to the guardianship of minors (Chal. III); they are forbidden to accept military or civil office (Chal. VII); they are forbidden to meddle with ecclesiastical business, except by direction of their Bishop (Chal. III, IV); they are forbidden to negotiate simoniacal contracts (Chal. II); they are forbidden to marry (Chal. XVI); or to wash in a bath with women (Laod. XXX); they are forbidden to enter a tavern (Laod. XXIV).

A Monk going to Constantinople, and causing disturbances there, is to be expelled from the City (Chal. XXIII).

Vid. also *Ascetic.*

MONTANISTS.—Montanists desiring reconciliation to the Catholic Church, are to be received as heathen (Const. VII).

MOPSUESTIA, THEODORE OF.—The heresies of Theodore of Mopsuestia are anathematized (Eph. VII).

MOTHER.—The mother of a Clergyman may reside with him (Nic. III).

MUNICIPAL DISTRICTS.—Ecclesiastical districts in a new or rebuilt City, are to coincide with the municipal divisions (Chal. XVII).

MURDERERS.—Wilful murderers can only be admitted to communion at the point of death (Anc. XXII).

MUTILATION.—Vid. *Castration.*

MYSTERIES, HOLY.—Heretics, who are reconciled to the Catholic Church, are, after Chrism, to communicate in the Holy Mysteries (Laod. VII).

NATIVITIES OF MARTYRS.—Nativities of Martyrs are forbidden to be celebrated during Lent (Laod. LI).

NEEDY.—Vid. *Poor.*

NEGLIGENCE.—Negligence of his duties, by a Bishop or Priest, is punishable by suspension, and if continued, by deposition (Ap. Can. LVIII).

NEO-CÆSAREA.—The Canons of Neo-Cæsarea are confirmed by Chal. I.

NEOPHYTE.—A Neophyte is not to be made a Bishop (Ap. Can. LXXX); he is not to be made a Bishop or Priest without a time of probation (Nic. II); he is not to be ordained (Laod. III).

Neophytes are to learn the Creed by heart, and recite it to the Bishop on Maundy Thursday, before being baptized (Laod. XLVI).

NESTORIUS.—A Metropolitan, who professes the heresies of Nestorius, is to be deposed and excommunicated, and to be subject to his own Bishops and the neighbouring Orthodox Metropolitans (Eph. Encyc., Can. I); a Provincial Bishop, for the same cause, is to be deposed (Eph. Encyc., Can. II, Can. VII); also a Priest, Deacon, or Minor Clergyman (Eph. Encyc., Can. IV, Can. VII); and a layman is to be excommunicated (Eph. VII).

Prohibitions by Nestorius are declared to be void (Eph. III); and also restorations by him of deposed Clergymen (Eph. V).

NEW ROME.—The Bishop of Constantinople is to have precedence next to the Bishop of Rome, because Constantinople is New Rome (Const. III, Chal. XXVIII).

NEW TESTAMENT.—Vid. *Testament.*

NICÆA.—The Creed of Nicæa is confirmed at Constantinople (Const. I), and at Ephesus (Eph. VII), and Chalcedon (Chal. Encyc.); the Creed of Nicæa is to be the only Declaration of Faith demanded of converts from heathenism, Judaism, or heresy, and the composition of any other Creed is stringently forbidden (Eph. VII, Chal. Encyc.); the decision of Nicæa, regarding the time for celebrating Easter, is reaffirmed (Ant. I); the Canons of Nicæa are confirmed (Chal. I).

NIECE.—Marriage with a niece disqualifies a man for being ordained (Ap. Can. XIX).

NON-ATTENDANCE.—A Bishop who does not attend a Provincial Synod, is to be admonished, unless his attendance was impossible (Chal. XIX); non-attendance of a Bishop at a Provincial Synod, is condemned, unless it is unavoidable (Laod. XL).

NONES.—The same Office of Prayers is to be used both at Nones and at Vespers (Laod. XVIII).

NON-RESIDENCE.—For the Canons directed against non-residence of the Clergy, see *Parish.*

NOVATIANS.—Vid. *Cathari.*

NOVELTIES.—The introduction of novelties is condemned (Gang. XXI).

NOVICE.—A novice is forbidden to be made a Bishop (Ap. Can. LXXX, Nic. II), or Priest (Nic. II); or to be ordained at all (Laod. III).

NUN.—Vid. *Virgin.*

NUPTIALS.—A Priest is forbidden to attend as guest the nuptials of a digamist (Neo-Cæs. VII).

OATH.—The Egyptian Bishops who refused to sign the letter of Leo, Archbishop of Rome, before the appointment of a Bishop of Alexandria, were required to take an oath that they would not leave Chalcedon until the appointment had been made (Chal. XXX).

OBEDIENCE.—Obedience to Bishops is enjoined on Clergymen (Ap. Can. XV, XXXI, XXXIX, Chal. VIII, Ant. III, Anc. XVIII); and on Monks and laymen (Chal. VIII).

A Bishop who is convicted of anything contrary to religion or morals, forfeits his claim to the obedience of his Clergy (Ap. Can. XXXI). A Metropolitan who falls into the heresy of Nestorius or Celestius, forfeits his claim to the obedience of his Provincial Bishops (Eph. I).

OBLATION.—The word *Oblation* (*προσφορά*) is in the Canons commonly used for the Holy Communion, and is indifferently applied to the celebration and to the reception of the Sacrament. *Eucharist* is used with reference to the Holy Gifts, and *Communion* to the status of the Communicant which entitled him to be present at the celebration, and to receive the Sacrament.

The Oblation is forbidden to be made in a private house (Laod. LVIII); or in Lent, except on Sabbaths and Sundays (Laod XLIX).

It is to come last in Divine Service (Laod. XIX); and Communicants are required to remain in Church for the Oblation, as well as for the reading of Scripture (Ap. Can. IX, Ant. II).

At the time of the Holy Oblation, incense may be offered at the Altar (Ap. Can. III).

The Oblation is not to be offered by a lapsed Priest, even if restored (Anc. I); nor by one who has been promoted after confession of bodily sin (Neo-Cæs. IX); nor by a Deacon (Nic. XVIII); nor by a country Priest in a City Church,

OBLATION—*Continued.*

in the presence of the Bishop and City Presbyters (Neo-Cæs. XIII); but this may be done by a Chorepiscopus (Neo-Cæs. XIV).

A married Priest may make the Oblation (Gang. IV).

All Clergymen are required to partake when the Oblation is made, or to give sufficient reasons for abstaining (Ap. Can. VIII); and its reception is always to follow Baptism and Confirmation (Laod. VII, XLVIII).

The Deacon is forbidden to receive before the Bishop or Priest; and it is to be administered to the Deacon by the Bishop or Priest (Nic. XVIII).

It is not to be granted to persons under penance (Nic. XI, XII, Anc. IV, V, VI, VII, VIII, IX, XXII, XXIV); but it is not to be refused to the dying in any case (Nic. XIII), even though they may be under penance (Anc. VI, XVI, XXII, Neo-Cæs. II); but the dying are to be examined by the Bishop before receiving the Oblation (Nic. XIII).

Bishops and Priests are forbidden to admit the Oblation of heretics (Ap. Can. XLVI).

See also *Eucharist* and *Communion;* and for particulars of persons excluded from the Oblation, see *Penance.*

OCTOBER.—Provincial Synods are to be held on the twelfth of October (Ap. Can. XXXVII); they are to be held on the Ides of October (Ant. XX).

ŒCUMENICAL SYNOD.—Vid. *Synod.*

OFFENCES, ECCLESIASTICAL.—For regulations as to persons who may bring accusations of ecclesiastical offences against a Bishop, see *Accusers.*

OFFERING.—Vid. *Oblation.*

OFFERINGS.—Vid. *First-fruits.*

OFFICE.—Clergymen and Monks are forbidden to accept any civil or military office (Chal. VII).

—OF PRAYERS.—The same Office of Prayers is to be used both at Nones and at Vespers (Laod. XVIII).

OIL.—Oil for the Altar lamps may be offered at the Altar (Ap. Can. III); the misappropriation of oil of the Church is forbidden (Ap. Can. LXXII).

Christians are forbidden to take oil into a temple of the heathen, or a synagogue of the Jews, at their festivals (Ap. Can. LXXI).

OLD TESTAMENT.—Vid. *Testament.*

ONESIMUS.—Onesimus is mentioned as having been ordained, after manumission by his master (Ap. Can. LXXXII).

OPPOSITION.—Factious opposition, of a minority of the Bishops of a Province, to the election of a Bishop, is to be disregarded (Ant. XIX).

ORARIUM.—A Sub-deacon has no right to wear an Orarium (Laod. XXII); nor a Reader or Singer (Laod. XXIII).

ORATORY.—An Oratory cannot be established without the consent of the Bishop of the Parish (Chal. IV).

ORDAINER.—Simony in an Ordainer is punishable by deposition (Ap. Can. XXIX, Chal. II), and excommunication (Ap. Can. XXIX). A Bishop who grants a second ordination, is to be deposed, unless the first ordination was void (Ap. Can. LXVIII).

ORDINATION.—Ordination is generally believed to remit past sins (Neo-Cæs. IX).

A Bishop is forbidden to ordain for money (Ap. Can. XXIX, Chal. II); he is forbidden to ordain beyond his own Parish (Ap. Can. XXXV, Const. II, Eph. VIII, Ant. XXII); or beyond his own Province, unless on the written invitation of the Bishops of the Province in which the ordination is made (Ant. XIII); a Chorepiscopus is forbidden to ordain Priests beyond his own District (Anc. XIII); he is forbidden to ordain Priests or Deacons (Ant. X).

A Bishop is to be ordained by two or three Bishops (Ap. Can. I); he is to be ordained by at least three Bishops (Nic. IV); and with the consent of a majority of the Bishops of the Province, and especially of the Metropolitan (Nic. IV, VI, Ant. XIX); he is to be ordained by the Provincial Synod (Ant. XXIII); he is to be ordained to his See within three months of its becoming vacant (Chal. XXV).

A Chorepiscopus is to be ordained by a Bishop (Ant. X).

A Priest, or Deacon, is to be ordained by a Bishop (Ap. Can. II); he is to be ordained by the Bishop of the Parish (Ant. IX).

The Minor Clergy are to be ordained by a Bishop (Ap. Can. II); but Readers, Sub-deacons, and Exorcists, may be ordained by a Chorepiscopus (Ant. X).

The ordination of those who have been steadfast throughout the persecutions, though forced to seem otherwise, is permitted (Anc. III).

Bishops may consent in writing, to the ordination of a Bishop, if personal attendance is difficult (Nic. IV, Ant. XIX).

ORDINATION—*Continued.*

Imposition of hands is necessary to the validity of ordination (Nic. XIX).

Ordinations by heretics are void (Ap. Can. LXVIII); ordinations by Paulianists are void (Nic. XIX); ordinations by Maximus the Cynic are declared to be void (Const. IV); ordinations by the Cathari are valid (Nic. VIII).

For the disqualifications for ordination, see *Disqualifications.*

ORPHANS.—Clergymen acting under their Bishop's directions may undertake the guardianship of orphans (Chal. III).

OUTLYING PARISH.—Vid. *Parish.*

PACIFICAL LETTERS.—Vid. *Letters.*

PARENTS.—Parents, who forsake or neglect their children, are anathematized (Gang. XV); also children, who forsake their parents (Gang. XVI).

PARISH.—A Bishop is forbidden to leave his own Parish, except under special circumstances, and by special request (Ap. Can. XIV); he is forbidden to do so without any exception (Nic. XV, Chal. V, X, XX, Ant. XXI).

A Bishop is to have charge of his own Parish (Ant. IX); but he is not to perform official acts beyond it (Ap. Can. XXXIV, XXXV, Ant. IX, XXII), unless authorized by the proper Bishop (Ant. XXII); he is to retain his jurisdiction over outlying and rural Parishes; but such jurisdiction must have existed for thirty years, to give a good title (Chal. XVII); he has a veto on the establishment of a Monastery or Oratory within his Parish (Chal. IV); he is to have control over the Monks within his Parish (Chal. IV); also over the Clergy of Poorhouses, Monasteries, and Martyries (Chal. VIII); he is to ordain Priests and Deacons within his own Parish (Ant. IX); he may authorize another Bishop to act within his Parish (Ant. XXII).

A Bishop who refuses to proceed to his Parish, is to be suspended (Ap. Can. XXXVI, Ant. XVII), and judged by the Synod (Ant. XVII); a Parish rejecting its Bishop, is to be punished by the suspension of its Clergy (Ap. Can. XXXVI); it is to be judged by the Synod (Ant. XVIII).

A Priest, Deacon, or Minor Clergyman, is forbidden to leave his own Parish without his Bishop's consent (Ap. Can. XV, Ant. III); he is forbidden to do so without any exception (Nic. XV, Chal. V, X, XX); and if he do so, he must return, or be suspended (Nic. XVI).

PARISH—*Continued.*

A Steward is to be appointed in each Parish from among its Clergy (Chal. XXVI).

Eulogiæ are forbidden to be sent from one Parish to another at Easter (Laod. XVI).

Vid. also *See.*

PASCASINUS.—A Bishop named Pascasinus was present at Chalcedon, as one of the legates from Rome (Chal., Introduction to Can. XXIX, also Can. XXX).

PATRIARCH.—See *Exarch.*

PATRIARCHAL SYNOD.—Vid. *Synod.*

PAULIANISTS.—Paulianists seeking reconciliation to the Catholic Church must be rebaptized (Nic. XIX); their Clergy, after Baptism, may, if worthy, be ordained, and, if unworthy, they are to be deposed (Nic. XIX).

PEACE, KISS OF.—The Kiss of Peace is to follow the prayers for full Communicants in Divine Service (Laod. XIX).

PENALTIES, ECCLESIASTICAL.—Vid. *Suspension, Deposition, Degradation, Expulsion, Excommunication, Anathema.*

PENANCE, DEGREES OF.—Penitents are received first as Hearers, then as Prostrators, and finally as Co-standers. These are the ordinary degrees of penance (Nic. XI, XII, XIV, Anc. IV, VI, IX); the term of penance as Hearers is, however, sometimes omitted (Anc. V, VII, VIII, XVI, XXII, XXIV); and there is, besides these, a still lower degree of penance, viz., that of the Hiemantes (Anc. XVII).

PENANCE.—The penance of offenders is to be proportionate to the nature of their offences (Anc. XVI, Laod. II); the penance of the lapsed varies from two to thirteen years, according to circumstances (Nic. XI, XII, XIV, Anc. IV—IX); an adulteress or an adulterer must fulfil seven years of penance (Anc. XX); women who use or prepare drugs for abortion are to fulfil ten years of penance (Anc. XXI); wilful murderers are to remain under penance till the end of life (Anc. XXII); involuntary homicides are to fulfil five years of penance (Anc. XXIII); diviners, sorcerers, and astrologers, are also to fulfil five years (Anc. XXIV); a woman who marries two brothers is to remain under penance till the hour of death (Neo-Cæs. II); the penance of those who contract many marriages is mentioned as being well known (Neo-Cæs. III); a digamist is to fulfil a short term of prayer and fasting (Laod. I); he is declared to be worthy of penance (Neo-Cæs. VII); a Priest who commits adultery is to be cast out and brought to pen-

PENANCE—*Continued.*

ance (Neo-Cæs. I); a certain case of seduction is mentioned as having entailed ten years of penance in the parties before they were received as Co-standers (Anc. XXV).

Penance is not to be readily allowed to the survivor of an unlawful marriage, when the other party dies out of communion (Neo-Cæs. II).

A person who is excommunicated in one City, and not yet admitted to penance, is not to be received in another City (Ap. Can. XII).

Prayers, for those who are under penance, are to follow the prayers for Catechumens, in Divine Service; and persons under penance are to leave the Church before the prayers for the faithful (Laod. XIX).

PENITENCE.—True penitence is a cause for remission of penance (Nic. XII, Anc. II); it is also a necessary condition for admission to penance (Laod. II).

PENITENTS.—Bishops and Priests are directed to receive penitents (Ap. Can. LII); but not without earnest entreaty (Ant. II); a Clergyman who repents of having denied his office, is to be received as a layman (Ap. Can. LXII); persons who are excommunicated for attending the Martyries of heretics, are to be readmitted if penitent (Laod. IX).

PENTAPOLIS.—The Bishop of Alexandria is to have jurisdiction in Pentapolis (Nic. VI).

PENTECOST.—Provincial Synods are to be held in the fourth week of Pentecost (Ap. Can. XXXVII, Ant. XX).

Kneeling at Prayer, during Pentecost, is forbidden (Nic. XX).

PERJURY.—A Clergyman who commits perjury is to be deposed (Ap. Can. XXV).

PERMISSION.—Vid. *Consent.*

PETITION.—A Clergyman cannot present a petition to the Emperor, without the consent of the Metropolitan and Provincial Bishops (Ant. XI).

PHOTINIANS.—The heresy of the Photinians is anathematized (Const. I).

Photinians are admitted to the Catholic Church by Chrism, after anathematizing all heresies, and especially their own, and after having learned the Symbols of the Faith (Laod. VII).

PHRYGIANS.—Phrygians, seeking reconciliation to the Catholic Church, are to be received as heathen (Const. VII); both

PHRYGIANS—*Continued.*

the Clergy and laity of Phrygians are to be instructed and baptized before admission to communion (Laod. VIII).

PHYLACTERIES.—Clergymen are forbidden to make or wear phylacteries (Laod. XXXVI).

PLAINNESS.—Plainness in dress is commended (Gang. XXI).

PLAYS.—Clergymen are forbidden to attend plays at weddings and banquets (Laod. LIV).

PLOTTING.—Plotting against the Bishop or Clergy is punishable, in Clergymen by deposition, and in Monks by excommunication (Chal. XVIII).

PNEUMATOMACHI.—The heresy of the Pneumatomachi is anathematized (Const. I).

POLITICAL DISTRICTS.—Ecclesiastical Districts, in a new or rebuilt City, are to coincide with the political divisions (Chal. XVII).

PONTUS.—The jurisdiction of the Bishop of Pontus is confined to his own Diocese (Const. II); the Metropolitans of Pontus are to be elected according to custom, and to be ordained by the Patriarch of Constantinople; and they are to ordain their own Bishops (Chal. XXVIII).

POOR.—The poor are to be relieved by the Bishop, from the funds of the Church (Ap. Can. XXXVIII, XLI, Ant. XXV); poor Clergymen are to be supplied with necessaries (Ap. Can. LIX).

The poor, when on a journey, are, after examination, to receive Letters Pacifical, not Letters Commendatory (Chal. XI).

The tradition of the Church inculcates charity to the poor (Gang. XXI).

POORHOUSES.—The Clergy of Poorhouses are to be subject to the Bishop of the Parish (Chal. VIII).

POSSESSION.—A man who is possessed of a devil, can neither be ordained, nor received to communion, until he is dispossessed (Ap. Can. LXXIX).

Uninterrupted possession for thirty years, by a Bishop, of jurisdiction over outlying or rural Parishes, gives a good title (Chal. XVII).

POSTURE.—The posture during Prayer is to be standing (Nic. XX).

PRAYER.—Communicants are forbidden to join in Prayer with the excommunicated (Ap. Can. X); Clergymen are forbidden to join in Prayer with a deposed Clergyman (Ap. Can. XI); Bishops, Priests, and Deacons are forbidden to join in Prayer

PRAYER—*Continued.*

with heretics (Ap. Can. XLV, LXIV, Laod. IX, XXXIII); the Minor Clergy and laity are under the same restriction (Ap. Can. LXIV, Laod. IX, XXXIII); Prayer with Jews is forbidden to Clergy and laity (Ap. Can. LXIV); also Prayer with schismatics (Ant. II, Laod. XXXIII).

A Sub-deacon is forbidden to leave the doors to join in Prayer (Laod. XLIII).

Communicants must remain in Church for Prayer, as well as for the reading of Scripture (Ap. Can. IX, Ant. II).

Prayer is enjoined on Monks (Chal. IV).

Prayers on Sunday, and during Pentecost, are to be offered standing (Nic. XX); the same Office of Prayers is to be used both at Nones and at Vespers (Laod. XVIII); in Divine Service the Prayer for the Catechumens is to follow the Bishop's sermon; and after this Prayer, is to come the Prayer for those who are under penance; which is to be followed by three Prayers for the Faithful, the first offered in silence, and the second and third with response (Laod. XIX).

Digamists may be admitted to communion after a short period of prayer and fasting (Laod. I); those who commit many sins, may be admitted to penance, if they give themselves to prayer with fasting and penitence (Laod. II).

Communion in Prayers only is the last degree of penance (Nic. XI, XII, Anc. XVI, XXIV).

PREACHING.—Preaching is forbidden to lapsed Priests, even after they have been restored (Anc. I).

PRECEDENCE.—The Bishop of Jerusalem is to have precedence next to the Metropolitan (Nic. VII).

A Metropolitan is to have precedence within his own Province (Ant. IX).

For the precedence of the Bishops of Rome and Constantinople, see *Rome*, *Constantinople.*

PREGNANT WOMAN.—A pregnant woman may be baptized whenever she will (Neo-Cæs. VI).

PREROGATIVES.—The prerogatives of all Churches are to be retained, according to the ancient customs (Nic. VI, Const. II, Eph. VIII, Chal. XII, XVII).

PRESBYTERATE, DISQUALIFICATIONS FOR THE.—Vid. *Disqualifications.*

PRESBYTERESSES.—Presbyteresses are forbidden to be appointed (Laod. XI).

PRESIDENTS.—Female Presidents are forbidden to be appointed (Laod. XI).

PRESIDING BISHOP.—The Presiding Bishop of a country is to be consulted by the Bishops under him, before they do anything of importance, and he is not to act without their consent (Ap. Can. XXXIV).

Vid. also *Metropolitan.*

PRETENDED ASCETICISM.—Vid. *Asceticism.*

PRIEST.—I. Disqualifications for the Office of a Priest.—

A person to be ordained Priest, must not, after Baptism, have been twice married, nor have had a concubine (Ap. Can. XVII); he must not have married a widow, a divorced woman, a harlot, a slave, or an actress (Ap. Can. XVIII); he must not have married two sisters, nor a niece (Ap. Can. XIX).

He must not have committed adultery, fornication, or any other forbidden act (Ap. Can. LXI); one whose wife has committed adultery cannot be ordained (Neo-Cæs. VIII).

He must not have castrated himself (Ap. Can. XXII, Nic. I); but if castrated by force, or for surgical purposes, he may be ordained; and if so castrated after ordination, he may remain among the Clergy (Nic. I).

He must not be possessed of a devil; but if dispossessed, and worthy, he may be ordained (Ap. Can. LXXIX).

A neophyte cannot be made a Priest without a time of probation (Nic. II, Laod. III); but former profession of heathenism is not in itself a disqualification (Anc. XII).

A slave, unless manumitted by his master, cannot be ordained (Ap. Can. LXXXII).

One who has lapsed cannot be ordained (Nic. X); and if he lapse after ordination, and is subsequently restored, he cannot officiate (Anc. I); but those who have been steadfast throughout the persecutions, though forced to seem otherwise, may be ordained (Anc. III).

A Priest is not to be ordained without examination, nor after confession of crimes (Nic. IX); and if ordained after confession of bodily sin, he cannot make the Oblation (Neo-Cæs. IX).

One who has received Clinic Baptism, cannot be made a Priest, unless on account of special qualifications, or because of lack of men (Neo. Cæs. XII).

A Priest is not to be ordained under thirty years of age (Neo. Cæs. XI); nor without a charge (Chal. VI).

PRIEST—II. Of the Election of a Priest.—

A Priest is not to be elected by the multitude (Laod. XIII).

—III. Of the Ordination of a Priest.—

A Priest is to be ordained by a Bishop (Ap. Can. II); he is to be ordained by the Bishop of the Parish (Ant. IX); he is not to be ordained by a Bishop beyond his jurisdiction (Ant. XXII); nor by a Chorepiscopus, beyond his own Parish, without the Bishop's permission (Anc. XIII); he is not to be ordained by a Chorepiscopus without the Bishop (Ant. X).

He is not to be ordained in another Church, after leaving his own (Nic. XVI).

—IV. Of the Duties of a Priest.—

Offerings not made at the Altar, are to be taken to the house of the Bishop and Priest, and to be shared by them with the other Clergy (Ap. Can. IV); a Priest is to join with his Bishop in the administration of Church funds (Ant. XXV).

He is to act as the Bishop's Almoner (Ap. Can. XLI), and to supply necessaries to Clergymen in need (Ap. Can. LIX).

He is to baptize persons who have been polluted by the impious (Ap. Can. XLVII); to baptize according to the catholic formula (Ap. Can. XLIX); and by trine-immersion (Ap. Can. L); he is to instruct and baptize reconciled Phrygians (Laod. VIII).

He is to receive penitents (Ap. Can. LII).

He is to administer the Eucharist to Deacons (Nic. XVIII); and when it is celebrated, he must partake himself, or give sufficient reasons for refusing (Ap. Can. VIII).

He is to fast during Lent, and on Wednesdays and Fridays, unless prevented by bodily weakness (Ap. Can. LXIX).

He is to give the Kiss of Peace to the Bishop, at the close of Divine Service, before the laity do so (Laod. XIX).

The Priests of Poorhouses, Monasteries, and Martyries, are to remain subject to their Bishop (Chal. VIII).

—V. Of the Privileges of a Priest.—

A Priest is to receive his share of Offerings not made at the Altar (Ap. Can. IV); when in need, he is to be supplied with necessaries (Ap. Can. LIX).

A Priest who is deposed by Nestorius or his followers, is to be restored (Eph. III).

A Priest may communicate at the Altar (Laod. XIX).

Clergymen are forbidden to insult a Priest (Ap. Can. LVI).

PRIEST.—V. Of the Privileges of a Priest.—*Continued.*

A Priest is superior to a Deacon; and a Deacon may not sit amongst the Priests (Nic. XVIII); nor may he sit in the presence of a Priest, without permission (Laod. XX).

Ecclesiastical acts cannot be performed by private persons, against the will of the Bishop and Priest (Gang. VI).

A Priest has a right of appeal to a Provincial Synod, against a sentence of his Bishop (Nic. V, Ant. VI, XII, XX).

A Priest who has a complaint against another Clergyman, may lay it before his Bishop; and if he have a complaint against a Bishop, he may lay it before the Provincial Synod (Chal. IX); if he have a difference with a Metropolitan, he may bring it before the Exarch of the Diocese, or the Throne of Constantinople (Chal. IX, XVII).

A Priest owes no obedience to a Bishop who is convicted of anything contrary to religion or morals (Ap. Can. XXXI).

A Priest is to be informed by his Bishop which is and which is not Church Property (Ant. XXIV).

A married Priest may offer the Oblation (Gang. IV).

Country Priests are forbidden to officiate in a City Church, in the presence of a City Priest (Neo-Cæs. XIII).

A Priest who has been steadfast throughout the persecutions, though forced to seem otherwise, is entitled to all his former privileges (Anc. III).

—VI. Things Forbidden to a Priest.—

A Priest is forbidden to divorce his wife under pretext of religion (Ap. Can. V); or to marry after ordination (Ap. Can. XXVI, Neo-Cæs. I); or to abstain from marriage, except for discipline (Ap. Can. LI); or to have any woman dwelling with him, except such relations, or other persons, as are beyond suspicion (Nic. III); or to wash in a bath with women (Laod. XXX).

He is forbidden to engage in worldly business (Ap. Can. VI, LXXXI); unless called by the law to the guardianship of minors (Chal. III); he is forbidden to meddle with any other than ecclesiastical business, and with that only by direction of his Bishop (Chal. III); he is forbidden to serve in the army (Ap. Can. LXXXIII); or to accept military or civil office (Chal. VII).

He is forbidden to become security (Ap. Can. XX); or to exact usury (Ap. Can. XLIV, Nic. XVII, Laod. IV).

He is forbidden to read false and heretical books in Church, as Scripture (Ap. Can. LX); or to compose, or use, any other than the Nicene Creed (Eph. VII, Chal. Encyc.); or

PRIEST.—VI. Things Forbidden to a Priest.—*Continued.*

to join in prayer with heretics (Ap. Can. XLV, Laod. XXXIII); or to employ them as Clergymen (Ap. Can. XLV); or to admit the Baptism or Sacrifice of heretics (Ap. Can. XLVI); or to receive the Eulogiæ of heretics (Laod. XXXII); or to attend the Cemeteries or the Martyries of heretics (Laod. IX); or to marry his children to heretics (Laod. X, XXXI); or to observe, or receive gifts from, festivals of heretics (Laod. XXXVII); or to enter a synagogue of Jews or heretics, for prayer (Ap. Can. LXIV); or to celebrate Easter before the Vernal Equinox, as the Jews do (Ap. Can. VII, Nic. Encyc., Ant. I); or to observe, or receive gifts from, Jewish fasts or festivals (Ap. Can. LXX, Laod. XXXVII); or to receive unleavened bread from the Jews (Ap. Can. LXX, Laod. XXXVIII); or to feast with the heathen (Laod. XXXIX); or to join in prayer with schismatics (Ant. II, Laod. XXXIII); or to adhere to the maintainers of conventicles (Ap. Can. XXXI).

He is forbidden to submit to the jurisdiction of Nestorius or his partisans (Eph. III).

He is forbidden to gather a separate congregation, and raise another Altar (Ap. Can. XXXI, Ant. V).

He is forbidden to communicate with the excommunicated (Ap. Can. X, Ant. II); or with a Clergyman who is deposed for celebrating Easter before the Vernal Equinox (Ant. I); or with a Bishop who has obtained his Church through secular rulers (Ap. Can. XXX); or with a Clergyman who, after deposition, meddles with his former ministry (Ant. IV); or to join in prayer with a deposed Clergyman (Ap. Can. XI).

He is forbidden to remove from his own Parish (Nic. XV, Chal. V, XX), without his Bishop's consent (Ap. Can. XV, Ant. III), or unless he is driven by necessity from his own country (Chal. XX); and if he do so, he cannot act officially (Ap. Can. XV, Nic. XV, XVI, Ant. III), nor be received by another Church (Nic. XVI); he is forbidden to be enrolled in two Churches (Chal. X); and if lawfully transferred to another Church, he is forbidden to meddle with the affairs of his former ministry (Chal. X).

He is forbidden to act without the consent of his Bishop (Ap. Can. XXXIX); he is forbidden to act without the consent of the Bishop of the City (Laod. LVII); or to address the Emperor without the consent of the Metropolitan and Provincial Bishops (Ant. XI); or to travel without his Bishop's consent (Laod. XLI); or without Letters Canonical

PRIEST.—VI. THINGS FORBIDDEN TO A PRIEST.—*Continued.*

(Laod. XLII); or to officiate in another City, without Letters Commendatory from his Bishop (Chal. XIII).

He is forbidden to carry off wax or oil from the Church (Ap. Can. LXXII); or to appropriate consecrated vessels to private purposes (Ap. Can. LXXIII).

He is forbidden to seize his Bishop's property on his death (Chal. XXII).

He is forbidden to offer anything at the Altar, except new ears of grain and clusters of grapes (Ap. Can. III).

He is forbidden to receive the Eucharist from a Deacon (Nic. XVIII); he is forbidden to make the Oblation in private houses (Laod. LVIII); country Priests are forbidden to make the Oblation in a City Church, in the presence of the Bishop and City Priests (Neo-Cæs. XIII).

He is forbidden to rebaptize one who has true Baptism, or to refuse to baptize one who has been polluted by the impious (Ap. Can. XLVII).

He is forbidden to receive a second ordination, unless the first was void (Ap. Can. LXVIII).

He is forbidden to commit simony (Ap. Can. XXIX, Chal. II); or to negotiate simoniacal contracts (Chal. II).

He is forbidden to abstain from flesh or wine, except for discipline (Ap. Can. LI); especially on festival days (Ap. Can. LIII); but after tasting flesh once, he may abstain, if he wishes to do so (Anc. XIV); he is forbidden to eat flesh with the blood, or the flesh of animals which have been slain by beasts, or have died a natural death (Ap. Can. LXIII); or to fast on Sunday, or on any Sabbath except Easter Even (Ap. Can. LXVI); or to join in forming drinking clubs (Laod. LV); or to eat in a tavern, except on a journey (Ap. Can. LIV); or to enter a tavern (Laod. XXIV).

He is forbidden to be a guest at the marriage of a digamist (Neo-Cæs. VII).

If invited to a Lovefeast, he is forbidden to take away his portion (Laod. XXVII); he is forbidden to attend plays at weddings and banquets (Laod. LIV).

He is forbidden to castrate himself (Ap. Can. XXIII, Nic. I).

He is forbidden to strike backsliders or unbelievers (Ap. Can. XXVII).

If deposed, he is forbidden to touch his former ministry (Ap. Can. XXVIII, Ant. IV).

He is forbidden to insult his Bishop (Ap. Can. LV); or to insult a Priest or Deacon (Ap. Can. LVI); or the Emperor,

PRIEST.—VI. THINGS FORBIDDEN TO A PRIEST.—*Continued.*

or a Magistrate (Ap. Can. LXXXIV); or to mock the infirm (Ap. Can. LVII).

He is forbidden to neglect his duties (Ap. Can. LVIII).

He is forbidden to deny his Clergy (Ap. Can. LXII).

He is forbidden to practice magic, enchantment, or mathematics, or to make or wear phylacteries (Laod. XXXVI).

He is forbidden to enter the Bema before his Bishop (Laod. LVI).

If he have a complaint against another Clergyman, he is forbidden to forsake his Bishop and run to secular courts (Chal. IX).

A country Priest is forbidden to send Letters Canonical, except to neighboring Bishops (Ant. VIII).

—VII. OF THE TRIAL OF A PRIEST.—

A Priest cannot be convicted of any bodily sin on the evidence of a single witness (Nic. II); nor can he be convicted of any offence on the evidence of those who are themselves under accusation (Const. VI); accusers of a Priest are to be examined as to character (Chal. XXI).

A Priest who appeals to the Emperor, instead of to a Synod, against a sentence of deposition, cannot be restored, nor can his cause be reheard by a Synod (Ant. XII).

A Priest who misappropriates Church Property, is to be judged by the Synod (Ant. XXV).

—VIII. PENALTIES TO BE INFLICTED ON A PRIEST.—

Vid. *Suspension of a Priest*, *Deposition of a Priest*, *Excommunication*, and *Anathema.*

—IX. GENERAL REGULATIONS AS TO A PRIEST.—

A Priest who is suspended or excommunicated by his Bishop, cannot be restored by any other Bishop (Ap. Can. XXXII, Nic. V), unless the Bishop who suspended him should die (Ap. Can. XXXII); nor can he be received by others, unless restored by his Bishop, or unless the sentence is reversed by a Synod (Ant. VI); nor, if suspended or excommunicated in one City, can he be received in another, without Letters Commendatory (Ap. Can. XII); nor, if suspended or deposed for leaving his own Parish, can he be received as a Clergyman (Ap. Can. XVI, Ant. III).

A Priest is not to be received from abroad without Commendatory Letters, nor, even if he bring them, without examination (Ap. Can. XXXIII).

A heretic cannot be employed as a Priest in the Catholic Church (Ap. Can. XLV).

PRIEST.—IX. General Regulations as to a Priest.—*Continued.*

The restoration by Nestorius or his followers, of a deposed Priest, is declared void (Eph. V).

An excommunicated Priest cannot bring accusations against a Bishop (Const. VI); a Priest bringing charges against a Clergyman, is to be examined as to character (Chal. XXI).

A lapsed Priest, if restored, is entitled to his former honours, but he cannot officiate (Anc. I), nor, if ordained after the commission of bodily sin, can he make the Oblation (Neo-Cæs. IX).

A Priest going to Constantinople and causing disturbances there, is to be expelled from the City (Chal. XXIII).

A Priest who is deposed for celebrating Easter before the Vernal Equinox, is to be deprived of the external honour due to the Priesthood (Ant. I).

A Priest who abstains from flesh, must taste it at least once (Anc. XIV).

If the wife of a Priest commit adultery, he must divorce her, or desist from his ministry (Neo-Cæs. VIII).

A Priest who is guilty of maintaining conventicles, is to be admonished three times by his Bishop before punishment (Ap. Can. XXXI, Ant. V).

A Bishop is forbidden to be reduced to the rank of a Priest (Chal. XXIX).

Bishops are described as of the Priesthood (Const. VI, Eph. II, Chal. XXVI).

A Priest of the Cathari, if reconciled to the Catholic Church, retains his orders, and his rank amongst other reconciled Clergymen (Nic. VIII); a Bishop of the Cathari, if reconciled, is to rank as a Priest whilst within the jurisdiction of a Catholic Bishop, and is entitled to employment as a Chorepiscopus or Priest (Nic. VIII).

A Priest of the Paulianists, reconciled to the Catholic Church, is, if worthy, to be ordained, and if unworthy, to be deposed (Nic. XIX).

A Priest ordained by Maximus the Cynic, is declared not to be a Clergyman (Const. IV).

A Priest of the Phrygians, seeking reconciliation to the Catholic Church, is to be instructed and baptized before admission (Laod. VIII).

PRIESTHOOD.—Bishops are included in the Priesthood (Const. VI, Eph. II, Chal. XXVI, Laod. XIX); the expression "the Priesthood of the Episcopate" is used in Chal. XXIX.

PRIVATE JUDGMENT.—Private judgment is forbidden to be maintained against the decision of the Church, as to the time of celebrating Easter (Ant. I).

—PSALMS.—Private Psalms are forbidden to be read in Church (Laod. LIX).

—HOUSE.—Vid. *House.*

PROBATION.—A Bishop is not to be appointed until after long probation, both of faith and life (Laod. XII).

PROCLAMATIONS.—Lapsed Deacons, who have been restored, are forbidden to make proclamations (Anc. II).

PROPERTY.—The property of a Bishop is to be kept distinct from that of the Church (Ap. Can. XL, Ant. XXIV); at his death, it is not to be seized by Clergymen, for the Church (Chal. XXII).

—ECCLESIASTICAL.—

Bishops are to have charge of ecclesiastical property (Ap. Can. XXXVIII, Ant. XXIV); they are forbidden to alienate it, or to bestow it upon their own relatives (Ap. Can. XXXVIII); they are to keep it distinct from their private property (Ap. Can. XL, Ant. XXIV).

Ecclesiastical property, which has been sold by Priests during the vacancy of a See, is to be reclaimed by the Bishop (Anc. XV).

The property of a Church having a Bishop, is to be managed by a Steward (Chal. XXVI).

The property of Monasteries is to be secured to them (Chal. XXIV).

PROSELYTE.—Vid. *Neophyte.*

PROSTRATORS.—Vid. *Degrees of Penance.*

PROVINCE.—No Bishop may act officially beyond his own Province, without the written invitation of the Metropolitan and Provincials of the Province in which he acts (Ant. XIII); but the Bishops of one Province may take part in the trial of a Bishop of another Province, if the Com-provincials of the accused Bishop cannot agree (Ant. XIV).

A Bishop is forbidden to obtain from the secular power the division of a Province, and the erection of a new Metropolis (Chal. XII).

For regulations as to the Bishops of particular Provinces, see *Alexandria*, *Antioch*, *Asia*, *Constantinople*, *Cyprus*, *Egypt*, *the East*, *Jerusalem*, *Libya*, *Pentapolis*, *Pontus*, *Rome*, *Thrace.*

PROVINCIAL CHURCHES.—The rights of Provincial Churches are to be maintained according to ancient custom (Nic. VI, Eph. VIII).

—SYNODS.—Vid. *Synods.*

—BISHOPS.—Vid. *Bishops.*

PSALMS.—The Psalms are not to be read consecutively, but with a Lesson after each (Laod. XVII).

Private Psalms are forbidden to be read in Church (Laod. LIX).

PUBLIC BUSINESS.—Bishops and Priests are forbidden to engage in public business (Ap. Can. LXXXI).

QUARTODECIMANS.—Quartodecimans are admitted to the Catholic Church by Chrism, after renouncing all heresies, and especially their own (Const. VII, Laod. VII); and after learning the Symbols of the Faith (Laod. VII).

RAPE.—One who has committed rape on a virgin who is not betrothed, must marry her (Ap. Can. LXVII); but if she be betrothed, he must restore her to the man to whom she is betrothed (Anc. XI).

Rape is punishable, in Clergymen, by deposition, and in laymen, by anathema (Chal. XXVII).

RATIFICATION.—Ratification by the Metropolitan is necessary to the validity of the election of a Bishop (Nic. IV, VI).

RAVISHER.—A Clergyman, who ravishes a woman, under pretence of marriage, is punishable by deposition; and a layman, by anathema (Chal. XXVII).

Vid. also *Rape.*

READER.—A Reader may be ordained by a Chorepiscopus (Ant. X).

He is to fast during Lent, and on Wednesdays and Fridays, unless prevented by bodily weakness (Ap. Can. LXIX).

He may marry after ordination (Ap. Can. XXVI); in certain Provinces (Chal. XIV).

He is forbidden to intermarry with, or to give his children in marriage to, a heretic (Chal. XIV); if given to dice or drunkenness, he is to be suspended (Ap. Can. XLIII); he is forbidden to enter a tavern (Laod. XXIV); he is forbidden to officiate in another City, without Letters Commendatory (Chal. XIII); he is forbidden to read wearing the Orarium (Laod. XXIII).

READING.—The reading of heretical and spurious books, publicly, in Church, as Scripture, is forbidden (Ap. Can. LX); the reading of uncanonical books in Church, is forbidden (Laod. LIX).

REBAPTISM.—A Bishop or Priest is forbidden to rebaptize one who has true Baptism (Ap. Can. XLVII).

Paulianists, who are reconciled to the Catholic Church, must be rebaptized (Nic. XIX); also Phrygians (Laod. VIII).

REBELLION.—Rebellion against their Bishops, is punishable, in Clergymen, by deposition, and in laymen or Monks, by excommunication (Chal. VIII).

RECEPTION.—The reception of a suspended or excommunicated person, who is not furnished with Letters Commendatory, is forbidden (Ap. Can. XII); the reception by a Bishop, of suspended Priests, in their clerical capacity, is forbidden (Ap. Can. XVI); the reception by a Bishop, of excommunicated persons, is forbidden (Ant. IV); the reception of a stranger, without Letters Commendatory, is forbidden (Ap. Can. XXXIII); the reception of a stranger, without Letters Pacifical, is forbidden (Ant. VII); the reception of candidates for Baptism, after the second week in Lent, is forbidden (Laod. XLV).

RECEIVER.—The receiver of a person who is under ecclesiastical censure, and who is not furnished with Letters Commendatory, is to be suspended (Ap. Can. XII).

The unlawful receiver of the Offerings of the Church, is to be anathematized (Gang. VIII).

RECLAMATION.—The reclamation by a Bishop, of Church Property, sold by Priests, during the vacancy of the See, is ordered (Anc. XV).

RECONCILIATION OF HERETICS.—Vid. *Heretics*.

REFEREE.—A referee, in disputes between Clergymen, may be appointed by the parties, subject to the Bishop's approval (Chal. IX).

REFORMATION OF THE CHURCH.—The reformation of the Church is one of the objects of Synods (Laod. XL).

REFUGE, HOUSES OF.—A Clergyman, who is lawfully transferred from his own Parish to another, is forbidden to meddle with the Houses of Refuge in his former ministry (Chal. X).

REFUGEES.—Clergymen who have been driven by necessity from their own country, are allowed to officiate in the country of their adoption (Chal. XX).

RELATIONS.—A Bishop is forbidden to bestow Church Property upon his own relations; if they are poor, he is to relieve them like the rest of the poor (Ap. Can. XXXVIII); he is

RELATIONS—*Continued.*

forbidden to ordain them to the Episcopate from personal motives (Ap. Can. LXXVI); or to entrust them with the management of Church Funds (Ant. XXV); he is to provide for them out of his private property (Ap. Can. XL, Ant. XXIV).

RELIGION.—Mutual examination by the Bishops, concerning the doctrines of Religion, is one of the objects of Synods (Ap. Can. XXXVII).

REMOVAL.—Removal of a Bishop from his own Parish, is forbidden, except under special circumstances, and by special request (Ap. Can. XIV); it is forbidden without any exception (Nic. XV, Chal. V, Ant. XXI).

Removal of a Priest or Deacon from his own Parish, without his Bishop's consent, is forbidden (Ap. Can. XV, Ant. III); it is forbidden without any exception (Nic. XV, Chal. V, X, XX); and if they leave their own Church, they cannot be received by another (Nic. XVI).

Removal of a Minor Clergyman from his own Parish, without his Bishop's consent, is forbidden (Ap. Can. XV); it is forbidden without any exception (Chal. V, X, XX); and after removal, they cannot be received by another Church (Nic. XVI).

Removal of a Monk from his Monastery, is forbidden (Chal. IV).

RENUNCIATION.—Renunciation of all heresies, and especially their own, is required from heretics, before their admission to the Catholic Church (Nic. VIII, Const. VII, Laod. VII).

REORDINATION.—Reordination is forbidden, unless the first ordination was void (Ap. Can. LXVIII).

REPENTANCE.—Vid. *Penitence.*

RESCRIPT.—A Bishop is forbidden to obtain an Imperial Rescript for dividing a Province (Chal. XII).

RESIDENCE.—For the Canons which enjoin permanent residence on the Clergy, see *Removal.*

RESPONSE.—The second and third Prayers for full Communicants, in Divine Service, are to be offered with response (Laod. XIX).

RESTING.—Resting on the Sabbath is forbidden, and resting on Sunday, when possible, is enjoined (Laod. XXIX).

RESTORATION.—A Bishop who is unjustly removed from his See, is to be restored (Chal. XXIX); a deposed Bishop cannot be restored, if, after the sentence, he meddles with his former

RESTORATION—*Continued.*

ministry (Ant. IV); nor if he appeals to the Emperor, instead of to a Synod, against the sentence of deposition (Ant. XII).

A Priest or Deacon, who is deposed for the contumacious maintaining of conventicles, cannot be restored (Ant. V); a Priest or Deacon, who is suspended by his Bishop, cannot be restored by another Bishop, unless the Bishop who suspended him should die (Ap. Can. XXXII); persons who are excommunicated by their Bishops cannot be restored by any other Bishop (Nic. V); nor can they be received, until restored by their own Bishops, or by a Synod (Ant. VI); a deposed Clergyman cannot be restored by Nestorius or his partisans (Eph. V).

Those who have been steadfast throughout the persecutions, and are unjustly punished as if they had lapsed, are to be restored to all their former rights (Anc. III).

For regulations as to the restoration of the lapsed, see *Lapsed.*

Priests, Deacons, and Minor Clergy, who leave their own Parishes, are to be restored to them (Nic. XVI).

The ravisher of a betrothed virgin, is to restore her to the man to whom she is betrothed (Anc. XI).

REVENUES.—The revenues of the Church are to be under the control of the Bishops (Ap. Can. XLI, Ant. XXV); acting with the consent of the Priests and Deacons (Ant. XXV); they are to be used for the support of the Bishop and his guests (Ap. Can. XLI, Ant. XXV).

The revenues of a vacant See are to be accumulated by its Steward (Chal. XXV).

RIGHTS.—Provincial and Diocesan rights are to be maintained, according to ancient custom (Eph. VIII).

ROME.—The Bishop of Rome is to have his ancient and customary jurisdiction (Nic. VI).

The Bishop of Constantinople is to rank next after the Bishop of Rome, because Constantinople is New Rome (Const. III, Chal. XXVIII); the precedence of Rome is declared, by the Council of Chalcedon, to have been rightly conceded by the Fathers of Constantinople, because Rome was the capital of the Empire (Chal. XXVIII).

The Throne of Rome is spoken of as apostolic (Chal. XXV).

Bishops Pascasinus and Lucensius, with the Priest Boniface, attended the Council of Chalcedon as legates of Rome

ROME—*Continued.*

(Chal., Introduction to Can. XXIX). Pascasinus is mentioned again in the same way (Chal. XXX).

RURAL PARISH.—Vid. *Parish.*

SABBATH.—Communicants are forbidden to fast on any Sabbath except Easter Even (Ap. Can. LXVI); they are forbidden to judaize by resting on the Sabbath (Laod. XXIX).

There is to be no Oblation of Bread in Lent, except on Sabbaths and Sundays (Laod. XLIX); commemorations of Martyrs are to be made, in Lent, only on Sabbaths and Sundays (Laod. LI).

The Gospels and other Scriptures are to be read on the Sabbath (Laod. XVI).

SABBATIANS.—Sabbatians are admitted to the Catholic Church by Chrism, after renunciation of all heresies (Const. VII).

SABELLIANS.—The heresy of the Sabellians is anathematized (Const. I); Sabellians, who desire reconciliation to the Catholic Church, are to be received as heathen (Const. VII).

SACERDOTAL LIST.—Vid. *List.*

SACRIFICE.—This word is applied twice in the Apostolical Canons to the celebration of the Eucharist (Ap. Can. III, XLVI). The term in ordinary use is "Oblation," which see.

SACRILEGE.—To reduce a Bishop to the rank of a Presbyter is sacrilege (Chal. XXIX).

SAINT LEO.—Vid. *Leo.*

SAINTS' DAYS.—Those who despise the services on Saints' days, are anathematized (Gang. XX). See also Synod. Ep. of same Council.

SANCTUARY.—Women are forbidden to enter the Sanctuary (Laod. XLIV); Priests are forbidden to enter the Sanctuary before their Bishops (Laod. LVI).

Vid. also *Bema.*

SCHISM.—(NOTE.—Under this head is included the maintaining of conventicles.)

Schism is punishable in Clergymen by deposition (Ap. Can. XXXI, Eph. II, Chal. VIII, Ant. V); and in laymen by suspension (Ap. Can. XXXI); it is punishable in Monks or laymen by excommunication (Chal. VIII); it is punishable in Clergymen by final deposition; and, if contumaciously persisted in, it is to be treated as sedition by the civil power (Ant. V).

A Metropolitan, who joins the schismatical assembly at Ephesus, is to be deposed and excommunicated, and to be

SCHISM—*Continued.*

subject to his own Bishops and the neighbouring orthodox Metropolitans (Eph. I).

Schismatics are anathematized (Gang. VI, Laod. XXXV).

Schismatics are not allowed to bring charges of ecclesiastical offences against a Bishop; for this purpose they are classed with heretics (Const. VI).

Communicants are forbidden to join in prayer with schismatics (Ant. II, Laod. XXXIII).

Schismatics are to be admonished by the Bishop before punishment (Ap. Can. XXXI, Ant. V).

Vid. also *Heretics.*

SCRIPTURE.—Only the Canonical Books of Scripture are to be read in Church (Ap. Can. LX, Laod. LIX); the Gospels and other Scriptures are to be read on the Sabbath (Laod. XVI).

Communicants must remain in Church for Prayer and the Holy Communion, as well as for the reading of Scripture (Ap. Can. IX, Ant. II).

SEAL.—Chrism is declared to be the Seal of the Gift of the HOLY GHOST (Const. VII).

SECOND BAPTISM.—Vid. *Baptism.*

—ORDINATION.—Vid. *Ordination.*

—MARRIAGE.—Vid. *Marriage.*

SECULAR POWER.—

A Bishop is forbidden to obtain his Church through secular rulers (Ap. Can. XXX); or to obtain from them the division of a Province, and the erection of a new Metropolis (Chal. XII).

The secular power is to treat contumacious persistence in schism as sedition (Ant. V).

—OFFICE.—

Clergymen and Monks are forbidden to accept secular office (Chal. VII).

—USES.—

Monasteries, once consecrated, are forbidden to be used for secular uses (Chal. XXIV).

—AFFAIRS.—Vid. *Business, worldly.*

—COURTS.—Vid. *Courts.*

SECURITY.—Clergymen are forbidden to become security (Ap. Can. XX).

Security was to be given by the Egyptian Bishops at Chalcedon, that they would not leave the City before signing Archbishop Leo's letter (Chal. XXX).

SEDITION.—A Bishop, acting as Priest, who stirs up sedition against the constituted Bishop, is to be deposed (Anc. XVIII).

Contumacious persistence in schism is to be treated by the secular power as sedition (Ant. V).

SEDUCER.—The seducer of a virgin, who is not betrothed, must marry her (Ap. Can. LXVII); but if she be betrothed, he must restore her to the man to whom she is betrothed (Anc. XI).

A Clergyman, who seduces a woman under pretence of marriage, is punishable by deposition, and a layman by anathema (Chal. XXVII); a certain case of seduction is mentioned as having involved ten years of penance in the parties, before they were received as co-standers (Anc. XXV).

SEE.—A Bishop is forbidden to obtain his See through secular rulers (Ap. Can. XXX); or to bequeath it (Ap. Can. LXXVI, Ant. XXIII); or to seize upon a vacant See (Ant. XVI).

A vacant See is described as "widowed;" and it is to be filled within three months of the vacancy, during which time the revenue is to be accumulated by the Steward (Chal. XXV); the property of a vacant See, which the Priests may have sold during the vacancy, is to be reclaimed by the Bishop (Anc. XV).

Provincial Sees are to retain their ancient and customary prerogatives (Nic. VI).

SELF-CASTRATION.—Self-castration is forbidden to both Clergy and laity (Ap. Can. XXII, XXIII, XXIV, Nic. I).

SEMI-ARIANS.—The heresy of the Semi-Arians is anathematized (Const. I).

SENSUAL SIN.—Vid. *Sin.*

SENTENCE.—A Synod may pass sentence on a Bishop in his absence, if he refuse to attend, after being summoned three times (Ap. Can. LXXIV).

A Bishop's sentence of excommunication may be appealed to the Provincial Synod (Nic. V, Ant. VI, XII); a sentence passed on a Bishop, by his Provincial Synod, may be appealed to a greater Synod (Ant. XII); unless the sentence was unanimous, in which case it is to be final (Ant. XV); it cannot be appealed to the Emperor (Ant. XII)

Vid. also *Verdict.*

SERMON.—The Bishop's sermon is to come first in Divine Service (Laod. XIX).

SERVICE.—For the regulations for the conduct of Divine Service, see Laod. XVII, XVIII, XIX.

Those who despise the services in honour of the Martyrs, are to be anathematized (Gang. XX); Communicants are forbidden to attend the Martyries of heretics, for prayer or service (Laod. IX).

Military service is forbidden to Bishops, Priests, and Deacons (Ap. Can. LXXXIII, Chal. VII).

A master is declared to be entitled to his slave's service (Gang. III).

SIMONY.—Simony is punishable by deposition and excommunication (Ap. Can. XXIX); it is punishable by deposition (Chal. II); and the negotiation of simony is punishable, in Clergymen, by deposition, and in laymen and Monks by anathema (Chal. II).

SIN.—Sensual sin is punishable in Bishops and Priests by deposition (Nic. II); a Priest, who has been promoted after confession of bodily sin, cannot make the Oblation (Neo-Cæs. IX); a Deacon, under the same circumstances, is to rank as a Subdeacon (Neo-Cæs. X).

A Catechumen, who falls into sin whilst he is a Kneeler, may be admitted to penance; but if he sin whilst he is a Hearer, he is to be cast out (Neo-Cæs. V).

Those who have been guilty of many sins may be admitted to penance, if they apply themselves to prayer with fasting and penitence (Gang. II).

Baptism washes away sin (Anc. XII).

SINGER.—A Singer is to fast during Lent, and on Wednesdays and Fridays, unless prevented by bodily weakness (Ap. Can. LXIX); he is to sing in the Ambo (Laod. XV).

A Singer may marry after ordination (Ap. Can. XXVI); in certain Provinces (Chal. XIV).

A Singer who is given to dice or drunkenness, is to be suspended (Ap. Can. XLIII); he is forbidden to intermarry with, or give his children in marriage to, heretics (Chal. XIV); he is forbidden to sing wearing the Orarium (Laod. XXIII); he is forbidden to enter a tavern (Laod. XXIV).

SISTER.—The sister of a Clergyman may reside with him (Nic. III).

SISTER-IN-LAW.—A man who marries his sister-in-law, cannot be ordained (Ap. Can. XIX); a woman who marries her husband's brother, can be admitted to communion only at the point of death (Neo-Cæs. II).

SLANDER.—Persons who bring slanderous accusations against a Bishop, are to suffer the penalty to which he would have been liable, had the accusations been proved (Const. VI).

SLAVE.—A man who marries a slave cannot be ordained (Ap. Can. XVIII).

A slave cannot be ordained, unless his master manumit him (Ap. Can. LXXXII); nor can he be received as a Monk, without his master's consent (Chal. IV); if castrated by his master, he is not thereby disqualified for ordination (Nic. I).

Persons who attempt to withdraw slaves from their masters' service, are anathematized (Gang. III).

A Bishop is to provide for his slaves out of his private property (Ap. Can. XL).

SLEEPING.—Sleeping in Church is forbidden (Laod. XXVIII).

SONS.—A Bishop is forbidden to ordain his own sons to the Episcopate from personal motives (Ap. Can. LXXVI); or to employ them in the management of Church Funds (Ant. XXV). Vid. also *Children.*

SORCERERS.—Sorcerers are to fulfil five years of penance (Anc. XXIV).

SPIRITS.—Spirits are forbidden to be offered at the Altar (Ap. Can. III).

SPURIOUS BOOKS.—Vid. *Books.*

STANDING.—Prayers on Sunday, and during Pentecost, are to be offered standing (Nic. XX).

STEWARD.—Every Church that has a Bishop, is to have a Steward among its Clergy (Chal. XXVI).

The Steward of a See is to accumulate its revenues during a vacancy (Chal. XXV); he is to take charge of the Offerings (Gang. VII, VIII).

A Steward who obtains his office for money, is to be deposed (Chal. II).

Clergymen and Monks are forbidden to act as stewards to laymen (Chal. III).

STOLE.—Vid. *Orarium.*

STRANGER.—A stranger is not to be received without Letters Commendatory (Ap. Can. XXXIII); he is not to be received without Letters Pacifical (Ant. VII).

STRANGLED.—The flesh of animals that have been strangled, is forbidden to be eaten (Gang. II).

STRIKING.—The striking of backsliders or unbelievers, is forbidden to Bishops, Priests, and Deacons (Ap. Can. XXVII).

SUBDEACON.—A Subdeacon may be ordained by a Chorepiscopus (Ant. X).

A Subdeacon is forbidden to give the Bread or to bless the Cup (Laod. XXV); he is forbidden to leave the doors (Laod. XXII, XLIII); he is forbidden to wear an Orarium (Laod. XXIII); he is forbidden to sit in the presence of a Deacon, without his permission (Laod. XX); he is forbidden to enter the Diaconicum, or to touch the sacred vessels (Laod. XXI); he is forbidden to enter a tavern (Laod. XXIV); if given to dice or drunkenness, he is to be suspended (Ap. Can. XLIII).

A Deacon who, before ordination, has committed bodily sin, is to rank as a Sub-deacon (Neo-Cæs. X).

SUBJECTION.—A woman's hair is the token of her subjection (Gang. XVII).

SUBMISSION.—Cathari, seeking reconciliation to the Catholic Church, must promise submission to her decrees (Nic. VIII).

SUCCESSOR.—A Bishop is forbidden to ordain a relation as his successor (Ap. Can. LXXVI), or to appoint his successor at all (Ant. XXIII).

SUFFRAGE.—The suffrage of Bishops, on the election of a Bishop, may be given in writing, if personal attendance is difficult (Nic. IV, Ant. XIX).

SUMMONS.—A summons to a Bishop, to appear for trial, must be served by two Bishops; and it must be served three times, if necessary (Ap. Can. LXXIV).

Bishops are forbidden to neglect a summons to attend a Provincial Synod (Chal. XIX, Laod. XL).

SUNDAY.—Communicants are forbidden to fast on Sunday (Ap. Can. LXVI, Gang. XVIII); they are to rest on Sunday, if possible (Laod. XXIX).

Prayers on Sunday are to be offered standing (Nic. XX).

There is to be no Oblation of Bread in Lent, except on Sabbaths and Sundays (Laod. XLIX); Commemorations of Martyrs are to be made, in Lent, only on Sabbaths and Sundays (Laod. LI).

SUPERCILIOUSNESS.—Superciliousness is condemned (Gang. XXI).

SUPPER, THE LORD'S.—See *Oblation*.

SUPPORT.—I. Of a Bishop.—

A Bishop is to receive his share of Offerings which are not made at the Altar (Ap. Can. IV); he is to be supported from the Funds of the Church (Ap. Can. XLI, Ant. XXV); when in need, he is to be supplied with necessaries (Ap. Can. LIX).

SUPPORT.—II. OF A PRIEST, DEACON, OR MINOR CLERGYMAN.—

Priests, Deacons, and the Minor Clergy, are to receive their share of Offerings which are not made at the Altar (Ap. Can. IV); when in need they are to be supplied with necessaries (Ap. Can. LIX).

SURETY.—Vid. *Security.*

SURGICAL OPERATION.—A eunuch, who is so made by a surgical operation, is not disqualified for ordination (Nic. I).

SUSPENDED PERSONS.—A person who is suspended in one City, is not to be received in another, without Letters Commendatory (Ap. Can. XII); suspended Clergymen are not to be received by a Bishop in their clerical capacity (Ap. Can. XVI); a Priest or Deacon, who is suspended by his Bishop, is not to be restored by any other Bishop, unless the Bishop who suspended him should die (Ap. Can. XXXII).

SUSPENSION.—I. OF A BISHOP.—

The penalty of Suspension is pronounced against a Bishop who joins in prayer with heretics (Ap. Can. XLV); or communicates with the excommunicated (Ap. Can. X, Ant. II); or receives suspended or excommunicated persons, without Letters Commendatory (Ap. Can. XII); or receives suspended Clergymen in their clerical capacity (Ap. Can. XVI); or receives a Clergyman of another Bishop (Chal. XX).

Or who refuses, without sufficient reason, to partake when the Oblation is made (Ap. Can. VIII).

Or who neglects his duties (Ap. Can. LVIII); or refuses to enter upon his ministry (Ap. Can. XXXVI, Ant. XVII); or refuses to relieve Clergymen who are in need (Ap. Can. LIX).

Or who misappropriates wax or oil of the Church (Ap. Can. LXXII); or appropriates consecrated vessels to private purposes (Ap. Can. LXXIII).

Or who divorces his wife under pretext of religion (Ap. Can. V).

Or who eats in a tavern, unless when he is on a journey (Ap. Can. LIV).

Or who insults a Priest or Deacon (Ap. Can. LVI); or mocks the infirm (Ap. Can. LVII).

Or who ordains a relative to the Episcopate from personal motives (Ap. Can. LXXVI).

Suspension, when contumaciously disregarded, is to be prolonged (Ap. Can. XIII).

SUSPENSION.—II. Of a Priest.—

The penalty of Suspension is pronounced against a Priest who joins in prayer with heretics (Ap. Can. XLV); or communicates with the excommunicated (Ap. Can. X, Ant. II); or receives suspended or excommunicated persons, without Letters Commendatory (Ap. Can. XII).

Or who refuses, without sufficient reason, to partake when the Oblation is made (Ap. Can. VIII).

Or who neglects his duties (Ap. Can. LVIII); or refuses to enter upon his ministry (Ap. Can. XXXVI); or refuses to relieve Clergymen who are in need (Ap. Can. LIX).

Or who leaves his Parish, and refuses to return when summoned by his Bishop (Ap. Can. XV, Nic. XVI, Chal. V, Ant. III); or visits another City without Letters Commendatory (Chal. XIII); or is received by any other than his own Bishop (Chal. XX).

Or who misappropriates wax or oil of the Church (Ap. Can. LXXII); or appropriates consecrated vessels to private purposes (Ap. Can. LXXIII).

Or who divorces his wife under pretext of religion (Ap. Can. V).

Or who eats in a tavern, unless when he is on a journey (Ap. Can. LIV).

Or who insults a Priest or Deacon (Ap. Can. LVI); or mocks the infirm (Ap. Can. LVII.)

If the people of a See refuse to receive a Bishop who is ordained over them, the Clergy of the See are to be suspended (Ap. Can. XXXVI).

Suspension, when contumaciously disregarded, is to be prolonged (Ap. Can. XIII).

—III. Of a Deacon.—

The penalty of suspension is pronounced against a Deacon who joins in prayer with heretics (Ap. Can. XLV); or communicates with the excommunicated (Ap. Can. X, Ant. II); or receives suspended or excommunicated persons, without Letters Commendatory (Ap. Can. XII).

Or who refuses, without sufficient reason, to partake when the Oblation is made (Ap. Can. VIII).

Or who refuses to enter upon his ministry (Ap. Can. XXXVI); or refuses to relieve Clergymen who are in need (Ap. Can. LIX).

Or who leaves his Parish, and refuses to return when summoned by his Bishop (Ap. Can. XV, Nic. XVI, Chal. V, Ant. III); or visits another City without Letters Commenda-

SUSPENSION.—Of a Deacon.—*Continued.*

tory (Chal. XIII); or is received by any other than his own Bishop (Chal. XX).

Or who misappropriates wax or oil of the Church (Ap. Can. LXXII); or appropriates consecrated vessels to private purposes (Ap. Can. LXXIII).

Or who divorces his wife under pretext of religion (Ap. Can. V).

Or who eats in a tavern, unless when he is on a journey (Ap. Can. LIV.)

Or who insults a Priest or Deacon (Ap. Can. LVI); or mocks the infirm (Ap. Can. LVII).

If the people of a See refuse to receive a Bishop who is ordained over them, the Clergy of the See are to be suspended (Ap. Can. XXXVI).

Suspension, when contumaciously disregarded, is to be prolonged (Ap. Can. XIII).

—IV. Of a Reader.—

A Reader who is given to dice or drunkenness, is to be suspended (Ap. Can. XLIII).

A Reader who visits another city without Letters Commendatory, is *ipso facto* suspended (Chal. XIII).

—V. Of a Subdeacon or Singer.—

A Subdeacon or Singer, who is given to dice or drunkenness, is to be suspended (Ap. Can. XLIII).

—VI. Of the Minor Clergy.—

The penalty of Suspension is pronounced against those of the Minor Clergy who communicate with the excommunicated (Ap. Can. X, Ant. II); or receive suspended or excommunicated persons, without Letters Commendatory (Ap. Can. XII).

Or who refuse, without sufficient reason, to partake when the Oblation is made (Ap. Can. VIII).

Or who leave their own Parish, and refuse to return when summoned by the Bishop (Ap. Can. XV, Nic. XVI, Chal. V); or visit another City without Letters Commendatory (Chal. XIII); or are received by any other than their own Bishops (Chal. XX).

Or who misappropriate wax or oil of the Church (Ap. Can. LXXII); or appropriate consecrated vessels to private purposes (Ap. Can. LXXIII).

Or who eat in a tavern, unless when on a journey (Ap.

SUSPENSION—*Continued.*

Can. LIV); or are given to dicing or drunkenness (Ap. Can. XLIII).

Or who insult a Priest or Deacon (Ap. Can. LVI); or mock the infirm (Ap. Can. LVII).

If the people of a See refuse to receive a Bishop who is ordained over them, the Clergy of the See are to be suspended (Ap. Can. XXXVI).

Suspension, when contumaciously disregarded, is to be prolonged (Ap. Can. XIII).

SUSPENSION FROM COMMUNION.—I. OF A BISHOP, PRIEST, DEACON, OR MINOR CLERGYMAN.—

A Clergyman of any rank, who enters a synagogue of Jews or heretics to pray, is to be suspended from communion (Ap. Can. LXIV).

—II. OF A LAYMAN.—

The penalty of Suspension from Communion, is pronounced against a layman, who leaves Church after the reading of Scripture, and does not remain for prayer and the Holy Communion (Ap. Can. IX, Ant. II).

Or who joins in prayer with the excommunicated (Ap. Can. X); or adheres to the maintainers of conventicles (Ap. Can. XXXI); or attends the Cemeteries or Martyries of heretics, for prayer or service (Laod. IX); or enters a synagogue of Jews or heretics to pray (Ap. Can. LXIV); or observes, or receives gifts from, Jewish fasts or festivals (Ap. Can. LXX).

Or who fasts on Sunday, or on any Sabbath except Easter Even (Ap. Can. LXVI); or neglects to fast during Lent, and on Wednesdays and Fridays, unless prevented by bodily weakness (Ap. Can. LXIX).

Or who is given to dice or drunkenness (Ap. Can. XLIII); or commits manslaughter (Ap. Can. LXV); or rape (Ap. Can. LXVII).

Or who misappropriates wax or oil of the Church (Ap. Can. LXXII); or appropriates consecrated vessels to private purposes (Ap. Can. LXXIII).

Or who castrates himself (Ap. Can. XXIV).

Or who divorces his wife and takes another; or marries a divorced woman (Ap. Can. XLVIII).

Or who mocks the infirm (Ap. Can. LVII); or insults the Emperor or a Magistrate (Ap. Can. LXXXIV).

Or who eats flesh with the blood thereof, or the blood of animals which have been slain by beasts, or have died a natural death (Ap. Can. LXIII).

SUSPENSION.—From Communion, of a Layman.—*Continued.*

Or who is possessed of a devil (Ap. Can. LXXIX).

Suspension, when contumaciously disregarded, is to be prolonged (Ap. Can. XIII).

SYMBOL.—See *Creed.*

SYNAGOGUE.—Christians are forbidden to take oil into, or light lamps in, a synagogue of the Jews, at their festivals (Ap. Can. LXXI); Clergymen and laymen are forbidden to enter a synagogue of Jews or heretics to pray (Ap. Can. LXIV).

SYNEISACTÆ.—Syneisactæ are forbidden to reside with the Clergy (Nic. III, Anc. XIX).

SYNOD.—Œcumenical.—

Charges against a Bishop are not to be brought before an Œcumenical Synod (Const. VI).

—Diocesan.—

Charges against a Bishop may be brought before a Diocesan Synod, if the Provincial Synod cannot decide them satisfactorily (Const. VI).

—Provincial.—

Provincial Synods are to be held twice a year, the first in the fourth week of the Pentecost, and the second on the twelfth of October (Ap. Can. XXXVII); the first is to be held after the third week of Easter, and the second on the Ides of October (Ant. XX); the first is to be held before Lent, and the second during Autumn (Nic. V); the Metropolitan is to decide where they shall be held (Chal. XIX); and they cannot be held without him (Ant. XVI, XX).

They are to guard the purity of Doctrine (Ap. Can. XXXVII); to give and receive instruction, and provide for the reformation of the Church (Laod. XL); to determine disputes (Ap. Can. XXXVII); to determine disputes as to a Bishop's jurisdiction over outlying Parishes (Chal. XVII); to decide what shall be done when a Bishop is prevented from entering upon his ministry (Ant. XVIII); to act as a Court of Appeal in revising sentences of individual Bishops (Nic. V, Ant. VI, XX); to try Bishops accused of offences (Ap. Can. LXXIV, Const. VI); to try the complaint of a Clergyman against a Bishop (Chal. IX); to try a Bishop who refuses to enter upon his ministry (Ant. XVII); to investigate the accounts of a Bishop or Priest who is charged with malversation (Ant. XXV); to punish Bishops who receive deposed Clergymen in their clerical capacity (Aht. III); or who act beyond their jurisdiction (Ant. XXII); to appoint Bishops (Nic IV, Ant. XIX, XXIII).

SYNOD.—PROVINCIAL.—*Continued.*

A Provincial Synod is forbidden to rehear the case of a deposed Clergyman, who, after deposition, meddles with his former ministry (Ant. IV); or that of a Priest or Deacon who is deposed for the contumacious maintaining of conventicles (Ant. V); or that of a Clergyman who appeals to the Emperor against a sentence of deposition (Ant. XII); a Provincial Synod is forbidden to appoint a Bishop in the absence of the Metropolitan (Ant. XIX).

A sentence by a Provincial Synod, is final, if unanimous (Ant. XV).

The consent of the Synod is necessary to the occupation of a See, even by a Bishop who is without a See (Ant. XVI).

A Synod is not to be accounted full without the presence of the Metropolitan (Ant. XVI).

Bishops are to attend Provincial Synods, unless prevented by unavoidable business (Chal. XIX); or ill health (Chal. XIX, Laod. XL).

SYSTATIC LETTERS.—Vid. *Letters Commendatory.*

TAVERN.—Clergymen are forbidden to eat in a tavern, unless when they are on a journey (Ap. Can. LIV); Clergymen of every grade, and Monks, are forbidden to enter a tavern (Laod. XXIV).

TEACHING.—Teaching of the Clergy and people is enjoined on Bishops and Priests (Ap. Can. LVIII).

Teaching is one of the objects of Synods (Laod. XL).

TEMPLE, HEATHEN.—Christians are forbidden to take oil into, or light lamps in, a temple of the heathen, at their festivals (Ap. Can. LXXI).

TESTAMENTS.—For lists of the Canonical Books of the Old and New Testaments, see Ap. Can. LXXXV, Laod. LX.

The Old and New Testaments are alone permitted to be read in Church (Laod. LIX).

TETRADITES.—Tetradites are admitted to the Catholic Church by Chrism, after renouncing and anathematizing all heresies (Const. VII).

THEFT.—Theft is punishable in Clergymen by deposition (Ap. Can. XXV).

THEODORE OF MOPSUESTIA.—The heresies of Theodore of Mopsuestia are anathematized (Eph. VII).

THRACE.—The Metropolitans of Thrace are to be elected according to custom, and to be ordained by the Bishop of Constantinople (Chal. XXVIII); their jurisdiction is confined to their own Diocese (Const. II); within which they are to ordain their own Bishops (Chal. XXVIII).

THURSDAY, MAUNDY.—Vid. *Maundy Thursday.*

TIME.—The time within which a Bishop's jurisdiction over outlying Parishes can be questioned, is limited to thirty years (Chal. XVII).

For regulations as to the time for holding Provincial Synods, see *Synod.*

TITLE.—A Clergyman cannot be ordained without a title (Chal. VI).

TOME.—The Tome of Saint Leo is approved (Chal. Encyc., and Can. XXX); the Tome of the Western Bishops is approved by the Church in Antioch (Const. V).

TORTURE.—Priests, who have lapsed under torture, may be restored to their honours, but are not permitted to officiate (Anc. I).

Persons who have remained steadfast under torture, though forced to seem otherwise, are entitled to all their former privileges (Anc. III).

TRADITION.—Ancient Tradition entitles the Bishop of Jerusalem to honour (Nic. VII).

The authority of Bishops is founded on Tradition (Chal. VIII).

The Tradition of the Church inculcates charity (Gang. XXI).

Apostolic Tradition is mentioned as of authority (Gang. XXI).

TRANSLATION.—The Translation of Bishops is forbidden (Nic. XV, Chal. V, X, XX, Ant. XXI).

TRAVELLING.—A Clergyman is forbidden to eat in an inn, unless when he is travelling (Ap. Can. LIV); he is forbidden to travel without his Bishop's consent (Laod. XLI); or without Letters Canonical (Laod. XLII).

TRIAL OF A CLERGYMAN.—Vid. *Bishop*, *Priest*, *Deacon*, *Clergy*, *Minor*.

TRINE-IMMERSION.—Initiation (*i. e.*, Baptism) is to be by Trine-Immersion (Ap. Can. L).

TRINITY.—The doctrine of the Trinity is acknowledged by Ap. Can. XXXIV, Const. V; it is to be acknowledged in the formula of Baptism (Ap. Can. XLIX).

UNANIMITY.—A unanimous verdict, by a Provincial Synod, on the trial of a Bishop, is final (Ant. XV).

UNBELIEVERS.—Bishops, Priests, and Deacons are forbidden to strike unbelievers (Ap. Can. XXVII).

UNCANONICAL BOOKS.—Uncanonical books are forbidden to be read in Church (Ap. Can. LX, Laod. LIX).

UNINTERRUPTED POSSESSION.—Uninterrupted possession for thirty years, by a Bishop, of jurisdiction over outlying or rural Parishes, gives a good title (Chal. XVII).

UNLEAVENED BREAD.—Communicants are forbidden to receive unleavened bread from the Jews (Ap. Can. LXX, Laod. XXXVIII).

UPRIGHTNESS.—Uprightness in the enjoyment of wealth is commended (Gang. XXI).

USURPATION.—The usurpation of a Province, by an Exarch, is forbidden (Eph. VIII); also the usurpation of a vacant See by a Bishop (Ant. XVI); also the usurpation, by a Bishop, of metropolitical power, by means of state interference (Chal. XII).

USURY.—The exaction of usury is forbidden to Bishops, Priests, and Deacons (Ap. Can. XLIV, Nic. XVII, Laod. IV); and to the Minor Clergy (Laod. IV).

VACANT SEE.—Vid. *See.*

VEGETABLES.—Vegetables are forbidden to be offered at the Altar, except new ears of grain, and clusters of grapes (Ap. Can. III).

A Priest or Deacon who refuses to eat vegetables served with meat is to be deposed (Anc. XIV).

VERDICT.—If the Provincial Bishops cannot agree to a verdict on the trial of a Bishop, the Metropolitan is to call in some of the Bishops of the neighbouring Provinces to re-hear the case (Ant. XIV).

Vid. also *Sentence.*

VERNAL EQUINOX.—Bishops, Priests, and Deacons, are forbidden to celebrate Easter before the Vernal Equinox as the Jews do (Ap. Can. VII, Ant. I). See also Nic. Encyc.

VESPERS.—The same Office of Prayers is to be used both at Nones and at Vespers (Laod. XVIII).

VESSELS.—The appropriation of consecrated vessels to private purposes is forbidden (Ap. Can. LXXIII); a Subdeacon is forbidden to touch the sacred vessels (Laod. XXI).

VESTMENTS.—The vestments worn by Deaconesses are mentioned in Nic. XIX.

A Subdeacon has no right to wear an Orarium (Laod. XXII); nor has a Reader nor a Singer (Laod. XXIII).

VETO.—A Metropolitan has a veto on the election of a Bishop (Nic. IV, VI); a Bishop has a veto on the establishment of a Monastery in his Parish (Chal. IV).

VIATICUM.—The Viaticum is never to be refused to the dying (Nic. XIII).

VILLAGE.—A village is not to have an independent Bishop, and such as are already appointed are to consult the City Bishop before acting (Laod. LVII).

VIRGIN.—A man who ravishes a virgin who is not betrothed, must marry her (Ap. Can. LXVII); but if she be betrothed, he must return her to the man to whom she is betrothed (Anc. XI).

A dedicated Virgin, who marries, is to be excommunicated (Chal. XVI); a professed Virgin, if corrupted, is to fulfil the penance of a digamist (Anc. XIX).

Virgins are forbidden to reside with men as sisters (Anc. XIX).

Virgins are forbidden to insult the married (Gang. X).

VIRGINITY.—Virginity is forbidden to be maintained from abhorrence of marriage (Ap. Can. LI, Gang. IX); though declared to be in itself holy and excellent (Gang. IX); it is commended when accompanied by humility (Gang. XXI); and professed Virgins who disregard their vows are to fulfil the penance of digamists (Anc. XIX).

VISITORS.—Itinerant visitors are to be appointed in villages and country districts, and they are to consult the Bishop before acting (Laod. LVII).

VOWS.—See *Virginity.*

WAX.—The misappropriation of wax of the Church is forbidden (Ap. Can. LXXII).

WEAKNESS.—Bodily weakness is a sufficient excuse for not observing the fasts of the Church (Ap. Can. LXIX, Gang. XIX).

WEALTH.—Uprightness and beneficence in the enjoyment of wealth is commended (Gang. XXI).

WEDDINGS.—A Priest is forbidden to be a guest at the wedding of a digamist (Neo-Cæs. VII).

Communicants are forbidden to join in wanton dances at weddings (Laod. LIII); Clergymen are forbidden to attend plays at weddings (Laod. LIV).

WEDNESDAY.—Fasting on Wednesdays is ordained (Ap. Can. LXIX).

WEST AND EAST.—The identity of the doctrine of the Trinity in the Eastern and Western Churches is affirmed (Const. V).

WHITSUNTIDE.—Vid. *Pentecost.*

WIDOW.—Marriage with a widow disqualifies a man from being ordained (Ap. Can. XVIII).

WIDOW—*Continued.*

Clergymen, acting under the direction of their Bishops, are allowed to undertake the guardianship of widows (Chal. III).

WIFE.—The wife of a Bishop, Priest, or Deacon, is not to be divorced under pretext of religion (Ap. Can. V); but if she commit adultery, she must be divorced (Neo-Cæs. VIII); the wife of a Bishop is to be provided for out of his private property, if he have any (Ap. Can. XL); the wife of a Reader or Singer must not be a heretic (Chal. XIV).

The wife of a man who dies in an unlawful marriage, and out of communion, is not to be easily admitted to penance (Neo-Cæs. II).

A Communicant is forbidden to put away his wife and take another, or to marry another man's divorced wife (Ap. Can. XLVIII).

A wife who forsakes her husband from abhorrence of marriage is to be anathematized (Gang. XIV).

The ravisher of a virgin who is not betrothed, must take her to wife (Ap. Can. LXVII).

WIFE'S SISTER, DECEASED.—Vid. *Sister-in-law.*

WINE.—Wine may be offered at the Altar (Ap. Can. III).

Abhorrence of wine is a blasphemous slander of God's work; and abstinence because of such abhorrence is punishable, in Clergymen, by deposition and excommunication, and in laymen by excommunication (Ap. Can. LI); if such abstinence be practised by a Clergyman on festival days, it is punishable by deposition (Ap. Can. LIII).

WITNESS.—Vid. *Accuser.*

WOMAN.—A woman who marries two brothers, is to be admitted to communion only at the point of death (Neo-Cæs. II); marriage with a divorced woman disqualifies a man for being ordained (Ap. Can. XVIII); a woman who forsakes her husband from abhorrence of marriage is to be anathematized (Gang. XIV).

A pregnant woman may be baptized whenever she will (Neo-Cæs. VI).

A woman who procures abortion, is to fulfil ten years of penance (Anc. XXI).

A woman who assumes the dress of a man, is anathematized (Gang. XIII); also a woman who cuts off her hair under pretence of religion (Gang. XVII).

Bathing with women is forbidden to men of every class (Laod. XXX).

WOMAN—*Continued.*

Women are forbidden to reside with the Clergy, unless, from relationship or otherwise, they are beyond suspicion (Nic. III); women who are professed Virgins, are forbidden to reside with men as sisters (Anc. XIX).

Women are forbidden to go into the Sanctuary (Laod. XLIV).

WORLDLY BUSINESS.—Vid. *Business, Worldly.*

WRITING.—The votes of Bishops, on the election of a Bishop, may be given in writing, if personal attendance is difficult (Nic. IV, Ant. XIX).

The consent of a Bishop, to ordinations by a Chorepiscopus beyond his district, must be in writing (Anc. XIII).

The invitation by a Metropolitan, to his provincial Bishops, to attend a Synod for the election of a Bishop, should be in writing (Ant. XIX).

The invitation of the Metropolitan and Provincial Bishops of a Province, to a Bishop of another Province, to act within their jurisdiction, must be in writing (Ant. XIII).

INDEX TO THE INTRODUCTION.

www.ingramcontent.com/pod-product-compliance
Lightning Source LLC
Chambersburg PA
CBHW050610300426
44112CB00012B/1441
* 9 7 8 1 6 2 5 6 4 8 8 1 5 *